Divining the Future

Divining the Future
Prognostication from Astrology to Zoomancy

EVA SHAW

GRAMERCY BOOKS
NEW YORK

The Law of Readiness:

When the Student is ready,
The Teacher will come.

◆

This 1999 edition is published by Gramercy Books™, an imprint of Random House Value Publishing, Inc.
201 East 50th Street, New York, N.Y. 10022, by arrangement with Facts on File, Inc., New York.

Gramercy Books™ and design are trademarks of Random House Value Publishing, Inc.

Random House
New York • Toronto • London • Sydney • Auckland
http://www.randomhouse.com/

Printed and bound in the United States of America.

Library of Congress Cataloging–in–Publication Data
Shaw, Eva, 1947-
Divining the future : prognostication from astrology to zoomancy / Eva Shaw.
p.   cm.
Originally published : New York : Facts on File, c1995.
Includes bibliographical references and index.
ISBN 0-517-19462-7
1. Divination.   2. Fortune-telling.   I. Title.
[BF1751.S48   2000]
133.3'03—dc21   99-12539
CIP

8 7 6 5 4 3 2 1

CONTENTS

———◆———

PREFACE

◆

Since time began, people have questioned what will happen next, why an event is taking place and why an incident has occurred. Predictions from the minds and mouths of Kabbalistic seers to tea shop card readers have warned of evil, answered lovers' questions and decided innocence or guilt.

Wanting to know the future and how to predict it has been the constant quest of civilization. Long before recorded history, cave paintings show people who lived in the caverns of the Sahara using divining rods to psychically locate water. It is documented that the roots of Judaism are anchored with the philosophy of a 13th-century mystic. And while it seems irrational by contemporary standards, at one time the serious business of the future was foretold by tiron-mancy, prediction by the placement of holes in cheese.

Divination was as commonplace in the past as split-second communication is today. As any student of history or literature knows, Julius Caesar was warned of the Ides of March by a soothsayer. In the Middle Ages, smoke from laurel branches thrown on a fire provided ways to determine the cause of action. On Saint Valentine's Day in Regency England, unmarried women were known to toss molten lead into icy water. The letter formed by the metal was believed to coincide with the first letter of the man's name each would marry. Even today in some parts of the United States, a teaspoon that is suspended by a string and hung directly in front of a pregnant woman's belly is thought to be able to foretell the unborn child's sex.

The compulsion to know the what and why of the future is timeless. The renewed fervor perhaps can be attributed to the instantaneous reporting of the media. We expect to see instantly what is happening in China, Russia or Iraq and in our own city or town, and often we become anxious when we are unable get the news *now*. It is quite understandable, therefore, that we want to know what will happen in the coming days and months ahead. It follows, too, that the most sophisticated, educated and successful are often the first to consult with psychics and those able to predict forthcoming events.

More than ever before, men and women are returning to psychics, mystics, metaphysical therapists and others to help solve some of the mysteries of life in these turbulent times. They come with such questions as "When will I get a raise?" and "Will I ever find true love?" They also want to know, "Will the tarot reveal the past life relationship between my stepchild and myself? How will this help strengthen the ties?" and "Which crystals can be used to help control unwanted eating?" "When should I return to college?" "What career path should I take?"

The metaphysical sections of bookstores have experienced a steady increase in the last five years, with books specializing on topics as commonplace as rune stones and astrology to the meanings of out-of-body experiences and use of elixirs concocted with gemstones. One reference librarian explained that she "hates the new age area" of the large metropolitan library where she works. It's not that she's a disbeliever; she reads Sidney Omarr first thing each morning in the *Times*. It's simply that the metaphysical books she wants to refer to patrons are never on the shelves; those in the reference section sometimes "vanish," although patrons are not allowed to take them from the library.

Divining the Future is a source book for prediction methods and techniques and the people, places and events relating to predictions. It does not divine the future. *Divining the Future* is much like the telephone book's Yellow Pages. It is a resource directory of metaphysical information. It provides a means to expand knowledge about the use and usefulness of predictions, from an academic view rather than a metaphysical opinion.

Divining the Future contains:

- Concise definitions of the terms and words used in the realm of predictions
- People and places pertinent to predictions
- Succinct details on concepts, techniques and forms of prediction
- "Further Reading" with books the reader may find of interest on a specific entry subject
- Cross-referenced information and an index.

As with other encyclopedias, you can read the specific entry to answer a question on a prognostication method or read through the book to add to your knowledge on prediction technique.

Throughout the text there are certain words that are used to define the topic. One of those is *querant*. Simply put, a querant is anyone who asks a question. It comes from the root word *query*, meaning to ask or to seek. In metaphysics, a querant who is receiving a psychic reading is referred to as the querant. Those who search for inspirational advice and enlightenment are constantly asking questions. When applied to prognostication, a querant is one who specifically asks for knowledge or advice through the use of a prognostication method or with the help of a psychic.

The endings or suffixes on many of the terms are *-mancy* and *-scopy*. Each originally had its own meaning and in scientific terms still does. In metaphysics and throughout history, the suffixes have often been misused. They are now almost interchangeable. Historically the suffix *-mancy* indicates a form of divination by a definite means or in a particular manner. For instance, in chiromancy or necromancy, one seeks metaphysical knowledge from the hand or from the dead. The suffix comes from the Middle English and Old French *-mancie*, derived from the Late Latin *-mantia*, which is descended from the Greek *manteia*, meaning divination. *Manteia* came from the word *manteuesthia* (meaning to predict) and from the word *mantis*, meaning a prophet. The suffix *-scopy* means to view, see or observe. For example, ceraunoscopy means prediction by observation of lightening patterns during thunderstorms. The suffix *-scopy* comes from the Greek *-skopia* and *skopein*, meaning to look into, to behold. Many other terms are defined within the pages of this book, and general definitions of terms not defined in the text can often be found in a comprehensive dictionary.

On a personal note, the words "thank you" hardly express the gratitude I feel to all those who have helped me during the researching and writing of this book. Many have shared, inspired, and discussed the realm of metaphysics. Many have graciously opened their private libraries as I attempted to categorize a millennium of metaphysical information.

Special appreciation goes to my husband Joe and our son Matt for listening, asking questions, and providing an environment in which the mystical is possible—and to Zippy, our Welsh Terrier and my self-appointed guide to adding more fun into my life. Next, to one who is never far from my literary thoughts—Bert Holtje, literary agent extraordinaire, for seeing the nugget of a book idea and encouraging me to write the proposal. To my editor Randy Ladenheim-

Gil for her help and quick response to all my queries, and for polishing my words. To Katherine Torres, Msc.D., a special spiritual woman and translator of the Sacred Path Wheel. And to Carlsbad's Mystical Dragon II's Lena Jorman, and to all the incredibly supportive, loving friends—I give a warm hug and a genuine thank you.

ABULAFIA, ABRAHAM BEN SAMUEL *(1240–1291) Kabbalistic mystic.*

Born in the Spanish city of Saragossa, Abulafia represented himself as both Christian and Jew. He fervently believed that he was the Messiah long foretold in Scripture. Christians passionately disagreed, and when Abulafia confronted Pope Nicholas III with his news, he was persecuted, hounded and harassed. It was announced by the Church that Abulafia would burn in hell for spreading his blasphemous belief to other citizens.

Abulafia's approach to the mystical arts was practical and methodical. Throughout his life, he studied the KABBALAH (also known as the Tree of Life). Abulafia is said to have taken great pains to balance precisely the mental with the spiritual.

Abulafia believed in the divine symbolism of the Hebrew alphabet (part of the Kabbalah) and wrote many books, including *The Book of the Righteous* and *The Book of Life.*

Further reading

Drury, Nevill. *Dictionary of Mysticism and the Esoteric Traditions.* Dorset, England: Prism Press, 1992.

Epstein, Perke. *Kabbalah: The Way of the Jewish Mystic.* Boston: Shambhala, 1988.

Ponce, Charles. *Kabbalah: An Introduction and Illumination for the World Today.* Wheaton, Ill.: Theosophical Publishing House, 1973.

ACHAD, FRATER

See JONES, CHARLES STANSFELD.

ADAMS, EVANGELINE *(1865–1932) American astrologer.*

Called the "first American astrologer," Adams is considered to have been the leading astrologer of her time. During a visit to New York City, she observed that the hotel in which she had a reservation was built under "the worst possible combination of planets, with conditions terrifying in their unfriendliness." That night the hotel burned to the ground; Adams escaped unhurt.

In 1914, Adams was brought to trial for fortune-telling. As part of the court proceedings, the judge asked that she read an anonymous horoscope. The horoscope was that of the judge's son (some records say it was actually the judge's horoscope that was read), and the reading was so accurate in its details that he released her, dropping all charges. By 1930, Adams was one of the most popular radio personalities of the day with her program on astrology. Her clients are said to have included the rich and famous of that era, including Britain's King Edward VII and Enrico Caruso, the opera singer.

At the peak of her fame Adams is reported to have received more than 300,000 letters a year from people asking for advice and assistance from the stars. Her book *Astrology for Everyone,* while hard to find today, is still available in used-books stores and is a classic in astrology.

Further reading

Adams, Evangeline. *Astrology: Your Place among the Stars.* New York: Dodd, Mead & Co., 1930.
———. *Astrology for Everyone.* 1931. Reprint. New York: Permabooks, 1943.
Brown, Slater. *The Heyday of Spiritualism.* New York: Hawthorn, 1970.
Godwin, John. *Occult America.* New York: Doubleday, 1972.
Woolfork, Joanna Martine. *The Only Astrology Book You'll Ever Need.* Landham, Mass.: Scarborough, 1992.

AEROMANCY
May also be referred to as NEPHELOMANCY *(from the Greek nephele, meaning cloud), divination using the formation of clouds and other patterns in the skies and predicting events by wind direction.*

Sometimes used in conjunction with ceraunoscopy (predictions made from the patterns of lightning during thunderstorms), aeromancy focuses on the forms and shapes made by clouds. The predictor intuitively interprets the configurations to answer questions or predict events. As with many other prediction methods, including tasseography (teacup reading), the symbols in the sky can be deciphered in many ways. Ancient mantic arts, aeromancy, ceraunoscopy and sciomancy (predictions made from the shapes of shadows) are no longer widely practiced; however, every child has at one time or other looked to the heavens and been amazed by the gliding shapes and stories the sky can tell. Like many of the archaic prediction methods, though the actual method of divination has been lost, the omens continue. The practice of aeromancy can still be noted in the child's poem beginning "The North wind doth blow, and we shall have snow."

Many people who grew up in New England know the saying "See a mackerel sky and in three days there will be rain." A "mackerel" sky is one with small, thin lines of clouds, much like the bones on a fish skeleton. Similarly, "Red skies at night, sailors delight. Red skies in the morning, sailors take warning" indicates that clouds in the morning could herald a storm's arrival.

Part of the group of earth-related prediction methods also known as geomancy, aeromancy is practiced by the answering of questions. After a question is posed, divination is sought by throwing dirt or sand into the wind. The answer is told in the shape of the dust cloud caused by the flying particles. Aeromancy is also practiced by throwing seeds in the air to foretell the future. In the case of seeds or any other lightweight objects, the placement of the fallen material or seeds reveals the answer to the question.

See also AUSTROMANCY, FENG SHUI and GEOMANCY, prediction methods that utilize shapes and forecasts discerned from earth patterns.

Further reading

Bletzer, June G. *The Donning International Encyclopedic Psychic Dictionary.* West Chester, Pa.: Whitford Press, 1986.
Maven, Max. *Max Maven's Book of Fortunetelling.* New York: Prentice-Hall, 1992.
Morgan, Chris. *Fortune Telling: How to Predict Your Own Future.* London: Quintet Publishing and Random House, 1992.
Opie, Iona, and Moira Tatem. *A Dictionary of Superstitions.* Oxford: Oxford University Press, 1992.
Rossbach, Sarah. *Feng Shui: The Chinese Art of Placement.* New York: Arkana/Penguin, 1991.
Stewart, R. J. *The Elements of Prophecy.* Dorset, England: Element Books, 1990.

AGRIPPA, VON NETTESHEIM, HEINRICH CORNELIUS (1486–1535)
German mystic, metaphysical scholar, numerologist and astrologer

Agrippa was rumored to possess magical powers and is said to have practiced NECROMANCY (divination by speaking to the spirits of the dead). He is the author of one of the earliest books on the occult, *De Occulta Phiulosophia*, a comprehensive volume dealing with divine names, natural magic and cosmology. He refined the classic system of NUMEROLOGY, eliminating the number nine, because according to Agrippa it is supposed to be associated exclusively with matters of divinity.

See also GEMATRIA.

Further reading

Ancient Wisdom and Secrets Sects. Mysteries of the Unknown. Alexandria, Va.: Time Life Books, 1990.

Drury, Nevill. *Dictionary of Mysticism and the Esoteric Traditions.* Dorset, England: Prism Press, 1992.

Maven, Max. *Max Maven's Book of Fortunetelling.* New York: Prentice-Hall, 1992.

AKASHIC RECORDS *The records of all experiences encountered in all ways throughout every existence and experience, which are incorporated into records located in the storehouse of spiritual knowledge.*

The Akashic Records, whose name comes from the Sanskrit word *akasha,* meaning primary substance, are considered by many to be ethereal records that chronicle attitudes, concepts, emotions and the senses of smell, taste, feel, sight and sound from past lives or previous incarnations. Even the minutest details are recorded. These records are preserved in the spirit world, to be recalled or rekindled when needed; thus the deja vu experience: a feeling of having experienced an incident before. It is thought that through study of these records, in this earth plane existence, we will be able to improve ourselves using the knowledge of previous experience and build new experiences, which are then also recorded in the Akashic Records.

Contemporary mystics sometimes compare Akashic Records to the hard drive on a personal computer. In computer terms, even when information is deleted on the hard drive, it actually remains there forever. It has only been coded that it should not be recalled. Therefore, when an incident of any magnitude has been placed in the Akashic Records, even if it has been found to be useless in the earth plane, it continues to exist and can be retrieved at another time.

The information in the Akashic Records is thought to be available to anyone who is moving toward perfectness of spirit. Although it takes sensitivity to be able to delve into the record, mystics assert that it is possible. Most psychics conclude that the Akashic Records travel on waves of light, and they maintain that with the proper training anyone can access the information. One can recognize experiences documented in the Akashic Records if one is attuned to the Holy Spirit, the universal consciousness, and the other side. As every thought vibration is sensed and recorded, the impressions can be delved into if one is familiar with the language of the records—that is, able to listen to the advice of guides, angels or the information of intuition.

The American psychic Edgar Cayce (1877–1945) is said to have had the power to examine the Akashic Records. Sometimes referred to as the "Sleeping Prophet," because he channeled information from the spirit world when in a sleeplike state, Cayce revealed that he referred to the Akashic Records as one might refer to books in the reference section of a library. In an out-of-body experience, as documented in *Edgar Cayce on Reincarnation* by Noel Langley, Cayce described seeing himself leave his body and move through a lighted path toward the record room. Both sides of the pathway were cloudy with smoke or fog. Voices called for help or assistance, trying to tempt him from his designated course, as he maneuvered the path, but he continued to move forward to a shaft of light. Arriving at a hill, he climbed the slope to a great temple and entered a room that was like a magnificent library. Without consulting any other entity, he located and read the volume that could unravel concerns for the client regarding past-life experiences specifically applied to health, marital problems and personal attitudes and questions. Cayce interchangeably called the Akashic Records the "Universal Memory of Nature" and the "Book of Life."

Calling them the "Akashic Chronicle," philosopher Rudolf Steiner explored the Akashic Records. He described the results of that exploration with details specifically on the fabled civilizations of Lemuria and Atlantis in his autobiography.

See also CAYCE, EDGAR; KARMA.

Further reading

Bailey, Alice. *A Treatise on White Magic.* New York: Lucis, 1951.

Bletzer, June G. *The Donning International Encyclo-*

pedic Psychic Dictionary. West Chester, Pa.: Whitford Press, 1986.

Cavendish, Richard, ed. *The Encyclopedia of the Unexplained.* New York: McGraw-Hill, 1974.

Cayce, Hugh Lynn, ed. *The Edgar Cayce Collection.* New York: Bonanza, 1986.

Guiley, Rosemary Ellen. *Harper's Encyclopedia of Mystical and Paranormal Experience.* San Francisco: HarperSan Francisco, 1991.

McDermott, Robert, ed. *The Essential Steiner.* San Francisco: Harper & Row, 1984.

ALBERTUS MAGNUS *(1205–1280)*
German mystic and alchemist.

Also known as the "Universal Doctor," Albertus Magnus claimed to have magical powers, especially in the realm of alchemy. He is remembered for supposedly having had the power to turn base metal into gold through an alchemical process, an ability sought long before and after Albertus Magnus's lifetime.

Further reading

Cosmic Connection. Mysteries of the Unknown. Alexandria, Va.: Time Life Books, 1990.

Drury, Nevill. *Dictionary of Mysticism and the Esoteric Traditions.* Dorset, England: Prism Press, 1992.

Alectromancy includes predictions through changes in weather patterns.

ALECTROMANCY *Forecasting the future through atmospheric or celestial conditions.*

Alectromancy was used in ancient Egyptian times. For example, if a comet or other celestial condition was viewed at the time of a noble person's birth, a psychic was consulted to determine if the atmospheric or celestial event was an omen that foretold of the eventual success or failure of the child, the family or the entire monarchy.

Alectromancy was also used to predict the downfall of an enemy using an eclipse. This divination method is grouped with others known as GEOMANCY.

Alectromancy also includes predictions through changes in weather patterns and encompasses AEROMANCY and NEPHELOMANCY, which both foretell the future through cloud patterns in the sky. The rhyme "Starlight, star bright, first star I see tonight," recited when wishing on a falling star, employs a form of alectromancy.

Alectromancy is occasionally referred to as astrometeorology. Astrometeorology uses astrology and alectromancy to forecast future weather patterns and national disasters.

See also GEOMANCY and other earth-related prognostication methods.

Further reading

Bletzer, June G., *The Donning International Encyclopedic Psychic Dictionary.* West Chester, Pa.: Whitford Press, 1986.

Morgan, Chris. *Fortune Telling: How to Predict Your Own Future.* London: Quintet Publishing and Random House, 1992.

ALECTRYOMANCY *Divination involving the behavior of animals.*

More than 2,400 years ago, the Etruscans practiced alectryomancy utilizing a hen or rooster. Poultry, it was theorized, was used because of the cock's habit of crowing as the sun rises each morning, foretelling the birth of the day. The Etruscan psychics drew a circle on the ground around which were drawn the 20 letters of the Etruscan alphabet. A kernel of grain (probably corn or wheat) was placed in front of each letter. The hen or cock was placed within the circle and allowed to eat. As the bird ate the grain, the psychic noted the sequence of letters next to the kernels to predict the future or answer the querant's question.

The ancient Babylonians used a variation of alectryomancy. By splashing water three times on a sleeping ox's head, a psychic could divine the future through 17 possible reactions and types of response. Each reaction had its own meaning. For example, if both eyes remained open, the answer was yes. If only one eye stayed open, the answer was maybe. The answer was no—or there was no answer at all—if the eyes stayed closed. The Hittites, an ancient people of Asia Minor and Syria who flourished from 1600 B.C. to 1200 A.D., used alectryomancy to divine the future by studying the movements of an eel within a tank of water.

Alectryomancy is still used today in many parts of the world. In the central African tribe of Zande, answers are discerned by the behavior of ants. Two long, thin leaves are inserted into an ant hill. If the ants eat the leaf on the left first, the answer to the querant's question is yes. If the leaf on the right is consumed first, the answer is no.

The Dogon, another African tribe who live in the western part of the continent, draw a design on the ground at nightfall and sprinkle nuts around it. In the morning the seers or tribal wise men and women return to inspect the paw patterns left by the jackals who have come during the night to eat the nuts.

In Polynesia, some tribal leaders believe that crimes can be solved when a beetle is allowed to crawl over the grave of a murder victim. It is claimed that the beetle's tracks can tell the murderer's name and identity when the tracks are psychically interpreted.

In Great Britain folklore tells us that a maiden can foretell the direction from which her lover will arrive if she cups a spotted ladybug in her hands and then watches its course as it flies away.

Although alectryomancy is still practiced in various parts of the world, North Americans think of it as luck, rather than a form of predicting the future, when they interpret animal behavior. In the United States, whether or not a groundhog sees its shadow on February 2 indicates the number of weeks before winter will end. Other lucky omens include meeting a goat or a flock of sheep (and making a wish when seeing the black sheep in the flock) and seeing a white horse in a field. Unlucky animal omens range from hearing a bat squeal as it flies over-

Using alectryomancy, divination involving the behavior of animals (especially poultry), many civilizations predicted the future.

head to meeting a hare (but only if you are a sailor on your way to your ship).

In most urban centers of the world, there are people who practice a variation of alectryomancy. For a small fee in many cities, including New York, Milan and Singapore, a querant asks a question and the fortune merchant's trained bird picks an answer from the papers located on a rack or branch.

Alectryomancy is a form of APANTOMANCY. Apantomancy foretells the future through an accidental meeting with animals, such as a black cat crossing one's path or a gull brushing against one's shoulder, which is said to predict death.

See also GEOMANCY; HIPPOMANCY; ORNITHOMANCY.

Further reading

Bethards, Betty. *The Dream Book: Symbols for Self-Understanding.* 9th printing. Petaluma, Calif.: Inner Light Press, 1992.

Levey, Judith S., with Agness Greenhall, eds. *The Concise Columbia Encyclopedia.* New York: Avon, 1983.

Maven, Max. *Max Maven's Book of Fortunetelling.* New York: Prentice-Hall, 1992.

Morgan, Chris. *Fortune Telling: How to Predict Your Own Future.* London: Quintet Publishing and Random House, 1992.

ALEUROMANCY *Divination through the messages baked inside and then found in cakes or cookies.*

Messages are written on bits of paper, placed in the cookies or cakes and then offered to the querant. The theory is that the question on the querant's mind will be answered by the forces encouraging him or her to select a specific baked good. The fortune cookie offered as an after-dinner treat in an American Chinese restaurant is an example of aleuromancy.

Aleuromancy began in ancient China, where it was a game for the nobility. Essays based on bits of philosophical tenets were baked into tea cakes. The Greeks used this method to provide answers to the future, wherein predictive phrases were written on slips of paper and baked into round, hard cakes. A cake was then chosen by

the querant to foretell a future event or offer the solution to a troubling predicament.

The European custom of baking a silver coin into a cake is derived from this archaic mantic art. The individual who finds the coin will have good luck (immediately or throughout the coming year, depending on the rules or guidelines traditionally followed by the cake-eating party). Sometimes those sharing the cake will each make a wish; the wish will come true for the one who discovers the coin.

CRITOMANCY takes this divination practice further, providing a means of foretelling events by examining the unusual behavior of the grain, the dough or the cakes and cookies themselves.

Good luck omens that may have originated from aleuromancy and are still known today include:

- Sleeping with wedding cake beneath your pillow will make you dream of your future husband or wife.
- The future can be divined from the shapes produced by combining the white of an egg with glass and then adding water, covering and shaking vigorously.
- Dropping an egg and having it break foretells bad luck; if the egg doesn't break, good luck is forthcoming.
- Ragged edges produced when bread is cut prognosticate a turn of misfortune for the one who takes a grave chance slicing this divining loaf of bread.

Further reading

Maven, Max. *Max Maven's Book of Fortunetelling.* New York: Prentice-Hall, 1992.

Morgan, Chris. *Fortune Telling: How to Predict Your Own Future.* London: Quintet Publishing and Random House, 1992.

Opie, Iona, and Moira Tatem. *A Dictionary of Superstitions.* Oxford: Oxford University Press, 1992.

ALPHITOMANCY *Divination that proves guilt or innocence through the use of a loaf of barley bread.*

An offshoot of ALEUROMANCY, in alphitomancy a loaf of barley is broken into pieces and shared by all those who may be connected to or suspected of a misdeed. Before each participant takes a bite of the bread, he or she repeats, "If I am deceiving you, may this piece of bread choke me." The guilty party will, of course, choke while swallowing.

Further reading

Bletzer, June G. *The Donning International Encyclopedic Psychic Dictionary.* West Chester, Pa.: Whitford Press, 1986.

AMNIOMANCY *Method of predicting the future happiness, or sadness, of an individual at his or her birth according to the caul that sometimes covers a newborn's head.*

Through amniomancy, a psychic interprets the caul (the fetal membrane that sometimes remains on an infant's head immediately after birth). If the caul is red, the child will grow strong and have a happy life. If the caul is lead colored, great misfortune will befall the child. An offshoot of amniomancy is the luck foretold when a baby is born with a caul, regardless of the color, promising protection against harm, especially drowning.

Other omens concerning the birth of a child include that it's unlucky for the mother to anticipate the sex of the unborn infants, and disaster will result from bringing a pram (baby carriage) into the house prior to a birth. If a baby cries at his or her christening, it means that any evil spirits are leaving the baby's body, and a baby born on a Sunday is the most fortunate of all children. A baby born with an open hand will be generous later in life. And if one of a pair of twins dies, the other will soon perish (as they share the same soul) *or* the surviving twin will be twice as smart (or lucky), as he or she receives all the strength from the other's soul. It was, at one time, a Scottish tradition to induce a sneeze in a newborn because until a baby had sneezed, it was more susceptible to evil forces.

Further reading

Bletzer, June G. *The Donning International Encyclopedic Psychic Dictionary.* West Chester, Pa.: Whitford Press, 1986.

Daniels, Cora Linn, and C. M. Stevans, eds. *Encyclopedia of Superstitions, Folklore and the Occult Sciences of the World.* Detroit: Gale Research, 1971.
Guiley, Rosemary Ellen. *The Encyclopedia of Ghosts and Spirits.* New York: Facts On File, 1992.
Morgan, Chris. *Fortune Telling: How to Predict Your Own Future.* London: Quintet Publishing and Random House, 1992.

ANSELM DE PARMA *(?–1440) Italian astrologer, healer and author.*

De Parma was regarded as a powerful sorcerer and a gifted astrologer. He is the author of *Astrological Institutions,* a classic in the field of astrology.

See also ASTROLOGY; LAYING ON OF HANDS.

Further reading

Drury, Nevill. *Dictionary of Mysticism and the Esoteric Traditions.* Dorset, England: Prism Press, 1992.
Krippner, Stanley, and Alberto Villoldo. *The Realms of Healing.* 3d ed. Berkeley, Calif.: Celestial Arts, 1986.
Meek, George W., ed. *Healers and the Healing Process.* Wheaton, Ill.: Theosophical Publishing House, 1977.
Powers of Healing. Mysteries of the Unknown. Alexandria, Va.: Time Life Books, 1990.
Woolfork, Joanna Martine. *The Only Astrology Book You'll Ever Need,* Landham, Mass.: Scarborough, 1992.

ANTHROPOMANCY *The ancient art of divination using entrails, the inner organs—specifically the intestines—of human sacrifices.*

The entrails, or viscera, were interpreted by psychics to forecast future events. Practiced by the ancient Babylonians, Sumerians, Japanese, Greeks and Romans, anthropomancy is an offshoot of HEPATOMANCY, divination by studying the livers of animals. Some say the ancient Druids, the priestly caste of the Celts, practiced anthropomancy late in the cult's existence. It is probably one of the most ancient mantic arts, likely more than 5,000 years old. Visceral interpretation was practiced by the Comanche Indians, the Incas and the Armenians, to name a few. The practice is said to continue today: The livers of farm animals are studied by psychics in Borneo and Burma.

Not involving death yet still considered a version of anthropomancy are any of the prediction methods employing bodily fluids, specifically blood. In the Middle Ages, an unprovoked nosebleed was considered a prophetic sign, foretelling misfortune or considerable luck, depending on the circumstance. An example of the widely held belief of the unfortunate possibilities of a nosebleed is referenced in Shakespeare's *Merchant of Venice*.

More recently, in the late 1970s, Masahiko Nomi wrote the Japanese best-seller *Good Combination of Blood Types*, proposing that personality traits could be directly related to the blood type of the individual. This concept is called blood-typing. While most North Americans know their astrological sun sign, most Japanese know their blood type regardless of their belief in the system.

It is thought that PALMISTRY (divining the future by looking at the hand) and ANTHROPOSOMANCY and PHYSIOGNOMY (divining the future by studying facial features) are variations of anthropomancy.

See also SCAPULOMANCY.

Further reading

Carr-Gomm, Philip. *The Elements of the Druid Tradition*. Dorset, England: Element Books, 1991.

Guiley, Rosemary Ellen. *Harper's Encyclopedia of Mystical and Paranormal Experience*. San Francisco: HarperSan Francisco, 1991.

"Japanese Success? It's in the Blood." *Newsweek*, page 45, April 18, 1985.

Mangnall, R. Curtis. "Pisces Out, Type O In." *Psychology Today*, page 88, October 1984.

Robinson, Rita. *The Palm: A Guide to Your Hidden Potential*. Los Angeles: Newcastle, 1988.

ANTHROPOSOMANCY

Divination by the interpretation of a person's face and/or body characteristics, sometimes referred to as PHYSIOGNOMY.

Anthroposomancy may also include the reading of moles, the lines on the face or the definition of a profile. PALMISTRY, PHRENOLOGY and body-

Anthroposomancy is divination by interpretation of a person's face and/or body characteristics.

typing are sometimes included in this category of mantic arts.

Published in the Sung dynasty, *Ma-Yee-Shang-Fa (The Simple Guide to Face-Reading)* was the first book on the topic of anthroposomancy, although the art had been practiced more than 3,200 years ago during the Chou dynasty. The book is still used as the basic source of information on a skill that continues to be practiced today in Asia with far more credence than palmistry. However, Confucius and the military theorist Sun-Tze both criticized and questioned the practice. More recently, the Chinese Communist regime attempted to eliminate anthroposomancy completely.

Aristotle commended the practice, stating that human faces could be interpreted with correlations drawn between characteristics and features of the face. Hippocrates, the "Father of Medicine," also believed that there was some certainty to the belief that one's face revealed traces of future disease. Face reading continued throughout history. In the 1500s facial interpretations proliferated and books on the subject increased. In 1658 in Paris, Jerome Cardan published *Metoposcopia*, a guide to face reading and, specifically, divining the future by use of the lines on the forehead. Calling the practice the metaphysical science of metoposcopy, the book had more than 800 illustrations to substantiate Cardan's thesis.

In 1775, Johann Levater (sometimes spelled Lavater), a Swiss minister, devised a distinctly different system of anthroposomancy and published a book on the topic. Dr. Levater interpreted the shape of the head and facial features of European nobility, including Edward, duke of Kent, the father of Queen Victoria. However, not everyone accepted the practice, and at one time the British Parliament officially condemned this mantic art.

Most psychics (as well as hairdressers, salespeople, teachers, therapists, physicians and parents of teenagers) reveal that they continue to use this ancient mantic art along with other ways to "read" the faces of those with whom they come in contact. A tired, drawn look betrays an individual who is worried or overtaxed. A glowing face speaks of good fortune, romance, a promotion or a happy disposition. Eyes that refuse to focus on another person often indicate the telling of lies even though the person's words may appear to be the truth.

The Japanese break down anthroposomancy into an adaptation called *ninso,* or person aspect, and practice it widely today. Like palmistry, which considers more than the lines on the palm, *ninso* takes into account the shape, contour and texture of the face, eyes and hair, as well as the coloring.

People with "circle" faces are said to be emotional, optimistic and social and to have a highly defined moral instinct, often possessing finely tuned business skills as well. According to Japanese face readers, these people may not be self-starters and often look toward others to help them along.

People with "square" faces tend to be practical and quick to move on a concept or business idea. They are said to be stubborn at times but with strong leadership abilities.

Those with "oval" faces are blessed with the abilities of both the "circle" and the "square." They have a strong ethical sense, fine business skills and the practical nature necessary to succeed.

"Triangle" faces indicate people who quickly grasp a situation, yet they bore easily. They are supposedly analytical and have questioning minds, although they can become distracted before completing a project. They tend to be somewhat awkward in social situations but are highly ingenious.

People with faces that resemble a "trapezoid" are considered to be bright, creative and intelligent but are slow to succeed because they may not be able to follow through on those bright, creative, intelligent ideas. Often the trapezoid-faced person does best working alone.

Other aspects of the face are also considered in *ninso.* The forehead's lines can indicate one who is honest (with long, unbroken lines) or has a desire for travel (wavy lines). An S-curve marks a devious personality; short, abrupt lines show changes forthcoming.

In China, a very straight nose signifies a successful marriage, and it is said that Napoleon Bonaparte and the duke of Wellington, in the tradition of their time, chose army officers on the basis of certain facial features, specifically the nose. A turned-up nose speaks of someone who is congenial. A turned-down nose reports that a person may be conservative and fastidious. Nostril size indicates strong character (large) or idealism and insecurity (small).

Someone with a "weak" chin is often considered, even by contemporary standards, to be weak in character. This may have been passed down from the mantic art of anthroposomancy; a receding chin reportedly demonstrates a person without strong ethics. A strong chin bespeaks one who is firm and assertive. A pointed chin indicates one who quickly makes decisions, and a cleft in the chin marks a person for life as one who has secrets or devious ambitions.

The eyes can tell everything, according to anthroposomancy, so much so that the specific mantic arts of OCULOMANCY and IRIDOLOGY have been devoted to them. Not only is color a factor, but size and shape indicate a person's characteristics and denote his or her fortune in life. Wide-set eyes indicate reliability. Glibness is shown in bulging eyes, and small eyes symbolize someone who is deceptive and calculating.

Heavy eyebrows announce a person's strength, along with the ability to be overbearing; thin brows indicate a personality that can be fussy and detail oriented. Gently curving brows provide a key to someone who is balanced and calm. Arched brows show a questioning nature. Those who have had the karma to be born with brows that grow thickly together above the nose are said to be most unfortunate indeed.

Ears are a favorite feature on which to base the practice of anthroposomancy. Large earlobes indicate affluence in the future; smaller ones indicate poverty. Ears that are small toward the top but with large lobes on the bottom tell of someone who is bright, with a good memory. Those born without lobes are destined to go through life aimlessly according to face readers, and are often wishy-washy in nature. In Japan, ears that are set low on the head are a sign of nobility, perhaps a carryover from a previous lifetime.

The mouth is a barometer of personal nature. A curving upward shows a good temperament; a downward curve indicates an unhappy disposition. A large mouth is considered to show extravagance and a small one a miserly, persnickety nature.

Babies born with teeth are often considered to have strong leadership qualities but a dark, overbearing and destructive side to their personality. Julius Caesar, Hannibal and Napoleon Bonaparte were all born with slightly developed teeth.

Hair color, even today, has specific meaning and can divine a personality trait. Traditionally, before we were told that blonds had more fun, darker hair colors indicated strength and courage. Red hair indicated someone with a strong emotional propensity. Coarse hair showed boldness, thin hair a gentle nature.

Another hair omen once considered to foretell the future concerns the hairline of women. A hairline that came to a point in the middle of the forehead was said to indicate an unfortunate event, specifically in marriage. While we currently discount this omen, we still call the point at the hairline a "widow's peak."

In medieval Europe children's hair was left uncut for many years to ensure their strength through childhood. Gypsies advised the lovelorn to snip a lock of the beloved's hair and wear it as a ring or in a locket to fuel passion. And in voodoo cults those who want to possess power over another's soul are told to get a piece of their enemy's hair.

Further reading

Bary, William Theodore de, ed. *Sources of Chinese Traditions.* New York: Columbia University Press, 1960.

Leland, Charles Godfrey. *Gypsy Sorcery and Fortune Telling.* New York: University Books, 1962.

Maven, Max. *Max Maven's Book of Fortunetelling.* New York: Prentice-Hall, 1992.

Walker, Barbara G. *The Woman's Encyclopedia of Myths and Secrets.* New York: Harper Collins, 1983.

APANTOMANCY *Divination interpreted by chance encounters with animals. (See also* ALECTRYOMANCY.*)*

In the United States, when a black cat crosses one's path, it foretells bad luck; in Britain, on the other hand, such an occurrence is a sign of good fortune. When a groundhog sees its shadow on February 2, it still makes headlines in newspapers and the six o'clock news throughout the United States. Omens such as this find their basis in ancient mantic arts, including apantomancy.

Animals have had a strong influence on a number of cultures. American Indians were often named for the first animal a mother saw after giving birth. In ancient Europe an accidental meeting with a squirrel, a white mouse or a hedgehog indicated good luck. The sighting of a pig, a bat or a hare told of impending doom. In prehistoric Arabian times, to encounter a camel or donkey out of the ordinary circumstances of the day—remembering that these animals were used as transportation—was considered to be supremely propitious.

The ancient Babylonians used apantomancy as a means of prophesy when a dog happened to enter a palace. Depending on the canine's coat color, important events, ranging from wars to natural disasters, were foretold by the psychics of the time. And should the dog actually lie down on the priest's throne, it was a clear message that the building would be demolished by fire.

Encountering any type of reptile was said to be a message of trouble, except, of course, for a tortoise or a turtle, which could charm away that unfortunate circumstance. Finding a ladybug (especially one with seven black spots) almost guaranteed success. And meeting a pig on the way to one's wedding was to be avoided at all cost: Ill fortune in the relationship was foretold. Yet seeing a dove, a peacock, a robin, a swallow or a woodpecker was such good luck that it would probably cancel out that passing pig.

Additionally, chance meetings with animals were used to predict rain or a change in the weather. For example, fish that bite more enthusiastically, swallows flying low to the ground and gophers digging up more than one hole were said to indicate that one should carry an umbrella; rain was sure to come.

Further reading

Bardens, Dennis. *Psychic Pets.* Boca Raton, Fla.: Globe Communications, 1992.

Green, Marian. *The Elements of Natural Magic.* Dorset, England: Element Books, 1989.

Stewart, R. J. *The Elements of Prophecy.* Dorset, England: Element Books, 1990.

APPARITION *A mistlike vision seen by psychics or sensed clairvoyantly that foretells future events. Sometimes referred to as ghosts or spirits, apparitions may appear as the likeness of a living or dead person or an animal.*

There is no one theory about apparitions. Some say that the patterns are produced by the subconscious mind without any help from the spirit world. It may also be that apparitions are astral or ethereal bodies of spirits manifesting themselves to divine events, whether forthcoming or in the past. Some experts say that apparitions are truly the dead speaking through those who are sensitive enough to audit the message.

Almost every civilization honors the dead, believing in some sort of apparition. Some Chinese believe that ancestral ghosts can be dangerous, as do a number of the African tribal cultures. In Christianity, angels, saints, the Virgin Mary and Jesus are believed to be examples of mystical apparitions allowed by God so that followers can become closer to the religion.

Psychics often sense an apparition rather than see it. There may be a touch, a sound, a presence, an animal noise or an unexplained smell that accompanies the appearance. Modern psychical researcher Andrew MacKenzie suggests that the ability to have apparitional experiences is a function of the personality structure. Some people are more apt to have them than others. Apparitional experiences, MacKenzie found through experiments, happened when the reality of the present was shut out, such as when falling asleep, upon waking, when concentrating on a book or when doing mundane chores.

Apparitions are also known as astral shells, shades, confused soul-minds, visionary appearances, specters, astral bodies, spirits, world intelligences and ghosts.

Further reading

Auerbach, Lloyd. *ESP, Hauntings and Poltergeists: A Parapsychologist's Handbook.* New York: Warner, 1986.

Guiley, Rosemary Ellen. *The Encyclopedia of Ghosts and Spirits.* New York: Facts On File, 1992.

Jaffe, Aniela. *Apparitions: An Archetypal Approach to Death, Dreams and Ghosts.* Irving, Tex.: Spring Publications, 1979.

MacKenzie, Andrew. *Hauntings and Apparitions.* London: Heinemann, 1982.

AQUARIUS *One of the 12 astrological signs of the zodiac. The symbol is the water bearer.*

Those who are born between January 20 and February 20 are natives of the sign of Aquarius and have specific traits indicative of the time and date on which they were born. Divination of events can also be charted through this astrological sign.

AQUARIUS

Astrologers divine what is in store throughout life through the time, date and place in which the individual was born as they coordinate the influences with other signs, the planets, the sun, the moon and other powers.

In traditional Western astrology, Aquarius is the 11th sign of the zodiac. Personality characteristics typical of those born in the sign of Aquarius include having a generous, humanitarian approach to life. Aquarians shy away from trouble but are tolerant and broad minded. These are not the rabble-rousers of the zodiac, and almost any kind of dissension disturbs them. Both men and women born within this sign are said to be just and generous, and they consider ethical practices to be most important.

The sign of the zodiac in which an individual is born is responsible for only one fragment of the qualities he or she receives at birth. Psychics are quick to point out that a general forecast based solely on the stellar position of the Sun on the day an individual was born is unlikely to provide an accurate glimpse of the future.

Although traditional astrologers use books to

This ancient symbol represents the astrological sign of Aquarius.

calculate a personal birth chart based on the position of the Sun, Moon and planets at a distinct time, computer software has replaced most of this time-consuming work. The correct term for calculating a birth chart is to "cast" it. In order to fully comprehend the extent of traits, potential and attributes, the exact time and place of birth must be known and interpreted.

See also ASTROLOGICAL SYMBOLS; ASTROLOGY.

Further reading

Cosmic Connections. Mysteries of the Unknown. Alexandria, Va.: Time Life Books, 1990.

Goodman, Linda. *Linda Goodman's Sun Signs*. New York: Fawcett/Columbine, 1978.

Morgan, Chris. *Fortune Telling: How to Predict Your Own Future*. London: Quintet Publishing and Random House, 1992.

Omarr, Sydney. *Aquarius*. New York: New American Library, 1992.

———. *My World of Astrology*. New York: Fleet, 1965.

Verlagsanstalt, Datura. *Aquarius Astro Analysis*. New York: Grossett & Dunlap, 1976.

Woolfork, Joanna Martine. *The Only Astrology Book You'll Ever Need*. Landham, Mass.: Scarborough, 1992.

ARCANA *The division of major and minor cards in the tarot pack of divining cards.*

The major arcana includes 22 cards; the minor arcana has 50. Psychics report that when most of the major arcana cards appear during a tarot reading, the querant is a seeker of spiritual knowledge. Minor arcana cards often indicate that less consequential questions are being asked.

Further reading

Buckland, Raymond. *Secrets of Gypsy Fortunetelling*. St. Paul, Minn.: Llewellyn, 1988.

Giles, Cynthia. *The Tarot: History, Mystery and Lore*. New York: Paragon House, 1992.

Secrets of the Alchemists. Mysteries of the Unknown. Alexandria, Va.: Time Life Books, 1990.

ARIES *One of the 12 astrological signs of the zodiac. The symbol is the ram.*

Those who are born between March 21 and April 20 are natives of the sign of Aries and have

ARIES

specific traits indicative of the time and date on which they were born. Divination of events can also be charted through this astrological sign.

Astrologers divine what is in store throughout life through the time, date and place in which an individual was born as they coordinate the influences with other signs, the planets, the Sun, the Moon and other powers.

In traditional Western astrology, Aries is the first sign of the zodiac. Those born during the period typically exhibit qualities of determination and ambition and, like their symbol in the zodiac, tend to ramrod their desires. Aries is a fire sign, and thus the Aries native may exhibit an instantaneous temper, but as often he or she is fast to forgive and forget. The Aries native is able to make astute determinations in very logical ways, yet sometimes all the decision is based on is intuition. This person is said to be idealistic and self-reliant, with an intense sense of responsibility and duty.

The sign of the zodiac in which an individual is born is responsible for only one fragment of

This ancient symbol represents the astrological sign of Aries.

the qualities he or she receives at birth. Psychics are quick to point out that a general forecast based solely on the stellar position of the Sun on the day an individual was born is unlikely to provide an accurate glimpse of the future.

Although traditional astrologers use books to calculate a personal birth chart based on the position of the Sun, Moon and planets at a distinct time, computer software has replaced most of this time-consuming work. The correct term for calculating a birth chart is to "cast" it. In order to fully comprehend the extent of traits, potential and attributes, the exact time and place of birth must be known and interpreted.

See also ASTROLOGICAL SYMBOLS; ASTROLOGY.

Further reading

Cosmic Connections. Mysteries of the Unknown. Alexandria, Va.: Time Life Books, 1990.

Goodman, Linda. *Linda Goodman's Sun Signs.* New York: Fawcett/Columbine, 1978.

Morgan, Chris. *Fortune Telling: How to Predict Your Own Future.* London: Quintet Publishing and Random House, 1992.

Omarr, Sydney. *Aries.* New York: New American Library, 1992.

———. *My World of Astrology.* New York: Fleet, 1965.

Verlagsanstalt, Datura. *Aries Astro Analysis.* New York: Grosset & Dunlap, 1976.

Woolfork, Joanna Martine. *The Only Astrology Book You'll Ever Need.* Landham, Mass.: Scarborough, 1992.

ARITHMANCY *Using letters or numbers in a specific combination to divine the future of a person, an event or a country; another term for NUMEROLOGY.*

As with numerology, letters and numbers are grouped and formatted to combine in a prearranged pattern, depending on the arithmanic or numerological method used. The converting of letters and other numerical sequences was developed in medieval times; arithmancy and numerology were refined by the German occultist Cornelius Agrippa during the 14th century.

Those who accept arithmancy and numerology believe that the future is planned, although people are able to make conscious changes and decisions that affect these preordained plans; the numbers foretell the future.

Further reading

Lawrence, Shirley Blackwell. *Behind Numerology.* San Bernardino, Calif.: Borgo, 1989.
Psychic Powers. Mysteries of the Unknown. Alexandria, Va.: Time Life Books, 1990.

ARMOMANCY *Divination used to predict the possibility for psychic abilities by inspecting the shoulders of the aspirant.*

Unlike anthroposomancy, which is still used today, other methods of education and information have replaced armomancy as a determining factor for psychic abilities or mediumships. Some believe that one is specifically born with the ability to foretell the future and recount the past. Others theorize that all people have the aptitude to reach deeply into the metaphysical world and use psychic powers to further their own knowledge. Psychic abilities are often considered to be intuition.

See EXTRASENSORY PERCEPTION (ESP); INTUITION.

Further reading

Bevan, E. *Sibyls and Seers: A Survey of Some Ancient Theories of Revelation and Inspiration.* London: George Allen & Unwin, 1982.
Buckland, Raymond. *Secrets of Gypsy Fortunetelling.* St. Paul, Minn.: Llewellyn, 1988.
Cheetham, E. *The Prophecies of Nostradamus.* London: Corgi, 1981.
Psychic Powers. Mysteries of the Unknown. Alexandria, Va.: Time Life Books, 1990.

ASTRAGALOMANCY *Divination by throwing dice or dominoes, or other objects with sides, to determine the future.*

This practice is more commonly known as ASTRAGYROMANCY and also by the contemporary title of sortilege.

See also DICE; I CHING; RUNE STONES; SORTILEGE SYSTEMS.

Further reading

Mind over Matter. Mysteries of the Unknown. Alexandria, Va.: Time Life Books, 1990.

ASTRAGYROMANCY *Divination of the future or the answering of a querant's question employing objects with sides.*

Ancient practitioners of astragyromancy used knucklebones, and the root word *astragalos* is Greek for vertebra or knucklebone. Records of the use of astragyromancy date from 5,000 years ago, with the tossing of bones to the ground. The position of the bones, including which side came up, revealed what the future held. This method was used in Mesopotamia.

The use of astragyromancy is mentioned in mythology when Greek goddess of fate Tyche, whom the Orphics called Eurydice, employed her powers to select sacrificial victims by the casting of lots or dice and to predict the future.

"Bone tossing" is still used today to forecast events and disclose life lessons by various cultures throughout the world. In West Africa, Bantu psychics use a set of 26 bones that are engraved with special symbols. Zulu psychics use 18 pieces in their set; numbers are engraved on 13, and 5 have symbolic messages.

The dice that are commonly used for games and gambling have a rich tradition that originated in astragyromancy. The slang for dice is "bones," which is appropriate because carved bones with dots, used to predict the future, were the actual origin of dice.

See also CLEROMANCY; SORTILEGE SYSTEMS.

Further reading

Mind over Matter. Mysteries of the Unknown. Alexandria, Va.: Time Life Books, 1990.
Visions and Prophecies. Mysteries of the Unknown. Alexandria, Va: Time Life Books, 1990.
Walker, Barbara G. *The Woman's Encyclopedia of Myths and Secrets.* New York: Harper Collins, 1983.

ASTRAL BODIES
See AURAS.

ASTRAL PLANE *Plane of existence and perception paralleling the physical plane, but one phase removed from it.*

It is said that the astral plane can be accessed during normal sleeping hours and typically involves out-of-body experiences. During these times the spirit/soul is able to move into other dimensions, perceiving things yet to happen and events that have occurred. Thus, the astral plane and out-of-body experiences can be used to divine upcoming events or circumstances that foretell the future.

In this mental world of the astral plane, everything is made of thoughts rather than atomic particles, as with the earth plane. Thus, the psychic, mental or astral "world" is not a three-dimensional realm but rather an area that is all around and all encompassing.

Carl Jung, the famous psychologist, reportedly regularly accessed the astral plane with what he termed "active imagination" and spoke with a spirit named Philemon. Jung explained that talking with this entity helped him to maintain objectivity in the psychic world. Jung was not alone in documenting communication in the astral plane. Robert Monroe, in *Journeys Out of the Body*, described the astral plane, complete with a host of "inhabitants," including those who had the appearance of demons, goblins and strange, "rubbery" entities, who supposedly possessed the ability to make Monroe's life miserable. Some psychics believe that fairies and elves also inhabit the astral plane, and humans must pass through the dominion before entering heaven, hell or an afterlife.

The astral plane is also, known in Vedic or metaphysical dialect as the kama world and *kamaloca*, which is said to be the second lowest plane, a place of emotions, desires and passions. The earth plane is even lower. In the astral plane, emotions become visible and tangible, as are material objects in the earth plane. When clairvoyantly perceived by psychics, the astral plane is said to look like Earth, with people, roads, means of transportation, schools and buildings; however, in this plane people do not need to eat, sleep or function as humans. Love prevails, but there is no physical love, as all inhabitants are genderless.

Further reading

Bletzer, June G., *The Donning International Encyclopedic Psychic Dictionary.* West Chester, Pa.: Whitford Press, 1986.

Monroe, Robert A. *Journeys Out of the Body.* New York: Doubleday, 1971.

Psychic Voyages. Mysteries of the Unknown. Alexandria, Va.: Time Life Books, 1990.

Watson, Donald. *The Dictionary of Mind and Spirit.* New York: Avon, 1991.

———. *Far Journeys.* Garden City, N.Y.: Dolphin/Doubleday, 1985.

ASTROLOGICAL SYMBOLS *Specific marks or glyphs used as symbols for planets, signs and aspects of the zodiac. They are used in place of words in casting (producing) an astrological birth or event chart.*

There are 10 planets, 12 signs of the zodiac, and 6 aspect symbols. Each of the planets and zodiac signs in its own way designates a specific position on a birth chart. The aspects indicate angles between planets. Astrology is an ancient metaphysical science once grouped with astronomy. According to those who practice the art, in astrology celestial bodies exert forces and display personalities and characteristics that influence people and events. See ASTROLOGY.

The Planets

The original seven planets viewed by the ancient astrologers are used to discern personal characteristics. They include the Sun, the Moon (although neither is a planet, both were once thought to be), Mercury, Venus, Mars, Jupiter and Saturn. The planets of Uranus, Neptune and Pluto, discovered later, do, according to astrologers, influence lives and events but have a more subtle effect.

The Sun, as a source of life and energy, has the most powerful effect on the individual born during a specific sign of the zodiac and indicates masculine qualities that are balanced with the Moon's more feminine characteristics. Most

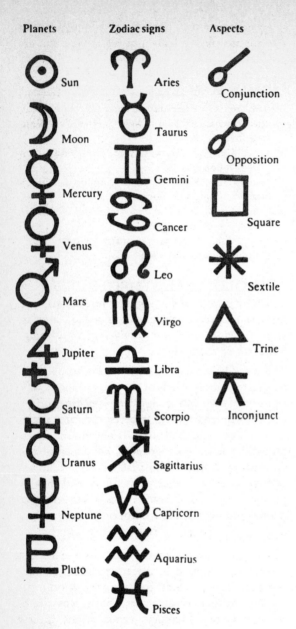

Planets	Zodiac signs	Aspects
Sun	Aries	Conjunction
Moon	Taurus	Opposition
Mercury	Gemini	Square
Venus	Cancer	Sextile
Mars	Leo	Trine
Jupiter	Virgo	Inconjunct
Saturn	Libra	
Uranus	Scorpio	
Neptune	Sagittarius	
Pluto	Capricorn	
	Aquarius	
	Pisces	

ASTROLOGICAL SYMBOLS
There are 10 planets, 12 signs of the zodiac and
6 aspect symbols. Each designates a specific position
on a birth chart.

Americans know their sun sign, whether it is Capricorn or Cancer. The Sun has the most dominance over personality; it represents career and power. The Sun affects the astrological signs (see specific astrological signs for more information) as it passes through them.

The Moon, a feminine influence in the universe, represents moods and emotions. It is said to control the characteristics of intuition, love, affection and spirituality. The Moon is said to control the rhythms of the natural patterns of life; it affects, for example, water and the tides.

Mercury is considered the messenger of the zodiac. It controls communication. Those born under Mercury are said to be quick witted, to communicate well and to be bright and potentially volatile. Sometimes it is associated with youth because it is the smallest planet and can, at times, be a trickster.

Venus's concern is harmony and unity; it is the most feminine of the planets, but astrologers point out that that does not mean strictly female but rather a love of sensitivity and solidarity. This is often reflected in individuals born with Venus in their sign, who are artistic, elegant, peace loving and romantic. They can also have tendencies toward shyness and passivity.

Mars rules the active nature of people and exemplifies strong passions. Often the individual with a strong influence of Mars in his or her sign has a quick temper but just as quickly forgives a wrongdoer. Mars also influences fearlessness, persistence and directness in words and actions.

Jupiter, the largest of the planets, is characterized by individuals exhibiting cheerfulness, optimism, expansion and candid behaviors. It brings out giving and trusting natures and has a strong drive for success in career and personal endeavors.

Saturn is said to be the "old man of the Zodiac," careful and considerate; responsibility and capability are characteristics shown from this planet's control. It is said to have an influence over thriftiness.

Uranus, according to some astrologers, signals change, newness and originality, and since it spends seven years in each sign as it passes through the solar system, Uranus may have great control over individuals. Other astrologers negate its effect. Uranus is said to produce a willingness to learn about metaphysical events and concepts.

Neptune is believed to have even less control on a birth chart than Uranus. It is a mystical planet and indicates characteristics of mysterious ways, heightened sensitivity and intuition. Because it moves so slowly, Neptune has only been in some of the constellations during this century, so astrologers do not know its true influence as yet.

Pluto is truly considered the planet of the unknown. It signifies change and metamorphosis, and since astrologers believe that those with the Pluto influence in their charts need to address these influences alone, it can signal a time of great revolution and transmutation.

The Signs

The following *general* characteristics are shown in natives of the sun signs:

Aries (March 22–April 20): Industrious, opinionated and sometimes confrontational; enjoys taking command.

Taurus (April 21–May 21): Tenacious and clever; may be stubborn and have a quick temper.

Gemini (May 22–June 22): Versatile, inconsistent, imaginative and quick witted.

Cancer (June 23–July 23): Innovative, thrifty, family oriented; may be shy and moody.

Leo (July 24–August 23): Powerful and poised; likes to be the star; may be egotistical.

Virgo (August 24–September 23): Modest and practical; tends to be fastidious; may be meddlesome.

Libra (September 24–October 23): Diplomatic and outgoing; may be wishy-washy and vacillate.

Scorpio (October 24–November 22): Intense and secretive; may be overly moody and suspicious.

Sagittarius (November 23–December 22): Outgoing and tolerant; may be too outspoken and restless.

Capricorn (December 23–January 19): Pragmatic and reliable; may be too serious and self-centered.

Aquarius (January 20–February 19): Individualistic and self-reliant; may be defiant and seek unorthodox lifestyles.

Pisces (February 20–March 21): Caring and gentle; may be secretive and shy.

The Aspects

There are six angular relationships of importance in casting a birth chart. These are the aspects. They detail the relationships between the other influences of the zodiac. Some astrologers use more than the following and study their use throughout a lifetime. The descriptions below are meant to be a jumping-off point for those who are interested in any phase of metaphysics.

Conjunction: This is when the planets of the same sign act in the same way. It is a concentration of energies. It is the strongest aspect in astrology.

Opposition: Said to indicate conflict between opposite signs. It has the latent quality to aid self-examination. It is often considered unharmonious.

Trine: The most harmonious aspect; however, an individual with too many trine aspects may lack motivation.

Square: Produces tension between planets and provides an opportunity for change. It indicates challenges.

Sextile: Planets in this combination are a signal for change and restyling. A sextile is thought to bring out opportunities.

Inconjunct: Indicated when planets have nothing in common or show a need to reconcile or reorganize traits of the personality and life.

Further reading

Bosanko, Susan, ed. *Predicting Your Future.* New York: Ballantine Books/Diagram Group. Visual Information Limited, 1983.

Cosmic Connection. Mysteries of the Unknown. Alexandria, Va.: Time Life Books, 1990.

Goodman, Linda. *Linda Goodman's Star Signs.* New York: St. Martin's, 1987.

———. *Linda Goodman's Sun Signs.* New York: Fawcett/Columbine, 1978.

Morgan, Chris. *Fortune Telling: How to Predict Your Own Future.* London: Quintet Publishing and Random House, 1992.

Stewart, R. J. *The Elements of Prophecy.* Dorset, England: Element Books, 1990.

Watson, Lyall. *Supernature.* Garden City, N.Y.: Anchor Press/Doubleday, 1973.

Woodruff, Maurice. *Maurice Woodruff Futurecaster: The Secrets of Foretelling Your Own Future.* Cleveland, Ohio: World Publishing Company, 1969.

Woolfork, Joanna Martine. *The Only Astrology Book You'll Ever Need.* Landham, Mass.: Scarborough, 1992.

ASTROLOGY *Divination using the study of the placement of the planets, Moon and stars at the time of birth or the time of a particular event.*

An astrologer is someone who has been specially trained to cast a birth or event chart using the ancient science and art of astrology. To have a complete and correct chart formatted, one must know the exact time, date and place of birth, including whether or not daylight saving time was in effect. Using precise calculations, astrologers can predict future happenings and interpret the nature or character of the individual or event. Many spend their entire lives studying astrology because there are many nuances to be considered, including the psychic's ability to decipher the information provided by the mathematical configurations required by the chart.

Unfortunately there are no simple "how to's" involved in instructing someone on how to cast a birth chart (sometimes called a natal chart). Typically, today's astrologer uses computer software in which the information of time, date and place of birth is input; the cost of a computer-generated chart produced by a company that specializes in charts is about $10. Astrologers charge from $40 to thousands of dollars to do a complete chart with the interpretations. Many books, however, give the manual method, which is too complex to outline here. An ephemeris, a book giving the positions of the Sun, Moon and planets at a particular time, is used in the calculating process. An ephemeris can be purchased at most metaphysical book stores; however, a basic class on astrology is probably the best method to learn the most simple techniques of casting a horoscope.

Almost every American knows his or her astrological sign. In a Gallup poll taken in 1990, it was found that more than half of those who answered the survey had read the astrological forecast offered in the daily newspaper. There are more than 10,000 astrologers in the United States, and astrologers have been used by both politicians and celebrities as well as everyday people looking for a way to avoid the bumps of life and foretell the future.

Proper understanding of astrology can provide a key to character and personality to control and minimize all that is negative. Claudius Ptolemy, an astrologer of the second century A.D., said, "You can take precautions against your own temperament just as you can against bad weather," when you know what is in your astrological chart. Additionally, the chart imparts understanding of the feelings and temptations of others, gives foreknowledge of the dangers to which, by reason of the moment of birth, one may be predisposed, and makes one aware of potential talents and abilities so that time might be spent fine-tuning those qualities. Moreover, it enables students of astrology to recognize the moment when good fortune will strike and pinpoints fortunate times in which to balance work, health and love.

The exact beginning of astrology is a topic on which there is much speculation, and the legends are filled with romance, mystery, contradictions and quests for ethereal information and power. For thousands of years, astrology and astronomy (the mathematical science of charting the planets and stars, without psychic interpretation) were actually considered one and the same.

As early as 8000 B.C., people looked to the heavens to understand life and perhaps plot future events. The Assyrians, Babylonians, Egyptians, Mayans, Incas and other ancient peoples believed that their fate could be determined from the activities taking place on high. All of these groups and many others that have since disappeared employed astrologers to record and predict the positions of the stars and the timing of events, looking heavenward to assist in their survival and prosperity.

The oldest astrology "textbook" was written around A.D. 150 by the astrologer-astronomer Ptolemy, working in Egypt, but unfortunately it is lost in time. The Greeks were the first to construct an ephemeris. The Romans continued the practice of astrology, and it was not until forecasting events by the movements in the sky was thought to be profane by the early Christians that astrology began to recede as the leading method of prognostication. Saint Augustine and others attacked astrology, and the art declined for the next 800 years. In the 13th century, astrology slowly revived. It would seem that true practitioners and astrologers simply went "underground" with their study, as the knowledge was not lost.

In the 17th century, interest increased. It is claimed by some (again, contradictions enter the picture) that Queen Elizabeth I turned to astrologer Dr. John Dee for counsel. And British astrologer and psychic William Lilly wrote *Astrological Predictions* in 1648, predicting, among other things, "sundry fires and consuming plague" for London, which was charted to occur about 1665. He was subsequently imprisoned because it was believed he somehow caused the Great Plague (of 1665, which wiped out a great mass of the English and European population) and the fire of London in 1666, although he was later exonerated. Francis Moore, author of *Vox Stellarum*, which was published at approximately the same time and later became *Old Moore's Almanac,* is still published annually and continues to be consulted by astrologers today. In 1784, Ebenezer Sibley wrote *The Celestial Art of Astrology,* perhaps the most ambitious book on the subject up to that point in history.

Astrology slowly declined in popularity and for a time only a few true believers cast horoscopes. When Madame Helena Blavatsky started the Theosophical Society in 1875, to study the unexplained laws of nature, including astrology, this occult art received new interest (see BLAVATSKY, HELENA P.), with the revival of spiritualism continuing into the early 1900s. But it was not until 1931 that astrology became fashionable once more. When Princess Margaret of Great Britain was born, the London *Sunday Express* hired an astrologer to chart her birth signs and tell the world about the characteristics of this newest royal princess. Suddenly it was chic and

trendy to know one's sun sign, and astrology has continued to gain in popularity ever since.

Psychologist Carl G. Jung often consulted horoscopes to assist patients, and today metaphysical counselors seek to advise of character factors said to be determined by the stars and the planets in the hope that current concerns and problems can be resolved.

While Western astrology looks to advise, the astrology practiced in the Far East often is seen as a way to blueprint coming events and divine future happenings.

See also CHINESE ASTROLOGY.

Further reading

Baigent, Campion, and Harvey Baigent. *Mundane Astrology: An Introduction to the Astrological Nations and Groups.* London: Aquarian Press, 1984.

Bosanko, Susan, ed. *Predicting Your Future.* New York: Ballantine Books/Diagram Group. Visual Information Limited, 1983.

Cornell, H. L. *Encyclopedia of Medical Astrology.* St. Paul, Minn.: Llewellyn, 1972.

Forrest, Steven. *The Changing Sky: The Dynamic New Astrology for Everyone.* New York: Bantam, 1984.

Goodman, Linda. *Linda Goodman's Star Signs.* New York: St. Martin's, 1987.

———. *Linda Goodman's Sun Signs.* New York: Fawcett/Columbine, 1978.

Lewis, Grant. *Heaven Knows What.* St. Paul, Minn.: Llewellyn, 1962.

Luce, Robert de. *The Complete Method of Prediction.* New York: ASI, 1978.

Stewart, R. J. *The Elements of Prophecy.* Dorset, England: Element Books, 1990.

Watson, Lyall. *Supernature.* Garden City, N.Y.: Anchor Press/Doubleday, 1973.

Wilson, James. *The Dictionary of Astrology.* New York: Samuel Weiser, 1974.

Woodruff, Maurice. *Maurice Woodruff Futurecaster: The Secrets of Foretelling Your Own Future.* Cleveland, Ohio: World Publishing Company, 1969.

Woolfork, Joanna Martine. *The Only Astrology Book You'll Ever Need.* 5th printing. Landham, Mass.: Scarborough, 1992.

ASTROLOGY, EMOTIONAL

ASTROLOGY, EMOTIONAL *A type of astrology that specifically deals with the emotional aspects of divination as it involves the study of the placement of the planets, the Moon* *and the stars at the time of birth or the occasion of a particular event.*

With emotional astrology, practitioners calculate specific periods for undertaking matters such as an engagement, a marriage, the conceiving of a child or the purchasing of property or a house. Emotional astrology can also be used to calculate the best date for taking a vacation or trip.

See also ASTROLOGY.

ASTROLOGY, HORARY *Divination using the placement of the planets, the Moon and the stars to calculate future events, such as earthquakes and floods.*

See also ASTROLOGY.

ASTROLOGY, INCEPTIONAL *Divination using the placement of the planets, the Moon and the stars to foretell the outcome of an event whose location, date and time of occurrence are known.*

For example, inceptional astrology might be used when predicting the outcome of a sporting event, a business meeting or a lawsuit.

See also ASTROLOGY.

ASTROLOGY, MEDICAL *Divination using the placement of the planets, the Moon and the stars to advise on the health of the querant.*

This branch of astrology correlates the signs of the zodiac and other planetary influences with disease and problems with the human body. Each of the 12 signs influences specific areas of the body.

Aries: Head and face
Taurus: Neck and throat
Gemini: Arms and shoulders
Cancer: Breast and stomach
Leo: Heart, back and neck area
Virgo: Internal organs
Libra: Kidneys, lower back and spine area
Scorpio: Reproductive organs
Sagittarius: Hips and large muscles of the body
Capricorn: Knees and skin

Aquarius: Legs and ankles
Pisces: Feet, toes and mucous membranes of the body

See also ASTROLOGY.

ASTROLOGY, MUNDANE *Divination using the placement of the planets, the Moon and the stars to advise on events that have a large-scale effect on people, such as wars, peace conferences, pollution, disasters, social trends and national political changes.*

This branch of astrology concerns itself with how such changes affect the population and various groups of people, along with the structure of the Earth.

See also ASTROLOGY.

ASTROLOGY, NATAL *Divination using the placement of the planets, the Moon and the stars to predict the future and other events using the personal astrological or natal chart of the querant.*

See also ASTROLOGY.

ASTROLOGY, PREDICTIVE *Divination using the placement of the planets, the Moon and the stars to predict future events in one's life.*

Although many astrologers also use predictive astrology to foretell things that will happen in the future, most look to astrology simply to divine character traits that, in turn, help the querant respond to their influences.

See also ASTROLOGY.

ASTROMANCY *An ancient divination method that involves observing the stars.*

A psychic or seer interprets the messages, answers a querant's questions or forecasts the future by looking at the stars and planets on a clear night. As with other astrologically oriented methods, astromancy probably originated more than 7,000 years ago, even before the Sumerians began producing complex astronomical charts.

See ALECTROMANCY; ASTROLOGY.

Further reading

Daniels, Cora Linn, and C. M. Stevans, Ph.D., eds. *Encyclopedia of Superstitions, Folklore and the Occult Sciences of the World.* Detroit: Gale Research, 1971.

Woolfork, Joanna Martine. *The Only Astrology Book You'll Ever Need.* Landham, Mass.: Scarborough, 1992.

AUGUR *One who can forecast or foretell the future.*

Other names for such individuals include clairvoyant, psychic, mystic, oracle, prophet or diviner. They may also be referred to as metaphysical counselors.

In ancient Rome, more than 2,000 years ago, augurs were specifically royal spiritualists who divined the future using birds: the route the birds flew, their speed, their species and number, along with the sounds made in flight or when they landed. When Julius Caesar came to power, augurs practiced on the government's payroll. Intriguingly enough, Roman augurs never directly watched the birds but sat on a nearby hill, often blindfolded, with assistants who explained to them what was happening.

Further reading

Maven, Max. *Max Maven's Book of Fortunetelling.* New York: Prentice-Hall, 1992.

Sinnigen, William G., and Arthur E. R. Boak. *A History of Rome to A.D. 565.* 6th ed. New York: Macmillan, 1977.

Visions and Prophecies. Mysteries of the Unknown. Alexandria, Va.: Time Life Books, 1990.

AURAS *Electromagnetic energy fields completely surrounding all living entities, including people, plants, animals and minerals. Also known as astral bodies, auras emanate color.*

Some psychics believe that only they, with their specifically learned skills or God-given talents, can see an aura; others maintain that anyone can see auras. As with other metaphysical topics, the viewing of auras is controversial because most people claim they cannot see them. Most psychics agree, however, that an aura can change, grow and produce various colors. There are overlapping colors and colors that are a blend of other colors. An aura is sometimes compared to a personal rainbow.

One explanation of an aura is that at different energy frequencies coming from the body, the colors blend and change. An aura is often said to be bipolar, receiving negative as well as positive energy, and unable to exist without the entity. According to psychics, the aura's major function is to protect the entity from invisible rays of light, acting as a shield against any harm from the ethereal world. Auras are said to disappear when a person dies, or "passes over."

In the early 1990s, it became popular to have one's aura read; the various colors emanating from the aura were said to indicate personality strengths and weaknesses, health and disease, even possible careers and emotional adaptability. Additionally, colors in an aura can change by the minute. For example, if one is in an angry mood, the aura might be a completely different color than if one is lounging by a lake on a glorious Sunday afternoon. Since each psychic (and each person) sees color in a slightly different manner, there are no absolutes on exactly what each color means, and there are often major differences of opinion.

Viewing and divining characteristics by the use of the aura is not a new concept. Medieval saints and mystics distinguished four different types of aura: the nimbus, the halo, the areola and the glory. The first two streamed from the head, the areola emanated from the entire body and the glory was seen as a combination of the two. Others believe that there are five divisions: the health aura, the vital aura, the karmic aura, the aura of character and the aura of spiritual nature. One of the first documented experimental investigations on auras was recorded in *Ten Years with Spiritual Mediums* by Francis Gerry Fairfield, an American researcher, in 1874. He claimed that all organic structures have a special nerve atmosphere. Though greeted with skepticism, the same conclusion that there is an aura surrounding living energies was established by Dr. Walter J. Kilner, and his findings were published in *The Human Atmosphere* in London in 1911. Dr. Kilner devised a screen and various lighting apparatuses that allowed the human eye to see the aura, regardless of the psychic ability of the observer. Kilner reported that his curiosity was peaked on this topic when he viewed old paintings of holy figures which showed them standing in a surrounding luminous glow long before Christians invented the halo.

Psychics often see the aura as a chronicle of past, present and future events, with the vibrations denoting the degree of energy each event mirrors in the life of the querant. They also view the aura according to texture, blemishes and intensity, each indicating a specific trait or concern. Some believe that the more mentally alert an individual is, the more intense the aura will be; conversely, if one is more physical than intellectual, the aura will take on grayish tones.

Auras were photographed through an electrographic system devised by electrician-inventor Semyon Kirlian in the 1930s.

Some people see a special type of aura around the head and body of psychics and mystics. Referred to as an areola, it is circular or oblong in shape. The oblong areola was especially associated with Jesus Christ.

See also KIRLIAN PHOTOGRAPHY.

Further reading

Ancient Wisdom and Sects. Mysteries of the Unknown. Alexandria, Va.: Time Life Books, 1990.

Bailey, Alice. *A Treatise on White Magic.* New York: Lucis, 1951.

Bowers, Barbara. *What Color Is Your Aura?* New York: Simon & Schuster, 1989.

Fodor, Nandor. *Encyclopedia of Psychic Science.* New York: University Books, 1966.

Kilner, Walter J. *The Aura.* New York: Samuel Weiser, 1973.

Krippner, Stanley, and Daniel Rubin. *The Kirlian Aura.* New York: Doubleday, Anchor Press, 1974.

Watson, Lyall. *Supernature.* Garden City, N.Y.: Anchor, 1973.

AUSTROMANCY
Divination by listening to the sound of the wind and interpreting the messages. Austromancy is part of the collective prediction methods grouped with GEOMANCY.

In ancient China and Tibet, austromancy was practiced by holding a seashell to the ear and

In ancient China and Tibet, austromancy was practiced by holding a shell to the ear. The sounds were interpreted to foretell future events or define an omen.

was considered an extremely serious method of divination. Today, as with many occult divination practices, the method has been passed down but has lost its divination meaning. As any child can attest, one can listen to the "waves" or the sound of the sea crashing to the shore by holding a shell to the ear.

Further reading

Lip, Evelyn. *Chinese Geomancy.* New York: Times Books International, 1979.

Maven, Max. *Max Maven's Book of Fortunetelling.* New York: Prentice-Hall, 1992.

O'Brien, Joanne, with Kwok Man Ho. *The Elements of Feng Shui.* Dorset, England: Element Books, 1991.

AUTOMATIC WRITING
Writing produced without the control of the conscious self; unconscious movement attributed to supernatural guidance.

This system of forecasting the future, or providing knowledge of events that will affect humanity, allows the spirits of the ethereal world to direct the writing of one's hand and arm with pencil and paper.

Not to be confused with inspirational writing (writing coming from one's own higher energy, which is often somewhat esoteric and poetic), automatic writing is a form of communication with the spirit world using the human body as a vehicle to provide written information.

Psychics and those who have experienced automatic writing describe it in much the same way: After feeling sleepy, prickly or tingly, or after going into a trance, the psychic allows the spiritual entity to use his or her body as a tool. One of the first documented automatic-writing incidents was described in a book, *Spirit Identity*, written by the Reverend Stainton Moses in 1872. He wrote, "My right arm was seized up and down with a noise resembling that of a number of factors at work. It was the most tremendous exhibition of 'unconscious muscular action' I ever saw. In vain I tried to stop it. I distinctly felt the grasps, soft and firm, round my arm, and though perfectly possessed of senses and volition, I was powerless to interfere, although my hand was disabled for some days by the bruising it then got. The object we soon found was to get up the force."

A number of writers have admitted that they have written in a semitrance state, and attributed it to automatic writing. Harriet Beecher Stowe, author of *Uncle Tom's Cabin*, said, "I didn't write it: It was given to me. It passed before me." Parts of the Old Testament were supposedly written through automatic writing: "And there came a writing to him from Elijah the prophet saying . . ." (2 Chron. 21:12). In 1883, a book produced by the German Augustinian nun Anna Catherine Emmerich, *The Lowly Life and Bitter Passion of Our Lord Jesus Christ and His Blessed Mother*, was accepted by Catholics as divinely written. The remarkable contents of the book were said to have come to the nun through visions that directed her hand.

One of the earliest accounts of automatic writing in the United States was a book of inspirational messages called *The Pilgrimage of Thomas Payne and Others to the Seventh Circle*, published in 1852 by Rev. C. Hammond, and automatic writing has continued with writings by Ruth Montgomery and Alice Bailey, among others.

While there has been a recent renewal of interest in this mantic art, especially through the works of Ruth Montgomery, automatic writing reached its peak during the late 1800s when the efficiency of the method (over the more arduous table tipping, where a different number of thumps stand for each letter of the alphabet) became evident. Alfred, Lord Tennyson and William Butler Yeats were among those who, psychics believe, used automatic writing to increase the poetry of their prose (however, it may have been inspirational writing, in their case, rather than automatic writing).

In the early 1900s in England, Frederick Bligh Bond, director of excavation at Glastonbury Abbey, and a colleague, John Allyne, used automatic writing, which came in Latin and Middle English, concerning the architectural design of the medieval chapel completely hidden beneath the abbey. When excavations began years later, the writings proved to be incredibly accurate, specifically in the detailed accounts of the structures and sizes of the building.

Some metaphysical experts insist that automatic writing is the way a discarnate spirit communicates; opponents believe that the writing comes from the psychic's own mind. Critics of automatic writing warn that the psychic using this method of divination may connect with an evil or demonic spirit. Skeptics believe that the only evil inherent in automatic writing is the possibility of dredging up the unconscious thoughts of the psychic.

Although those who instruct others in the mantic art of automatic writing warn that results take time and patience, it is possible to achieve the skill. It is said that by meditating or relaxing with pencil or pen in hand, and opening one's thoughts to information from the ethereal world, writing will begin. Some suggest using a typewriter or personal computer to make the process more readable, as often the script is illegible.

Additionally, there have been cases of automatic painting, automatic speaking and automatic piano playing. Rosemary Brown, a mediocre pianist at best, suddenly discovered that in a trancelike state she could play beautifully. She claimed that composers such as Beethoven, Chopin and Liszt were taking her over and using her hands "like a pair of gloves."

Automatic writing is a facet of the mantic art of automatism, which encompasses automatic writing, automatic musical ability, automatic literature and automatic art ability.

See also OUIJA BOARDS; TABLE TIPPING.

Further reading

Brown, Rosemary. *Immortals at My Elbow.* London: Bachman & Turner, 1974.

Fodor, Nandor. *Encyclopedia of Psychic Science.* New York: University Books, 1966.

Guiley, Rosemary Ellen. *Harper's Encyclopedia of Mystical and Paranormal Experience.* San Francisco: HarperSan Francisco, 1991.

Montgomery, Ruth. *A Search for the Truth.* New York: Bantam, 1968.

Psychic Powers. Mysteries of the Unknown. Alexandria, Va.: Time Life Books, 1990.

Search for the Soul. Mysteries of the Unknown. Alexandria, Va.: Time Life Books, 1990.

Watson, Donald. *The Dictionary of Mind and Spirit.* New York: Avon, 1991.

AUTOMATISM *Writing, drawing, painting or musical abilities produced without the control of the conscious mind; unconscious movement attributed to supernatural guidance.*

See AUTOMATIC WRITING.

AXINOMANCY *Use of an ax to locate that which is hidden.*

Axes were used specifically to find buried treasure or for finding out where something was hidden. In axinomancy, the ax is balanced on the wrist, and information is said to come directly from the spirit world to the psychic who is performing the rite. Or the ax is balanced on the wrist of the psychic, and the direction of the handle when the tool falls to the ground determines the basis for gauging future events.

In ancient Greece, the ax may also have been heated and studied to foretell the placement of an object. In a variation of this method, a piece of agate or a special stone is balanced on the edge of the blade. When the metal blade cooled, the stone fell to the ground and the direction and placement of the stone was analyzed.

See also BELOMANCY; DOWSING.

Further reading

Bletzer, June G. *The Donning International Encyclopedic Psychic Dictionary.* West Chester, Pa.: Whitford Press, 1986.

Mysterious Lands and Peoples. Mysteries of the Unknown. Alexandria, Va.: Time Life Books, 1990.

B

BAILEY, ALICE *(1880–1949) English psychic and author who specialized in automatic writing.*

Bailey often produced the books and articles attributed to her using the divination method of automatic writing. She also channeled information from the spirit world.

Bailey founded the Arcane School to study the secret knowledge of the ethereal world and wrote (using AUTOMATIC WRITING) and published a multitude of material from the masters, including Koot Hoomi and another entity called "the Tibetan."

Her books include *A Treatise on Cosmic Fire, A Treatise on White Magic, Letters on Occult Meditation* and *Unfinished Autobiography,* published after her death in 1951.

Further reading

Bailey, Alice. *A Treatise on White Magic.* New York: Lucis, 1951.

Brown, Rosemary. *Immortals at My Elbow.* London: Bachman & Turner, 1974.

Fodor, Nandor. *Encyclopedia of Psychic Science.* New York: University Books, 1966.

BELOMANCY *Divination using arrows.*

In this ancient method of prognostication, which originated in Arabia, Greece and/or Chaldea, arrows are thrown in the air. Predictions about the future or answers to an individual's questions are determined by the direction in which the arrows point; this is the direction the querant should take.

A form of sortilege in which an object is thrown into the air or dropped to the ground to determine future happenings (see SORTILEGE SYSTEMS), belomancy was common in many primitive cultures, where it was not unusual to use arrows for hunting game and for sport. Historians of the mantic arts compare the sport of archery to the use of belomancy, in which one would take aim on the future rather than on a target.

Originally, belomancy was only used to provide yes or no answers. For example, if the arrows crossed, the answer was no; if they did not touch, then an affirmative answer was received. Sometimes the arrows were actually marked with the words *yes* or *no,* and in that case, whichever arrow was side up revealed the forecast. In time a third arrow was used which was blank. Thus, if yes and no were face down on the ground, the addition of the third arrow indicated that the question could not be answered. The use of the blank arrow was the beginning of other systems that also included an indecisive answer.

In Tibet, a two-arrow system, called dahmo, was used. In dahmo, a length of white cloth was

Belomancy began in ancient Arabia, Greece and/or Chaldea. After a question was posed, arrows were thrown in the air. Interpretation was done by the direction and placement of the fallen arrows.

BIBLICAL PROPHETS AND DIVINATION METHODS *In the New Testament, prophecies were distrusted and the occult outlawed. However, the Old Testament is filled with prophecies and references to diviners, dream interpreters, magicians, soothsayers and psychics who played a role in the development of the Israelite society and religion.*

Two well-known practices of the metaphysical arts were used in ancient Mesopotamia. One of the most developed of the mantic arts, according to Bible scholars, was hepatomancy, the art of predicting the future by studying the color and shape of the livers of sacrificial animals (also called HEPATOSCOPY). The Prophet Ezekiel refers to this practice in 21:21, "For the king of Babylon stood at the parting of the way, at the head

tied onto the center of one arrow; this was the affirmative answer. A strip of black cloth was tied to the other arrow and indicated a negative response. The arrows were shot or plunged into a mound of barley. As the barley fell to the sides, the arrows were allowed to fall. The final placement of the arrows was interpreted to divine the future or answer a querant's questions.

Arrows and similar belomantic systems have been used in what is now Mexico and Korea, and there are references to belomancy and other divination tools as used by psychics in the Old Testament.

See also BIBLICAL PROPHETS AND DIVINATION METHODS.

Further reading

Maven, Max. *Max Maven's Book of Fortunetelling.* New York: Prentice-Hall, 1992.

Morgan, Chris. *Fortune Telling: How to Predict Your Own Future.* London: Quintet Publishing and Random House, 1992.

BIBLICAL PROPHETS AND DIVINATION METHODS
Jesus Christ was acclaimed as a prophet (Matt. 21:11 and other references throughout the New Testament) and regarded himself as one (Mark 6:4 and elsewhere).

of the two ways, to use divination: he made his arrows bright, he consulted with images, he looked in the liver." Intricate instructions regarding how to employ hepatomancy to divine, including the use of clay models, have been discovered by archaeologists. One such model was uncovered in a Canaanite temple at Hazor in northern Israel and dated at about 1500 B.C.

In the Old Testament, astrology and prognostication are found in Isaiah 47:13: "Let now the astrologers, the stargazers, the monthly prognosticators, stand up and save thee from these things that shall come upon thee." Dream interpretation is referred to in Daniel 2:2–3: "Then the king commanded to call the magicians, and the astrologers, and the sorcerers, and the Chaldeans, for to shew the king his dreams. So they came and stood before the king. And the king said unto them, I have dreamed a dream, and my spirit was troubled to know the dream."

There are numerous passages in the Old Testament that offer direct references to "dreamers," "sorcerers," "enchanters" and "magicians." Biblical texts on these topics include Exodus 7:11 (the use of psychics by the Egyptians) and Isaiah 47:9–15 (their use by the Babylonians). A special class of priests in ancient Egypt practiced, and were specifically trained in the forecasting of future events, as documented in the Book of Genesis.

Often prophesies were spoken, such as those thought of today as being channeled. It is also thought that priests and other psychics of the time used a method similar to TASSEOGRAPHY (interpreting the dregs of tea leaves or coffee grounds, as in teacup reading). This mantic art was used to divine the future through the patterns formed by oil poured on top of water in a bowl or cup, a skill Genesis 44:5 and 15 attributed to Joseph.

Numbers 12:5–6 deals with dream interpretation: "And the Lord came down in a pillar of cloud, and stood at the door of the Tent, and called both Aaron and Miriam and they both came forth.

"And He said, Hear now my words: if there be a prophet among you, I the Lord will make myself known unto him in a vision, I will speak with him in a dream."

Not only men of the Bible were prophets: A number of women known to have psychic abilities are mentioned. In the Old Testament, Miriam (Exod. 15:20) and Deborah (Judg. 4:4) were prophets. However, some scholars believe these mentions were made to honor the women, not to infer that they actually had prophetic abilities. Nevertheless, Huldah (2 Kings 22:12–20) was consulted by the priest at the command of Josiah, king of Judah, in regard to interpreting the Book of Law.

When Jerusalem was destroyed, prophecy in the Holy Land ceased, yet a revival has been forecast.

In the New Testament, John the Baptist is called "the prophet of the Most High" (Luke 1:76); in Matthew 3:4 he is described wearing the clothes of a prophet, a "garment of camel's hair, and a leather girdle around his waist." Many prophets and priests wore breastplates (loose robes with leather belts) with a pocket that contained a Urim and Thummin, which are said to have been used as a sortilege method, a way of casting lots to divine the future or deciding the innocence or guilt of an accused.

Jesus was acclaimed as a prophet (Matt. 21:11 and other references throughout the New Testament) and regarded himself as one (Mark 6:4 and elsewhere).

The use of prophecy and the words of prophets contributed to the development and evolution of the Jewish and Christian faiths.

See also CHANNEL.

Further reading

Bouqet, A. C. *Everyday Life in New Testament Times.* New York: Scribner's, 1954.

Everyday Life in Bible Times. Washington, D.C.: National Georgraphic Society, 1967.

McKenzie, John L. *Dictionary of the Bible.* Milwaukee: Bruce, 1965.

Miller, Madeleine S., and J. Lane Miller, eds. *Harper's Encyclopedia of Bible Life.* San Francisco: Harper & Row, 1978.

Tinney, Merrill C., ed. *The Zodervan Pictorial Encyclopedia of the Bible.* Grand Rapids, Mich.: Zondervan Publishing House, 1977.

BIBLIOMANCY *Divination by using a sacred book—though not necessarily the Bible—to forecast the future or provide answers to a querant's question.*

The term *bibliomancy* was derived from the Greek *byblos*, meaning book or paper, originating from the Phoenician city of that name, which specialized in the export of paper products.

With eyes closed, a book is opened at random or where fate will direct the querant or psychics. When they are opened, the eyes are to be directed to a certain passage; sometimes a finger is run down the page and stopped before the eyes are opened. The paragraph or verse is the correct answer to the question at hand.

In ancient times both Jews and Christians used the Bible for divination purposes. Particularly in the 4th through the 14th centuries, it was used repeatedly by kings, bishops and saints. Saint Augustine, in so many words, recommended taking omens from the Bible for guidance and in cases of spiritual difficulty or bewilderment.

Today, some groups and religious orders still use a form of bibliomancy for sustenance, advice or guidance, soliciting help from the verses or prophecies found in holy books.

See also RHAPSODOMANCY.

Further reading

Agrippa, Cornelius. *The Ladies' Oracle*. London: Hugh Evelyn Publishers, 1966.

Baring-Gould, Sabine. *Curious Myths of the Middle Ages*. New York: University Books, 1967.

Bevan, E. *Sibyls and Seers: A Survey of Some Ancient Theories of Revelation and Inspiration*. London: Allen & Unwin, 1982.

Cheetham, E. *The Prophecies of Nostradamus*. London: Corgi, 1981.

Hazlitt, W. Carew. *Faiths and Folklore of the British Isles*. 2 vols. New York: Benjamin Blom, 1965.

Maple, Eric. *The Dark World of Witches*. Cranbury, N.J.: A. S. Barnes & Co., 1964.

Opie, Iona, and Moira Tatem. *A Dictionary of Superstitions*. Oxford: Oxford University Press, 1992.

Walker, Barbara G. *The Woman's Encyclopedia of Myths and Secrets*. New York: Harper Collins, 1983.

BIOCORPOREITY *Term for the image of the body when it has been projected to another place.*

See also BILOCATION.

BILOCATION *The psychic method by which a person appears in two places at once, which sometimes foretells the death of the individual who sees the "double."*

Few recent accounts have been recorded concerning this phenomenon. It is said that in 1774, Saint Alphonsus Maria de'Ligouri was seen at the bedside of Pope Clement XIV as he was dying. Actually the saint was locked in a cell in a prison four days' journey from the terminally ill pontiff.

This ancient procedure is said to have been practiced by monks, holy people, saints, mystics and psychics. A person, whether in an exact image or in a foggy, ghostly form, materializes to group or an individual while also appearing in another place at the very same instant. Many Christian saints and monks were said to have used the art of bilocation. They include Saint Anthony of Padua, Saint Ambrose of Milan and Saint Severus of Ravenna.

The term used by psychics for the image of the duplicate form is *biocorporeity.*

Further reading

Ferguson, John. *An Illustrated Encyclopedia of Mysticism and the Mystery Religions*. New York: Seabury Press, 1976.

Fodor, Nandor. *Encyclopedia of Psychic Science*. New York: University Books, 1966.

BLAVATSKY, HELENA P. *(1831–1891) Psychic, mystic and one of the founders of the Theosophical Society.*

Madame Blavatsky, best known as H.P.B., demonstrated startling psychic powers and claimed personal contact with highly developed masters living in Tibet and India. Well versed in metaphysical and esoteric lore, H.P.B. is often attributed with bringing Eastern religion, philosophy and mythologies to the Western consciousness. She wrote profusely and eloquently about the

MADAME HELENA P. BLAVATSKY
Known as H.P.B., Madame Blavatsky was one of the founders of the Theosophical Society. Well versed in metaphysical and esoteric lore, she is often attributed with bringing Eastern religion, philosophy and mythologies to the Western consciousness.

information and thoughts channeled to her. Her own bohemian style of life had all the drama, excitement, suspense and mystery of a modern thriller.

The granddaughter of a White Russian princess, Blavatsky became the first internationally acclaimed professional psychic. Though she was often accused of being an occult con artist, she drew into her bizarre web George Bernard Shaw and William Butler Yeats. A fervent bohemian who traveled the world in search of enlightenment before the term *hippie* was ever coined, she was an obese shrew with a femme fatale's power to charm both men and women and attract them without question to her cause in order to establish the ultimate religious order.

Helena Petrovna Blavatsky was born on August 12, 1831, at Ekaterinoslav, Ukraine, Russia, the daughter of Colonel Peter Alexeyevich von Hahn and novelist Helena Andreyevna (nee de Fadeyev). In 1849, she married N. V. Blavatsky and shortly thereafter began more than 20 years of extensive travel, which brought her into contact with mystical and metaphysical traditions throughout the world. She was the co-founder, in 1875, of the Theosophical Society with Col. Henry Steel Olcott, a lawyer in New York City. She devoted her inexhaustible literary talents to its humanitarian and educational purposes until her death in London on May 8, 1891.

The Theosophical Society, founded in 1886 in New York City, continues to distribute information around the world from its headquarters based in Pasadena, California, as the Theosophical University Press. The society is based on the ancient occult teaching of Pythagoras, Plato, the Neoplatonists and the Gnostics. Many astrologers, psychics and other students of metaphysics contribute to and support the society today.

Madame Blavatsky's major works include *Isis Unveiled, The Secret Doctrine, The Key to Theosophy* and *The Voice of the Silence;* they are considered classics in the metaphysical world. Madame Blavatsky used automatic writing to produce much of her work. While writing *Isis Unveiled,* she reported, "I sit with my eyes open and to all appearance see and hear everything real and actual around me, and yet at the same time I see and hear that which I write. I feel short of breath; I am afraid to make the slightest movement for fear the spell might be broken. Slowly century after century, image after image, float out of the distance and pass before me as if in a magic panorama; and meanwhile, I put them together in my mind."

Further reading

Caldwell, Daniel H., ed. *The Occult World of Madame Blavatsky: Reminiscences and Impressions by Those Who Knew Her.* Tucson, Ariz.: Impossible Dream Publications, 1991.

Cranston, Sylvia. *H.P.B.: The Extraordinary Life and Influence of Helena Blavatsky.* Los Angeles: Jeremy P. Tarcher, 1992.

Meade, Marion. *Madame Blavatsky: The Woman behind the Myth.* New York: Putnam's, 1980.

Ryan, Charles J. *H. P. Blavatsky and the Theosophical Movement.* Pasadena, Calif.: Point Loma, 1975.

Woolfork, Joanna Martine. *The Only Astrology Book You'll Ever Need.* Landham, Mass.: Scarborough, 1992.

BLETONOMANCY *Divination using the patterns of moving water.*

Psychics used bletonomancy (also known as bletonism) to provide answers to a querant's question or to foretell future events through the study of the currents of streams and rivers, in much the same way as Nostradamus used a bowl of water to divine the future.

Psychics used bletonomancy to provide answers to a querant's question or to foretell future events in the currents of streams and rivers.

Bletonomancy is a form of GEOMANCY which predicts the future by the use of earth-related objects or by utilizing things in nature.

The art of FENG SHUI (which translates as wind/water) is a form of bletonomancy. For example, in watching and forecasting the future by studying a river or stream, those who interpret *feng shui* may recommend the avoidance of building a house or dwelling at a river with a sharp bend. Ignoring or negating this information could lead to disease, a couple could end up childless or a spouse might perish, and even though children might be born into a rich family, they would ultimately become poor. However, if the same dwelling was built at a spot where the river divided and branched to the northeast, northwest, southeast or southwest, there would be great prosperity.

Further reading

Bletzer, June G. *The Donning International Encyclopedic Psychic Dictionary.* West Chester, Pa.: Whitford Press, 1986.

Feuchtwang, Stephen. *An Anthropological Analysis of Chinese Geomancy.* Taipei: Southern Materials Center, 1974.

O'Brien, Joanne, with Kwok Man Ho. *The Elements of Feng Shui.* Dorset, England: Element Books, 1991.

Rossbach, Sarah. *Feng Shui: The Chinese Art of Placement.* New York: Arkana/Penguin, 1991.

BOTANOMANCY *Divination through plant life; may include the burning of plants and foretelling of future events through the ashes or smoke generated from the burning or smoldering plants or trees.*

The ancient Druids, among other cults and religious groups, paid homage to plants and trees. Like similar groups, the Druids believed that trees contained spirits, and they worshiped the oak, as well as mistletoe. Oak groves are both traditional and contemporary places for Druids to gather and teach one another.

The lotus and the mimosa had divine status in many parts of ancient Asia. The Greeks believed that roses held luck-producing powers, and the Romans thought laurel leaves had abilities of protection.

BOTANOMANCY
Phyllomancy, a form of botanomancy, is divination by studying the patterns and veins on leaves.

Almost every child has taken a dandelion seed cluster, made a wish and blown the seeds off the stalk. In medieval times in England, young women used this same dandelion pastime in a slightly different way: The number of puffs needed to release the seeds to the wind indicated the number of years a woman would have to wait to find true love. In colonial America, a young woman would carefully peel an apple, leaving the skin in one long piece. With her eyes closed, she would throw the skin over her shoulder; the formation of the apple skin was said to indicate the first letter of the first name of the man she would eventually marry.

Many metaphysical historians believe that the attribution of divine qualities to plants and plant life is derived from plants as symbols of fertility; thus botanomancy is often employed in forecasting events in regard to marriage, conception and love. A lovelorn maiden may pull off the petals of a daisy and alternate saying, "He loves me; he loves me not," with the final petal revealing the depths of her lover's commitment. Likewise, schoolgirls twist the stems on apples, reciting a letter of the alphabet with each twist. The letter

mentioned when the stem comes free is supposed to be the first letter of her future husband's name.

According to the ancient Chinese art of FENG SHUI, it is recommended that those who find their wealth slipping away should grow a large plant with round leaves in their sitting room; pointed-leaf plants are to be avoided in this instance. The larger the plant, the better. Additionally, three coins, wrapped in red paper, are to be buried in the plant's soil, and all fading or dead leaves must be removed immediately to make sure that good luck continues.

Botanomatic variations and methods of divination are found in a myriad of plants. Cromniomancy is foretelling future events by interpreting the patterns of onions when sliced in two or by peeling back the layers. PHYLLOMANCY is divination by studying the patterns and veins on leaves. And there is also the Greek method of PHYLLORHODOMANCY, which is accomplished by placing a rose petal between the hands, clapping the hands together and then interpreting the look of the petal when the hands are opened (other variations include interpreting the sounds of the petal during the clapping).

The Old Testament includes a number of references to botanomancy. For example, in the Second Book of Samuel (5:23–24), David is given holy information regarding the timing of a battle with the Philistines through the rustling of trees.

In the southern portions of India and in Sri Lanka, the interiors of coconuts are examined and used to forecast birth results; for example, a rough interior might mean a difficult life, whereas a smooth interior would foretell ease and wealth. In the Pacific islands, the Trukese are said to divine using the knotted vines found in the forest.

Should you find a four-leaf clover, pluck it from the plant and make a wish, you are practicing botanomancy. The first published connection of a four-leaf clover and good luck was in 1580, in *Euphues and His England*. It provided the advice, "For as salfe being is it in the company of a trustie mate, as sleeping in the grass Trifole, where there is no serpent so venemous that dare venture." Additionally, according to folklore published in *Superstitions of Ireland* (c. 1880), the finder of a four-leaf clover will have luck in gaming and racing, and witchcraft will have no power over him or her. However, should the finder show it to anyone or give it away, that luck will run out.

Another variation of botanomancy is CAUSIMONANCY; divination occurs when objects such as plants or paper burn and the results are interpreted from the ashes. Variants of causimonancy are LIBANOMANCY (divination by the smoke produced when incense is burned), DAPHNOMANCY (divination by the crackle of burning laurel leaves), CAPNOMANCY (divination of poppy buds bursting on hot coals) and CRITOMANCY (divination of the pattern when corn is scorched in a pan over hot flames).

See also CRITOMANCY and GEOMANCY.

Further reading

Ancient Wisdom, Ancient Sects. Mysteries of the Unknown. Alexandria, Va.: Time Life Books, 1990.

Carr-Gomm, Philip. *The Elements of the Druid Tradition.* Dorset, England: Element Books, 1991.

O'Brien, Joanne, with Kwok Man Ho. *The Elements of Feng Shui.* Dorset, England: Element Books, 1991.

Opie, Iona, and Moira Tatem. *A Dictionary of Superstitions.* Oxford: Oxford University Press, 1992.

Rossbach, Sarah. *Feng Shui: The Chinese Art of Placement.* New York: Arkana/Penguin, 1991.

CABALA
See KABBALAH.

CAGLIOSTRO, COUNT ALESSAN-
DRO DI *(1743–1795) Italian psychic who
practiced scrying; an occultist, medium and
alchemist.*

Count Cagliostro, born Guiseppe Balsamo and
also known as the marquis di Pellegrini, gave
himself his own title. He traveled throughout
Europe and the Mediterranean area conducting
alchemical experiments. The child of a poor family, Cagliostro quickly turned his talent for precognition into a lucrative fortune-telling career.
With his flamboyant personality, he charmed
princes and paupers alike and enjoyed a high
style of living, mostly off others. After marrying
a wealthy socialite, Lorenza Feliciani, in Italy,
Cagliostro was a regular attendee at aristocratic
events and noble courts throughout Europe. Feliciani is reported to have been his partner in
numerous occult deceptions and worked with
Cagliostro utilizing various metaphysical arts
such as crystal gazing, healing by the laying on
of hands, conjuring spirits and even predicting
winning lottery numbers.

Further, Feliciani and Cagliostro sold a myriad of magic potions said to lengthen life. At the
same time, Cagliostro made money by supposedly transmuting metal to gold, casting out
demons and sharing his psychic gifts. These applications are said to have led many to call him
the "Divine Cagliostro"; others said he was
merely a charlatan, a trickster and a quack.

Count Cagliostro formulated one of the most
comprehensive dream interpretation charts until
that time. The chart correlated dreams with numbers; upon paying a price, the purchaser was
guaranteed to win the French lottery.

In his thirties, Cagliostro became interested in
Freemasonry. It was at this time that he became
a medium and a faith healer. A few years later,
he was arrested for stealing a diamond necklace,
but the charges, which were false, were dropped.
He was arrested again in 1789 for his involvement
in Freemasonry (Freemasonry was considered
heresy by the Holy Office). He was sentenced
to spend the rest of his days in prison, in the
Castle of San Leo, near Montefeltro. (Cagliostro's wife also perished in prison.) While history notes that the count died in prison, it was
long rumored that he actually mysteriously escaped. Count Cagliostro was "sighted" in Russia, Europe and America for years after his
reported death.

Further reading

Carroll, David. *The Magic Makers.* New York: Arbor
House, 1974.

Drury, Nevill. *Dictionary of Mysticism and the Esoteric Traditions.* Dorset, England: Prism Press, 1992.

Guiley, Rosemary Ellen. *Harper's Encyclopedia of Mystical and Paranormal Experience.* San Francisco: HarperSan Francisco, 1991.

Knight, Stephen. *The Brotherhood: The Secret World of the Freemasons.* New York: Stein & Day, 1984.

Magical Arts. Mysteries of the Unknown. Alexandria, Va.: Time Life Books, 1990.

Maven, Max. *Max Maven's Book of Fortunetelling.* New York: Prentice-Hall, 1992.

CALLOWAY, HUGH G.

See FOX, OLIVER.

CANCER
One of the 12 astrological signs of the zodiac. The symbol is the crab.

Those who are born between June 21 and July 22 are natives of the sign of Cancer (sometimes referred to as Moon Children) and are supposed to have specific traits indicative of the time and date on which they were born. Divination of events can also be charted through this astrological sign.

Astrologers divine what is in store throughout life through the time, date and place in which an individual was born as they coordinate the influences with other signs, the planets, the Sun, the Moon and other powers.

In traditional Western astrology, Cancer is the fourth sign of the zodiac. Those born during the period typically exhibit qualities that exemplify a gentle nature. Home and family are at the top of the list for Cancer natives, whether male or female, who love to nurture and care for things and people, children or, for instance, an exten-

CANCER

This ancient symbol represents the astrological sign of Cancer.

sive collection of Egyptian art. They typically want to decorate the world with love but can also be career driven, extremely ambitious and genuinely creative; however, with Cancerians, all these characteristics combine with a coaxing gentleness that encourages others to jump in and help. They can also be extremely moody and get depressed over imagined slights. They are easy to offend and can hold a grudge (real or imaginary) for a lifetime. Those born under this sign sometimes pretend that nothing bothers them, but they can become deeply hurt and moody at times when other signs would shrug off the same trouble or person.

Under the influence of the Moon, Cancers are drawn to the water and often feel the effects of the gravitational pull of the tides and the Moon. Cancerians are said to have moon-shaped faces and, because of their love of home and hearth, often have weight problems.

The sign of the zodiac in which an individual is born is responsible for only one fragment of the qualities he or she receives at birth. Psychics are quick to point out that a general forecast based solely on the stellar position of the Sun on the day an individual was born is unlikely to provide an accurate glimpse of the future.

While traditional astrologers use books to calculate a personal birth chart based on the position of the Sun, Moon and planets at a distinct time, computer software has replaced most of this time-consuming work. The correct term for calculating a birth chart is to "cast" it. In order to fully comprehend the extent of traits, potential and attributes, the exact time and place of birth must be known and interpreted.

See also ASTROLOGICAL SYMBOLS; ASTROLOGY.

Further reading

Cosmic Connections. Mysteries of the Unknown. Alexandria, Va.: Time Life Books, 1990.

Goodman, Linda. *Linda Goodman's Sun Signs.* New York: Fawcett/Columbine, 1978.

Morgan, Chris. *Fortune Telling: How to Predict Your Own Future.* London: Quintet Publishing and Random House, 1992.

Omarr, Sydney. *Cancer.* New York: New American Library, 1992.

———. *My World of Astrology.* New York: Fleet, 1965.

Verlagsanstalt, Datura. *Cancer Astro Analysis.* New York: Grosset & Dunlap, 1976.

Woolfork, Joanna Martine. *The Only Astrology Book You'll Ever Need.* Landham, Mass.: Scarborough, 1992.

CANDLE PROPHECY *Divination by interpreting visions using the flame of a candle.*

An ancient prognostication method used, along with scrying, in Old Testament times, candle prophecy (more commonly referred to as lampadomancy) involves meditating on a burning candle and interpreting how the flame burns and/or what is seen in the flame.

To practice candle prophecy, a burning candle, a quiet, darkened room without any wind currents and time for meditation on a specific question are necessary. (Some practitioners use three candles.) Turn off all the lights; you may need to use a flashlight in order to see the matches and light the candle. Light the candle (or all three, using only one match).

The following are some of the interpretations for one-candle prophecies:

If the candle burns brightly, the answer is yes.

If the candle seems to burn slowly or extinguishes itself, the answer is no, or there will be a negative result of the action under consideration.

If sparks flicker from the candle, caution should be taken.

If the candle should suddenly extinguish after it has been burning brightly, there is grave danger or perhaps disaster ahead.

The following are interpretations of the three-candle method:

If one candle burns more brightly than the others, the omen is good. There will be success ahead and the answer to the question is affirmative.

A candle with an extrabright sparkle at the tip of the flame is a very lucky omen.

If the flames move from side to side, a change of circumstances or even a journey is indicated. If only one flame moves from side to side while the others are still, a singular endeavor—an unaccompanied journey or a project one must take on alone—is foretold.

If only one candle extinguishes while the others continue to burn, an obstacle is approaching; perhaps a sign of danger, this is definitely a warning of caution.

If one of the flames spirals and twists, with or without smoke, there may be difficulties and/or plots against the querant.

After the singing of "Happy Birthday," what celebrant hasn't leaned over, made a secret wish and attempted to blow out all the candles? The whimsical birthday game is actually a form of candle prophecy that is still very much in practice today.

See also LAMPADOMANCY; LYNCHOMANCY; PYROMANCY.

Further reading

Dey, Charmaine. *The Magic Candle.* Bronx, N.Y.: Original Publications, 1989.

Morgan, Chris. *Fortune Telling: How to Predict Your Own Future.* London: Quintet Publishing and Random House, 1992.

Opie, Iona, and Moira Tatem. *A Dictionary of Superstitions.* Oxford: Oxford University Press, 1992.

Pajeon, Kala, and Ketz Pajeon. *The Candle Magic Workbook.* New York: Citadel Press, 1992.

CAPNOMANCY *Divination by the patterns of smoke made by burning various objects and/or sacrifices.*

Psychics using this mantic art threw or placed laurel leaves, jasmine, poppy seeds or some other flammable botanical material on hot coals or into a fire. The future was foretold in the wisps of

In New England, a form of capnomancy is still practiced among those who enjoy folklore. In capnomancy, weather conditions are forecast by the behavior of smoke coming from a chimney.

smoke or, in the case of the seeds, in the way they crackled, smoldered or burned. Capnomancy was originally practiced by the Babylonians as they studied the patterns of smoke generated from burning cedar branches or shavings. The Druids had a variation, called dendromancy, using the cuttings of the sacred oak and mistletoe. The burning of incense for the purpose of divination is called LIBANOMANCY.

Ancient civilizations that used human sacrifices to predict the future, including, some believe, the cult of the Druids, employed smoke generated from burning humans or animals to predict the future. If the smoke rose lightly from the altar on which the sacrifice was burned, then moved straight to the clouds, it meant that conditions were favorable for whatever was being asked. But if the smoke hung close to the altar or the ground, it was a sign that plans should be changed. Smoke that was inhaled from a sacrificial burning was said to increase good fortune.

In New England, a form of capnomancy is still practiced among old-timers in regard to forecasting weather conditions. If the smoke from a chimney rises straight to the sky, regardless of the time of day or climatic conditions, then the weather will be fair and good for sailors and farmers. However, if the smoke clings to the roof, filters around the house, pushes back down the chimney or moves to the ground, a storm is approaching and/or it is a bad omen for those who live in the house.

Another name for capnomancy is CAUSI-MONANCY, and variations of this mantic art are CRITOMANCY (burning of barleycorn), DAPHNO-MANCY (divination by the crackle of burning laurel leaves) and SIDEROMANCY (divination by interpreting the twisting and smoldering of pieces of straw when thrown on a red-hot grate).

See also CRITOMANCY.

Further reading

Bletzer, June G. *The Donning International Encyclopedic Psychic Dictionary.* West Chester, Pa.: Whitford Press, 1986.

Opie, Iona, and Moira Tatem. *A Dictionary of Superstitions.* Oxford: Oxford University Press, 1992.

Visions and Prophecies. Mysteries of the Unknown. Alexandria, Va.: Time Life Books, 1990.

CAPRICORN *One of the 12 astrological signs of the zodiac. The symbol is the goat.*

Those who are born between December 22 and January 19 are natives of the sign of Capricorn and have specific traits indicative of the time and date on which they were born. Divination of events can also be charted through this astrological sign.

Astrologers divine what is in store throughout life through the time, date and place in which an individual was born as they coordinate the influences with other signs, the planets, the Sun, the Moon and other powers.

In traditional Western astrology, Capricorn is the 10th sign of the zodiac. Those born during the period typically exhibit qualities of patience,

CAPRICORN

reserve and determination. They are highly ambitious, although many people miss that in the Capricorn personality because they are easygoing. Unlike other signs of the zodiac, Capricorns will use shrewd and ingenious methods to achieve their goals, and they are quick to see an opportunity and seize it.

Practical and pragmatic in nature, Capricorns are solemn as well. They often have to force themselves to have a good time. It is as if they are born adults with adult responsibilities even when they are children, and they may feel that they are the only human beings in the world on whom they can depend. While that is not necessarily true, the Capricorn native does have the reputation for being a sober, sensible, reserved individual. Yet beneath that foreboding stare is a surprise for many—a dry, keen sense of humor that, according to astrologers, has the knack of erupting when others least expect it. When something tickles the Capricorn funny bone, it produces peals of laughter that totally take over body and soul.

Cautious and conservative in friendship, career, love relationships and finance, Capricorn has a talent for attracting the best in life, including wealth. This sign may even marry for money and do quite well in the relationship. With a basic concern for security, the Capricorn feathers his or her nest with the finer things in life, always choosing carefully and always with a self-contained "I can handle this myself" attitude.

The sign of the zodiac in which an individual is born is responsible for only one fragment of the qualities he or she receives at birth. Psychics are quick to point out that a general forecast solely on the stellar position of the Sun on the day an individual was born is unlikely to provide an accurate glimpse of the future.

While traditional astrologers use books to calculate a personal birth chart based on the position of the Sun, Moon and planets at a distinct time, computer software has replaced most of this time-consuming work. The correct term for calculating a birth chart is to "cast" it. In order to fully comprehend the extent of traits, potential and attributes, the exact time and place of birth must be calculated and interpreted.

See also ASTROLOGICAL SYMBOLS; ASTROLOGY.

Further reading

Cosmic Connections. Mysteries of the Unknown. Alexandria, Va.: Time Life Books, 1990.

Goodman, Linda. *Linda Goodman's Sun Signs.* New York: Fawcett/Columbine, 1978.

Omarr, Sydney. *Capricorn.* New York: New American Library, 1992.

————. *My World of Astrology.* New York: Fleet, 1965.

Verlagsanstalt, Datura. *Capricorn Astro Analysis.* New York: Grosset & Dunlap, 1976.

Woolfork, Joanna Martine. *The Only Astrology Book You'll Ever Need.* Landham, Mass.: Scarborough, 1992.

CARD PREDICTIONS
See CARTOMANCY; TAROT.

CARTOMANCY *Divination using a pack of cards to predict the future or to respond to a question.*

This form of prognostication may have originated in ancient Egypt or in India; the exact beginning of playing cards is obscure, though some believe that playing cards and cards used for divination are a variation of the game of chess. The first report of the use of cards as a method of prognostication was in Europe around 1300 by gypsies (who were thought to have originated in ancient Egypt). As the gypsies began traveling widely, others copied the cards. Some metaphysical scholars believe that cards

This ancient symbol represents the astrological sign of Capricorn.

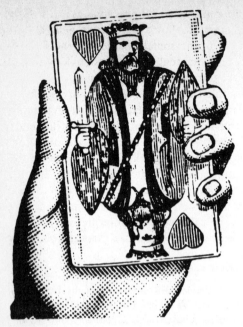

CARTOMANCY
The king or queen of each suit is used as a significator when playing cards are the psychic tool for a reading.

accompanied the returning Crusaders as they moved homeward from the Middle East. Although the exact root of cards and card prophecies is cloudy, after the 1300s gypsies and other psychics were using cards to foretell the future.

There are a number of popular card layouts, or spreads. Some of the layouts require all 52 cards in a regular pack; others use only 32. In the 32-card layout, twos, threes, fours, fives and sixes are discarded. According to psychics who use playing cards to foretell the future, the choice depends on individual preference and on the querant. Some people who read cards use different layouts and different decks depending on the querant. Some of the layouts use all the cards; others use only a few. While every reader or psychic doing a card reading uses his or her own specific talents and rules, most of the time the querant shuffles the deck before the cards are placed on the table.

A significator (sometimes known as a client card) is a playing card selected from the deck before the reading begins. The querant is asked to pick the card he or she wants to represent

him- or herself. Most of the time this card is chosen by the querant, although some card readers select the significator for the querant. The king or queen of each suit is used for this purpose when regular playing cards are the tool for the reading. Some readers feel that if the querant is an older person, either fair skinned or graying, the king or queen of diamonds should be used as the significator. If the querant is a younger person either fair skinned or with light-colored hair, the king or queen of hearts is to be used as the significator. If the querant is older and has dark hair and/or dark or olive skin, the king or queen of spades is to be used. And if the querant is a younger individual with dark hair and/or dark or olive skin, the king or queen of clubs is to be used as the significator.

If the querant is asked to place the cards, the psychic will instruct him or her on how to select the cards. Typically, querants are asked to pick cards that "speak" to them; that is, they stand out of the deck as feeling unusual—perhaps a card that will not shuffle smoothly.

The actual placement of the cards is often referred to as the spread. With most spreads, cards are dealt facedown and turned over by either the reader or the querant.

In the Pyramid spread, the cards are placed with seven cards as the foundation of the pyramid, with one less card on each subsequent row, and a final card on top. This is one of the most popular card layouts.

In the, SEVEN-POINT STAR spread the querant shuffles the cards from a 32-card deck and hands the deck to the reader. The reader counts out the first six cards and places the seventh card facedown, continuing to do this, reshuffling the deck as needed, until there are 12 cards placed facedown in a circle. The significator is often placed in the middle of this spread with the face up.

In a quick one card method, cards are spread out in a fan shape. The querant asks one question and draws one card. The psychic gives advice from that one card.

Other spreads include the Romanaï Star, the Lucky 13, the Nine Square and the Cross of the Year.

Regardless of the deck or layout, the influences of the suits remain the same.

Hearts are the lucky cards of the deck and indicate good fortune and success in business, career and love. Depending on the placement of the cards, hearts may signify strong ambitions or relationships.

Clubs are the cards of success, with a strong connection to money, prosperity and ambition. Depending on the placement, they may also foretell business problems and personal disappointment.

Diamonds are indicative of influences outside of the personal and other pulls or requirements for the querant's time and energy.

Spades indicate a caution signal and may warn of unforeseen difficulties in the querant's life. Depending on how the cards are read and the placement of the spades, this suit may symbolize unhappiness in a new love affair or caution before entering a new enterprise or career field.

Interpretation depends on the method the psychic or card reader uses. Often the psychic uses other metaphysical talents, such as CLAIRVOYANCE or channeled messages, to expound on what is happening in the querant's life and to answer his or her questions.

See also PSYCHIC READINGS; TAROT.

Further reading

Buckland, Raymond. *Secrets of Gypsy Fortunetelling*. St. Paul, Minn.: Llewellyn, 1988.

Innes, Brian. *The Tarot: How to Use and Interpret the Cards*. London: Orbis, 1979.

Secrets of the Alchemists. Mysteries of the Unknown. Alexandria, Va.: Time Life Books, 1990.

CASE, PAUL FOSTER (1884–1954)
American tarot reader.

Case made a comprehensive study of the tarot and produced an excellent book on metaphysics and the occult. *The Tarot: A Key to the Wisdom of the Ages* and a book on tarot meditations, *The Book of Tokens*, are his best-known works.

Case, who founded the occult center known as Builders of the Adytum (BOTA) in Los Angeles (the publisher of his many books), believed that the tarot was designed by a group of scholars about A.D. 1200 in Fez, Morocco. He theorized that the cards symbolized the mystery of the universe. His concepts and ideas are often thought to be eccentric by other metaphysical scholars.

Further reading

Case, Paul Foster. *Book of Tokens*. Los Angeles: Builders of Adytum Publishers, 1968.

———. *The Tarot: A Key to the Wisdom of the Ages*. Los Angeles: Builders of Adytum Publishers, 1970.

Drury, Nevill. *Dictionary of Mysticism and the Esoteric Traditions*. Dorset, England: Prism Press, 1992.

Giles, Cynthia. *The Tarot: History, Mystery, and Lore*. New York: Paragon House, 1992.

Visions and Prophecies. Mysteries of the Unknown. Alexandria, Va.: Time Life Books, 1990.

CASTING OF LOTS *Divination by tossing dice, bones or other articles that have sides and markings.*

This method of forecasting the future is technically called ASTRAGYROMANCY and is part of the practice of sortilege (see SORTILEGE SYSTEMS). As with astragyromancy, casting of lots answers the querant's questions when he or she tosses an object with sides to a table or the ground. Interpretation is accomplished through the codes inscribed on the objects or by interpreting their placement.

See also CLEROMANCY.

Further reading

Diagram Group. *Predicting Your Future*. New York: Ballantine, 1983.

Maven, Max. *Max Maven's Book of Fortunetelling*. New York: Prentice-Hall, 1992.

Mind over Matter. Mysteries of the Unknown. Alexandria, Va.: Time Life Books, 1990.

Visions and Prophecies. Mysteries of the Unknown. Alexandria, Va.: Time Life Books, 1990.

Walker, Barbara G. *The Woman's Encyclopedia of Myths and Secrets*. New York: Harper Collins, 1983.

CATHERINE OF SIENA (1347–1380)
Catholic saint and mystic.

Although she had never been taught to write, Catherine of Siena dictated numerous metaphysical and inspirational works, including *The Dialogue of St. Catherine of Siena*. It is said that in 1375 she received on her body the stigmata marks of Christ's wounds from the cross, indicating she did have a holy bond.

Further reading

Drury, Nevill. *Dictionary of Mysticism and the Esoteric Traditions*. Dorset, England: Prism Press, 1992.

Tinney, Merrill C., ed. *The Zondervan Pictorial Encyclopedia of the Bible*. Grand Rapids, Mich.: Zondervan Publishing House, 1977.

CATOPTROMANCY *Divination by interpreting patterns or images produced by looking at a light source reflected in a shiny object, such as a mirror.*

Catoptromancy was used originally as a divination method, with a glass suspended over a well to foretell the future or reveal answers to questions. The early Christians used catoptromancy by discerning the patterns reflected on the glass from inside the consecrated water well, much like reading tea leaves.

Catoptromancy is a form of SCRYING; staring at a smooth, shiny surface, whether water or a mirror, meditating on what is seen and then interpreting the visions to predict the future or interpret events. With catoptromancy the psychic does not look directly at his or her image; the mirror is tilted to catch a light source and the patterns the light provides. Long before mirrors as we know them were invented, the Persians and the Chinese used this method of divining the future. The Greeks used polished plates made of bronze. Hebrew Kabbalists used a system that required seven high-polished mirrors made of a range of metals. Depending on the day of the week and the season, a specific polished metal surface came to be used.

The Thessalonians and Pythagoras would scry by moonlight, and when glass mirrors were developed in Venice, Italy, about 1200, they were quickly selected as the best instrument to forecast the future. Catoptromancy was used as a method of prognostication during biblical times. In the Book of Exodus, there is a mention of *Hoshen*

Early divination by catoptromancy involved the use of a glass suspended over a well to foretell the future or reveal answers to questions. Catoptromancy evolved to include the use of any specially prepared mirror.

Hishpat, or the breastplate of judgment, which was worn by the high priest Aaron, brother of Moses. Some Bible scholars and historians believe that the breastplate, along with the Urim and Thummin, were used in divining, to judge innocence or guilt by the way light caught on the shiny metal and inset of stones.

Many alchemists, seers and psychics developed their own rituals and rules for catoptromancy and scrying. In the 1500s, Theophrastus Bombastus von Hohenheim, also known as Paracelsus, developed an intricate scheme for fabricating just the right mirror. The formula requires that all of the metals used be of precise measurement and the mirror made at just the right alignment of the planets. The proper method of polishing the mirror was also outlined in Paracelsus's rules.

Other mirror variations were used by the Aztec shamans by polishing obsidian, the natural glass caused by quickly cooling volcanic lava. Dr. John Dee, who is said to have advised Queen Elizabeth I, used a black mirror of obsidian to consult and help the queen. Dee called the instrument a "shew-stone," and it, along with other metaphysical objects and tools, is on display at the British Museum.

It is interesting to note that scrying mirrors appear in many paintings of Rembrandt and Leonardo da Vinci.

To practice catoptromancy, the only requirements are a mirror, a question and a place for quiet meditation before questions are asked. With the mirror placed in front of the querant, the question is asked (either aloud or silently) and the answers are clairvoyantly perceived. Some psychics perceive past-life information, see auras and are able to speak to the souls of the dead through this mirror-gazing technique. Students of catoptromancy use the mirror to see visions of their spirit guides. Those who are learning how to become more clairvoyant sometimes are encouraged to use mirrors that are painted black on the back side. This supposedly makes reading easier.

There is metaphysical interest in mirrors even today. Breaking a mirror still indicates a period of seven years of bad luck. And there has been a resurgence of interest in scrying in mirrors, which are often referred to as magic mirrors.

See also CRYSTALLOMANCY; DEE, DR. JOHN; INTUITION.

Further reading

Butler, W. E. *How to Develop Clairvoyance.* 2d ed. New York: Samuel Weiser, 1979.
Fodor, Nandor. *Encyclopedia of Psychic Science.* New York: University Books, 1966.
Maven, Max. *Max Maven's Book of Fortunetelling.* New York: Prentice-Hall, 1992.
Psychics. Mysteries of the Unknown. Alexandria, Va.: Time Life Books, 1990.
Visions and Prophecies. Mysteries of the Unknown. Alexandria, Va.: Time Life Books, 1990.

CAUSIMONANCY *Another term for the prognostication form of* CAPNOMANCY, *divination by throwing flammable objects into a fire or onto hot coals.*

The future or answer to a querant's question is arrived at from the way the object burns. If it burns quickly, the answer is yes; if it smolders and burns slowly, the response is unfavorable.

Further reading

Visions and Prophecies. Mysteries of the Unknown. Alexandria, Va.: Time Life Books, 1990.

CAYCE, EDGAR *(1877–1945) American psychic.*

One of the best-known psychics, Cayce was nicknamed the "Sleeping Prophet," because the trancelike states he would enter seemed like sleep until he spoke. While in a trance he could diagnose illnesses of people all over the world, without ever meeting or even seeing them. Cayce practiced a form of long-distance healing for more than 43 years, diagnosing and then curing the person he was thinking about. His diagnosis and the drugs he prescribed were said to be more than 90% accurate, even though he only had a limited education and no training in medicine.

Cayce is said to have exhibited psychic abilities from birth. Once he recognized his gift, he was consulted by thousands of people regarding their health problems. Often he was able to cure those whom doctors had reported to be terminally ill. Transcripts of the healing readings are included in *Edgar Cayce on Healing.*

Cayce believed in the symbolic content of dreams and placed great emphasis on the value of an individual's personal study of his or her own dreams. More than 600 of his readings on dreams are included in the book *Edgar Cayce on Dreams.*

Edgar Cayce on Diet and Health details Cayce's philosophy that "the body is the temple of the soul" and it must be cared for properly. The book encompasses his theories on proper diet and health for a great sense of well-being and includes recipes.

Additionally, during his trance state, Cayce viewed other beings and changed his strongly Christian philosophy to one accepting of reincarnation. He taught followers about the AKASHIC RECORDS, the ethereal library where all post-life information is stored. He founded the Association for Research and Enlightenment in Virginia Beach, Virginia, and wrote and dictated many books. *Edgar Cayce on ESP* provides information about the psychic, along with his hypothesis on AURAS, AUTOMATIC WRITING and hypnosis, among a host of other metaphysical topics as pertinent today as when Cayce revealed the information in the early 20th century.

See also IATROMANCY; LAYING ON OF HANDS.

Further reading

Carter, Mary Ellen. *My Years with Edgar Cayce.* New York: Warner, 1974.

Cayce, Edgar. *Edgar Cayce on Diet and Health.* Virginia Beach, Va.: ARE Press, 1969.

———. *Edgar Cayce on Dreams.* Virginia Beach, Va.: ARE Press, 1968.

———. *Edgar Cayce on ESP.* Virginia Beach, Va.: ARE Press, 1969.

———. *Edgar Cayce on Healing.* Virginia Beach, Va.: ARE Press, 1969.

Stern, Jess. *Edgar Cayce, the Sleeping Prophet.* New York: Bantam, 1968.

Woodward, Mary Ann. *Edgar Cayce's Story of Karma: God's Book of Remembrance.* New York: Coward, McCann & Geoghegan, 1971.

CELTIC CROSS *A tarot card spread.*

The Celtic Cross is thought to be one of the oldest and most powerful of the spreads, or layouts. The origin of this card placement, like others in tarot and playing-card divination, is obscure. However, many believe that it began with Druid priests as a means to foretell the future, a segment of their religious beliefs.

The Celtic Cross can be used to interpret a specific question or for a complete reading of the past, present and future influences on the querant's life. Some readers place two cards at every spot on the Celtic Cross spread.

The spread of the Celtic Cross is complex and there are a number of variations. The following is the simplest spread with four rows of cards, all in various positions. One should think of the placement of numbers on a clock while placing the cards. The first card is placed in the middle (where the hands of the clock would join). The second card is placed directly below the first; the third directly below the second. The fourth card is placed in the nine o'clock spot and the fifth card is placed on the twelve o'clock spot. The sixth card is in the three o'clock position. The reader or the querant then places the seventh card directly to the right of the third card and builds a row up from seven with cards eight, nine and ten.

Cards one and two reflect the present situation, card three the foundation of one's life. Card four represents the past, card five the appearance of one's life. Card six is supposedly the future. Card seven is the self. Card eight tells about others. Card nine discusses one's hopes and fears. Card ten tells the querant the outcome of his or her problem or answers a question.

See also CARTOMANCY; PSYCHIC READINGS; TAROT.

Further reading

Giles, Cynthia. *The Tarot: History, Mystery and Lore.* New York: Paragon House, 1992.

King, Francis, and Stephen Skinner. *Techniques of High Magic.* Rochester, Vt.: Destiny Books, 1991.

Thierens, A. E. *Astrology and the Tarot.* Los Angeles: Newcastle, 1975.

Waite, Arthur Edward. *The Pictorial Key to the Tarot.* New York: Samuel Weiser, 1973.

Walker, Barbara G. *The Secrets of the Tarot: Origins, History and Symbolism.* New York: Harper & Row, 1984.

CEPHALOMANCY *Divination using the study of the shape of the human skull as a means to define character and personality traits. Commonly known as PHRENOLOGY.*

Cephalomancy may also refer to the ancient prognostication method of boiling the head of a sheep, goat or donkey and then examining the skull for information in order to foretell the future. A variation known as OINOMANCY was developed in 13th-century Europe, in which an animal skull was boiled in wine. The future was interpreted through the study of the remaining bones.

See also HARUSPICY.

Further reading

Cumont, Franz. *Oriental Religions in Roman Paganism.* New York: Dover, 1956.

Opie, Iona, and Moira Tatem. *A Dictionary of Superstitions.* Oxford: Oxford University Press, 1992.

CERAUNOSCOPY *Divination through the study of the patterns of lightning during a thunderstorm.*

See also AEROMANCY.

Further reading

Opie, Iona, and Moira Tatem. *A Dictionary of Superstitions.* Oxford: Oxford University Press, 1992.

Rossbach, Sarah. *Feng Shui: The Chinese Art of Placement.* New York: Arkana/Penguin, 1991.

Stewart, R. J. *The Elements of Prophecy.* Dorset, England: Element Books, 1990.

CEROMANCY *Divination through interpreting the patterns made when molten wax is poured into water.*

This method of prognostication was probably developed in ancient Rome and continued to be very popular during the Middle Ages. In the 1700s there was a resurgence in this method's reputation, and in Spain at one time, ceromancy became the divination method of choice, using hot sealing wax. Ceromancy was passed on to other Spanish-speaking countries, and it continues to be used today in Mexico, Puerto Rico and some parts of Haiti, where it is said to be used in voodoo rituals.

To practice ceromancy, a red candle is necessary, along with a shallow dish of water, patience and a quiet area in which to meditate on the results. The candle must be lighted and allowed to burn for an hour as the querant contemplates the questions on his or her mind. By this time, the quantity of hot wax around the wick will be

Using ceraunoscopy, predictions for future events were made by deciphering the patterns of lightning during thunderstorms.

sufficient to provide the message. The candle is carefully tipped into the dish of water from at least eight inches above the plate.

Interpretation of the congealed wax is similar to that found in tasseography, or psychic translation of the shapes that are formed. For example, a wax shape in the form of a heart means love. A shape in the form of a letter of the alphabet might mean one will hear or speak to a person whose name begins with that letter.

Further reading

Bletzer, June G. *The Donning International Encyclopedic Psychic Dictionary.* West Chester, Pa.: Whitford Press, 1986.

Davis, Wade. *The Serpent and the Rainbow.* New York: Warner, 1985.

Denning, Melita, and Osborne Phillips. *Voudou Fire: The Living Reality of Mystical Religion.* St. Paul, Minn.: Llewellyn, 1979.

CHAKRAS *The spiritual nerve network of the body with energy centers believed necessary to maintain inner balance.*

Psychics often talk about chakras with regard to healing. Some psychics provide healing readings when a querant asks questions regarding health.

There are seven major chakras of the body and hundreds of minor ones. Each chakra is associated with a specific area of the body and radiates a specific color that can be seen by some psychics. The chakras are often thought to look like petals of a flower or sections of a color wheel. Each chakra is said to vibrate at a different rate; as the spirit moves through each incarnation and understands his or her life lesson, the crown chakra grows stronger. Additionally, some psychics believe that if an individual has a specific lesson on which to work in his or her current life that lesson is often indicated in the intensity of vibration or color emanating from that specific chakra. For example, an issue concerning sexuality might be manifest in one's scral chakra.

With the Sanskrit word in parentheses before the description, the chakras are:

The root *(muladhara)*, located at the base of the spine.

The scral *(svadhisthana)*, located near the genitals and associated with reproduction and sexuality.

The solar plexus *(manipurna)*, slightly above the navel.

The heart *(anahata)*, located between the shoulder blades and the chest.

The throat *(visuddha)*, the center of creativity and self-expression, located in the throat area.

The brow *(ajna)*, located between the eyebrows and called the third eye.

The crown *(sahasrara)* swirls just above the head and reveals the level of one's spiritual consciousness.

Further reading

Avalon, Arthur. *Shakti and Shakta.* New York: Dover, 1978.

Gunther, Bernard. *Energy, Ecstasy, and Your Seven Vital Chakras.* North Hollywood, Calif.: Newscastle, 1983.

Karagulla, Shafica and Dora van Gelder Kunz. *The Chakras and the Human Energy Fields.* Wheaton, Ill.: Theosophical Publishing Co., 1989.

CHANNEL *A person who is said to be in contact with the spirit world and who transmits information through this spiritual contact.*

A channel may or may not go into a trance to relay information. The channeled information is done through voice channeling, often in the accent or dialect of the spirit said to be channeled, through AUTOMATIC WRITING or during PSYCHIC READINGS. Channeling may be done involuntarily or may be induced by the use of mind-altering drugs. Typically the personality and/or speech pattern of the channel changes while the outside entity enters his or her body to speak through the psychic.

The nonhuman spirits may be angels, nature spirits, guardian spirits, deities, demons or spirits of the dead. Sometimes the messages are transmitted from the higher self, soul intelligence, or from other entities that often have exotic names.

Channeling is the term used to describe the relaying of information from outside the Earth plane. This is not an innovative concept first practiced by New Age metaphysicians; throughout history, there has been documentation of channeled information. The priests of ancient Egypt were highly adept channelers, and the Greeks, Tibetans, Japanese, Babylonians, Druids and Assyrians, along with early Christians, Muslims and Jews all practiced channeling.

While channeling fell out of favor during medieval times, its popularity increased with the 19th-century interest in spiritualism. Madame Helena P. Blavatsky, Alice Bailey and Jane Roberts were channels, as are contemporary psychics such as JZ Knight.

As with other metaphysical practices, channeling is controversial. Some medical professionals believe it is New Age trickery; others believe that it indicates a severe medical disorder. On the other hand, some Christian groups cite examples of channeling in the Bible. For example, the book of Revelation was supposedly "channeled" from an angel to St. John. Metaphysical experts believe channeling is like a long-distance cordless telephone connection to the spirit world, conveying information to help those on Earth become better educated about the ethereal world we will return to after death.

See also BAILEY, ALICE; BLAVATSKY, HELENA P.; KNIGHT, JZ; LEONARD, GLADYS OSBORNE.

Further reading

Kautz, William H., and Melanie Branon. *Channeling: The Intuitive Connection.* San Francisco: Harper & Row, 1987.

Klimo, John. *Channeling: Investigations on Receiving Information from Paranormal Sources.* Los Angeles: Jeremy P. Tarcher, 1987.

Leonard, Gladys Osborne. *My Life in Two Worlds.* London: Two Worlds Publishing, 1931.

Rodegast, Pat, and Judith Stanton, comp. *Emmanuel's Book: A Manual for Living Comfortably in the Cosmos.* New York: Bantam, 1987.

Stewart, R. J. *The Elements of Prophecy.* Dorset, England: Element Books, 1990.

CHEIRO *(1866–1939) Palmist and occultist.*

Cheiro was the professional or stage name of "Count" Louis le Warner de Harmon. He is considered to have been the world's leading palmist. Controversy surrounds his background. Cheiro claimed that his father was Greek and his mother Irish; some reports indicate that Cheiro came from a middle-class family of Irish farmers. Regardless, he is considered the most gifted palmists the world has ever known.

Living in London, Cheiro became known for predicting the future for many well-known and noble celebrities of his time, including King Edward VIII of Great Britain (later the duke of Windsor), King Leopold II of Belgium, Czar Nicholas II of Russia, Pope Leo XIII, Lord Kitchener and Mark Twain. He read thousands of palms a year, his fame spreading throughout the world.

One of his most famous predictions, made after reading King Edward's palm, was that he would abdicate the throne to follow his heart. Another prediction came through so strongly after a reading that Cheiro continued to try to sway a British journalist from making any type of sea voyage in the spring of 1912. Though he listened to Cheiro, and read his warnings in letters the palmist wrote to him, W. T. Stead sailed on the *Titanic* and perished along with many others when the ocean liner struck an iceberg on April 14, 1912.

Although Cheiro did not live to see many of his predictions come true, he did foretell the time, date and place of his own death, exactly as he had predicted, quietly in his bed.

Cheiro's works are still the basis for modern palmistry and include *Confessions of a Modern Seer, Cheiro's Guide to the Hand, The Language of the Hand* and *Cheiro's Book of Numbers,* some of which are in print today; others can be found at used-books stores.

See also GEMS; LAYING ON OF HANDS; PALMISTRY.

Further reading

Altman, Nathaniel. *Palmistry Workbook.* New York: Sterling, 1990.

Benham, William G. *Hands.* Los Angeles: Newcastle, 1988.

Cheiro. *Cheiro's Book of Numbers.* New York: Prentice-Hall, 1988.

———. *The Language of the Hand.* New York: Prentice-Hall, 1987.

Fitzherbert, Andrew. *Hand Psychology.* Garden City, N.Y.: Avery, 1989.

CHINESE ASTROLOGY *Divination of personal characteristics based on a 12-year animal system.*

Still widely practiced in Asia and increasingly in the West, this ancient Chinese system establishes that people born during a particular year exhibit similar qualities, and these qualities are determined through the influence of a specific animal. Each animal sign is dominant for one year every 12 years. It is the Year of the Rooster as this book is being written, and the book will be published in the Year of the Pig.

Chinese Astrology provides keys to the traits of those who are born during the 12 animal signs. Psychics divine upcoming incidents and events, combined with other mantic practices, as they consider an individual's trait.

The true basis for dividing years into 12 different animal signs, and not into monthly segments, as with Western astrology, has been lost in time. It is said that one Chinese New Year, Buddha invited all the animals in the kingdom to come to visit. Why only 12 arrived is obscure. In gratitude for their loyalty, Buddha identified time in 12-year cycles and gave each year of the cycle an animal's name.

Depending on the practitioner of Chinese astrology, the animal names may vary slightly. Thus, Chinese astrology is made up of Rats, Oxen (or Buffalo), Tigers (or Cats), Rabbits (or Hares), Dragons, Snakes, Horses, Goats (or Sheep), Monkeys, Roosters, Dogs and Pigs. Additionally, those who closely study and interpret Chinese astrology have the years broken down by specific dates within each year period.

The following provide a sketch of Chinese astrology. For a more complete understanding, consult the books included at the end of the entry.

The Rat (Years: 1900, 1912, 1924, 1936, 1948, 1960, 1972, 1984, 1996). Those born during the Year of the Rat are often said to be ambitious and persistent. They seek opportunities well before others and are quick to comprehend their financial importance. The Rat is said to make an excellent, determined entrepreneur and is happiest when setting his or her own routines.

The Ox (Years: 1901, 1925, 1937, 1949, 1961, 1973, 1985, 1997). Those born during the Year of the Ox are hardworking and feel best when life is lived on a schedule. They tend to be loners and individual thinkers who exhibit strong, patient natures, sometimes with oversized egos. They are goal setters and goal achievers.

The Rabbit (Years: 1903, 1915, 1927, 1939, 1951, 1975, 1987, 1999). Those born during the Year of the Rabbit are said to move easily in and out of difficult situations. They possess highly refined social skills, enjoy being with people and are often the creative and innovative geniuses behind shrewd business deals. This is considered to be an extremely lucky sign.

The Dragon (Years: 1904, 1916, 1928, 1940, 1952, 1964, 1976, 1988, 2000). Those born during the Year of the Dragon have no trouble standing up for themselves or any cause, business or relationship in which they are involved. Once they are committed, little sways them. They are dependable, sincere and somewhat more ambitious than people born in other signs.

The Snake (Years: 1905, 1917, 1929, 1941, 1953, 1965, 1977, 1989, 2001). Those born during the Year of the Snake are individual thinkers who often do not share themselves or ideas with anyone but their loved ones. Somewhat like the snake, they quietly ingest information to use it at a later date. They can be reflective and extremely secretive at times, too.

The Horse (Years: 1906, 1918, 1942, 1954, 1966, 1978, 1990, 2002). Those born during the Year of the Horse are the attention grabbers of Chinese astrology. They are naturally charismatic, which is a great help because many enter the fields of entertainment and politics. The negative position of the sign is that they may have an exaggerated sense of self-importance.

The Sheep (Years: 1907, 1919, 1931, 1943, 1955, 1967, 1979, 1991, 2003). Those born during the Year of the Sheep are deeply caring and considerate. They form lasting friendships and relationships in which they can grow and blossom. They move through life with a somewhat timid nature. The Sheep prefers working in a group and is a true team player.

The Monkey (Years: 1908, 1920, 1932, 1944, 1956, 1968, 1980, 1992, 2004). Those born during the Year of the Monkey possess a delightful nature; playful regardless of their age, they attract the most interesting people and careers. They are children at heart and do well in areas that require a sense appreciation or understanding of the old.

The Rooster (Years: 1909, 1921, 1933, 1945, 1957, 1969, 1981, 1993, 2005). Those born during the Year of the Rooster are much like their animal counterpart: They let the world know exactly where they are and what they are doing. They are committed, adventurous and outgoing and have a stubborn streak that sometimes gets in the way of their common sense.

The Dog (Years: 1910, 1922, 1934, 1946, 1958, 1970, 1982, 1994, 2006). Those born during the Year of the Dog are much like their animal counterpart—devoted, loving and dependable. They often exhibit a deep patriotic streak and are considered extremely trustworthy. They can often be found in careers dedicated to community service and their fellow human beings.

The Pig (Years: 1911, 1923, 1935, 1947, 1959, 1971, 1983, 1995, 2007). Those born during the Year of the Pig are unafraid to speak up for what they believe in. Sometimes considered to be retiring in nature, in actuality, they choose their friends and commitments with care because once they pledge energy, money or their life, there is no turning back.

Further reading

Alleau, Rene. *History of Occult Sciences.* London: Leisure Arts, 1965.
Cosmic Connections. Mysteries of the Unknown. Alexandria, Va.: Time Life Books, 1990.
Somerville, Neil. *Your Chinese Horoscope.* London: Aquarian Press, 1992.

CHIROMANCY *Divination and character analysis through studying the nails, lines and fingers of a person's hand.*

See also CHEIRO; PALMISTRY.

CHRESMOMANCY *Divination through the interpretation of the chance encounter with a series of magic sounds, utterances or foreign words.*

Popular during the height of the Roman Empire, chresmomancy included interpreting omens, answering questions and foretelling the future from the sounds. Less common was omen interpretation from the mutterings of the mentally ill.

See also GELOMANCY.

Further reading

Maven, Max. *Max Maven's Book of Fortunetelling.* New York: Prentice-Hall, 1992.
Visions and Prophecies. Mysteries of the Unknown. Alexandria, Va.: Time Life Books, 1990.

CHRESMONANCY *Divination through a voice from the ethereal world, transmitted through a psychic, providing knowledge or other wisdom.*

Chresmonancy was used with absolute assurance during Roman times by augurs. Paid by the government, augurs interpreted omens and predicted the future using various mantic arts.

Those who channel information in this way sometimes report that they fall into a deep trance and do not know what is being said; other psychics report that they do hear the words being transmitted but have nothing to do with the thoughts or energy behind them. They are a vehicle for another being's voice and/or communications. Also referred to as voice trance, the psychic's neck area is taken over by a spirit and the vocal chords serve as an amplification system to bring the spirit voice to a level humans can hear.

Chresmonancy is also known as channeling (see CHANNEL) and is sometimes referred to as a voice trance.

Further reading

Knight, JZ. *A State of Mind: My Story.* New York: Warner, 1987.
Montgomery, Ruth. *A Search for Truth.* New York: Bantam, 1968.
———. *Strangers among Us.* New York: Fawcett Crest, 1979.

CLAIGUSCIENCE *Tasting of a specific food by someone who is psychic without actually eating the food. May be used as a way to divine an upcoming event or incident in the querant's life.*

Claiguscience is often considered to be a divine message from the ethereal world that must be interpreted by a psychic. Often the food or substance is smelled as well as tasted by the psychic.

Those who practice palm reading support the theory that characteristics and attitudes, among other things, are reflected in the palm of the hand.

It is also considered symbolic, for example, if during a psychic reading the psychic tastes something extremely bitter, it might mean that the querant is coping with a very traumatic matter or that he or she is bitter about someone or something in life.

Someone with this psychic ability is called a clairgustant.

Further reading

Psychic Powers. Mysteries of the Unknown. Alexandria, Va.: Time Life Books, 1990.

CLAIRAUDIENCE *The ability to hear voices and messages from the dead, only audible*

to the psychic, as a means to advise the querant of cautions or to provide guidance.

Clairaudience can also be associated with other sounds: a rushing stream or wind in the trees that can be interpreted as messages for the querant. Sometimes the sounds are of knocking, bells ringing, music playing or voices speaking or singing in a choir.

Psychics say that the messages come out of their head and can be heard as clearly as if someone was standing next to them talking. Because those who are able to receive clairaudient messages must also deal with the world, typically these voices and messages are kept under control unless specifically requested to be received during a psychic reading.

Further reading

Fodor, Nandor. *Encyclopedia of Psychic Science.* New York: University Books, 1966.

Psychics. Mysteries of the Unknown. Alexandria, Va.: Time Life Books, 1990.

CLAIRSENTIENT *One who receives information through the body instead of the mind.*

Often clairsentient feelings are interpreted through the stomach; when one gets a "gut feeling" that something will happen, it could be an instance of clairsentience.

See also INTUITION.

Further reading

Bro, Harmon. *Edgar Cayce on Religion and Psychic Experience.* New York: Warner, 1988.

Burns, Litany. *Develop Your Psychic Abilities.* New York: Pocket Books, 1987.

Vaughn, Frances. *Awakening Intuition.* Garden City, N.Y.: Anchor/Doubleday, 1979.

CLAIRVOYANCE *Psychic ability to become aware of something or someone without the normal perception of the senses and without any outside influences.*

Clairvoyance is the umbrella term that designates all the ways in which a psychic knows of upcoming events or things that have happened in the past. It is a common psychic ability and includes everything from hunches to telepathy. Throughout history, prophets, soothsayers, fortune-tellers, clairvoyants, spiritualists and those who consider themselves to be sensitive to other depths of thinking and knowing use forms of clairvoyance. Clairvoyance is said to have been the gift of the soothsayer who tried to warn Caesar of the Ides of March, and clairvoyance is the particular gift of many psychics, including Jeane Dixon.

The use of clairvoyance is ancient and has guided the nobility as well as the masses. The Bible documents many clairvoyant prophecies.

During the mid-1800s, there was a revival period of mysticism in the United States. Psychics who practiced clairvoyance and other prognostication methods traveled the country giving seances for groups of people.

Sometimes a trancelike state is necessary to induce clairvoyance; for others, the information is readily available, as if someone has spoken in the psychic's ear. There are a number of variations of clairvoyance, including an obscure form known as CLEDONOMANCY: knowing what will be said in the first few minutes of a conversation and predicting the future by the context of the remarks.

In the late 1800s Professor Charles Richet began testing people for clairvoyance, and the study continues today using ESP cards. The subject of clairvoyance, as with other metaphysical topics, is highly controversial. Some scientists consider the entire subject a hoax; others believe that clairvoyance is simply a sense, like hearing, seeing and touching, that some human beings can use more capably than others.

See also EXTRASENSORY PERCEPTION (ESP); INTUITION.

Further reading

Alleau, Rene. *History of Occult Sciences.* London: Leisure Arts, 1965.

Butler, W. E. *How to Develop Clairvoyance.* 2d ed. New York: Samuel Weiser, 1979.

Guiley, Rosemary Ellen. *Harper's Encyclopedia of Mystical and Paranormal Experience.* San Francisco: HarperSan Francisco, 1991.

LeShan, Lawrence. *The Medium, the Mystic, and the Physicist: Toward a General Theory of the Paranormal.* New York: Viking, 1974.

CLEDONOMANCY *The art of predicting, from the first few minutes of a conversation, what remarks will follow.*

See also CLAIRVOYANCE.

CLEIDOMANCY *Divination using the swinging of a pendulum to foretell the future or answer a querant's question.*

See also DOWSING; KELIDOMANCY; PENDULUM PREDICTIONS.

Further reading

Fodor, Nandor. *Encyclopedia of Psychic Science.* New York: University Books, 1966.

Geller, Uri, and Guy Lyon Playfair. *The Geller Effect.* New York: Henry Holt, 1986.

Roberts, Kenneth. *Henry Gross and His Dowsing Rod.* Garden City, N.Y.: Doubleday, 1951.

CLEROMANCY *Divination using objects with sides that are thrown on a table, onto a cloth with specific divination markings or to the ground in order to foretell the future.*

Originating more than 5,000 years ago, cleromancy is still a common divination method. Many cultures have used a variation of it. The ancient Chinese system is called *chiao-pai*, and it is still very much in use in Hong Kong, Singapore and throughout Asia; many American travelers have seen practitioners on street corners foretelling the future. Using *chiao-pai*, two curved bamboo blocks are thrown to the ground as a question is asked. Should both blocks land with curved sides up, the answer is yes. If the blocks land with flat sides up, the response is negative. And when the blocks land with one flat side and one curved side up, the response is thought to be extremely positive. The blocks should be tossed three times in order to achieve a comprehensive reading.

Bones are also used in cleromancy, with a history going back more than 3,500 years in Egypt and 3,000 years in Greece. The casting of lots, bone casting and foretelling the future with dice of various shapes and sizes are still practiced by the Zulu and the West African tribe of the Bantu. As with other sortilege methods, it is the placement or the inscription on the objects that psychics interpret to answer a querant's question.

Objects used in cleromancy vary as to from what they are made and the number of sides. For instance, in *chiao-pai*, the objects have two sides. The ancient Egyptians used dice with eight sides; in the Middle Ages dice with 12 sides were used. The Romans predicted the future using dice with as many as 14 sides. The most commonly used dice to forecast the future are the six-sided ones available throughout the United States; sides are arranged so that any pair of opposite surfaces add up to the number seven.

Foretelling the future using dice has changed little since the days of ancient Egypt. A pair of dice and a 12-inch circle, drawn on a paper or a cloth, are all that is required. (Traditionally, the circle is drawn with chalk on a piece of cloth, although some cultures use a stick or knife to draw the circle on bare ground.)

The dice are shaken in a specially designated cup. Some say the cup and dice must be held in the left hand of the querant; gypsies insist it is the right hand that must throw the dice. The dice are poured or tossed into the circle. If either die rolls out of the circle, the number appearing on the top side doesn't count. If both roll out of the circle, the toss must be repeated. If this happens twice, the session should be stopped and resumed at another time, since this could indicate a bad omen for those involved. If both the dice roll out of the circle, an argument or an estrangement will occur. Additionally, some practitioners of this system say the dice should not be consulted on a Monday or a Wednesday, in hot weather or when there is a storm brewing. And while throwing of dice may seem a somewhat absurd method of predicting the future, those who practice it assert that the dice never lie and consultation must be done in complete silence.

The following are the responses of the two-dice system:

1. The answer to the question is yes (if the other die lands outside the circle, it isn't counted).
2. The answer to the question is no.
3. Extreme care must be taken in handling the situation.
4. Think before acting.
5. Excellent results; good fortune arriving soon.
6. Very favorable; the outcome is smooth.
7. Continue as you are for a favorable result.
8. Be patient; the answer is yes over time.
9. Success in the enterprise.
10. There may be disappointment in the situation.
11. At this time, it is not possible.
12. The chance for success is slim.

A three-dice method that was used by the ancient Tibetans developed into a system used in the United States today to forecast future events and answer questions. The practice is similar to the two-dice system, in that if the die falls outside the circle's line, it is not counted. As an added facet, if two of the dice land and balance on top of each other, it means that the querant will either receive a gift or something of great value or be forewarned of problems in a relationship. This omen is interpreted by the psychic.

The number of dots on the face of the dice that point toward the querant are said to provide the answer to questions or indicate:

1. Problems with family.
2. Rethink your situation.
3. A pleasant surprise.
4. Bad luck is about to begin.
5. A wish will be realized.
6. Money or something of value will be lost or taken.
7. Distress with a relationship.
8. Unjust disapproval.
9. Love and romance are favorable.
10. A birth, of a person, idea or concept.
11. There will be a separation.
12. News will be received that is fortunate.
13. There will be a cause of distress and grief.
14. Someone new will help you.
15. Temptation; do not be deterred from your plan.
16. A journey will have favorable results.
17. A change in plans; favorable for business.
18. All good things are coming.

Along with simple cleromancy systems, there are more intricate methods, including those that divide the 12-inch circle into 12 segments. The placement of the die as it falls to one of the segments provides a more detailed answer to the querant's question. In addition to dice, shells, crystals, rocks and coins can also be thrown. Flipping a coin to decide an answer or to see which sports team will begin play is derived from the practice of cleromancy.

See also ASTRAGALOMANCY; ASTRAGYROMANCY; I CHING; RUNE STONES; SORTILEGE SYSTEMS.

Further reading

Buckland, Raymond. *Secrets of Gypsy Fortunetelling.* St. Paul, Minn.: Llewellyn, 1988.
Mind over Matter. Mysteries of the Unknown. Alexandria, Va.: Time Life Books, 1990.
Morgan, Chris. *Fortune Telling: How to Predict Your Own Future.* London: Quintet Publishing and Random House, 1992.
Visions and Prophecies. Mysteries of the Unknown. Alexandria, Va.: Time Life Books, 1990.
Walker, Barbara G. *The Woman's Encyclopedia of Myths and Secrets.* New York: Harper Collins, 1983.

CLIDOMANCY *Divination of the guilt or innocence of an accused by the use of a key, a holy book—typically a Bible—and the index finger of a virgin.*

Using clidomancy, the psychic writes a description of the crime that has been committed onto a key. The key is tied to a Bible or other holy book, and both are hung from the finger of a virgin. The movement of the key and the book, determined by a formula, forecasts the guilt or innocence of the accused. This ritual was performed, in the Middle Ages, only when the Sun or Moon was in Virgo.

See also BIBLIOMANCY.

Further reading

Bevan, E. *Sibyls and Seers: A Survey of Some Ancient Theories of Revelation and Inspiration.* London: Allen & Unwin, 1982.

Visions and Prophecies. Mysteries of the Unknown. Alexandria, Va.: Time Life Books, 1990.

COFFEE GROUND READING *Divination by interpreting the dregs of coffee in a cup.*

Similar to TASSEOGRAPHY, or teacup reading, coffee ground reading uses the grounds of coffee beans in the same basic ritual as with tea leaves. As with teacup reading, patterns and formations of grounds and their placement indicate what will happen in the querant's future and/or the answer to his or her question.

Coffee ground reading became popular in cultures that drank strong coffee instead of tea. It continues to be preferred by people who do not like tea but want a reading, and some psychics choose coffee ground reading as their only method of prognostication.

COFFEE GROUND READING
Divination by interpreting the dregs of coffee in a cup is known as coffee ground reading. It utilizes techniques similar to those of tasseography.

Further reading

Buckland, Raymond. *Secrets of Gypsy Fortune Telling.* St. Paul, Minn.: Llewellyn, 1988.

Visions and Prophecies. Mysteries of the Unknown. Alexandria, Va.: Time Life Books, 1990.

COLLECTIVE UNCONSCIOUS *The term used by Dr. Carl Jung to describe memories that are experienced and shared by people.*

The collective unconscious is often referred to as the universal consciousness and is considered to be a library of thoughts accessible to all people—though usually only realized by psychic and believers in reincarnation—including images and patterns of instinctive behavior. Jung also believed that the collective unconscious was reflective of archetypal symbols, images passed down from humans' prehuman and animal ancestors. Some believe that the archetypal images and symbols are the memories of past lives.

See also JUNG, DR. CARL G.

Further reading

Fordham, Frieda. *An Introduction to Jung's Psychology.* 3d ed. Harmondsworth, England: Penguin Books, 1966.

Guiley, Rosemary Ellen. *Harper's Encyclopedia of Mystical and Paranormal Experience.* San Francisco: HarperSan Francisco, 1991.

Jung, Carl G., ed. *Man and His Symbols.* New York: Anchor Press/Doubleday, 1988.

COLOROLOGY *The study of colors and/or AURAS.*

Divination may be made by interpreting the colors sensed in the mind of the querant or by interpreting the colors in the halolike field surrounding one's body, which psychics call the aura. The colors are psychically interpreted. Generally, a red aura shows an outgoing nature, blue shows a nurturing spirit, yellow indicates one with a strong imagination, green is a people person, violet a creative person, brown tells of a dependable individual and black is a rebellious person.

COLORS

See AURAS; COLOROLOGY.

COLOR TELEPATHY *The ability to send the thoughts or sensations of a specific color from one person to another.*

The receiver is said to be able to sense the color without having been directed to the specific word for it through the use of clairvoyance.

See also CLAIRVOYANCE.

COOK, FLORENCE *(1904–1956) English psychic.*

Cook was a popular psychic who began to demonstrate her talent as a teenager during her mother's tea parties. Cook is supposed to have summoned spirits and channeled their voices and images, including that of Katy King, the daughter of buccaneer Henry Morgan. She was applauded for her abilities in many circles but denounced by other psychic investigators as a charlatan.

See also CHANNEL.

Further reading

Drury, Nevill. *Dictionary of Mysticism and the Esoteric Traditions.* Dorset, England: Prism, 1992.
Spirit Summonings. Mysteries of the Unknown. Alexandria, Va.: Time Life Books, 1990.

COSCINOMANCY *Divination using a sieve and a pair of scissors to determine guilt or innocence.*

Practiced in biblical times to ascertain innocence or guilt among a group of people, coscinomancy was a complex process. Two people held, by their thumbnails, a pair of shears or tongs that supported a sieve. The group of accused people were placed directly in front of the sieve and asked the question "Who is guilty?" The sieve would turn, and when the handle pointed at someone in the group, he or she was considered to be the guilty party.

This divination method was but one of those used during the time chronicled in the Old Testament.

See also BIBLICAL PROPHETS AND DIVINATION METHODS; BIBLIOMANCY; SCRYING.

Further reading

Bletzer, June G. *The Donning International Encyclopedic Psychic Dictionary.* West Chester, Pa.: Whitford Press, 1986.
McKenzie, John L. *Dictionary of the Bible.* Milwaukee: Bruce, 1965.
Miller, Madeleine S., and J. Lane Miller, eds. *Harper's Encyclopedia of Bible Life.* San Francisco: Harper & Row, 1978.
Tinney, Merrill C., ed. *The Zondervan Pictorial Encyclopedia of the Bible.* Grand Rapids, Mich.: Zondervan Publishing House, 1977.

CRITOMANCY *Divination by observing grain and flour in various ways to predict the future.*

A variation of CAUSIMONANCY, critomancy (also referred to as crithomancy) involved observing the results of sprinkling various grains and flours over sacrificial victims, sprinkling the grains and flours in a fire or over hot coals or by watching the dough and cakes as they baked.

See also ALEUROMANCY.

Further reading

Maven, Max. *Max Maven's Book of Fortunetelling.* New York: Prentice-Hall, 1992.
Morgan, Chris. *Fortune Telling: How to Predict Your Own Future.* London: Quintet Publishing and Random House, 1992.
Visions and Prophecies. Mysteries of the Unknown. Alexandria, Va.: Time Life Books, 1990.

CROISET, GERARD *(1909–1980) Dutch clairvoyant.*

A gifted psychic, Croiset helped police departments find missing bodies and missing persons and helped bring criminals to justice throughout Europe and in the United States. He used a form of psychometry, in that he touched an object owned by the missing or murdered individual, "reading" the messages left as hidden vibrations on the objects, which directed him to the person or body.

As with many psychics, Croiset's talent is disputed. However, it was studied for 20 years and found to be authentic by Professor W. H. C. Tenhaeff at Utrecht University, the Netherlands, who was an investigator of paranormal phenomena.

Further reading

Marks, David, and Richard Kammann. *The Psychology of the Psychic.* Buffalo, N.Y.: Prometheus, 1980.

Pollack, Jack Harrison. *Croiset the Clairvoyant.* Garden City, N.Y.: Doubleday, 1964.

Psychic Powers. Mysteries of the Unknown. Alexandria, Va.: Time Life Books, 1990.

Wilson, Colin. *The Psychic Detectives.* San Francisco: Mercury House, 1985.

CROWLEY, ALEISTER *(1875–1947)*
British occultist.

Crowley's contribution to the study of metaphysics is still controversial even though it has been more than 45 years since his death. He was either one of the great thinkers and occultists of his age or a notorious charlatan. During his lifetime, he was held in great esteem, but he was called "the wickedest man in the world" by the media.

As a young man, he developed a lifelong interest in the occult, ritual magic, torture and sexual degradation. Crowley was initiated as a novate in the Hermetic Order of the Golden Dawn, a secret society that studied magic, the occult and the Kabbalah, attracting many notable people of the time. When there was dissent over the course of the society, Crowley moved in a different direction and became known internationally as a leading figure in the occult.

During a trip to Cairo, Egypt, in 1904 with his wife, Rose, Crowley performed a magical ritual learned during his days with the Hermetic Order of the Golden Dawn. Rose channeled information regarding a statue of Horus, which was on exhibit at a nearby museum. The exhibit was number 666. Crowley believed that this statue was the Great Beast referred to in the Book of Revelation and that he had been chosen as the Antichrist.

Rose Crowley subsequently fell into another trance, and in it she began channeling a volume known as *The Book of the Law,* which was said to confirm that Crowley was the new Lord. It is of little surprise that Crowley's acknowledgment of this position was not accepted by the Christian church; however, that did not stop him. He had, he believed, been initiated into a new secret organization that only inducted new members every 2,000 years. The new secret order was called the Argenteium Astrum, and it claimed special knowledge of Egyptian magic and ritual sources. At its height, the new order had about 100 members, including some of the best-known occultists of the time, among them Victor Neuberg, Austin Spare, Pamela Hansford-Johnson and Louis T. Cullings, all famous mediums of the day.

Crowley believed he was the reincarnation of Eliphas Levi (1810–1875). A sometime magician, Levi is best remembered for determining that the 22 cards of the tarot's major arcana have a symbolic relationship with the Kabbalah.

Crowley is said to have died with his thoughts and theories in conflict, addicted to drugs, in poor health and in poverty.

Crowley's major works include *Magick in Theory and Practice, The Book of Thoth* and *Qabalah of Aleister Crowley.*

See also SPARE, AUSTIN OSMAN.

Further reading

Cavendish, Richard, ed. *The Encyclopedia of the Unexplained.* New York: McGraw-Hill, 1974.

Giles, Cynthia. *The Tarot: History, Mystery and Lore.* New York: Paragon House, 1992.

Guiley, Rosemary Ellen. *The Encyclopedia of Witches and Witchcraft.* New York: Facts On File, 1989.

MacKenzie, Norman. *Secret Societies.* New York: Holt, Rinehart & Winston, 1967.

Symonds, John, and Kenneth Grant, eds. *The Confessions of Aleister Crowley: An Autobiography.* London: Routledge & Kegan Paul, 1979.

CRYSTALLOMANCY *An ancient divination practice of casting lots or sortilege, using small stones or small crystals (see SORTILEGE SYSTEMS).*

Unlike crystalomancy, by which images or messages are received by meditating in a crystal ball or a mirrorlike pool, prognostication occurs here depending on the placement of the stones, as with CASTING OF LOTS.

See also DICE; GEMS.

Further reading

Markham, Ursula. *The Crystal Workbook: A Complete Guide to Working with Crystals.* Northamptonshire, England: Aquarian Press, 1988.

———. *Fortune-Telling by Crystals and Semiprecious Stones.* Northamptonshire, England: Aquarian Press, 1987.

Matteson, Barbara J. *Mystic Minerals.* Seattle: Cosmic Resources, 1985.

Walker, Dael. *The Crystal Book.* Sunol, Calif.: Crystal Col, 1983.

CRYSTALOMANCY *Divination by studying a crystal ball.*

A form of SCRYING, crystalomancy (sometimes incorrectly grouped with crystallomancy, or casting of lots) is an ancient practice developed about 1000 B.C. as a means to foretell the future or forthcoming events.

As with other applications of scrying, psychics stare into a crystal ball until a vision appears, specifically to the psychic (the querant typically cannot see the vision). The vision or message is then interpreted or provided to answer the querant's question.

Meditation should occur before the crystal is consulted. Consultation is usually done in a darkened room with a light source bouncing off the crystal ball. Initially, the crystal ball may appear clear, but as the psychic stares at the ball, it may become misty or foggy.

Dr. John Dee, psychic to Queen Elizabeth I of England, is said to have used a crystal ball and a blackened mirror for scrying. He warned the queen against a plot by Spanish agents to burn the forests of England. Because ships were made of wood at that time, this was of grave concern, and extra military was assigned to the protection of the forests. Had the forests been burned, England might have fallen against the Spanish Armada of 1588.

Contemporary psychic Jeane Dixon uses a crystal ball for forecasting future events; one of her predictions was that John F. Kennedy would be slain in 1963.

Today, the most popular crystal balls are available in metaphysical stores and through catalogs that sell metaphysical tools. The preferred size is one or two inches in diameter, although some psychics use crystal balls that are well over 12 inches in diameter. Most crystal balls are round, though some are egg shaped or conical.

See also CATOPTROMANCY; LITHOMANCY.

Further reading

Encyclopedia of Religion. New York: Macmillan, 1987.

King, Frances, and Stephen Skinner. *Techniques of High Magic.* Rochester, Vt.: Destiny, 1991.

Magickal Almanac. St. Paul, Minn.: Llewellyn, 1989.

The Psychics. Mysteries of the Unknown. Alexandria, Va.: Time Life Books, 1990.

Walker, Dael. *The Crystal Book.* Sunol, Calif.: Crystal Col, 1983.

CRYSTAL PREDICTIONS *Divination using natural crystal stones.*

Foretelling future events through the use of jewels and crystals is technically known as LITHOMANCY, a form of scrying. It is considered by many to be one of the oldest forms of prognostication.

Natural crystals and gemstones were used for the purpose of divination by most ancient civilizations, including the Aztecs, the Incas, the Babylonians and the Egyptians. In addition to their use in scrying, crystals are still used for meditation, heightening intuition and in healing rites, including healing chakras.

Some astrologers believe that each sign of the zodiac is attached to a specific natural crystal; more commonly, these are known as birthstones. The following is a list of natural crystals and the astrological sun sign typically associated with them:

Aries: Diamond, ruby, red jasper
Taurus: Sapphire, lapis lazuli

Gemini: Citrine, yellow agate
Cancer: Pearl, moonstone
Leo: Tiger's eye, dendritic agate
Virgo: Green jasper, sardonyx
Libra: Sapphire, aquamarine
Scorpio: Ruby, opal, red jasper
Sagittarius: Topaz
Capricorn: Turquoise, smokey quartz
Aquarius: Amethyst
Pisces: Moonstone, rose quartz

Specific crystals have specific divination or helping qualities. Thus if a person wears or carries a certain crystal, he or she will be assisted by the crystal's power. For example, to increase psychic ability, it is suggested that a diamond or peridot be worn or carried. A bronze or sapphire crystal will help in channeling. And a Herkimer diamond or fire opal should be worn or carried to enhance clairaudience.

See also GEMS.

Further reading

Baer, Randall N., and Vick V. Baer. *The Crystal Connection.* San Francisco: Harper & Row, 1986.
Bravo, Brett. *Crystal Healing Secrets.* New York: Warner, 1988.
Bryant, Page. *Crystals and Their Use.* Santa Fe, N.Mex.: Sun Publishers, 1984.
Daya, Sarai Croshon. *Healing with Crystals and Gemstones.* New York: Samuel Weiser, 1983.
Markham, Ursula. *The Crystal Workbook: A Complete Guide to Working with Crystals.* Northamptonshire, England: Aquarian Press, 1988.

CUMMINGS, GERALDINE *(1890– 1969) Irish medium.*

Cummings (also known as Geraldine Cummins) believed she could contact the spirits of those involved in early Christianity, including Philip the Evangelist. Although Cummings never studied or visited the Middle East, she could clearly define areas there and knew even greater details of early Christian figures mentioned in the Bible. Tested by a number of metaphysical research groups, such as the Society for Psychical Research in London, and psychical investigators, including Dr. R. H. Thouless and Professor C. D. Broad, Cummings was considered to be a legitimate psychic. She was sometimes referred to as the "medium with integrity."

She chronicled her thoughts and the messages from the spirits in a number of books. Best known are *The Scripts of Cleophas, The Road to Immortality, They Survive, Unseen Adventures* and *Mind in Life and Death.*

Further reading

Drury, Nevill. *Dictionary of Mysticism and the Esoteric Traditions.* Dorset, England: Prism Press, 1992.
Search for the Soul. Mysteries of the Unknown. Alexandria, Va.: Time Life Books, 1990.

CUSP *In ASTROLOGY, the cusp is the theoretical line where each sign of the zodiac begins and ends.*

The word *cusp* is derived from the Latin word *cuspis,* meaning point. For example, if one is born when the Sun is in Capricorn, but the birth is on the last day of that sign, he or she is said to be born on the cusp and will manifest characteristics of both Capricorn and Aquarius, the next sun sign of the zodiac.

The cusps can also refer to the beginning and ending points in the houses of the zodiac. There are twelve houses, each depicting various areas in the querant's life.

See also ASTROLOGICAL SYMBOLS.

Further reading

Goodman, Linda. *Linda Goodman's Sun Signs.* New York: Fawcett/Columbine, 1978.
Omarr, Sydney. *My World of Astrology.* New York: Fleet, 1965.
Woolfork, Joanna Martine. *The Only Astrology Book You'll Ever Need.* Landham, Mass.: Scarborough, 1992.

CYCLOMANCY *Divination using a wheel or revolving circle to foretell the future.*

The practice of cyclomancy may have been the origin of the roulette wheel as a game of chance.

CYLICOMANCY *Divination through the use of a cup of water.*

It is said that Old Testament prophet Joseph used a variation of cylicomancy to foretell the future by placing a small amount of oil in a dish filled with water (Gen. 44:5, 15).

See also BIBLICAL PROPHETS AND DIVINATION METHODS; HYDROMANCY; SCRYING.

Further reading

McKenzie, John L. *Dictionary of the Bible*. Milwaukee: Bruce, 1965.

Pajeon, Kala, and Ketz Pajeon. *The Candle Magic Workbook*. New York: Citadel Press, 1992.

Visions and Prophecies. Mysteries of the Unknown. Alexandria, Va.: Time Life Books, 1990.

DACTYLOMANCY *Divination using a tripodlike tool that moves with the answer to a querant's question around a board or basin on which letters of the alphabet are inscribed.*

An ancient method of divination, dactylomancy was originally used by the Greek psychics and Dactyls (a sect of Phrygian soothsayers and sorcerers) around 50 B.C. Our contemporary OUIJA BOARDS are a version of dactylomancy.

See also DACTYOMANCY.

Further reading

Drury, Nevill. *Dictionary of Mysticism and the Esoteric Traditions.* Dorset, England: Prism Press, 1992.
Witches and Witchcraft. Mysteries of the Unknown. Alexandria, Va.: Time Life Books, 1990.

DACTYOMANCY *Divination using a suspended object, particularly a finger ring, as a pendulum above a round table to foretell the future or answer a querant's question.*

With the technique of Dactyomancy, a wedding ring, a plain gold band or another ring of some sentimental or metaphysical importance is suspended on a string and used as a pendulum. The dactyomancer holds the string by his or her index finger and thumb over a round table on which is inscribed the letters of the alphabet, forming a circle on its top. The answers to questions are revealed by the pendulum swinging over or to the letters, spelling at a message. Depending on the psychic, the pendulum will rotate or swing forward and backward and to either side. It is said that for a pendulum to work, one must be sensitive to the vibrations found in all living energy fields, nonliving energy fields and energy fields outside one's presence.

Dactyomancy is similar to DOWSING in that a pendulum is used to predict the future and/or answer questions. Other systems are less time consuming and have gained more popularity, since dactyomancy takes patience and time for the messages to be spelled out, read and interpreted.

A variation of dactyomancy, called DACTYLOMANCY, is still in use today in OUIJA BOARDS. The updated Ouija board (a trademark of the manufactured board sometimes sold in toy stores) used under the guidance of a dactyomancer, medium or someone practicing mediumship taps into unconscious radiations to divine the future and answer questions. Instead of a pendulum, the Ouija board uses a small-wheeled device that slides over the board to the letters, numbers and yes and no responses printed on the board. A wine glass or a planchette has also been used as the pointing device.

DACTYOMANCY
Greek professional soldier, historian and prolific writer Ammianus Marcellinus (c. 330–390) describes a table with a slab, engraved with letters of the alphabet, above which a ring was suspended by a thread. This is a direct reference to dactyomancy.

Dactyomancy has been in documented service since about 540 B.C., when Pythagoras used it. According to a historical account of the philosopher's life, his sect held frequent seances or circles at which a mystic table, set on wheels, moved toward signs, which the philosopher and his pupil, Philolaus, interpreted for the audience as being revelations from the unseen world.

Tertullian (c. A.D. 160–230), the Roman Christian theologian, also knew about table communications. Greek professional soldier, historian and prolific writer Ammianus Marcellinus (c. 330–390) described a table with a slab engraved with letters of the alphabet above which a ring was suspended by a thread. This is a direct reference to dactyomancy.

See also AUTOMATIC WRITING; PENDULUM PREDICTIONS.

Further reading

Fodor, Nandor. *Encyclopedia of Psychic Science.* New York: University Books, 1966.

Geller, Uri, and Guy Lyon Playfair. *The Geller Effect.* New York: Henry Holt, 1986.

Guiley, Rosemary Ellen. *Harper's Encyclopedia of Mystical and Paranormal Experience.* San Francisco: HarperSan Francisco, 1991.

Ostrander, Sheila, and Lynn Schroeder. *Psychic Discoveries behind the Iron Curtain.* Englewood Cliffs, N.J.: Prentice-Hall, 1970.

DAPHNOMANCY *Divination using the smoke of burning branches of the laurel tree to answer questions and forecast upcoming events.*

As in CAPNOMANCY, the smoke and fire were interpreted by psychics. However, in daphnomancy, if the branches and laurel wood crackled, it was said that the response to the querant's question was favorable. If the fire was quiet or the smoke did not rise but hung close to the floor or ground, it was considered a negative omen. This form of daphnomancy is still heeded in contemporary New England by those who believe in the validity of folklore.

Further reading

Drury, Nevill. *Dictionary of Mysticism and the Esoteric Traditions.* Dorset, England: Prism Press, 1992.

Johnson, Clifton. *What They Say in New England and Other American Folklore.* Boston: Lee & Shepherd, 1896. Reprinted ed., Carl A. Withers, ed. New York: Columbia University Press, 1963.

Kittredge, George. *Witchcraft in Old and New England.* Cambridge: Harvard University Press, 1929. Reprint. New York: Atheneum, 1972.

Visions and Prophecies. Mysteries of the Unknown. Alexandria, Va.: Time Life Books, 1990.

D'ARPETIGNY, CASIMIR STANIS-LAUS *(1789–?) French palmist and psychic.*

D'Arpetigny is said to have had the most beautiful hands in Europe in his day. As a palmist, mystic and psychic, he developed a theory that the thumb was an indicator of ego and genius. He refined palmistry and added his innovative thoughts on the way fingers and thumbs revealed personal characteristics. His works include *La Chirognomonie* and *Le Science de la Main.*

Further reading

King, Francis. *Palmistry: Your Fate and Fortune in Your Hand.* New York: Crescent, 1987.

Sorell, Walter. *The Story of the Human Hand.* Indianapolis: Bobbs-Merrill, 1967.

Waite, Arthur Edward. *The Occult Sciences.* 1881. Reprint. London: K. Paul, Trench, Trubner & Co., 1923.

DAVIS, ANDREW JACKSON *(1826–1910) American clairvoyant and psychic.*

Davis became intrigued with metaphysics at an early age and went on to become one of the most well known (at that time) of the psychic healers. He was often referred to as the "Poughkeepsie Seer," channeling information on the health of querents while in a trance. Davis was greatly affected by the work of Mesmer regarding hypnosis and the power of the mind, and he became a leader in the spiritualism movement that occurred in the United States in the late 1800s.

The Principles of Nature (published in 1847) is considered Davis's most important work.

Further reading

Fodor, Nandor. *Encyclopedia of Psychic Science.* New York: University Books, 1966.

Powers of Healing. Mysteries of the Unknown. Alexandria, Va.: Time Life Books, 1990.

DEE, DR. JOHN *(1527–1608) British astrologer, psychic and scryer.*

Dee was intrigued by a number of different mantic arts and in magic. In order to divine the future and provide consultation to his noble clients, he used CATOPTROMANCY, a scrying method. Dee calculated an astrological chart for Queen Elizabeth I when she came to the throne in 1558.

It is said that Dee positioned a shiny black mirror or a crystal ball in a light source and interpreted the patterns of light that reflected off the mirror. Some sources refer to Dee using a black mirror; others state that he used a black crystal ball, or even a natural crystal, to scry.

Dee is reported to have used 007 as a code name (the same as fictional spy James Bond).

The two zeros were meant to symbolize the human eyes, while the seven symbolized the sum of the two eyes, the four other senses and a mystical equation of intelligence.

Further reading

Butler, W. E. *How to Develop Clairvoyance.* 2d ed. New York: Samuel Weiser, 1979.

Fodor, Nandor. *Encyclopedia of Psychic Science.* New York: University Books, 1966.

Psychics. Mysteries of the Unknown. Alexandria, Va.: Time Life Books, 1990.

Smith, C. F. *John Dee.* London: Constable, 1909.

DEJA VU *The feeling or ability to know that one has experienced a thought or incident before, often in regard to reincarnation.*

Deja vu, from the French words "already seen," is a common phenomenon. It is the quality of knowing that there is a repetition of any of the senses, without a logical explanation. For example, if one visits a cathedral for the very first time, without ever having seen the building even in photos or drawings, and knows that he or she has seen the uniquely columned construction before, this is referred to as deja vu. The feelings or senses experienced in deja vu are often attributed to past lives and the occurrences of those lives imprinted in our AKASHIC RECORD.

See also KARMA; REINCARNATION.

Further reading

Cavendish, Richard, ed. *The Encyclopedia of the Unexplained.* New York: McGraw-Hill, 1974.

Cayce, Hugh Lynn, ed. *The Edgar Cayce Collection.* New York: Bonanza, 1986.

Time and Space. Mysteries of the Unknown. Alexandria, Va.: Time Life Books, 1990.

Wolman, Benjamin B., ed. *Handbook of Parapsychology.* New York: Van Nostrand Reinhold, 1977.

DICE *Instruments or tools used to predict the future or answer a querant's question.*

The word *dice* is plural; *die* is the singular term. Correctly known as a form of sortilege (see SORTILEGE SYSTEMS), this divination tool originated in the casting of bones more than 5,000 years ago; thus, in today's games of chance, dice are referred to as bones.

See also ASTRAGALOMANCY; ASTRAGYRO-MANCY; CASTING OF LOTS; CLEROMANCY; I CHING; RUNE STONES.

Further reading

Mind over Matter. Mysteries of the Unknown. Alexandria, Va.: Time Life Books, 1990.
Visions and Prophecies. Mysteries of the Unknown. Alexandria, Va.: Time Life Books, 1990.
Walker, Barbara G. *The Woman's Encyclopedia of Myths and Secrets.* New York: Harper Collins, 1983.

DIRECT-VOICE MEDIUM *A psychic, or channel, who becomes the vehicle through which an entity can speak, without using the psychic's own powers of speech or moving the psychic's mouth.*

Typically, the direct-voice medium channels a dead spirit known to others in the room rather than a guru or wise person of another time or place. Often the medium's voice will take on the same tone and accent as the one being channeled; at other times, it is sensed that the voice is coming from someplace close to the psychic but not from his or her throat.

This form of divination was popular during the mid-1800s, the height of spiritualism in the United States. One of the most famous direct-voice mediums was Leslie Flint. Flint, an English man, had been accused repeatedly of performing a ventriloquist's fraud, yet no evidence was ever substantiated that Flint was doing anything but somehow using his body as an antenna, channeling information, in ghostly words, from deceased spirits.

See also CHANNEL.

Further reading

Brown, Slater. *The Heyday of Spiritualism.* New York: Hawthorn, 1970.
Godwin, John. *Occult America.* New York: Doubleday, 1972.
Guiley, Rosemary Ellen. *Harper's Encyclopedia of Mystical and Paranormal Experience.* San Francisco: HarperSan Francisco, 1991.

DIVINATION *The ability to forecast the future by intuitive rather than unscientific or irrational means. Interpreting omens is a form of divination.*

Those who practice a form of divination and counsel or advise querants say that one form of divination should be used and stayed with, immersing oneself in the method and spiritual tradition of that form.

Some forms of divination are CLAIRVOYANCE, AUTOMATIC WRITING, channeling and interpreting omens or events—for example, dream interpretation or translating the movement of an object, such as with candle prophecies (LAMPADOMANCY), clouds (CERAUNOSCOPY) or tea leaves (TASSEOGRAPHY). Other divination systems include the use of dowsing sticks, pendulums, coins and hexigrams (such as with I CHING) or dice (such as with RUNE STONES).

Some of the oldest divination systems are PALMISTRY, GEOMANCY, CLEROMANCY and AEROMANCY, which were practiced before recorded history. Some of the newest forms of divination are based on methods practiced in antiquity, such as the use of computer software to read tarot, interpret an astrological chart or decode dreams.

Further reading

Aylesworth, Thomas G. *Astrology and Foretelling the Future.* New York: Franklin Watts, 1973.
Bethards, Betty. *The Dream Book: Symbols for Self-Understanding.* Petaluma, Calif.: Inner Light Press, 1992.
Glass, Justine. *The Story of Fulfilled Prophecy.* London: Cassell, 1969.
King, Francis, and Stephen Skinner. *Techniques of High Magic.* Rochester, Vt.: Destiny Books, 1991.
Loewe, Michael, and Carmen Blacker, eds. *Divination and Oracles.* London: Allen & Unwin, 1981.
Logan, Jo, and Lindsey Hodson. *The Prediction Book of Divination.* Dorset, England: Blandford Press, 1984.
Stern, Jess. *Edgar Cayce, the Sleeping Prophet.* New York: Bantam, 1968.
Stewart, R. J. *The Elements of Prophecy.* Dorset, England: Element, 1990.
Woods, R., ed. *Understanding Mysticism.* New York: Doubleday, 1980.

DIXON, JEANE (1918–) *American astrologer, scryer and psychic.*

A popular and world-famous contemporary psychic who has gained media attention for various predictions, Dixon foretold the assassinations of John F. Kennedy, Robert Kennedy and Martin Luther King, Jr. She "saw" the 1967 Apollo AS-204 disaster in which Virgil I. Grisson, Edward H. White II and Roger B. Chaffee died in a flash fire that destroyed their spacecraft as it underwent routine tests at Cape Kennedy. (The men were to have been the first astronauts in the Apollo program.) She also predicted Lyndon Johnson's withdrawal from the presidential race (which most people would not have considered possible) in that same year. Using astrology, a crystal ball, dreams, psychometry and telepathy, as well as intuition, she has read for thousands of people throughout the years.

Dixon believes deeply in her religious faith and upbringing and says that she uses her gift of divination only for the good of humankind, firmly rejecting monetary compensation for her personal readings.

Her autobiography, *Jean Dixon: My Life and Prophecies*, discusses her philosophies and gift for foretelling future events.

Further reading

Brian, Denis. *Jeane Dixon: The Witnesses.* New York: Warner, 1976.

Dixon, Jeane, and Rene Noorbergen. *Jeane Dixon: My Life and Prophecies.* New York: Morrow, 1969.

Montgomery, Ruth. *A Gift of Prophecy.* New York: Bantam, 1966.

DOMINOES *Divination by casting the dotted lots (or counters) known as dominoes and interpreting the meaning revealed through the wooden rectangles.*

Although dominoes are now marketed as a game for children, they are a lesser-known method of prognostication and a form of CLEROMANCY and sortilege (see SORTILEGE SYSTEMS). Casting the future using dominoes is said to have been practiced in 12-century China, and dominoes are still widely used as a prognostication tool in some provinces of China, Korea and India. As with tarot, dice, runes and scrying, dominoes are a tool for the psychic. Often psychics choose a specific tool to indicate to the querant that a process is going on, while in actuality the psychic is quietly channeling the information.

To answer a question or respond to a querant's needs for direction, the dominoes are all placed facedown. A question should be asked and meditated upon for a period of time. Three tiles are drawn. It is consided bad to consult with dominoes more than once a month, because the messages are powerful and will take that long to completely understand.

When the tiles are turned over, each combination has a specific meaning, the numbers corresponding to the quantity of dots on the tiles.

Six/six is the luckiest of all the combinations. It means assured success and happiness; the question or query will have a positive result.

Six/five means that a favor or a kindness will bring one good fortune, but patience may be tested.

Six/four means that there is an unfavorable aspect, perhaps a lawsuit or some other litigation forthcoming.

Six/three means the prospect for travel—possibly unexpected travel of a positive nature—or a gift that has to do with travel.

Six/two means good fortune; the future assures betterment of finances and/or health.

Six/one means that there may be a wedding, a possible joint venture or a union with a positive result.

Six/blank means one should beware of false friendships.

Five/five means there will be a change in financial standing in a beneficial way.

Five/four means financial gain.

Five/three means a period of serenity and/or the querant will receive helpful advice or assistance.

Five/two means there will be a birth, perhaps of an idea that will bring about joy.

Five/one means there is the possibility of new love, but with it comes a warning that the affair may have an unhappy ending.

Five/blank means there may be the necessity to comfort a friend regarding a sadness.

Four/four means a time of celebration, thanksgiving and happiness is forthcoming.

Four/three means there will be happiness and success but possible problems on the domestic front or in relationships.

Four/two means there may be an unhappy change of events or a relationship that goes awry.

Four/one means there may be challenging financial times ahead.

Four/blank means there may be a setback in a relationship, along with a temporary disappointment. However, there should be a reconciliation.

Three/three means there are obstacles forthcoming in love and career, but the outcome is beneficial.

Three/two means there will be happy changes, including in home and career, especially with money.

Three/one means the answer to the querant's question is no.

Three/blank means there may be unanticipated invitations and requirements that will challenge the querant's ethics and strengths.

Two/two means there will be much to celebrate in all areas, especially in career and personal relationships.

Two/one means the possible loss of something of value; however, love, friendship and a career move will come as a result of the loss.

Two/blank means there will be a time of anxiety, then the development of new friendships, travel and a business enterprise that will be fruitful. Beware of false advice.

One/one means there will be harmony in all aspects of life, but one should avoid making any snap decisions.

One/blank means heed warnings and be especially careful. All is not what it seems.

Blank/blank means that for a period of time there will be road blocks, challenges and difficulties that must be overcome in order to achieve the predictions of the other dominoes.

See also CASTING OF LOTS.

Further reading

Buckland, Raymond. *Secrets of Gypsy Fortune Telling.* St. Paul, Minn.: Llewellyn, 1988.

Heywood, R. *Beyond the Reach of Sense.* New York: Dutton, 1961.

Magickal Almanac. St. Paul, Minn.: Llewellyn, 1989.

Maven, Max. *Max Maven's Book of Fortunetelling.* New York: Prentice-Hall, 1992.

Pajeon, Kala, and Ketz Pajeon. *The Candle Magic Workbook.* New York: Citadel Press, 1992.

Visions and Prophecies. Mysteries of the Unknown. Alexandria, Va.: Time Life Books, 1990.

DOWSER *One who employs the prediction method of* DOWSING *to find objects, minerals, water supplies and missing persons.*

Henry Gross is said to have been one of the world's most gifted dowsers; Uri Geller is probably the most famous.

Further reading

Geller, Uri, and Guy Lyon Playfair. *The Geller Effect.* New York: Henry Holt, 1986.

Roberts, Kenneth. *Henry Gross and His Dowsing Rod.* Garden City, N.Y.: Doubleday, 1951.

DOWSING *The method used to search for hidden objects, subterranean springs, sites, precious metals, lost treasure and missing people using dowsing sticks or rods.*

Traditionally, the rods were made of hazelwood; modern dowsers use almost any form of rod from a coat hanger to a Y-shaped stick. This form of prediction is also known as RADIESTHESIA or CLEIDOMANCY.

It is not known when dowsing originated. Cave paintings in the Sahara, from about 6000 B.C., have shown a person holding a divining rod. Greek and Roman literature refers to RHABDOMANCY (dowsing with rods, arrows or wands), although there is speculation as to whether this is dowsing in the contemporary sense. Ancient myths and legends suggest magical rods were used by Hermes and Aaron; however, these are often considered more like magician's wands than the dowser's forked stick or rod. Other primitive cultures used dowsing rods. According to a Melanesian folk tale, the reason the dowsing

DOWSING
An 18th-century water diver with dowsing stick.

rod tremble is because a ghost has been conjured up and is directing the rod. In African lore, a stick was used to name a thief or ferret out hidden booty.

In the Bible (Exod. 17:6), when the Israelites needed water for survival in the desert, Moses was told by God to take his rod and "smite the rock and there shall water come out of it." This may be one of the earliest recorded uses of a dowsing rod, one of many divined prophecies in the Bible.

From the Middle Ages, dowsing was used to pinpoint natural underground rivers and springs. In the 15th century in the mountains in Germany, dowsing was practiced to unearth minerals; later Martin Luther denounced the practice as witchcraft.

In 1556, *De Re Metallica*, a book on metallurgy and mining written by George Agricola, discussed dowsing as an acceptable method of locating rich mineral sources. In 1635, the Baron and Baroness Beausoleil purportedly located more than 150 mineral veins through the use of a dowsing rod. They were also reported to be the first to document use of a dowsing rod to locate water, in their book *Les Baguettes Divinatoires* and again in 1640, in a book dedicated to Richelieu. A few years later, the aristocratic couple was imprisoned for sorcery.

By the late 17th century, dowsing was used as a psychic investigation tool by French authorities to locate the criminals involved in an ax murder, and the dowsing rod became a recognized scientific instrument that was used on a regular basis. Dowsers were in great demand during the gold rush in early California.

The Divining Rod (1926) by Sir William Barrett documented a number of experiences in the late 1890s involving the British dowser John Mullins. Mullins found abundant water on an estate in Sussex where engineers had previously been unable to locate water with the somewhat unsophisticated equipment of the time. Henry Gross, of Maine, was one of the United States' best-known dowsers. More recently, U.S. Marines in Vietnam located explosives and land mines using dowsing sticks.

Dowsing is still one of the methods used today to locate underground water and minerals, among other valuables. And dowsing is still sometimes used by metaphysical healers to intuitively identify and locate a sick organs or areas of illness that trouble a querant. This is known as medical dowsing.

A dowser normally walks slowly over the terrain in the area that is being searched. He or she holds a Y-shaped stick, a pair of bars or a pendulum. A few dowsers use no device at all but "know" when the object is close. It is said that they rely on sensations in their hands and arms.

Using rods, a stick or a suspended object, dowsers cover the terrain, walking slowly and concentrating on the object that is to be found. When it is located, the rods cross, the stick circles furiously or points straight down or the pendulum swings.

Dowsing is possible, it is believed, through the strong psychic energy radiated by the object and picked up by the individual holding the divining device. Some believe that dowsing is a variant of the instinct that pulls homing pigeons back to their starting points and sends domestic pets on treks across the country to their former homes. It is debated whether one must be a psychic to dowse, or whether the skill is available to all of us who use rods or a stick while concentrating on an objective.

Sometimes a dowser will hold a pendulum or indicator over a map. When the indicator moves rapidly, the object is said to be located. This is often considered a form of AUTOMATIC WRITING, because a spirit is guiding the indicator.

Some dowsers hold a similar object as they search. Thus, to locate underground water, a bottle of water might be held. To pinpoint a vein of gold ore, a golden nugget would be carried. Interestingly, a dowser may be unaware of a flowing subterranean stream nearby if he or she is attempting to locate buried treasure, and vice versa.

Those who doubt the ability of a dowser to predict placement of objects including treasure, missing persons, metals, oil and water insist that the dowsing rod's movement is caused by the dowser's own involuntary arm muscle action. As with other methods of prognostication, dowsing has its detractors, yet it continues to be used throughout the United States, especially by American Indians, as a way to cut the expense of drilling wells for water.

A wire coat hanger can be used to make a dowsing rod. Cut off the hook and cut the wire into two sections. Holding the short ends of the wire rods, the dowser slowly walks around an area concentrating on what he or she desires to find, including thoughts of how deeply the object might be buried. For example, in the case of underground water, the dowser should concentrate on locating a spring no deeper than a certain level.

See also CLAIRVOYANCE; PENDULUM PREDICTIONS.

Further reading

Cayce, Hugh Lynn, ed. *The Edgar Cayce Collection.* New York: Bonanza, 1986.

Fodor, Nandor. *Encyclopedia of Psychic Science.* New York: University Books, 1966.

Geller, Uri, and Guy Lyon Playfair. *The Geller Effect.* New York: Henry Holt, 1986.

McKenzie, John L. *Dictionary of the Bible.* Milwaukee: Bruce, 1965.

Miller, Madeleine S., and J. Lane Miller, eds. *Harper's Encyclopedia of Bible Life.* San Francisco: Harper & Row, 1978.

Roberts, Kenneth. *Henry Gross and His Dowsing Rod.* Garden City, N.Y.: Doubleday, 1951.

Thomas, Keith. *Religion and the Decline of Magic.* New York: Macmillan, 1971.

DREAM INTERPRETATIONS
Divination by translating visions seen during the rapid eye movement (REM) segment of sleep, the deepest dream pattern state.

According to metaphysical beliefs, during the deepest phases of sleep the astral and mental bodies disconnect themselves from the physical and ethereal forms. Sleepers are free to move mentally and consider past lives and intuitive information that the mind may censor during waking hours. Psychologists and scientists, while still guessing why people dream, often like to compare the brain to a computer that needs time to process all that is experienced during waking hours.

According to metaphysical beliefs, the astral and mental bodies disconnect themselves from the physical and ethereal forms during the deepest phases of sleep.

Dream interpretation is an ancient divination practice. There are many references to the interpretation of religious dreams in the Bible, including Numbers 12:5–6 and Daniel 2:2 and 4:7. In Job 33:12, it is said, "God speaks to man in one way, and in two, though man does not perceive it. In a dream, in a vision of the night, when deep sleep falls upon men, while they slumber in their beds, then He opens the ears of men."

The *Bu'ya Sadiga* is a spiritual book of the dreams Mohammed had prior to revealing the Koran. The dreams are said to have appeared to Mohammed as "luminous impressions." The Uitoto Indians of Colombia believe that the world was created as a dream. For the Aborigines of Australia, the state of dreaming, or dreamtime, is the entire mythical past, the present and the future. They believe that anything outside of their dreams has no existence in reality.

Dreaming and dream interpretation was an essential part of the American Indian culture. The Iroquois recognized the dream as the language of the soul. The Maricopa attempted a dream journey to seek instruction in poetry and medicine, although it said that the pathway is dangerous and long.

The Greeks valued dream interpretation, and there were healing temples where one might sleep in order to dream about the proper cure for a specific ailment. The Pythagoreans believed that in sleep the soul is freed from the body, its tomb, and, soaring upward, is able to perceive and converse with higher beings on other ethereal planes. This theory is derived from the ancient Egyptian and Orphic doctrines where the *ba* (or *ka*), or spiritual double, left the body during the dream state to learn. Plato said that "spirits scattered in the ethereal regions come to rest near us to imprint on our souls ideas disengaged from the senses, and to transmit to us the orders of God." The Platonic philosophy was passed through metaphysical teachings and appeared again during the Renaissance, when psychics once more adopted it.

Sigmund Freud, the renowned psychoanalytical theorist, published an exhaustive book on dream interpretation. In *The Interpretation of Dreams*, Freud stated that dreams were the disguised fulfillment of the dreamer's infantile sexual needs. Many choose to believe in these theories. Carl G. Jung, one of the great psychologists, saw dreaming as a form of spontaneous and creative expression of the unconscious and continued to disagree with Freud's ideas.

Today, many still are tied to the idea that during the dream state, we are processing information sensed during our waking hours. Some psychics think of the dream state as playtime for the mind and pay little heed to what dreams foretell. Others support the theory that in our dreams our minds are unburdened and reveal visions to help, warn and inform.

In order to interpret dreams, one must become aware of what has occurred during the dream state. For most, this is the most difficult part of the interpretation because upon waking, the dream is often forgotten. Those who interpret dreams suggest meditating just before sleep and telling the subconscious mind that the dream will be remembered. They also recommend keeping a pencil and pad next to the bed in order to jot down the vision upon waking, even if that is in the middle of the night.

Contemporary dream interpreters caution that there are no "bad" or "good" dreams, and nothing seen or sensed in a dream should be judged. Thus, having even the most illicit-seeming dream should not be considered a character flaw.

Even though there may be other people involved in a dream, dream interpreters suggest that the main character, regardless of sex or even species, represents the individual having the dream. For example, if the dream involves a beach crab, it may mean that the dreamer is being instructed to move in an indirect way to solve a problem; it might also point out that he or she is crabby.

Typically, in a dream, there will be a series of events or visions. Dream interpreters suggest that notes be taken on everything remembered; then, through study or meditation, a correlation can be found.

The following are some archetypal dream interpretations.

Bathroom or Toilet Dreams: The dreamer may not be taking care of the troubles that are bothering him or her. For example, there is a need to get rid of a specific task or burden, yet the dreamer holds on to it.

Chase Dreams: The dreamer is trying to avoid or run away from something that is troubling him or her. This is unnecessary anguish, and the chase dream indicates that the dreamer must face the pursuer to overcome the obstacle.

Costume Dreams: The dreamer is thinking of or reliving past lives.

Flying Dreams: The dreamer is investigating new thoughts or avenues. If the dreamer feels he or she is going to fall, there is a fear of failure in the search.

Money Dreams: The dreamer will have some changes coming in his or her life. When small change—pennies, nickels and dimes—are seen, the changes will be minor. If there is a large amount of paper money in large denominations, the changes will be significant.

Sexual Dreams: The dreamer is learning to balance the male and female intuitive forces in his or her life or the merger of energies. Typically, it has little to do with actual sexual intercourse.

Further reading

Bethards, Betty. *The Dream Book: Symbols for Self-Understanding.* 9th printing. Petaluma, Calif.: Inner Light Press, 1992.

Buckland, Raymond. *Secrets of Gypsy Dream Reading.* St. Paul, Minn.: Llewellyn, 1990.

Coxhead, David, and Susan Hiller. *Dreams: Visions of the Night.* New York: Thames & Hudson, 1976.

Garfield, Patricia, Ph.D. *Healing Power of Dreams.* New York: Fireside Books, 1991.

Johnson, Robert A. *Inner Work.* New York: Harper/San Francisco, 1986.

Jung, C. G. *Dreams.* Princeton, N.J.: Princeton University Press, 1974.

Maybrock, Patricia. *Romantic Dreams.* New York: Pocket, 1991.

Reed, Henry. *Dream Solution.* San Rafael, Calif.: New World Library, 1991.

Signell, Karen A. *Wisdom of the Heart.* New York: Bantam, 1990.

Ullman, M., ed. *Dream Telepathy.* New York: Macmillan, 1973.

DRUIDS *Prophetic group of Celtic priests who worshiped nature spirits, with their origins dating from more than 4,000 years ago.*

Except for isolated groups, the Druids were crushed when the Romans conquered Europe, and the practice of Druidism was outlawed. The Roman emperor Claudius banned Druidism in A.D. 43. The main tenet of the belief system was that after death the soul passed into the body of a newborn baby. Druid priests (both male and female) believed that they were descendants of a supreme being. The Druids were classed in three categories: Druids, Prophets and Bards.

There is considerable controversy surrounding the Druids, which means "knowing the oak tree" in Gaelic. Some believe that they were a bloodthirsty cult, burning and disemboweling human sacrifices. Others firmly contradict this notion and support the theory that the Druids originated as seers and psychics who lived sacred lives honoring nature, much like the American Indians before the intervention of European morality.

The Druids honored the oak tree and the mistletoe plant. However, contrary to popular thought, they did not build Stonehenge but rather used it for planetary observation and perhaps in divining the future using a form of ASTROLOGY. The Druids also practiced many methods of prognostication. They used a form of CAPNOMANCY that is called dendromancy, whereby branches of the oak tree or segments of the mistletoe plant are cut and placed on a fire or hot coals. Divination occurs when the smoke generated by the burning plant is interpreted. The Druids are also said to have developed RUNE STONES or rune dice as a tool for predicting the future. The Druids are believed to have looked for omens in the movement of birds and in the weather and to have practiced other GEOMANCY divination methods. They are also credited with divining the future through various sacrificial methods using human enemies as well as group members specifically chosen as a religious honor.

Contrary to popular belief, the Druids did not build Stonehenge. Rather they used it for planetary observation, celebration of celestial festivals and divining the future with astrology.

Most agree that the Druids were a mysterious group, and their legacy is often based in the imagination and in folklore rather than in fact, since fact was not documented at that time. According to traditional belief, Druidism was a religion practiced by the Celts in pre-Roman Gaul (what is now France) and in Britain. There are a number of references to Druids and Druidism in Greek and Roman writings, including in accounts by Julius Caesar.

Contemporary Druids, in small groups or groves, are now studying the ancient rites and rituals of Druidism in the United States and in Britain. They often celebrate the seasonal changes and festivals, including eight pagan holidays, in a traditional way, through the worship of nature outdoors or in groves of trees.

Further reading

Carr-Gomm, Philip. *The Elements of the Druid Tradition.* Dorset, England: Element, 1991.

Chadwick, Nora K. *The Druids.* London: University of Wales Press, 1966.

Goodman, Linda. *Linda Goodman's Star Signs.* New York: St. Martin's, 1987.

Nichols, Ross. *The Book of Druidry—History, Sites, Wisdom.* London: Aquarian, 1990.

Opie, Iona, and Moira Tatem. *A Dictionary of Superstitions.* Oxford: Oxford University Press, 1992.

Piggott, Stuart. *The Druids.* New York: Praeger, 1986.

Ruthford, Ward. *The Druids: Magicians of the West.*

Rev. ed. Northamptonshire, England: Aquarian, 1983.

DUNNE, JOHN WILLIAM *(1875–1949)*
Irish psychic.

Trained as a mathematician and airplane designer, in 1906 Dunne built the first British military aircraft. However, his main focus in life was a thirst for knowledge about spiritualism and the metaphysical laws. Preoccupied by dreams, Dunne began recording his own dream states, realizing that they were often predictive of upcoming events.

One of his most famous interpretive dreams forecasted and recorded a gigantic volcanic eruption on Martinque. Only one segment of the psychic dream was incorrect: He dreamed that 4,000 people would die, while in actuality more than 40,000 perished in the disaster.

Dunne believed that time existed on one plane of the universe and the experience of time existed on another. Consequently, events could be known before they happened. Though no longer in print, Dunne's best-known works include *An Experiment with Time* and *The Serial Universe*.

See also DREAM INTERPRETATIONS; LAWS OF METAPHYSICS.

Further reading

Coxhead, David, and Susan Hiller. *Dreams: Visions of the Night.* New York: Thames & Hudson, 1976.

Drury, Nevill. *Dictionary of Mysticism and the Eso-teric Traditions*. Dorset, England: Prism Press, 1992.

Ullman, M., ed. *Dream Telepathy*. New York: Macmillan, 1973.

Ullman, Montague, and Nan Zimmerman. *Working with Dreams*. Los Angeles: Jeremy P. Tarcher, 1979.

Visions and Prophecies. Mysteries of the Unknown. Alexandria, Va.: Time Life Books, 1990.

ECKHART VON HOCHHEIM (1260–c. 1328) *German psychic and religious mystic.*

Also referred to as Meister Eckhart, he was a Dominican friar in Erfurt, Germany. He took a strong stance that the immensity and the supreme excellence of the divine light was available to all; however, the believer must give up wealth and power to find the divine light, which was his God.

Since at that time, the nobility and the wealthy ruled the church, Eckhart was considered a heretic—one did not have to give up anything, the upper class felt, to find God. Rebels against the faith were often thrown into prison or ostracized. While Eckhart's religious commitment wasn't questioned, his writing was considered heretical. Near the end of his life, Eckhart Von Hochheim once more came into the embrace of the Catholic Church.

Further reading

Drury, Nevill. *Dictionary of Mysticism and the Esoteric Traditions.* Dorset, England: Prism Press, 1992.

Visions and Prophecies. Mysteries of the Unknown. Alexandria, Va.: Time Life Books, 1990.

EDWARDS, HARRY (1893–1976) *British psychic healer.*

Edwards was known throughout England for his psychic healing abilities. At one "performance" in Kings Hall, Manchester, a crowd of more than 7,000 people watched as he selected people from the audience, placed on hands and healed various ailments. He was said to be able to best heal arthritis, spinal lesions, paralysis and blindness and deafness. He claimed that the guides, or spirits, of Pasteur and other great medical practitioners guided him from the ethereal world (see GUIDE).

From his spiritual healing sanctuary in Shere, Surrey, England, Edwards continued throughout his life to provide his services, including the healing of members of British nobility and the royal family of Great Britain.

See also LAYING ON OF HANDS.

Further reading

Krippner, Stanley, and Alberto Villoldo. *The Realms of Healing.* 3d ed. Berkeley, Calif.: Celestial Arts, 1986.

Meek, George W., ed. *Healers and the Healing Process.* Wheaton, Ill.: Theosophical Publishing House, 1977.

Powers of Healing. Mysteries of the Unknown. Alexandria, Va.: Time Life Books, 1990.

West, D. J. *Eleven Lourdes Miracles*. New York: Helix, 1957.

Worral, A. *The Gift of Healing*. New York: Harper & Row, 1965.

EMPYROMANCY *Divination by interpreting the smoke generated by burning laurel leaves.*

This ancient mantic art is known to have been practiced as early as 550 B.C. by the Greek prophet, mystic and philosopher Pythagoras (582?–500? B.C.). Empyromancy was used to divine the future and answer a querant's questions, including those on reincarnation and of a metaphysical nature. A form of empyromancy known as DAPHNOMANCY is still practiced today, and the observance of omens concerning the behavior of smoke is still common in rural New England.

Further reading

Bulfinch, Thomas. *Myths of Greece and Rome*. New York: Viking/Penguin, 1979.

Johnson, Clifton. *What They Says in New England and Other American Folklore*. Boston: Lee & Shepherd, 1896. Reprinted ed., Carl A. Withers, ed. New York: Columbia University Press, 1963.

Kittredge, George. *Witchcraft in Old and New England*. Cambridge: Harvard University Press, 1929. Reprint. New York: Atheneum, 1972.

ENOPTROMANCY *The ancient divination method of using a shiny surface placed in water to foretell the recovery (or death) of someone.*

Enoptromancy is a form of CATOPTROMANCY, in which divination occurs through interpreting patterns or images produced by looking at a light source as it is reflected in a shiny object, such as a mirror. Using enoptromancy, the psychic or healer suspends a mirror into water. Only the base of the mirror was allowed to touch the water. The psychic would then gaze into the mirror, interpreting the vision that appeared on

ENOPTROMANCY
Enoptromancy requires a mirror and much patience. Divination is accomplished by interpreting patterns or images produced by a light source reflected in a shiny object such as a mirror.

the shiny surface, foretelling whether the patient would die or recuperate.

See also HYDROMANCY; SCRYING.

Further reading

Fodor, Nandor. *Encyclopedia of Psychic Science*. New York: University, 1966.

Krippner, Stanley, and Alberto Villoldo. *The Realms of Healing*. 3d ed. Berkeley, Calif.: Celestial Arts, 1986.

Meek, George W., ed. *Healers and the Healing Process*. Wheaton, Ill.: Theosophical Publishing House, 1977.

Powers of Healing. Mysteries of the Unknown. Alexandria, Va.: Time Life Books, 1990.

EPATOSCOMANCY *Divination through the examination of the entrails of animals.*

Epatoscomancy is a form of ANTHROPOMANCY, the ancient divination method of scrutinizing the inner organs, specifically the intestines, of human sacrifices. With epatoscomancy, as with HEPATOMANCY (the examination of the liver of animals that were sacrificed for this purpose), the viscera were interpreted by psychics to forecast future events. Practiced by the ancient Babylonians, Sumerians, Japanese, Greeks and Romans, there are more than 700 examples of epatoscomancy and hepatomancy in the Mesopotamian royal archives, and while it sounds ghoulish today, it was a well-established part of formal religion at that time. Additionally, there are a number of biblical references, including in the Book of Ezekiel, describing this mantic art as it was used by the king of Babylon, and a verse in the second book of Kings refers to epatoscomancy being used as a divination method by King Ahaz of Judah.

Epatoscomancy was also practiced by Native American tribes, including the Comanche. The Incas and Aztecs also may have used epatoscomancy. Today, in some remote parts of the world, this mantic art is still considered a valid divination method. In Borneo and Burma, psychics continue to view the livers of slaughtered farm animals when foretelling the future or forecasting the answer to a querant's question.

See also DRUIDS.

Further reading

Bevan, E. *Sibyls and Seers: A Survey of Some Ancient Theories of Revelation and Inspiration.* London: Allen & Unwin, 1982.

Cosmic Connections. Mysteries of the Unknown. Alexandria, Va.: Time Life Books, 1990.

Luck, G. *Arcana Mundi, Magic and the Occult in the Greek and Roman Worlds.* Wellingborough, England: Crucible Publishing, 1987.

Miller, Madeleine S., and J. Lane Miller, eds. *Harper's Encyclopedia of Bible Life.* San Francisco: Harper & Row, 1978.

Stewart, R. J. *The Elements of Prophecy.* Dorset, England: Element Books, 1990.

EXTISPICIOMANCY *Ancient divination method of forecasting the future by examining the viscera of animals, more commonly known as EPATOSCOMANCY.*

See also ANTHROPOMANCY; DRUIDS; HEPATOMANCY.

EXTRASENSORY PERCEPTION (ESP) *Perception and/or reception of information through a means other than the traditional senses.*

The passage of thought or the sensing of thought, emotions or visions from one mind to another, even at a distance and without any outside assistance, and the divination of forthcoming events or circumstances are grouped under the general category of ESP. It also includes such metaphysical gifts or talents as TELEPATHY, CLAIRVOYANCE, channeling, psychometry and psychic ability. These and other terms indicate an awareness without the support of information or data. ESP is the traditional term most people recognize for the "knowing" gift that psychics exhibit.

Three types of ESP have been recognized by those who study this science. They have been known since the beginning of civilization, though no specific terms were used to describe them. Clairvoyance is ESP of objects or events. PRECOGNITION is the knowing of events that will occur in the future. And telepathy is the direct experience of another person's mental condition or state of being.

ESP is sometimes referred to as PSI (parapsychological scientific investigation). Psychokinesis (PK) is the ability to affect objects at a distance by means other than known physical forces and is typically grouped with other acts of ESP.

The term *extrasensory perception* was attached to this concept by J. B. Rhine, often called the "Father of Modern Parapsychology." Rhine told friends, when selecting the name for telepathy, that he wanted to make it sound as normal as possible so that the study would be accepted within the scientific community. *Perception* was an established psychology term, and Rhine hoped to place ESP as an offshoot of perception, not something occult and mystical.

Rhine studied ESP throughout his life through carefully documented experiments and produced the Zener cards that test ESP ability which are still in use today. Rhine and other researchers have found that when the subject being tested for ESP is told that he or she is doing well reading the 25 Zener cards (similar to playing cards but with four unique shapes on the "picture" side), the results are often the same as with those who do not profess to have ESP. Additionally, the fear of failure in ESP tests has been shown to lower scores in clinical tests. Boredom lowers test scores; caffeine tends to increase test scores. Children are more receptive and perceptive than adults during testing.

Scientists continue to test subjects for ESP; however, objective proof that it exists is often impossible to obtain, since perception is highly subjective. The ever-present interest in ESP has been recognized throughout history to be an advantage in espionage and subversive control and during wartime.

Those who test ESP in the clinical setting say that their chief criticism is that the experiments on extrasensory perception are often impossible to duplicate. Those who support ESP and other parapsychological studies believe that the rigid testing required to make metaphysical topics scientific are too restrictive for exploring the unknown.

The Society of Psychical Research was founded in England in 1882, and a branch was opened in the United States in 1884. Both groups continue to publish papers and information on ESP, as they continue to investigate the survival of the personality or soul after death, mediumship, hauntings, apparitions, ghosts and spirits and out-of-body experiences, along with clairvoyance and telepathy. One of the earliest projects of the group was to investigate hypnosis, which was at that time used mainly in psychic trances and has now become a mainstay of the medical and psychological community. Other groups that investigate and test ESP include the American Society for Psychical Research, the Parapsychological Association, and the American Association for the Advancement of Science.

Most Americans believe in ESP, and more than 10% of a polled 1,000 people said that they had an experience involving ESP. Many of these include a personal experience of precognition of dreams. Most common are premonitory dreams of personal tragedies; these can also be found in records from antiquity. For example, King Coreus (d. about 546 B.C.), the last king of Lydia, an ancient country in Asia Minor, dreamed of the murder of his son, and the dream came to be reality. Abraham Lincoln claimed to have had a telepathic dream of his forthcoming death and is supposed to have "seen" himself in a coffin—exactly as he lay some days later.

Psychics like to point out that everyone has psychic and ESP abilities, although some are

It is said that Abraham Lincoln had a prophetic dream of his forthcoming death and is supposed to have "seen" himself in a coffin—exactly as he lay some days later.

more practiced or aware of the gift than others. There is a working view, among scientists who delve into the occurrence of ESP, that the ability is available to all; however, individual differences in attitude, habit and interest determine whether or not ESP and other psychic abilities will be expressed or inhibited.

Psychics explain that in order to receive ESP messages or visions or to be aware of dreams, their minds are often blank. This allows the thoughts to come through to their conscious mind. They also say that it takes patience and meditation to hone this ability.

See also CHANNEL; DREAM INTERPRETATION.

Further reading

Cavendish, Richard, ed. *Man, Myth and Magic: An Illustrated Encyclopedia of the Supernatural.* Vol. 7. New York: Marshal Cavendish Corporation, 1970.

Feyer, Dr. Ernest C. *The Call of the Soul: A Scientific Explanation of Telepathy and Psychic Phenomena.* San Francisco: Auto-Science Institute, 1926.

Halbourne, Max. *Mental Telepathy and ESP Powers for the Millions.* Los Angeles: Sherbourne Press, 1967.

Hintze, Naomi A., and J. Gaither Pratt. *The Psychic Realm: What Can You Believe?* New York: Random House, 1975.

Rhine, Louisa E. *ESP in Life and Lab.* New York: Collier-Macmillan, 1967.

Richet, Charles. *Thirty Years of Psychical Research.* London: William Collins Publishers, 1923.

Scott, Cyril. *An Outline of Modern Occultism.* London: Routledge & Kegan Paul, 1950.

Thouless, R. H. *Experimental Psychical Research.* New York: Penguin, 1963.

Tyrrell, G. N. M. *Science and Psychical Phenomena.* London, 1938. Reprint. New York: University Books, 1961.

Ullman, M., ed. *Dream Telepathy.* New York: Macmillan, 1973.

FAKIR *General term describing anyone with psychic or mystic qualities or a member of the Muslim mendicant (begging) orders, which is an extension of the Hindu order of India.*

A fakir (from the Arabic word *faqir*, meaning "poor man") is said to be both the traveler on life's pathway as well as the follower and the teacher.

It is said that even today, some fakirs go through life begging and preaching; most, however, simply live a strict monastic life. Like some other orthodox orders, these fakirs devote themselves primarily to meditation and prayer and live the most austere monklike existence. This severe existence is necessary, according to those who believe in this sect, in order to fuse the pineal and pituitary glands to produce psychic information that is used in healing and in the guidance of the fakir's followers.

In many parts of the Arab world, the fakir is known to practice prognostication through magic and sorcery.

See also LAYING ON OF HANDS.

Further reading

Encyclopedia of Religion. New York: Macmillan, 1987.
Krippner, Stanley, and Alberto Villoldo. *The Realms of Healing*. 3d ed. Berkeley, Calif.: Celestial Arts, 1986.
Meek, George W., ed. *Healers and the Healing Process*. Wheaton, Ill.: Theosophical Publishing House, 1977.
Mind over Matter. Mysteries of the Unknown. Alexandria, Va.: Time Life Books, 1990.
O'Flaherty, Wendy Doniger. *Hindu Myths*. Harmondsworth, England: Penguin Books, 1975.

FATE LINE *One of the many lines in the palm of the hand that is said to indicate specific characteristics.*

The fate line is sometimes referred to as the line of fate by palmists. Because there are many variations of the fate line, and since palmistry is complex as well as intriguing, it is recommended that one refer to a palmist or a book on the subject for a complete examination and interpretation of the hand.

The fate line is found generally from a point just above the wrist across the palm vertically to a place just below where the middle finger is joined to the hand. If there is no fate line, it may indicate that the individual's life is peaceful and quiet. If the line is clear, deep and straight, it may be because he or she is especially successful, but it may also indicate personal challenges. A wavy line may indicate a tendency to be argumentative, unsystematic and sloppy. Palmists believe that breaks in the fate line indicate unplanned changes. If the fate line begins from the heart or the head line, it is a sign that great success may come later in life, typically after the age of 40.

See also CHEIRO; PALMISTRY.

Further reading

Altman, Nathaniel. *Palmistry Workbook*. New York: Sterling, 1990.

Cheiro. *Cheiro's Book of Numbers*. New York: Prentice-Hall, 1988.

———. *The Language of the Hand*. New York: Prentice-Hall, 1987.

Robinson, Rita. *The Palm: A Guide to Your Hidden Potential*. North Hollywood, Calif.: Newcastle, 1988.

FELIDOMANCY *Divination through the observation of felines, including domestic and wild cats.*

If a cat sneezes, it means that it will rain. If a cat is on a ship (regardless of what he or she does), it foretells bad luck. And if a cat crosses ones path, particularly a black one, it can mean either good fortune (in the British Isles) or a turn of bad luck (in the United States). All these omens are derived from the mantic art of felidomancy.

Cats have always held a fascination for people, held in high (religious) esteem by some and cast out as evil by others. Thus prognostication by the actions of cats, as well as other animals, is only to be expected. Animals of all types play an important role in the mantic arts, and cats

In the mantic art of felidomancy, divination was practiced by observing both domestic and wild cats.

especially have been featured in rituals of magic.

In ancient Egypt there were cat goddesses. There was an extended period of mourning when a household cat died, and family members shaved off their eyebrows. It is not known if this custom was a ritual to honor the deceased cat or if it was performed to nullify a bad omen. The cat goddesses of Egypt were Bast and Skehmet, associated with fertility and sexual prowess. Because they were held in such high esteem by their owners and in religious circles, cats were often mummified, and Egyptian law forbade the removal of cats' graves, as all were thought to be sacred. Divination, during this period, occurred by watching cats for specific movements, which were interpreted by psychics according to their own evaluation.

Cats were revered as sacred by the Incas, and statues were built to cats during pre-Columbian times in South America. Cats often played a part in religious and occult ceremonies in India, and they were worshiped as deities in parts of China and India.

Cats and witches have traditionally been linked; since those who used metaphysical gifts and had psychic powers were often considered to be witches, it is not surprising that felines have this association.

The medieval folklore that says a cat has nine lives is supposed to have come from the Egyptian Ennead, the mythic figure of the Ninefold Goddess. The Dark Ages were a superstitious and turbulent time, and it was thought that a witch could assume a cat's shape nine times in her life. With its nocturnal habits and prowling instincts, the cat came to be feared. The Inquisitor Nicholas Remy said that all cats were born of the devil and were four-footed demons. Early Christians were sometimes known to torture cats and burn them along with purported witches.

The Middle Ages were difficult years for cats, as well as people. During this period cats became synonymous with the devil, and this may be the basis of contemporary omens, such as a cat crossing one's path. Other intriguing omens that have survived through time often concern cats. Some of the best known are: A black cat kept in a sailor's home will ensure that the seafarer will return safely. A cat at a wedding is considered to assure a long, happy marriage. In some parts of France, a strange white cat seen sunning itself on the doorstep means a hasty marriage for one of the house's residents. In the Midlands of England, it was said that bringing a cat as a wedding gift was a way of sharing prosperity with the newlyweds.

See also ALECTRYOMANCY; HIPPOMANCY; ICHTHYOMANCY; MYOMANCY; OPHIMANCY; ORNITHOMANCY.

Further reading

Budge, Sir E. A. Wallis. *Egyptian Magic*. New York: Dover, 1971.
———. *Gods of the Egyptians*. 2 vols. New York: Dover, 1969.
Cavindish, Richard. *The Powers of Evil*. New York: Putnam's, 1975.
Howey, W. Oldfield. *The Cat in the Mysteries of Magic and Religion*. New York: Castle, 1956.
Larousse Encyclopedia of Mythology. London: Hamlyn Publishing Group, 1968.
Necker, Claire. *The Natural History of Cats*. London: Thomas Yoseloff, 1970.
Opie, Iona, and Moira Tatem. *A Dictionary of Superstitions*. Oxford: Oxford University Press, 1992.
Walker, Barbara G. *The Woman's Encyclopedia of Myths and Secrets*. New York: Harper Collins, 1983.

FENG SHUI
The Chinese principle of yin and yang as applied to the land; a form of GEOMANCY.

Feng (meaning wind) and *shui* (meaning water) are said to form a system of understanding omens and changing those omens to produce the best luck. Using the qualities of positive and negative of yin and yang, those who practice *feng shui* actively shape their environment to produce the best omens possible. The term *feng shui* refers to the power of the natural environment, which is alive with hidden forces. By studying these influences and observing the natural patterns of the land, a *feng shui* master (or *hsien-shen*, a title of respect) can advise on favorable directions for a house, school or building to be erected and counsel on the forces at work in that area. Additionally, *feng shui* is a way of living in harmony

FENG SHUI
Feng shui *is based on the polarities of yin and yang. This is the ancient symbol.*

with the environment. Experts say that *feng shui* is a means of aligning with the Tao (the universal flow of energy surrounding the Earth and within all living things, including trees, water and air), and producing accord in the world.

Feng shui masters offered advice for the dead as well as the living, and when placement for a tomb was to be decided, the master was the first one called. Traditionally, the masters advised that the dead be buried on a south-facing slope, above the town and protected from malign spirits by mountains to the north.

While the symbols and philosophies of this prognostication form are far older, the actual history of *feng shui* began more than 3,000 years ago. It is mentioned in such ancient volumes as *The History of the Former Han Dynasty, The Golden Box of Geomancy* and *Terrestrial Conformations for Palaces and Houses*, none of which have survived. *Feng shui* is thought to be a combination of numerology, geomancy, astrology and other methods used by the Chinese in the placement of objects and buildings. *Feng shui* masters are no longer consulted officially on mainland China. However, in many modernized areas, including bustling Hong Kong, Seoul, the Philippines and high-tech areas of Malaysia and Thailand, these geomancers can still be found, not in flowing silk gowns, perhaps, but in suits, starched shirts and with a *feng shui* compass tucked within a smart leather briefcase.

Feng shui is an ancient practice still used today, balancing an eye for observation as well as a highly tuned psychic ability. It influences personal choices as well as the shape of cities, buildings and cemeteries. Through the forces of *feng shui*, people can achieve the three blessings of the universal flow (the Tao), which are health, happiness and prosperity.

The two elements of *feng shui*, wind and water, can shape the environment and, according to practitioners, affect human fortune and personal landscapes. *Feng shui* gets its power from the Ch'i, the life breath of the earth. If the Ch'i is blocked from entering a house, for example, because there is a tree growing directly in front of the main entrance, the family may suffer. However, following the practice of *feng shui*, moving the tree may be the best way to avoid terrible problems. Additionally, by positioning a wind chime, placing a mirror to reflect a light source, putting a specific type of plant in the dwelling or adding an aquarium to the room, *feng shui* can be changed. Sometimes furniture can be moved around, walls can be replaced (or blocked) and doors repositioned. Thus luck can be invited, encouraging the return of the Ch'i and the universal flow of energy.

In the United States we talk about the good feelings generated by clean air, fresh water and a relaxed environment. Sometimes in the West it is referred to as "earth magic"; sometimes the vibrations of a certain area of the country pulls people to it. This is the essence of *feng shui*.

Feng shui is traditionally practiced only by a *feng shui* master or expert. When a house is being built in China, it is quite customary to contract with a master before the plans are drawn. He or she will walk the land or area, read the signs and the landscape (a hill, a natural breeze, the directions where the doors and windows should be) and then make a recommendation to the architect. Those who practice *feng shui* design their homes, offices, businesses and even camping trips around the custom.

The study of *feng shui*, like astrology or tarot, requires years of instruction and meditation.

See also AEROMANCY; ALECTROMANCY; BLETONOMANCY; GEOMANCY.

Further reading

Bary, William Theodore de, ed. *Sources of Chinese Traditions.* New York: Columbia University Press, 1960.

Dore, Henry S. J. *Chinese Customs.* Translated by M. Kennelly. Singapore: Graham Brash, 1987.

Feuchtwang, Stephen. *An Anthropological Analysis of Chinese Geomancy.* Taipei: Southern Materials Center, 1974.

O'Brien, Joanne. *Chinese Myths and Legends.* London: Arrow, 1990.

O'Brien, Joanne, with Kwok Man Ho. *The Elements of Feng Shui.* Dorset, England: Elements Books, 1991.

Rossbach, Sarah. *Feng Shui: The Chinese Art of Placement.* New York: Arkana/Penguin, 1991.

FINGER TOUCHING *Fingers used as transmitters and receivers of psychic knowing and energy.*

Psychics use their fingers to heal as well as to forecast future events in a querant's life. For example, when a psychic's fingertips of both hands touch, it is said that the psychic's brain vibrations are stronger. Often we will see business people with their fingers in the steeple position, elbows down and fingers up, with just the tips pointing, an unconscious example of finger touching.

Various fingers have specific psychic qualities as transmitters and receivers. The index finger of the right hand is supposed to be able to take the energy from the brain and project it toward wherever the psychic is pointing. The index finger and the thumb are said to be the strength for communicating psychic information, after an object or person has been touched, and the left hand is said to be stronger for the purposes of healing.

It has long been known that blind people often can touch objects and "know" the color and the object's use in much the same way a psychic can finger an object belonging to another and sense its history. In metaphysics, the fingers are used for sightless readings, PSYCHOMETRY and faith healing (or LAYING ON OF HANDS). Palmists not only read the palm of the hand to reveal the querant's personality traits and prognosticate the future, they examine the fingers and their spacing and texture, skin, nails and joints.

See also PALMISTRY.

Further reading

Benham, William G. *Hands.* Los Angeles: Newcastle, 1988.

Bletzer, June G. *The Donning International Encyclopedic Psychic Dictionary.* West Chester, Pa.: Whitford Press, 1986.

Fitzherbert, Andrew. *Hand Psychology.* Garden City, N.Y.: Avery, 1989.

Krippner, Stanley, and Alberto Villoldo. *The Realms of Healing.* 3d ed. Berkeley, Calif.: Celestial Arts, 1986.

Meek, George W., ed. *Healers and the Healing Process.* Wheaton, Ill.: Theosophical Publishing House, 1977.

Powers of Healing. Mysteries of the Unknown. Alexandria, Va.: Time Life Books, 1990.

West, D. J. *Eleven Lourdes Miracles.* New York: Helix Press, 1957.

Worral, A. *The Gift of Healing.* New York: Harper & Row, 1965.

FORD, ARTHUR *(1897–1971) American psychic.*

One of the best-known U.S. psychics, Ford acquired an international reputation and claimed that he could contact the dead and transmit messages. He used a channel named Fletcher as his contact in the spiritual plane.

Ford consulted with Episcopalian clergyman Bishop James Pike when Pike's son disappeared and died. Ford located the body and explained how the death had occurred. Ford also held readings and is said to have contacted the spirit of Harry Houdini, claiming that he had broken the code that Houdini had left to test the proof of life after death.

Outgoing and personable, Ford was a popular media figure; however, he was plagued with a lifelong struggle with alcoholism and drug addiction. Later in life, he was accused of faking some of his readings and psychic experiences. He was the founder of several metaphysical organizations, the most prominent of which is the Spiritual Frontiers Fellowship.

Further reading

Ford, Arthur, as told to Jerome Ellison. *The Life beyond Death.* New York: Putnam's, 1971.

Ford, Arthur, and Marguerite Harmon Bro. *Nothing So Strange: The Autobiography of Arthur Ford.* New York: Harper & Brothers, 1958.

Spraggett, Allen. *Arthur Ford: The Man Who Talked with the Dead.* New York: New American Library, 1973.

FORTUNE, DION *(1891–1946) English psychic, ritualist magician and author.*

Fortune, born Violet Mary Firth, began studying occultism after suffering a nervous breakdown at about age 20. Having been raised in the strict teachings of the Christian Science faith, this turn to the occult is said to have been a bone of contention between her and her family, yet from all reports they did not stifle the child who dreamed of Atlantis and believed in past lives. Fortune turned to Madame Blavatsky's Theosophical Society and became a follower of the psychic, mystic and co-founder of the society.

Throughout her life, Fortune belonged to the Theosophical Society and the Hermetic Order of the Golden Dawn (considered to be the greatest magical order of all times) and then started the Fraternity of the Inner Light with her husband, Thomas Penry Evans. The fraternity (now called the Society of the Inner Light) is still based in London and is very popular among witches; however, the society continues to state that Fortune was not a witch. Fortune explained that metaphysics is the key to understanding psychology and psychology the key to the unknown world of the occult.

Fortune was one of the first to write novels on astral travel and magic. *The Mystical Qabalah,* written in 1935, is said to be her greatest work and is still considered the finest book on magic ever written. Other works include *The Secrets of Dr. Taverner, The Demon Lover, Glastonbury: Avalon of the Heart* and *The Cosmic Doctrine.*

Further reading

Fortune, Dion. *The Mystical Qabalah*. York Beach: Maine: Samuel Weister, 1935.

———. *Psychic Self-Defence*. 1930. 6th ed. Reprint. York Beach, Maine: Samuel Weister, 1957.

Guiley, Rosemary Ellen. *The Encyclopedia of Witches and Witchcraft*. New York: Facts On File, 1989.

Richardson, Alan. *Priestess: The Life and Magic of Dion Fortune*. Wellingborough, England: Aquarian Press, 1987.

Spiritual Summonings. Mysteries of the Unknown. Alexandria, Va.: Time Life Books, 1990.

FORTUNE-TELLING *Divination using various metaphysical methods to foretell the future or answer a querant's question.*

The attempts of people to know what will happen in the future, read others' minds, and contact loved ones who have died have been described in every culture since the beginning of recorded time. One of the earliest examples are cave paintings on the walls of a natural tunnel in the Sahara dating from about 6000 B.C. The figure is using a forked stick (as a divining rod) to discover the area where water could be found.

The contemporary perception of fortune-telling involves gypsies reading palms or tea leaves or scrying with a crystal ball. These fortune-telling arts are still employed in the United States and throughout the world. Fortune-tellers who ply their trade, for a price, use various systems.

To many psychics, the term *fortune-telling* has a negative connotation; they prefer to say they are doing a "reading." Those who see fortune-telling as a moneymaking scheme without any metaphysical element point out that anyone can tell fortunes by reading the body language clues of one's customers. There are some books that purport to offer the formula for telling fortunes and claim that the fortune-teller needs no special metaphysical gift. It is often said that attorneys, hairdressers, salespeople and teachers know how to "read" the people they work with in order to find the most credible approach to dealing with their clients.

While at one time interpreting ripples on water or puffs of smoke was the most accepted form of fortune-telling, today the most popular forms of fortune-telling, meaning divination and prognostication, are ASTROLOGY; TAROT, PALMISTRY and CLAIRVOYANCE.

Further reading

Buckland, Raymond. *Secrets of Gypsy Fortune Telling*. St. Paul, Minn. Llewellyn, 1988.

Butler, W. E. *How to Develop Clairvoyance*. 2d ed. New York: Samuel Weiser, 1979.

Morgan, Chris. *Fortune Telling: How to Predict Your Own Future*. London Quintet Publishing and Random House, 1992.

Palmer, Martin; Joanne O'Brien; and Kwok Man Ho. *The Fortune Teller's I Ching*. London: Century, 1986.

Stern, Jess. *Edgar Cayce, the Sleeping Prophet*. New York: Bantam, 1968.

Stewart, R. J. *The Elements of Prophecy*. Dorset, England: Element, 1990.

FOX, GEORGE *(1624–1691) English spiritual leader, healer and psychic; founder of the Society of Friends, the Quaker order.*

Fox was a quiet, religious child, born in Fenny Drayton, Leicestershire, to a Puritan family. At age 19, Fox began receiving psychic information that he believed was the voice of God instructing him to be directed by Christ alone; that is, it was not necessary, as was expected at the time, that God's voice be directed through the established route of a church spokesperson. Interpreting the revelations as meaning that people should follow their own inner light, he waited for a sign. This came, he believed, when after a long meditation, he began to quake because he was so filled with the spirit. In 1647 he started preaching his "inner light" message, formalizing it into a religious order. He spoke out against the doctrine of Presbyterianism and advocated divine communication with God and Jesus. He was fervently opposed to slavery, war and the persecution of any religious groups.

Jailed many times throughout his life for crimes against the organized religious groups of the time, Fox nonetheless attracted a large following. He is credited with many miracles of healing using only his hands. In 1649, he spoke out against a minister, and a year later was consequently jailed in Derby, England, on a false charge of blasphemy. Going before Justice Gervase Bennet, in 1650, Fox corrected the judge and said that he should tremble at the word of the Lord. Bennet ridiculed Fox and his followers, calling them "quakers," because of their agitated movements when speaking out during services, and the name continues to this day.

Although in ill health, Fox remained steadfast in his convictions and spread the word of the Friends, traveling to North America, establishing Quaker groups in the colonies and opening chapters of his religious order in Germany and Holland. Later in life, this psychic healer established Quaker schools and communities and was instrumental in passing the Act of Toleration, a measure that granted freedom of worship to all Christians except Catholics and Unitarians.

Fox is best known for his *Journal* (1694) and *Gospel Truth* (1706), both published after his death.

See also LAYING ON OF HANDS.

Further reading

Babour, Hugh, and J. William Frost. *The Quakers.* New York: Greenwood, 1988.

Krippner, Stanley, and Alberto Villoldo. *The Realms of Healing.* 3d ed. Berkeley, Calif.: Celestial Arts, 1986.

Meek, George W., ed. *Healers and the Healing Process.* Wheaton, Ill.: Theosophical Publishing House, 1977.

FOX, OLIVER (1885–1943) *English psychic, and pioneer in astral projection.*

Oliver Fox began having prophetic dreams as a child, dreams of knowledge and dreams that seemed so real that he felt that he had physically been with a deceased person he had dreamed about. In his dreams, he said he could command that he rise off the bed and glide around at the height of 100 feet, although he was always somehow called back to his body.

Fox reported in personal accounts in the *English Occult Review* (1920) and in his book *Astral Projection* (republished in 1962), that he could remain in his dreamlike state and travel to different time periods and places. According to Fox's

claims, to achieve an out-of-body experience one must send the body to sleep while keeping the mind awake. He explained that one must concentrate upon an imaginary trapdoor within the brain. However, in his books Fox cautioned, "No one with a weak heart should seek practical acquaintance with the phenomenon of separation and very excitable, nervous people would do well to leave the subject alone."

Fox dedicated his life to the investigation of prophetic dreams and out-of-body experiences and adopted Madame Blavatsky's philosophies.

Fox's work has contributed much toward the investigation of out-of-body experiences, and he is considered one of the earliest and best known to document this metaphysical technique.

See also BLAVATSKY, HELENA P.

Further reading

Fox, Oliver. *Astral Projection: A Record of Out-of-the-Body Experiences.* 1920. Reprint. Secaucus, N.J.: Citadel Press, 1962.

Guiley, Rosemary Ellen. *Harper's Encyclopedia of Mystical and Paranormal Experiences.* San Francisco: HarperSan Francisco, 1991.

Mitchell, Janet Lee. *Out-of-Body Experiences: A Handbook.* Jefferson, N.C.: McFarland, 1981.

Monroe, Robert A. *Far Journeys.* Garden City, N.Y.: Dolphin/Doubleday, 1985.

Psychic Voyages. Mysteries of the Unknown. Alexandria, Va.: Time Life Books, 1990.

FOX SISTERS *American psychic sisters, Kate (1841–1892) and Margarette (1838–1893).*

The Fox sisters are credited with promoting public awareness and acceptance of the concepts of spiritualism. In 1848, when the sisters were 7 and 10, the Fox family moved to a house in Arcadia, New York. According to local gossip, the Fox family had taken up residence in a place known for mysterious happenings. Within days, the girls began hearing rapping and tapping, and they devised a code to use to rap and tap back. One rap meant "no," two "yes," and three meant that the spirit who was rapping was uncertain or did not grasp the concept or question.

The rapping continued. By asking questions it was understood that they were in contact with the spirit of a peddlar who had been murdered for financial gain there by the previous owner of the house. Fragments of bone and hair, discovered buried in the basement, supported the girls' theory of a trapped spirit who wanted to communicate with the world. Mrs. Fox and the Fox sisters traveled around the country, giving talks and discussing the spirit world during a time of renewed interest in spiritualism, and they became extremely popular.

The Fox family, especially the girls, were accused of fraud, although nothing was ever proved confirming that they had lied about the happenings in the house in Arcadia. However, later in their lives Kate and Margarette confessed that the rappings were fraudulent, accomplished by secretly kicking the floor or chair legs. Still later, Margarette turned that confession around and stated that they really had communicated with spirits.

Regardless of the truth or falsity of their claims, the Fox sisters were two of the first and most popular spiritualists in the United States. They brought the idea of metaphysics into homes throughout the country.

Further reading

Brandon, Ruth. *The Spiritualists.* New York: Knopf, 1983.

Brown, Slater. *The Heyday of Spiritualism.* New York: Hawthorn, 1970.

Fodor, Nandor. *Encyclopedia of Psychic Science.* New York: University Books, 1966.

Fox, Oliver. *Astral Projection: A Record of Out-of-the-Body Experiences.* 1920. Reprint. Secaucus, N.J.: Citadel Press, 1962.

Hintze, Naomi A., and J. Gaither Pratt, *The Psychic Realm: What Can You Believe?* New York: Random House, 1975.

Spiritual Summonings. Mysteries of the Unknown. Alexandria, Va.: Time Life Books, 1990.

GARRETT, EILEEN *(1893–1970) Irish psychic.*

One of the best-known psychics of the 20th century, Garrett, unlike some other psychics, believed that she connected with spiritual forces of the unconscious mind during a channeling or a reading, rather than contacting the dead. This is what sets her philosophy apart.

Garrett is best known for her work in ESP, including AUTOMATIC WRITING and TELEPATHY. The spirit she channeled was Uvani, an Arab.

Garrett is remembered for her part in the study of psychic research at the British College of Psychic Science in London. Additionally, she was subjected to numerous tests at the Johns Hopkins University to test her psychic ability. Since no trickery was found, these studies concluded that Garrett might indeed have had psychic abilities. She also participated in psychic research studies with Dr. J. B. Rhine at Duke University and other leading psychic investigators, including Dr. Hereweard Carrington, Dr. Alexis Carrel and Dr. Nandor Fodor. Her abilities were never disproved.

In 1951, Garrett worked with a team to establish a meeting place to study ESP and other metaphysical teachings, founding the Parapsychology Foundation. Continuing her work in 1953, she organized the first International Congress of Parapsychology at the University of Utrecht in the Netherlands. Garrett dedicated her time to proceeding with research regarding metaphysical investigations and advancements, writing on topics relating to parapsychology and producing fiction under the pen name of Jean Lyttle.

Further reading

Angoff, Allan. *Eileen Garrett and the World beyond the Senses.* New York: Morrow, 1974.

Fodor, Nandor. *Encyclopedia of Psychic Science.* New York: University, 1966.

Garrett, Eileen. *Adventures in the Supernormal: A Personal Memoir.* New York: Garrett Publications, 1949.

Watson, Donald. *The Dictionary of Mind and Spirit.* New York: Avon, 1991.

GASTROMANCY *Divination during which a psychic transmits a baritone voice that is unlike the usual voice of the psychic.*

Because the deep voice used by the psychic or originating from the channeled spirit seems to be coming from deep within the belly, this form of channeling was termed gastromancy. Gastromancy is also called direct-voice mediumship, wherein the voice comes from somewhere near the psychic or through the use of the psychic's own vocal cords, while he or she has no knowledge of what is being said and no control of his or her body.

This form of metaphysics was extremely popular during the height of spiritualism in the United States in the late 1800s through the early 1900s, a time when seances were extremely popular. Madame Blavatsky (1831–1891), best known as H.P.B., demonstrated startling psychic powers and claimed personal contact with highly developed masters living in Tibet and India and channeled these and other spirits. In doing so, as with many other psychics who channel spirits, her voice was altered by the experience.

As with other forms of psychic consultations, the querant may ask questions and advice may be given. Often, a channel works before an audience, confering wisdom from the ethereal world or general or specific knowledge offered by the wise spirit who is being channeled. More recently, gastromancy has resurfaced, with channeled messages coming from well-known American psychic JZ Knight and her spirit Ramtha, the Enlightened One.

See also BLAVATSKY, HELENA P.; CLAIRVOYANCE; DIRECT-VOICE MEDIUM; KNIGHT, JZ.

Further reading

Butler, W. E. How to Develop Clairvoyance. 2d ed. New York: Samuel Weiser, 1979.
Caldwell, Daniel H., ed. The Occult World of Madam Blavatsky: Reminiscences and Impressions by Those Who Knew Her. Tucson, Ariz.: Impossible Dream Publications, 1991.
Knight, JZ. A State of Mind: My Story. New York: Warner, 1987.
Saxon, Kurt. Keeping Score on Our Modern Prophets. Eureka, Calif.: Atlan Formularies, 1974.
Visions and Prophecies. Mysteries of the Unknown. Alexandria, Va.: Time Life Books, 1990.

GELLER, URI (1946–) Israeli psychic.

Geller is probably the most widely known psychic in the world, with an international reputation for demonstrating his psychic abilities before the media and large audiences. He came to public attention through his ability to use his mental powers to bend metal objects, such as spoons, forks and keys, and he has fixed broken watches and clocks through this same energy. He does this by stroking or concentrating on the object but using no physical force. This gift has come to be known as the "Geller Effect."

Geller was five years old when he discovered his mental powers. He touched a funny spark from his mother's sewing machine as it was working and received an electrical shock. After the incident, he began to be able to read his mother's thoughts. Sometime later, he realized he could make the hands on his father's watch race around the dial, and shortly after that, he began bending spoons using his mind alone. In 1969, he became a performer in order to utilize his talents and share them with the world.

Geller has been a popular, somewhat flamboyant figure. He has displayed his techniques for researchers, submitting himself for experimental tests at the Stanford Research Institute and demonstrating his power under the supervision of leading scholars and scientists including Edgar D. Mitchell, Russell Targ, Harold Puthoff and Wilbur Franklin. The results were impressive. During the testing, Geller correctly identified the number on dice eight out of eight times. He was able to correctly identify objects hidden in metal containers 12 out of 14 times. However, under clinical conditions, he was unable to bend metal objects using his mental powers. It has been suggested that the metal bending was all a magician's trick, which has led some to denounce completely his psychic gifts.

In the 1970s, after years of living a controversial life, Geller withdrew from the public eye and turned his attention to consulting, becoming a noted dowser. His ability to locate oil and precious metals is known internationally. Geller is able to dowse land and maps using his hands. He believes that anyone can dowse if they are willing to concentrate and believe that they have the ability.

Geller's autobiography, My Story, is fascinating reading for anyone interested in the power of the mind.

Further reading

Geller, Uri. My Story. New York: Praeger, 1975.
Geller, Uri, and Guy Lyon Playfair. The Geller Effect. New York: Henry Holt, 1986.

Puharich, Andrija. *Uri: A Journal of the Mystery of Uri Geller*. New York: Bantam, 1975.

GELOMANCY *Divination through the interpretation of sounds other than those typically spoken, particularly laughter. Also known as geloscomancy and geloscopy.*

Gelomancy is derived from the Greek word *gelao*, to laugh, but this method of divination was not restricted only to laughter. Divination occurred in ancient Greece when the mutterings, animal sounds and howling, and utterances of those who were considered insane were psychically interpreted and used to answer a querant's questions regarding the future.

A variation of gelomancy is ololygmancy, divination by specifically interpreting the howls of dogs and wolves, which was practiced by augurs, psychics of the Roman Empire. CHRESMOMANCY, the psychic interpretation after repeating a series of magic words, literary quotes, utterances and/or foreign words, such as abracadabra or hokus pokus, is also sometimes grouped under the heading of gelomancy.

Chresmomancy was used with absolute assurance during the height of the Roman Empire by augers. These government-sanctioned psychics were the only ones who could interpret and predict the result of any contemplated human action through the use of divination systems such as this (see AUGUR).

Further reading

Krauss, Franklin Burnell. *An Interpretation of the Omens, Portents, and Prodigies Recorded by Livy, Tacitus and Suetonius*. Philadelphia: University of Pennsylvania Press, 1930.

Magical Arts. Mysteries of the Unknown. Alexandria, Va.: Time Life Books, 1990.

Maven, Max. *Max Maven's Book of Fortunetelling*. New York: Prentice-Hall, 1992.

Sinnigen, William G., and Arthur E. R. Boak. *A History of Rome to A.D. 565*. 6th ed. New York: Macmillan, 1977.

GEMATRIA *Divination through translating words or sentences of literature and holy books, into number values.*

Gematria is a primitive form of numerology that was used as a prognostication method as early as the eighth century B.C. by King Sargon II of Babylon. Ancient Greeks, Persians, Gnostics and early Christians also used gematria, often developing specific systems to suit their desires and doctrines. For instance, one system discounted all vowels, another assigned the number one to all vowels, and a third gave vowels a number depending on their placement in a given word.

Pythagoras, the ancient mystic and mathematician, believed that letters and numbers had mystical possibilities, and he and his followers, known as Pythagoreans, became intensely interested in numerology. Gematria was also practiced by the 13th-century mystics who followed the Kabbalah; they turned Hebrew words and phrases into a numerical message or prophecy.

See also KABBALAH; NUMEROLOGY.

Further reading

Drury, Nevill. *Dictionary of Mysticism and the Esoteric Traditions*. Dorset, England: Prism Press, 1992.

Giles, Cynthia. *The Tarot: History, Mystery and Lore*. New York: Paragon House, 1992.

Hall, Manly P. *The Secret Teachings of All Ages*. 1928. Reprint. Los Angeles: Philosophic Research Society, 1977.

Hitchcock, Helyn. *Helping Yourself with Numerology*. West Nyack, N.Y.: Parker, 1972.

Scholem, Gershom. *Kabbalah*. New York: New American Library, 1974.

Westcott, W. Wynn. *Numbers: Their Occult Power and Mystic Virtues*. London: Theosophical Publishing House, 1974.

GEMINI *One of the 12 astrological signs of the zodiac. The symbol is the twins.*

Those who are born between May 21 and June 20 are natives of the sign of Gemini and have specific traits indicative of the time and date on which they were born. Divination of events can also be charted through this astrological sign.

Astrologers divine what is in store throughout life through the time, date and place in which an individual was born as they coordinate the influences with other signs, the planets, the Sun, the Moon and other powers.

GEMINI

In traditional Western astrology, Gemini is the third sign of the zodiac. Those born during the period typically exhibit qualities of versatility, energy and adaptability. Gemini is an air sign and is quick to move to a new intellectual or physical interest and thus may seem to exhibit nervous energy. These are people who sometimes find it impossible to sit still or to finish a project.

Possessing flair and style, the Gemini native is a trendsetter, not a follower. Gemini is clever with words and spots trends well before other signs. He or she is able to communicate well, with the knack of being able to craft words to suit any situation. This person is said to have the gift of persuasion and works well in marketing and sales, entrepreneurial pursuits, the law and education. Because Gemini moves with the speed of light, he or she is often accused of being superficial, shallow and thoughtless, but it is a multifaceted interest, intellect and personality that is really in play here, not a frivolous nature.

This ancient symbol represents the astrological sign of Gemini.

The sign of the zodiac in which an individual is born is responsible for only one fragment of the qualities he or she receives at birth. Psychics are quick to point out that a general forecast solely on the stellar position of the Sun on the day an individual was born is unlikely to provide an accurate glimpse of the future.

While traditional astrologers use books to calculate a personal birth chart based on the position of the Sun, Moon and planets at a distinct time, computer software has replaced most of this time-consuming work. The correct term for calculating a birth chart is to "cast" it. In order to fully comprehend the extent of traits, potential and attributes, the exact time and place of birth must be calculated and interpreted.

See also ASTROLOGICAL SYMBOLS; ASTROLOGY.

Further reading

Cosmic Connections. Mysteries of the Unknown. Alexandria, Va.: Time Life Books, 1990.

Goodman, Linda. *Linda Goodman's Sun Signs.* New York: Fawcett/Columbine, 1978.

Morgan, Chris. *Fortune Telling: How to Predict Your Own Future.* London: Quintet Publishing and Random House, 1992.

Omarr, Sydney. *Gemini.* New York: New American Library, 1992.

———. *My World of Astrology.* New York: Fleet, 1965.

Verlagsanstalt, Datura. *Gemini Astro Analysis.* New York: Grosset & Dunlap, 1976.

Woolfork, Joanna Martine. *The Only Astrology Book You'll Ever Need.* Landham, Mass.: Scarborough, 1992.

GEMS *Divination according to the placement of gemstones when cast as lots or through the practice of* SCRYING.

Precious and semiprecious stones, cut or uncut, such as diamonds, amethysts, agates and rose quartz, have always played a role in metaphysics. Some gems are used for interpreting future events and are cast on a circle with specific areas determined to foretell certain things, as one might toss dice. Others are used in curing illnesses; amethyst is said to have healing qualities, and those who believe in the curing power of stones suggest that the infirm wear or sleep with this gem. Gems can be used to heal patients either through the use of a pendulum (see below) or as a diagnostic tool. This is referred to as analytical dowsing. They may also be used as a pendulum by circling the stone over specific CHAKRAS for the relief of illness or for deeper spiritual understanding.

Considered by many to be one of the oldest forms of prognostication, foretelling future events through the use of jewels and crystals is technically known as LITHOMANCY, a form of scrying. As with crystal balls, a specific gem is placed in a quiet area, with a light source reflected off the natural sides or cut facets of the stone. Through studying and interpreting the play of light, the visions seen in the stone or the messages received telepathically, the psychic is able to answer a querant's question, advise on a specific concern or prognosticate future events. In the case of casting lots with gems, each stone has a specific meaning and ability to divine.

Gems are sometimes used in DOWSING. A stone is suspended on a light cord held between the fingers; after a period of meditation, questions are asked. The suspended gem will swing back and forth or clockwise for yes; for no, it will swing from left to right or counterclockwise. If there is insufficient information to provide an answer, or if there is no answer at all, the suspended gem will be still.

In order to provide the best reading from a gem used as a pendulum, one should never swing it or exert any force. Questions need not be spoken aloud.

Before gems are used for any metaphysical purpose, psychics recommend cleaning the crystals by scrubbing them with salt and water or by boiling them in water and then rinsing them well. To energize the crystal or gem, one should leave it outdoors on a night with a full moon.

"Gem elixirs" are recommended by psychics in order to help restore the healthy energy of the body and for their curative powers. EDGAR CAYCE often suggested gem drinks. It should be noted that these recommendations and treatments do not replace medical assistance. For any health concerns, professional medical advice is always recommended.

To make a gem elixir, a psychic would select the correct gem, unpolished, uncut, in a crystal form if possible, and clean. The gem is then placed in the sunshine to activate its healing powers. The querant would sit in a quiet place to meditate. After a few moments, the gem is put in the center of a clear glass bowl; then the bowl is filled with distilled water. The bowl should be left on a natural surface (such as wood or glass), preferably in the sunshine, for about two hours. (The bowl can be covered with a piece of glass to keep the elixir clean.) The elixir may be stored in a tightly covered glass bottle or consumed immediately.

The most commonly used elixirs are:

- Amethyst for calming the disposition and reducing stress.
- Bloodstone for improvement of any bone marrow condition, and the health of testicles, ovaries, cervix and uterus.
- Citrine to reduce and/or remove toxins from the legs and feet.
- Diamond (an extremely powerful elixir) is said to remove any blockages and pockets of negativity, anxiety and insecurity.
- Jade provides a balance in the mind and the body to increase wisdom, psychic abilities and promote courage.
- Onyx helps restore the heart, kidneys and nerve tissues of the body.
- Rose quartz assists the body in reducing emotional disruptions and providing a feeling of balance and self-confidence.
- Turquoise is called the "master healer." It moves through the body quickly, strengthening and regenerating it, while protecting the colors of the aura.

See also CASTING OF LOTS; CRYSTAL PREDICTIONS; SORTILEGE SYSTEMS.

Further reading

Baer, Randall N., and Vick V. Baer. *The Crystal Connection*. San Francisco: Harper & Row, 1986.
Bravo, Brett. *Crystal Healing Secrets*. New York: Warner, 1988.
———. *Crystal Love Secrets*. New York: Warner, 1991.

[Cayce, Edgar.] *Gems and Stones: Readings of Edgar Cayce.* Virginia Beach, Va.: ARE Press, 1976.

Markham, Ursula. *The Crystal Workbook: A Complete Guide to Working with Crystals.* Northamptonshire, England: Aquarian Press, 1988.

———. *Fortune-Telling by Crystals and Semiprecious Stones.* Northamptonshire, England: Aquarian Press, 1987.

Matteson, Barbara J. *Mystic Minerals.* Seattle: Cosmic Resources, 1985.

Walker, Dael. *The Crystal Book.* Sunol, Calif.: Crystal Col, 1983.

GEOMANCY *Divination by interpreting the patterns and shapes of objects or events found in nature.*

The most ancient and basic form of geomancy is to hold a handful of seeds, pebbles or sand and gently toss them and then divine the future or answer a querant's question by interpreting the position of the objects as they fall to the ground. The results are sometimes read as with TASSEOGRAPHY. Geomancy is also applied to earth-related prognostication methods, including FENG SHUI, ALECTROMANCY and NEPHELOMANCY.

In the Middle East in ancient times, geomancy was practiced by psychics who examined the cracks in the dry earth to foretell the future. In ancient China, after careful consideration, handfuls of dirt were tossed and the resulting patterns

were interpreted. In Africa today, many groups still use geomancy. Those of the Yoruba tribe place a thin layer of sand in a flat dish and tap the sides, causing the sand to move into patterns; these formations are then interpreted. The members of the West African Dogon tribe, which resides about 60 miles south of the Niger River, still rely on geomancy to tell them when to plant and harvest and to foretell the result of critical decisions. They toss cowrie shells into a straw basket and then interpret the placement as a divination method.

To practice geomancy, one should meditate on a specific question and then take a handful of sand or dirt. Small pebbles are sometimes used too; this prognostication method is called PESSOMANCY and is used by the Masai of East Africa. Some psychics believe that one must use sand from a holy place or sand that has been specially cleansed; others believe that dirt or sand from one's own yard is best. Hold the sand or dirt, consider the question and then toss the sand to the ground. As with teacup reading or the reading of cloud patterns, one should use inborn intuitive skills to see images, letters and messages in the patterns that are made.

See also HALOMANCY.

Further reading

Ancient Wisdom and Secret Sects. Mysteries of the Unknown. Alexandria, Va.: Time Life Books, 1990.

Bletzer, June G. *The Donning International Encyclopedic Psychic Dictionary.* West Chester, Pa.: Whitford Press, 1986.

Morgan, Chris. *Fortune Telling: How to Predict Your Own Future.* London: Quintet Publishing and Random House, 1992.

Rossbach, Sarah. *Feng Shui: The Chinese Art of Placement.* New York: Arkana/Penguin, 1991.

GIRDLE OF VENUS *One of the many lines in the palm of the hand that are said to foretell specific characteristics.*

According to palmists, the Girdle of Venus lies beneath the fingers and just above the heart line. Often much fainter and thinner than the other lines of the palm, it indicates a character that enjoys good living and physical pleasures along

In ancient China, among other cultures, geomancy was used to foretell the future. After careful consideration, handfuls of dirt were tossed and the resulting patterns were interpreted.

with a sensual disposition. The person with this line is often extremely confident and knows well his or her abilities.

Although this line is not often found in the palm, those who do have it are friendly and outgoing, yet they can be overly sensitive to real or imagined wrongs. If there is more than one Girdle of Venus in the hand, it indicates a hypersensitive nature.

See also PALMISTRY.

Further reading

Altman, Nathaniel. *Palmistry Workbook.* New York: Sterling, 1990.

Cheiro. *Cheiro's Book of Numbers.* New York: Prentice-Hall, 1988.

———. *The Language of the Hand.* New York: Prentice-Hall, 1987.

Robinson, Rita. *The Palm: A Guide to Your Hidden Potential.* North Hollywood, Calif.: Newcastle, 1988.

GNOSIS *The general term for seeking to know.*

Like ESP, gnosis is information perceived without the use of the five traditional senses. Gnosis is said to have begun at the same time as Christianity and blends the metaphysical meaning of God with the ethereal; it is knowing with feeling and the sense of God, rather than learning about the Scriptures or the interpretation of Christianity from teachers. One who knows and uses the power of gnosis is called a Gnostic.

Gnosticism, a religious belief based on gnosis, was common during the second century A.D. Those who practiced it believed that through knowledge rather than faith the soul could be saved. It is often referred to as a dual philosophy of religion and metaphysics; however, Christians reject Gnosticism as a dissident, false religious order. According to scholars, the basis for Gnosticism may have actually been the original Christian approach to life and the afterlife, and the theories could be found in all major civilizations of the ancient world, well before the birth of Jesus Christ.

Those who practiced this religious belief were persecuted by the Christian church, especially during the Middle Ages, because Gnostics believed that people originated in the celestial realm and could return to this perfect place through ethereal knowledge and communication with other spirits. The philosophies of gnosis were hidden in the cults of the Freemasons, the Rosicrucians, the Kabbalists and other freethinkers.

Early in this century and continuing to the present, there has been a renewed interest in this antiquated theory of creation. Psychiatrist Carl G. Jung said he was a "neo-Gnostic," and believed Gnosticism embraced psychology. Some people believe that tarot cards originated with Gnosticism. Those who read the tarot point out that symbols of the major arcana have been interpreted as a representation of the major principles of Gnosticism. For instance, the Death card has nothing to do with dying, but rather with new perception through spiritual awareness. Thus, the symbols found in the tarot may actually represent the principles of gnosticism.

As religion moves forward into the 21st century, it may be that the ancient knowledge of gnosis will return as more people blend metaphysics and Christianity. The Madaeans (or Christians of Saint John) are a Gnostic sect, located in Baghdad, that is still active today.

See also EXTRASENSORY PERCEPTION (ESP); GEMATRIA; TAROT.

Further reading

Ferguson, John. *An Illustrated Encyclopedia of Mysticism and the Mystery Religions.* New York: Seabury Press, 1976.

Hoeller, Stephan A. *The Gnostic Jung and the Seven Sermons to the Dead.* Wheaton, Ill.: Theosophical Publishing House, 1982.

Raymond, Litzka. *How to Read Palms.* Garden City, N.Y.: Perma Books, 1950.

Rudolph, Kurt. *Gnosis: The Nature and History of Gnosticism.* San Francisco: Harper & Row, 1987.

Watson, Donald. *The Dictionary of Mind and Spirit.* New York: Avon, 1991.

GOODMAN, LINDA *(1925–) American astrologer.*

Goodman is probably the best-known astrologer of contemporary times. She is recognized for her witty writing style on the topic of astrology, especially the sun signs. *Linda Goodman's Sun Signs* contains descriptions of personality types as they reflect sun-sign astrology. Goodman was the first astrologer to have a book on the *New York Times* best-seller list, with *Linda Goodman's Sun Signs* selling more than 4 million copies. Her writing and astrological theories are known internationally, and much of her success is due to the readability and conversational style of her prose.

In addition to being an astrologer and providing astrological guidance to the rich and famous, including many Hollywood celebrities and Washington politicians, Goodman also founded a religion called Mannitou. Based on Native American beliefs, it focuses on the teachings of Saint Francis of Assisi.

Goodman's life has not been without tragedy, including the disappearance of a former lover and the alleged death of her 21-year-old daughter. Goodman firmly believes that they both will be returned to her.

Goodman's other works include *Venus Trines at Midnight: Verses about Lions, Rams, Bulls, Twins, Archers and Other Sun Signs and You*, said to be the first volume of astrological poetry; *Linda Goodman's Love Signs: A New Approach to the Human Heart* and *Linda Goodman's Star Signs*.

Further reading

Goodman, Linda. *Linda Goodman's Love Signs: A New Approach to the Human Heart*. New York: Harper & Row, 1978.
———. *Linda Goodman's Star Signs*. New York: St. Martin's, 1987.
———. *Linda Goodman's Sun Signs*. New York: Fawcett/Columbine, 1978.

GRANT, JOAN *(1907–1990) English author and psychic.*

Grant was able to verbalize her experiences in previous incarnations and lives and wrote about the experience. She interpreted her dreams as a form of prognostication, and through PSYCHOMETRY (pressing an object to one's forehead) she was able to see visions of where an object had originated.

Grant's novels contained stories of the people and places she professed to have met, known and traveled with during past lives, including existences in ancient Egypt, the Holy Land and South America before the Spanish conquest of the native peoples. She is best known for her novels *Winged Pharaoh, Lord of the Horizon, Return to Elysium* and her autobiographical works *A Lot to Remember, Far Memory* and *Many Lifetimes.*

Further reading

Denys, Kelsey and Joan Grant. *Many Lifetimes*. Garden City, N.Y.: Doubleday, 1967.
Grant, Joan. *Far Memory*. New York: Harper & Row, 1956.
Langley, Noel. *Edgar Cayce on Reincarnation*. New York: Castle, 1967.
Lenz, Frederick. *Lifetimes: True Accounts of Reincarnation*. New York: Fawcett Crest, 1977.

GRAPHOLOGY *Interpretation of personal characteristics through the study of handwriting, used by psychics as a key to personality.*

Also known as handwriting analysis, this method is not used to divine the future but to investigate personality traits.

While the study of graphology probably did not start at the same time, the act of writing began more than 5,500 years ago with the Sumerians and the beginnings of the alphabet as we know it today. A variation of graphology began about 539 B.C., when the Roman court appointed augurs to review signatures because of their uniqueness and reflection on the character of the individual who had signed his or her name. It is said that Aristotle, more than 2,000 years ago, studied graphology. Julius Caesar's augurs used it to test the faithfulness of Caesar's officers and advisors. Chinese philosopher Jo-Hau is said to have studied this mantic art. The first true study of graphology was done in 1632 by the Italian physician Camille Baldo in his book *How to Know the Nature and Qualities of a Person by Looking at a Letter He Has Written*. And the system of modern graphology is attributed to Abbe Flandrin, a French churchman, who in 1830 enlarged on Baldo's theories. In 1896, Ludwig Lages, a German physician, founded the Graphological Society; scientists and the government acknowledged graphology's ability to discern specific personal characteristics.

Whereas the practices of TAROT, ASTROLOGY and TASSEOGRAPHY, for example, have all been considered nondocumentable by the scientific community, graphology is a prognostication method that is well accepted. In 1906, psychologist Alfred Binet published papers proclaiming the validity of the uniqueness of writing and the reflection of specific personality types and characteristics. Graphology is currently used regularly by the U.S. government, psychologists and personnel managers when hiring employees. It is also used by forensic investigators to detect forgeries and to establish the authenticity of manuscripts. It is considered a logical science (compared with metaphysical science).

Graphology can detect more than 300 personality characteristics including introversion, egocentricity, imagination, ambition and enthusiasm. Graphologists—those who specialize in this field—analyze the slant, shape, size, pressure, margins and spacing of letters, along with the legibility of the writing. Writing that is clear indicates a personality that is aboveboard; an illegible writing style indicates a guarded nature. The color of the pen or pencil used also indicates personality traits, as does the flair and extra embellishments of the style.

Graphologists caution that the analysis of handwriting indicates personality traits and clues, not hard evidence of characteristics. For instance, large script indicates an outgoing personality; medium script shows a well-balanced ego; a small script style is said to show a perfectionist and rationalist, someone who is analytical.

Further reading

Green, Jane Nugent, with Ethel Erkkila Tigue. *You and Your Private I: Graphological Analysis Focused on the Personal Pronoun I*. St. Paul, Minn.: Llewellyn, 1975.

Hartford, Huntington. *You Are What You Write*. New York: Macmillan, 1973.

Leibel, Charlotte P. *Change Your Handwriting, Change Your Life*. New York: Stein & Day, 1972.

Roman, Clara. *Handwriting, a Key to Personality*. New York: Noonday Press, Farrar, Straus & Giroux, 1966.

Sonnemann, Ulrich. *Handwriting Analysis as a Psychodiagnostic Tool*. New York: Grune & Stratton, 1964.

GREATRAKES, VALENTINE (1628–?)
Irish magistrate and psychic healer.

Greatrakes believed that his healing powers were a gift from God, and he was widely known as a healer, with a special faculty for curing scrofula, a tuberculous of the lymphatic glands, known in his day as the "King's Evil." He was also known for being able to heal palsy, dropsy, epilepsy, ulcers, wounds and bruises, lameness, deafness and partial blindness.

Greatrakes was nicknamed the "Stroker" because of his unique ways of working with the infirm. To heal them, he slowly stroked and squeezed the limbs from the trunk to the fingers and toes, which he believed pushed the illness out. He was known for spiritual healing at large gatherings. Although a magistrate by profession, he was received by King Charles II of England who gave him permission to practice healing.

The Royal Society (of England) published accounts of Greatrakes's healing acts in its journal, *Transactions*. In 1660, Greatrakes published his autobiography, in a very small volume, and called it *Val. Greatrakes, Esq. of Waterford in the kingdom of Ireland, famous for curing several disease and distempers by the stroke of his hand only*.

Later in life, he abruptly discontinued psychic healing, saying that his powers had weakened.

See also LAYING ON OF HANDS.

Further reading

Drury, Nevill. *Dictionary of Mysticism and the Esoteric Traditions*. Dorset, England: Prism Press, 1992.

Fodor, Nandor. *Encyclopedia of Psychic Science*. New York: University Books, 1966.

Krippner, Stanley, and Alberto Villoldo. *The Realms of Healing*. 3d ed. Berkeley, Calif.: Celestial Arts, 1986.

Meek, George W., ed. *Healers and the Healing Process*. Wheaton, Ill.: Theosophical Publishing House, 1977.

The Psychics. Mysteries of the Unknown. Alexandria, Va.: Time Life Books, 1990.

GUIDE *A highly evolved spiritual source of energy that is said to protect and inform, often providing prognostication to those who know how to listen.*

Guides, sometimes known as guardian angels, are considered benevolent, protective sources of advice, knowledge, metaphysical information and love. The term *control* is used for a spirit that is channeled from the spiritual plane through to a psychic's mind so he or she can advise a querant.

The Greeks, among other ancient civilizations, including many Native American tribes, believed that each person has an individual guardian angel, which could also appear in an animal form. Traditionally, American Indians regard the guide as a specific class of spirit that, once acquired through a vision or a dream, continues to help by providing specific powers, abilities—including clairvoyance—and the knowledge of medicine or healing powers. With the appearance of Christianity, the guardian became a "familiar spirit." A Gallup poll, taken in the late 1970s, indicated that well over half of all people in the United States believe in angels.

Although there is no hard scientific evidence of the existence of guides, psychics insist that everyone has them and they are always ready to assist their own people. These manifestations of intelligence have been said to have lived many times on the earth plane and are more evolved than human beings. According to psychics, though a guide is there to assist, it will never interfere in a human's life without a specific request or invitation.

The guide can take on any form the psychic wishes to envision or any part of that vision. As an example, if the psychic expects to see the guide dressed as an Indian fakir, that is how the guide will appear.

Some psychics believe that we all have a number of guides, with one guide overseeing our entire life on this planet. The others, helping guides, are called forth when there is a specific

need, such as in healing or in a time of transformation.

To connect with one's guide, it is recommended that the querant select a quiet spot in which to clear his or her mind and meditate. One must ask for the guide's presence, and if one "knows" by a feeling that he or she is no longer alone, the guide has manifested itself. Many psychics communicate with their guides through tools such as the TAROT, the PENDULUM PREDICTIONS, meditation on crystals or by talking. Guides can also be channeled through a psychic through a DIRECT-VOICE MEDIUM or by visions, smells, tastes or sounds. Before a reading, most psychics call forth their guides to provide a connection with the information available in the ethereal plane or the AKASHIC RECORDS.

Guides are also referred to as archangels, spiritual guides, guardian angels, joy guides, doorkeepers, doctors, healers, teachers and protectors.

See also CHANNEL.

Further reading

Belhayes, Iris, with Enid. *Spirit Guides.* San Diego: ACS, 1985.

Bletzer, June G. *The Donning International Encyclopedic Psychic Dictionary.* West Chester, Pa.: Whitford Press, 1986.

Butler, W. E. *How to Develop Clairvoyance.* 2d ed. New York: Samuel Weiser, 1979.

Hirschfelder, Arlene, and Paulette Molin. *The Encyclopedia of Native American Religions.* New York: Facts On File, 1992.

Search for the Soul. Mysteries of the Unknown. Alexandria, Va.: Time Life Books, 1990.

Walker, Barbara G. *The Woman's Encyclopedia of Myths and Secrets.* New York: Harper Collins, Publishers, 1983.

GUPPY, MRS. AGNES (SAMUEL)
(1860?–1917) English psychic.

Guppy's talents were discovered by Dr. Alfred Russell Wallace, a Welsh naturalist and psychical researcher. Born Agnes Nichol, she was recognized while she was just a child as having the ability of a powerful psychic. She could move objects without touching them, working best when alone in a room. As she became more aware of her gifts, she was able to levitate objects and people.

Guppy's psychic gifts included being able to produce the spirits of flowers, gifts and animals at seances or readings. Manifestation of her gift are said to include showers of butterflies, uncooled fowl ready for the oven and a white cat; the animals (and other objects, such as jewelry, books and possessions) seen by others are called apports. They are grouped under the heading APPARITION. Apports are not said to be transported from the ethereal world but from one earth plane position to another in what seems to be thin air or through solid matter, such as a wall. They are produced by the power of the psychic's gift. One example of Guppy's ability to produce objects "out of thin air" was when Princess Marguerite of Naples is said to have wanted a specimen of prickly cactus. Suddenly more than 20 cacti dropped onto the table around which Guppy and the princess were seated.

Guppy was considered one of the most controversial psychics during the heightening of spiritual awareness in the late 1800s. But no claims of fraud were ever brought against her, nor did she ever gain financially from her gifts.

Guppy could, according to reports of the time, levitate and transport herself to other places. One such event occurred on June 3, 1871, in London, at her home in Highbury. Through meditation and her own talent, she transported herself more than 60 miles to another seance and was seen by those in attendance. They said that the room was brightly lit when Guppy appeared, with all the witnesses' stories matching in the account.

Guppy said she made other psychic flights; however, the undocumented ones attributed to her are considered disputatious.

See also LEVITATION.

Further reading

Brown, Slater. *The Heyday of Spiritualism*. New York: Hawthorn, 1970.
Chaney, Rev. Robert G. *Mediums and the Development of Mediumship*. Freeport, N.Y.: Books for Libraries, 1972.

Fodor, Nandor. *Encyclopedia of Psychic Science*. New York: University Books, 1966.
Guiley, Rosemary Ellen. *The Encyclopedia of Ghosts and Spirits*. New York: Facts On File, 1992.
Spirit Summonings. Mysteries of the Unknown. Alexandria, Va.: Time Life Books, 1990.

GYPSY 7 *Tarot card spread, deriving its name because only seven cards are used, far fewer than the typical layout.*

Like the Celtic Cross and other tarot card spreads, the Gypsy 7 has been used for a quick read and is a favorite among gypsy readers. In this method, all tarot cards are utilized and are shuffled by the querant while he or she considers the question to be asked. A card is drawn by the querant to serve as the significator, the card that represents him or her, and is placed faceup. Then seven more cards are drawn from the deck and placed facedown in a line from left to right, moving from the significator.

The first card is said to represent the internal spirit. The second reveals forces or energy at work around the querant. The third is an indication of past influences, challenges or occurrences in which the querant has been involved. The fourth signifies desires, dreams and goals. The fifth represents relationships, family and friends. The sixth indicates forces that are working against the querant. The seventh card in the Gypsy 7 reveals the realization of the querant's question or what is to come when all the other card forces are combined.

In order to interpret the cards, many readers and psychics suggest referring to a book specifically for tarot; others suggest using one's own psychic skills and doing an intuitive reading. In an intuitive reading, the psychic looks at the pictures on the cards, and those objects or figures or colors that come into his or her mind first are discussed.

See also CARTOMANCY.

Further reading

Buckland, Raymond. *Secrets of Gypsy Fortune Telling*. St. Paul, Minn.: Llewellyn, 1988.
Cavendish, Richard. *The Tarot*. New York: Putnam's, 1967.

Giles, Cynthia. *The Tarot: History, Mystery, and Lore.* New York: Paragon House, 1992.

Innes, Brian. *The Tarot: How to Use and Interpret the Cards.* London: Orbis, 1979.

King, Francis, and Stephen Skinner. *Techniques of High Magic.* Rochester, Vt.: Destiny Books, 1991.

Thierens, A. E. *Astrology and the Tarot.* Los Angeles: Newcastle, 1975.

Waite, Arthur Edward. *The Pictorial Key to the Tarot.* New York: Samuel Weiser, 1973.

GYROMANCY *Divination by moving in a circle until dizziness occurs.*

The future is foretold, or a question is answered, by interpreting the placement of the person or people after they are overcome with dizziness or exhaustion, or through the visions or messages received from this experience. Divination may also occur by interpreting the person's mutterings after exhaustion sets in. It is thought that the Druids used this form of prognostication.

While dancing in circles has been the custom in many civilizations, especially in Greece, and continues to be used throughout the world in celebrations and rituals, few people still practice the divination method of gyromancy. The Tarahumares Indians in Mexico are one of the few groups who believe in gyromancy. With a specific ritual and to music, those chosen to dance whirl and spin until they fall to the ground. The specific way they collapse produces the divination of future events.

Further reading

Grant, James. *The Mysteries of All Nations.* Detroit: Gale Research, 1971.

Maven, Max. *Max Maven's Book of Fortunetelling.* New York: Prentice-Hall, 1992.

Smith, Christine. *The Book of Divination.* London: Rider, 1978.

Visions and Prophecies. Mysteries of the Unknown. Alexandria, Va.: Time Life Books, 1990.

HALL, MANLY P. *(1901–1990) Spiritual teacher and author.*

A prolific writer, Hall produced thousands of books and pamphlets on various metaphysical subjects, such as karma and clairvoyance. He is considered by many people throughout the world to be the foremost teacher, lecturer and leader of the metaphysical movement for the 20th century. Some of his long-selling titles of more than 200 books include *Buddhism and Psychotherapy, From Death to Rebirth* and *Positive Uses of Psychic Energy.*

Hall founded the Philosophic Research Society, headquartered in Los Angeles, and his work and teachings continue to inform, inspire and motivate students of metaphysics.

Further reading

Hall, Manly P. *The Secret Teachings of All Ages.* 1928. Reprint. Los Angeles: Philosophic Research Society, 1977.

HALOMANCY *Divination by interpreting the formation of the crystals when salt is poured to the ground.*

Salt as a tool for psychics most likely originated with the ancient Egyptians, when the substance was a prized possession. As with GEOMANCY, psychics of the time interpreted how the salt landed after being poured or gently tossed. Those who practiced this method used crystals of salt that were much larger than the type that comes out of the shaker today; as in PESSOMANCY, the salt was probably the size of small pebbles, easily tossed into patterns that became obvious to the seers.

Salt has been used to frighten away evil spirits, counteract bad omens, produce luck, bring money to the house, protect sailors and babies and induce love spells. A substance now considered so mundane as salt has had a rich and intriguing history. Salt in divination and superstition has been with us since before the written word and was used by ancient Egyptians, Arabs and Christians alike.

In 800 B.C. Homer's *Iliad* mentions, "Patroclus scattered the embers and laid the spits above them . . . after he sprinkled the meat with holy salt . . . to sacrifice to the gods." This was part of a ritual conducted to interpret the future. Salt can also protect those we love, as suggested in the *Historical Guide to Scarborough* (published in England in 1787): "if one needed to appease the angry waves and obtain a propitious breeze favourable to the voyager's safe return, he must ask his fair spouse (or other anxious female friend) to proceed unaccompanied, about 40 paces along the pier. Here a small circular cavity among the stones, receives a saline libation which is poured into it, while the sacrificer, muttering her tenderest wishes, looks toward that quarter from whence the object of her anxiety is expected to return."

To obtain a reading by the use of halomancy, one should acquire coarse salt (much like that used on pretzels) and a square of smooth soil or a dark cloth on which the salt can fall. Cupping a handful, meditate on the question at hand for as much time as necessary until a clear understanding of the question is in the mind. Then toss the salt up in the air in a gentle manner. The formations are clues to the answers and can be read much like tea leaves or coffee grounds, that is, seeing actual pictures in the scattered salt crystals. If one is reading for another, he or she should go through the process of holding, meditating and tossing the salt; then the psychic can read the results.

See also TASSEOGRAPHY.

Further reading

Bletzer, June G. *The Donning International Encyclopedic Psychic Dictionary.* West Chester, Pa.: Whitford Press, 1986.

Cavendish, Richard. *The Visions of Heaven and Hell.* New York: Harmony, 1977.

Hartley, C. Gasquoine. *The Truth about Woman.* New York: Dodd, Mead & Co., 1913.

Opie, Iona, and Moira Tatem. *A Dictionary of Superstitions.* Oxford: Oxford University Press, 1992.

Walker, Barbara G. *The Woman's Encyclopedia of Myths and Secrets.* New York: Harper Collins, 1983.

HAMOND, COUNT LOUIS LE WARNER DE
See CHEIRO.

HAND ANALYSIS
See PALMISTRY.

HANDWRITING ANALYSIS
See GRAPHOLOGY.

HARTMANN, FRANZ (1838–1912) German-American mystic and psychic.

Hartmann was the founder of the Order of the Esoteric Rose Croix and the magical group that evolved into the Ordo Templi Orientis, still in existence today and located in England and California, which practices a form of ritual sexual magic. Aleister Crowley and Theodor Reuss were also involved in the organization.

Hartmann believed that everyone had psychic abilities, a thought considered novel at the time. He is best remembered for his works *Magic, Black and White* and *In the Pronaos of the Temple of Wisdom.*

Further reading

Cavendish, Richard, ed. *The Encyclopedia of the Unexplained.* New York: McGraw-Hill, 1974.

Drury, Nevill. *Dictionary of Mysticism and the Esoteric Traditions.* Dorset, England: Prism Press, 1992.

Wilson, Colin. *The Occult.* New York: Vintage, 1973.

HARUSPICY *Divination through the use of the cracks that appear in the shoulder blade of a roasted sheep.*

Also known as SCAPULOMANCY, haruspicy is sometimes grouped with HEPATOMANCY (examination of the livers and internal organs of animals). Divining the future using bones is one of the oldest methods of prognostication and has been found in all civilizations.

Haruspicy began with the ancient Chinese more than 5,000 years ago and may have originated as a prognostication method using what was left over after the sacrifice of an animal and a ceremonial dinner. With haruspicy, the shoulder bones were heated in an intense fire until the bones were dry and cracked (most likely after the sacrifice was burned). Later, haruspicy dictated that the psychics examined the charred bones without the sacrifice, depending on the psychic and the animals that were available, such as deer, horses, sheep, pigs and oxen. Because it provides a wide surface, the shoulder blade was the bone of choice.

The practice appears to have been used throughout the world. The Romans placed the shoulder blade of a sheep in hot coals and then "read" the cracks that appeared. The Druids and Celts preferred the shoulder blade of a pig. The native peoples residing in Labrador used what they had the most of: caribou. Haruspicy was practiced in ancient Japan and was called *futomani*.

It is said that haruspicy is still practiced in remote parts of Turkestan today, and a form of haruspicy continues to be used by the shaman of the Gurung, a farming people in Nepal. The shaman sacrifices a chicken and through examining the lungs can foretell the health of the people and the success or failure of various crops.

Even today (Turkestan and Nepal notwithstanding), there is a mystical quality about the bones of animals. For instance, at Thanksgiving in the United States, the furcula bone (or wishbone) of the turkey is saved and dried; then, when it is crisp, two people grasp the bone, one on each side, and break it—making a wish. The wish will come true for the one who ends up with the longest piece. The custom was developed among the Etruscans more than 2,400 years ago. They believed that chickens and fowl had unique metaphysical powers. Romans believed that to gain luck (or change a bad omen) one had to stroke a chicken bone.

Mother Bunch's Golden Fortune-Teller, published in England around 1840, advises the reader to use care when burning bones. "Burning beef boanes . . . brings sorrow through poverty; and to cast those of pork or veal into the fire, inflicts pains in the bones of the person so improvident." However, according to an English folk tale, presenting a bride with a chicken side bone called a "hug-ma-close" on her wedding day will ensure that she will be happy with her husband.

In years past, it was a tradition in Scotland to hang the shoulder blade (whether it was roasted is unclear) of a sheep over the front door of a pregnant woman's house. The sex of the baby was foretold by the sex of the first person to walk through the door the following day. Sailors in Scotland were reverent of fish bones, too, and in order to preserve their fishing harvests they would never, ever, throw fish bones into the fire.

See also CEPHALOMANCY; PHRENOLOGY.

Further reading

Budge, Sir E. A. Wallis. *Egyptian Magic*. New York: Dover, 1971.

Cumont, Franz. *Oriental Religions in Roman Paganism*. New York Dover, 1956.

Maven, Max. *Max Maven's Book of Fortunetelling*. New York: Prentice-Hall, 1992.

Opie, Iona, and Moira Tatem. *A Dictionary of Superstitions*. Oxford: Oxford University Press, 1992.

HEAD LINE
One of the many lines in the palm of the hand that are said to foretell specific characteristics.

The head line is located beneath the fingers between the heart line and the life line, and its endings and beginnings are important. The head line is said to indicate the intellect, disclosing the direction of potential. This line typically begins on the palm about one inch below where the index finger joins the hand.

A head line that runs less than half the way across the palm shows single mindedness; this is a person who becomes deeply involved in one area. If the head line runs across the palm and then moves toward the little fingers, it is considered a sign of intelligence and a logical mind. A head line that dips down to the mount of Luna indicates a personality that is creatively free, so much so that the creativity can run away with good intentions. A head line that curves down slightly toward the wrist and then moves back up toward the little finger shows someone who has the potential to be financially successful.

The head line is sometimes referred to as the "line of head" by palmists.

See also PALMISTRY.

Further reading

Altman, Nathaniel. *Palmistry Workbook*. New York: Sterling, 1990.

Cheiro. *Cheiro's Book of Numbers*. New York: Prentice-Hall, 1988.

———. *The Language of the Hand*. New York: Prentice-Hall, 1987.

Robinson, Rita. *The Palm: A Guide to Your Hidden Potential*. North Hollywood, Calif.: Newcastle, 1988.

HEART LINE
One of the many lines in the palm of the hand that are said to foretell specific characteristics.

One of the deepest lines of the palm, the heart line begins at the Mount of Jupiter (on the palm beneath the index finger) and crosses the palm. The heart line gives the palmist indications about the querant's behavior, especially in relationships that involve love, particularly how the querant expresses and receives love.

Basically, if the heart line begins on the mount of Jupiter, it suggests that one is looking for Mr. or Ms. Right, the perfect soul mate. If the line begins between the index and middle fingers, it indicates that one is willing to accept reality (instead of looking for a princess or a knight in shining armor). If the line is chained—that is, looks like a chain with two lines continuing to cross each other—this may indicate disappointment in love or reveal a nature that is cautious when it comes to matters of the heart. A drooping heart line may indicate trouble relating to the opposite sex. If the line is forked at the beginning, it indicates a self-reliant, extroverted nature, able to meet life and love with an open mind.

The heart line is sometimes referred to by palmists as the "line of the heart."

See also PALMISTRY.

Further reading

Altman, Nathaniel. *Palmistry Workbook*. New York: Sterling, 1990.

Cheiro. *Cheiro's Book of Numbers*. New York: Prentice-Hall, 1988.

———. *The Language of the Hand*. New York: Prentice-Hall, 1987.

Robinson, Rita. *The Palm: A Guide to Your Hidden Potential*. North Hollywood, Calif.: Newcastle, 1988.

HEIROMANCY *Divination through the use of sacred articles and by observing sacrifices.*

Heiromancy, practiced by the ancient Egyptian seers, used articles that were believed to be sacred, such as animals, gems and fountains (as with PEGOMANCY) for divination purposes. It is unclear whether it was the reflecting light that was deciphered to advise on the future or if the psychic knew through his prognostic metaphysical powers and thus was able to answer the querant's question or to furnish advice when scrutinizing the article.

In a contemporary form of heiromancy, a psychic dedicates a crystal ball (SCRYING) or TAROT cards to the higher consciousness or higher self. The items become sacred, providing advice or answers to a querant.

Heiromancy also includes divination of the future by observing sacrifices (humans and animals). The word *sacrifice* (in Latin, *sacrificium*) originally meant "something made holy." Sacrifices were the mainstay of many ancient religions. The ancient Greeks sacrificed goats, horses, dogs, cattle and sheep. Prior to the invasion of the Spanish, the Aztecs of Mexico offered human sacrifices to their sun god, which is said to have accepted more than 20,000 such sacrifices a year. In the early rituals of Hinduism, humans, animals and plants were offered during the Vedic period. Ancient Chinese religious ceremonies also included human sacrifices, as well as sacrifices of animals and food, to the gods.

Sacrificial killings were part of the ancient lives of Egyptians, Babylonians, Jews and Christians. Christians consider the cruxifiction of Jesus Christ to be a sacrificial death, offered to make amends for the sins of humanity. Biblical historians point out that throughout the Bible, Christ's death is referred to as a sacrificial offering (1 Cor. 5:7, Eph. 5:2, Heb. 10:12–13). In the Old Testament, Leviticus 17:11 talks about the soul being in the blood; thus blood was offered as a sacrifice. (Meat was a commodity that was never wasted needlessly. The slaughtered animal was often consumed before or after the ceremony.)

While this sounds grisly and pagan by our contemporary standards, not all sacrifices were human. Salt was sometimes sacrificed, as was corn and other grains. These items received a blessing and became sacred before being burned in order to reveal knowledge. CAPNOMANCY (divination through smoke), CAUSIMONANCY (divination by throwing combustible objects on a fire), CRITOMANCY (burning of barleycorn), DAPHNOMANCY (divination by the crackle of burning laurel leaves) and SIDEROMANCY (divination by interpreting the twisting and smoldering of pieces of straw or dried peas when thrown on a red-hot grate) were also used.

The Druids, as with many ancient cults, were said to have practiced heiromancy by interpreting the crackles of sound that were made when sacrifices (typically their enemies, or at times specially chosen members of the priesthood) were being burned at the stake.

Further reading

Bletzer, June G. *The Donning International Encyclopedic Psychic Dictionary.* West Chester, Pa.: Whitford Press, 1986.

Campbell, Joseph, ed. *Myths, Dreams and Religion.* New York: Dutton, 1970.

Cumont, Franz. *Oriental Religions in Roman Paganism.* New York: Dover, 1956.

McKenzie, John L. *Dictionary of the Bible.* Milwaukee: Bruce, 1965.

Nichols, Ross. *The Book of Druidry—History, Sites, Wisdom.* London: Aquarian Press, 1990.

Stewart, R. J. *The Elements of Prophecy.* Dorset, England: Element, 1990.

HEPATOMANCY *Divination through observance and interpretation of the surfaces and cavities of animal livers.*

Also known as "liver gazing," this was a common practice of the Etruscans, Hittites and Babylonians. Hepatomancy was performed on the livers of sacrificial animals, typically sheep and oxen, because this organ was thought to be the core of being, much as we believe the heart is the "feeling organ" of the body. The hepatomancy system evolved into the Sumerian method of looking for omens in livers, with more than 6,000 different variations on the size, shape, texture and health of the liver in order to foretell the future and as a means of understanding other omens. Archaeologists have uncovered hundreds of clay models of livers found in the Middle East that were used to train the psychics, called augurs, who practiced hepatomancy (see AUGUR). The Hittites, according to the archaeological discoveries in the central plateau of what is now Anatolian Turkey, performed hepatomancy on sheep as well as partridges; clay models of livers of both these species have been found.

The Etruscans made models out of bronze, as did the Roman and Hittite peoples, and they turned this mantic art into a more diverse system known as HARUSPICY, in which other internal organs were observed to forecast the future. These models have been found with elaborate inscriptions pertaining to and asking for specific blessings from the gods and the heavens etched into the metal. It was the *processus pyramidalis,* the liver's pyramid-shaped projection, that clearly provided the guidance for those who practice hepatomancy. If this area was large and firm, it was a good omen. A small, misshapen *processus pyramidalis* could foretell disaster.

The most spectacular example of the use of hepatomancy occurred in the time of Julius Caesar. In the second week of March, 44 B.C., Caesar's psychic, Spurinna Vestricius, performed hepatomancy with regard to Caesar's continued reign. The liver of a sacrificed sacred bull revealed the absence of the *processus pyramidalis.* Vestricius went straight to Caesar with the dire news. However, the emperor did not heed the Auger's advice to "beware of the Ides of March": Caesar was stabbed to death on March 15th, just as the liver's omen had foretold.

Variations of hepatomancy are practiced to this day.

Further reading

Cumont, Franz. *Oriental Religions in Roman Paganism.* New York: Dover, 1956.

Maven, Max. *Max Maven's Book of Fortunetelling.* New York: Prentice-Hall, 1992.

Opie, Iona, and Moira Tatem. *A Dictionary of Superstitions.* Oxford: Oxford University Press, 1992.

Visions and Prophecies. Mysteries of the Unknown. Alexandria, Va.: Time Life Books, 1990.

HERMETICA *A controversial series of metaphysical writings and dialogues based on the unity of all things.*

The Hermetica is a collection of writings by an unknown Christian author that combines Neoplatonic, Kabbalistic and Christian elements said to be based on ancient Egyptian wisdom. No one is sure of their origin or if they are fakes;

there has been continuing debate about their authenticity since the Renaissance.

The Hermetica has been translated into many languages, including English. The English translations were done by John Everard (1650), J. D. Chambers (1882) and G.R.S. Mead (1906). The Hermetica includes 14 sermons by Poimandres (or Pymander, who was called the "shepherd of men" and "the spiritual leader" of men). It also includes the "Perfect Sermon of Asklepios," 27 excerpts from a collection of the fifth-century writer Stobaeus, along with a selection of sermons or teaching messages on the mystery tradition from the church fathers. These teachings are said to be transcriptions of conversations with the Greek healing gods of Asklepios and Imhotep, along with Isis, Osiris and Thoth.

The name Hermetica is derived from Hermes Trismegistus, or "Thrice-greatest Hermes." Hermes Trismegistus is the principal figure in the Hermetic literature and is thought to be a combination of the Greek god Hermes and the Egyptian god of wisdom, Thoth. Hermes Trismegistus assumes the role of prophet and spiritual leader of the world, the god that will save the world from evil.

The Hermetica is still part of metaphysical teachings.

Further reading

Guiley, Rosemary Ellen. *The Encyclopedia of Witches and Witchcraft*. New York: Facts On File, 1989.

Hall, Manly P. *The Secret Teachings of All Ages*. 1928. Los Angeles: Philosophic Research Society, 1977.

Watson, Donald. *The Dictionary of Mind and Spirit*. New York: Avon, 1991.

HERMETIC ORDER OF THE GOLDEN DAWN *A mystical group dedicated to studying ritual magic and the occult.*

Founded in 1888 by S. L. MacGregor Mathers, in London, the Hermetic Order of the Golden Dawn was dedicated to studying the occult, but it was riddled with fear, intrigue and controversy. The original premise of the organization was to delve into the history of TAROT and NUMEROLOGY, with studies of the Bible, the KABBALAH and ritualistic magic. Later it became synonymous with atypical sexual and ritual practices.

Members of this occultists' society included Aleister Crowley, the poet W. B. Yeats, Arthur Edward Waite (famous for his tarot cards) and Bram Stoker (author of *Dracula*), among others.

See also CROWLEY, ALEISTER; WAITE, ARTHUR EDWARD.

Further reading

Guiley, Rosemary Ellen. *Harper's Encyclopedia of Mystical and Paranormal Experience*. San Francisco: HarperSan Francisco, 1991.

Harper, George Mills. *Yeat's Golden Dawn*. Wellingborough, England: Aquarian Press, 1974.

King, Francis. *Ritual Magic in England, 1887 to the Present Day*. London: Neville Spearman, 1970.

HIGHER SELF *A superintelligence providing knowledge and information, the soul, the self or "the God within."*

Those who divine the future often tap into their higher self in order to make contact with the ethereal world and other higher selves. Sometimes referred to as the overself, it is not to be confused with Freud's version of the superego, which is a socialized self. The higher self is not the conscience, which provides a decision-making process, but rather the voice that brings about creative, intuitive and telepathic thought. It is said to attract us to a higher thinking plane and a metaphysical awareness of all things, including the ability to connect with the AKASHIC RECORDS.

In order to connect with the higher self, it is recommended that the querant choose a quiet place, meditate in calm and stillness and ask for guidance to unite the mind with the higher self. The result, over a period of time, will be to bring the personality more in line with the soul.

Historically, ancient alchemists, in searching for the philosophers' stone (which could turn base metals into gold and then diluted to become the Elixir of Youth), discovered the higher self and considered it to be an all-knowing ability to provide answers to the future and generate the wisdom of all ages.

See also KARMA.

Further reading

Assagioli, Roberto. *Psychosynthesis.* Wellingborough, England: Turnstone Press, 1965.

Hardy, Jean. *A Psychology with a Soul.* London: Routledge & Kegan Paul, 1987.

Watson, Donald. *The Dictionary of Mind and Spirit.* New York: Avon, 1991.

HILTON, WALTER (?–1396) English mystic and psychic.

A member of a mystical group that functioned in the 14th century, Hilton was closely associated with Julian of Norwich, the medieval English mystic and theologian.

Hilton is best remembered for his work *Epistle to a Devout Man in a Temporal Estate.* This treatise offers the principles of spiritual guidance for the wealthy. Hilton believed that one should give up wealth to become close to God. It is a practical guide that considers how one can achieve spiritual transformation through meditation, prayer and contemplation.

Further reading

Happold, F. C. *Mysticism: A Study and an Anthology.* Rev. ed. New York: Penguin, 1970.

Molinari, Paul S. J. *Julian of Norwich: The Teaching of a 14th Century English Mystic.* New York: Longmans, Green & Co., 1958.

HIPPOMANCY *Divination involving the behavior of horses.*

With hippomancy, not only were the behavior and color of horses considered when forecasting the future, but the pattern of their hoof marks and even the amount of dust created by their movement were part of the divination process. It is thought that hippomancy originated in the time of the Celts, who dominated much of western and central Europe during the first millennium B.C. As the Celts moved to the British Isles, so did their prognostication methods, including hippomancy. The Celts are believed to have kept white horses in consecrated groves, training them to walk only in a certain area of the grove. After the horses passed by, psychics or priests interpreted the prints left in the dirt.

Hippomancy considers the behavior and coat color of horses to forecast the future. In addition, the pattern of hoof marks and perhaps even the amount of dust created by their movement were part of the divination process.

Early Germanic people are said to have kept special horses in their temples. The horses were let out of their stalls when the warlords were considering overtaking another tribe. If the first hoof to cross the sacred threshold was a left forefoot it was considered a bad omen; plans for war were put off for another time.

Although it might seem strange today, in England in the 1500s when a farm horse died, the farmer hung the hooves in the farmhouse as a charm against evil. Yet, we consider it extremely lucky to find a horseshoe, and often it is the custom, especially in the American West, to hang a horseshoe in the house or on the wall of a barn to preserve good luck. This is a folk custom dating from the time of hippomancy, with a detour taken when horses began to be shod.

See also ALECTRYOMANCY.

Further reading

Hazlitt, W. Carew. *Faiths and Folklore of the British Isles.* 2 vols. New York: Benjamin Blom, 1965.

Levey, Judith S., with Agness Greenhall, eds. *The Concise Columbia Encyclopedia.* New York: Avon, 1983.

Opie, Iona, and Moira Tatem. *A Dictionary of Superstitions.* Oxford: Oxford University Press, 1992.

HOME, DANIEL DUNGLAS (1833–1886) Scottish-American psychic.

Considered one of the most noted psychics because of his supposed ability to levitate objects and his body at will, Home was tested by the psychical researcher Sir William Crookes, who announced in 1871 that he was convinced of Home's genuine gift for moving objects without touching them. After his death, however, controversy surrounded Home's ability, and many accused him of performing magician's tricks.

Home was born in Scotland, and his psychic gift was apparent as early as four years old, when he predicted the death of his cousin. At age nine, he and his family moved to Connecticut. After his mother's death, Home was thought to be possessed by evil spirits and devils, because he could move objects using the power of his mind and seemingly communicate with the dead. His father hired an exorcist to eradicate the evil from the boy; however, this assistance failed. It is curious that Home's powers should be questioned by his family, since his mother was a noted clairvoyant who predicted the date of her own death. Throughout his life, Home maintained spiritual contact with his mother, and she continued to encourage him to use his psychic powers fully.

Home's psychic abilities included table tipping, rappings, making ghostly hands appear that could shake the hands of the seance participants, guitars that played their own music, moving objects and spelling out messages from the dead through the use of a set of alphabet cards. Home is said to have been able to stretch and shrink his physical body at will; in order to prove that this was not a magician's stunt, he had the sitters at his seances hold his hands and feet. At one event, he was able to stretch his body 11 inches and then reduce his size to less than five feet tall.

It is said that Home held seances in full daylight, thus dispelling any hint of trickery, such as the use of hidden pulleys to move the objects. He felt most psychics of the time were charlatans, swindling money from those who wanted to contact their deceased loved ones. He is noted as the most famous "physical medium" (demonstrating physical feats such as moving furniture or objects without touching them) of the Victorian era, and he also practiced the psychic art of channeling spirits through him.

Home traveled internationally, performing his psychic feats for the nobility, including the Russian czar Alexander II, Napoleon III and Empress Eugenie of France and Kaiser Wilhelm I of Germany. Pale, with light-colored hair, and often

DANIEL DUNGLAS HOME
Daniel Dunglas Home is regarded as one of the most noted psychics because of his ability to levitate his body and various objects at will.

weak from debilitating, recurrent bouts of tuberculosis, Home was a well-dressed figure, demonstrating his powers in the most glittering salons of Europe. In 1856, after giving a demonstration of his powers to Pope Pius IX, Home converted to Catholicism. Later, however, the Catholic Church began taking a dim view of Home's unexplainable gift (according to its doctrine) and expelled him from the church for practicing "sorcery."

The most incredible demonstration of Home's ability to levitate occurred in 1868, at the London home of Lord Adare. In full view of reputable witnesses, Home is said to have levitated out of a third-floor window, moved through space and reentered through another window. All this was reportedly accomplished without Home's ever touching the outside window ledge with any part of his body.

During the resurgence of interest in spiritualism in the 19th century there were many deceptions and hoaxes perpetrated by those with and without psychics gifts. However, Home was never caught cheating or performing any devious acts. While he accepted gifts for his services, Home did not charge fees, unlike other psychics of his and other times. Stage magicians, including Houdini, insisted that they could reproduce all the same "tricks" as Home, including his levitation, but duplications were never achieved, and Home is still considered one of the finest psychics of all time.

Home died of tuberculosis in Europe in 1886. His two autobiographies, *Incidents in My Life* (written in 1862) and *Incidents in My Life, 2d Series* (written in 1872), were published posthumously by his second wife, Julie de Gloumeline. She also published other accounts of her husband's life, including *D. D. Home: His Life and Mission* (1888) and *The Gift of D. D. Home* (1890).

See also LEVITATION; PSYCHIC.

Further reading

Brown, Slater. *The Heyday of Spiritualism.* New York: Hawthorn, 1970.
Edmonds, I. G. *D. D. Home: The Man Who Talked with Ghosts.* Nashville: Thomas Nelson, 1978.
Fairley, John, and Simon Welfare. *Arthur C. Clarke's World of Strange Powers.* New York: Putnam's, 1984.
Guiley, Rosemary Ellen. *Harper's Encyclopedia of Mystical and Paranormal Experience.* San Francisco: HarperSan Francisco, 1991.

HOROSCOPE *In* ASTROLOGY, *a map of the Sun, Moon and planets at the exact moment of one's birth.*

From the Latin and Greek word *horo,* meaning "hour," and *scope,* meaning "watcher," a horoscope can be charted, or cast, for a person, an idea, an event or a country. For example, the United States is said to be a Cancerian country, since the final version of the Declaration of Independence, stating that the original 13 colonies were forming a separate country, was written on July 4, 1776. Some astrologers believe that the United States exhibits the qualities of the Cancer personality and point out that these are illustrated by the country's strong commitment to helping the underdog through programs like the Peace Corps and other national volunteer organizations. Thus by casting a horoscope, one can better understand the qualities of a country.

A birth chart is a horoscope designed specifically for the birth of a person and is calculated from the placement of the Sun, Moon and planets in the zodiac (the part of the heavens that is studied in a horoscope), at the very moment he or she took that first breath. The 12 divisions of a horoscope that represent different categories or areas of life are referred to as houses; the 12 divisions of a horoscope that represent the qualities of the constellations are called signs.

The horoscope is based on mathematical calculations performed with the help of an ephemeris. An ephemeris, available at bookstores and libraries, is an almanac that lists the positions of the Sun, Moon and planets on each day of the year, typically running from 1900 to the year 2000.

Casting a horoscope is a complex process, and astrologers study for years to be able to cast charts. However, there are a number of books and systems that allow even beginning students of astrology to cast them. While casting an accurate chart is crucial, including knowing the exact time, date and place of birth, a gifted astrologer does more by interpreting other factors in the birth chart. Computer software programs now offer every personal computer user the expertise to cast horoscopes; however, the ability to interpret the chart still requires human attention. Computer-cast charts are available through mail-order services and at many metaphysical bookstores.

At one time in history, horoscopes were drawn in a square; today they are drawn in a circle and are divided into 12 houses. There is some controversy regarding this division. Some astrologers believe there should be only eight houses; others disagree on the dominions of each house; a few debate the way each should be divided. The 12 house system is the one most commonly used. Depending on where, the date when, and the hour when one is born, the planets, Sun, Moon and other influences are reflected in the houses. The 12 houses are:

- First house rules the self.
- Second house rules money and possessions.
- Third house rules communication.
- Fourth house rules home life and beginnings.
- Fifth house rules pleasure, creativity, sex.
- Sixth house rules service and health.
- Seventh house rules partnership, business, relationships.
- Eighth house rules death and changes.
- Ninth house rules mental explorations, self-discoveries.
- Tenth House rules career and the public view of the individual.
- Eleventh house rules friends, goals, desires.
- Twelfth house rules the undisclosed side of the individual, his or her personal sorrows and destruction.

Each house represents a different, distinct area of a person's life, unique for each person. Additionally, the astrologer charts in the placement of the Sun, Moon and planets and considers other influences including the aspects, the opposition of major aspects and the transit or passage of planets through the horoscope. It is said that, like blood types, finger prints and DNA, each horoscope is distinctive.

See also ASTROLOGICAL SYMBOLS.

Further reading

Baigent, Campion, and Harvey Baigent. *Mundane Astrology: An Introduction to the Astrological Nations and Groups.* London: Aquarian Press, 1984.

Bosanko, Susan, ed. *Predicting Your Future.* New York: Ballantine Books/Diagram Group. Visual Information Limited, 1983.

Forrest, Steven. *The Changing Sky: The Dynamic New Astrology for Everyone.* New York: Bantam, 1984.

Goodman, Linda. *Linda Goodman's Sun Signs.* New York: Fawcett Columbine, 1978.

Luce, Robert de. *The Complete Method of Prediction.* New York: ASI, 1978.

Wilson, James. *The Dictionary of Astrology.* New York: Samuel Weiser, 1974.

Woolfork, Joanna Martine. *The Only Astrology Book You'll Ever Need.* Landham, Mass.: Scarborough, 1992.

HORSESHOE SPREAD *A TAROT card spread that receives its name from the pattern of placing the cards in the shape of a horseshoe in readings.*

Like the Celtic Cross, Gypsy 7 and other tarot card spreads, the Horseshoe spread is said to be excellent for thorough but quick readings. It is used to answer specific questions, rather than to provide an overview of upcoming events in the querant's life.

In this method all the tarot cards are shuffled by the querant while he or she considers the question to be asked. Sometimes one card is picked by the querant before the reading. He or she will look closely at all the cards, and the one that "speaks" to the querant (i.e., is especially intriguing or inviting) should be used as the significator. This is the card that will represent him or her. It is placed faceup near where the cards in the Horseshoe pattern are spread on the table.

Seven additional cards are drawn from the deck and placed facedown in a semicircle, with the opening of the "horseshoe" facing away from the querant. Some readers draw the cards for the querant, whereas others have the querant place his or her own cards on the table. Working from left to right, the first card indicates past influences; the second presents circumstances and events; the third shows the prospects for the future; the fourth indicates the best way to utilize these prospects; the fifth card tells of relationships and the attitudes of others toward the querant; the sixth card states possible obstacles in the way of the outcome of the querant's question; the last card explains how the outcome of the question will be resolved.

In order to interpret the cards, many readers and psychics suggest referring to a book specifically for tarot. Others suggest using one's own psychic skills and conducting an intuitive reading. With an intuitive reading, the psychic looks at the pictures on the cards, and those objects or figures or colors that first come forward into his or her mind are discussed.

See also CARTOMANCY.

Further reading

Buckland, Raymond. *Secrets of Gypsy Fortunetelling.* St. Paul, Minn.: Llewellyn, 1988.

Cavendish, Richard. *The Tarot.* New York: Putnam's, 1967.

Giles, Cynthia. *The Tarot: History, Mystery and Lore.* New York: Paragon House, 1992.

Innes Brian. *The Tarot: How to Use and Interpret the Cards.* London: Orbis, 1979.

King, Francis, and Stephen Skinner. *Techniques of High Magic.* Rochester, Vt.: Destiny Books, 1991.

Thierens, A. E. *Astrology and the Tarot.* Los Angeles: Newcastle, 1975.

Waite, Arthur Edward. *The Pictorial Key to the Tarot.* New York: Samuel Weiser, 1973.

HYDROMANCY *Divination by staring at water and interpreting what is seen in it.*

Hydromancy is a form of SCRYING. A psychic places a dish of water in an indirect light source and looks at the water, with or without a film of oil added to the surface. He or she interprets the visions seen in the patterns on the surface or through a misty message in the water itself.

Hydromancy was a divination method practiced in ancient Greece. At one time it was so intertwined with Greek mythology that a Greek psychic would only accept water supposedly brought by the sea angel Nereus.

Apparently other psychics were not so choosy and began to practice hydromancy by examining a bowl of water. Other variations of hydromancy include divination by examining and deciphering according to their own set of metaphysical principles the colors, waves, turbulence of the ocean, running water in a stream or river and the pattern of the current in a brook. Some psychics in ancient Egypt preferred using rainwater to forecast the future or interpret omens. Other weather prediction methods include ALECTROMANCY, AEROMANCY and NEPHELOMANCY.

Another variation that was widely used up until the time that Christianity labeled scrying and other divination methods witchcraft was to pour a small amount of oil in a bowl. The future's events could be foretold from the patterns formed on the water. This is documented in the Old Testament (Gen. 44:5, 15), where Joseph used this type of hydromancy. Nostrodamus (1503–1566) used a bowl of water set upon a brass tripod when predicting more than 1,000 future events up to the year 3797, more than half of which are said to have come true.

Almost every child has at one time or other "skipped" a rock across water. If the rock skips three times, a wish will come true. This is actually a variation of the ancient prognostication method of hydromancy, when psychics interpreted the ripples made from drops of water and/or rain.

See also CATOPTROMANCY; ENOPTROMANCY; LECONOMANCY.

Further reading

Bletzer, June G. *The Donning International Encyclopedic Psychic Dictionary.* West Chester, Pa.: Whitford Press, 1986.

Cavendish, Richard, ed. *The Encyclopedia of the Unexplained.* New York: McGraw-Hill, 1974.

Miller, Madeleine S., and J. Lane Miller, eds. *Harper's Encyclopedia of Bible Life.* San Francisco: Harper & Row, 1978.

Roberts, Henry C. *The Complete Prophecies of Nostradamus.* New York: American Book–Stratford Press, 1969.

HYLOMANCY
See PSYCHOMETRY.

IATROMANCY *The art of diagnosing illness psychically.*

Practiced in various forms since early peoples related sickness with physical problems in the body and sought help from "doctors" of their tribes, iatromancy continues today within various tribes of Africa, in Haiti and in the Native American culture through the use of shamanism. Iatromancy, unlike psychic healing, only reveals what is wrong with the patient, but typically, the psychic who uses iatromancy will also heal the invalid. However, technically, those who practice iatromancy do not cure or perform psychic surgery (surgery performed with the bare hands in which the body is opened and closed without instruments and the patient is healed).

American psychic Edgar Cayce (1877–1945) was one of the world's best-known practitioners of iatromancy.

Those psychics who read auras can see when someone is ill because of specific color changes apparent only to the psychic; often they can diagnosis illness. Iatromancy is also practiced by clairvoyants who are able to psychically see and know the health of a querant or someone about whom the querant has questions. Possibly this is done by connecting with the AKASHIC RECORDS. Astrologers who use medical astrology interpret a birth chart to learn the influences on health and illness of a querant and are often able to tell what specific inclination a querant has to a disorder. Palmists look at a querant's life line to point out health challenges.

See also ASTROLOGY; AURAS; CAYCE, EDGAR; CLAIRVOYANCE; LAYING ON OF HANDS; LIFE LINE; PALMISTRY.

Further reading

Achterberg, Jeanne. *Imagery in Healing: Shamanism and Modern Medicine.* Boston: Shambhala, 1985.

Bowers, Barbara. *What Color Is Your Aura?* New York: Simon & Schuster, 1989.

[Cayce, Edgar.] *Edgar Cayce on Healing.* Virginia Beach, Va.: ARC Press, 1969.

Cornell, H. L. *Encyclopedia of Medical Astrology.* St. Paul, Minn.: Llewellyn, 1972.

Hirschfelder, Arlene, and Paulette Molin. *The Encyclopedia of Native American Religions.* New York: Facts On File, 1992.

Sherman, Harold. *"Wonder" Healers of the Philippines.* Los Angeles: DeVross, 1967.

Stern, Jess. *Edgar Cayce, the Sleeping Prophet.* New York: Bantam, 1968.

Weil, Andrew. *Health and Healing: Understanding Conventional and Alternative Medicine.* Boston: Houghton Mifflin, 1883.

I CHING *Chinese system of divination in which one tosses or selects objects that supply information for questions on business, personal or* *psychological concerns, with answers provided by* The Book of Changes.

I Ching (pronounced rather like *e jing*) is considered to be one of the most ancient and enduring of all methods of divination, originating well before written time (most likely prior to 2498 B.C.) and based on an oral divination system. The mystical Fu-Hsi, who is said to have produced the gifts of civilization and is supposed to have been the first emperor of China, supposedly devised the system.

One of the folklore theories of the mystical origin of I Ching explains that while Fu-Hsi was meditating at the side of the Yellow River, a tortoise surfaced and the trigrams (three-line patterns) that explained the yin and yang of I Ching were inscribed on the tortoise's belly plate. Another legend says that the system was revealed to Fu-Hsi through the mythical winged beast that was part horse and had the head of a dragon. The three-line patterns of the I Ching were said to be inscribed on the creature's side.

I Ching (which is loosely translated as *The Book of Changes*) is composed of 64 three-line patterns, made up of broken and unbroken lines, and the interpretation of the symbols. The unbroken is called yang and signifies a yes answer. Yang is active and is considered masculine. The broken is called yin and signifies a no answer. Yin is traditionally passive and is considered feminine.

The original trigram evolved into two sets of trigrams, which are now hexagrams, or six-line

One of the folklore theories on the beginning of the I Ching trigrams explains that while ancient emperor Fu-Hsi was meditating at the side of the Yellow River, a tortoise surfaced and the trigrams were inscribed on the reptile's belly plate.

patterns. During the Chou dynasty, King Wen formalized the system. King Wen's son, the duke of Chou, finished the system and produced the text that is referred to as the Chou-I (or *The Changes of Chou*), with a commentary on the symbols. Confucius, the great Chinese philosopher, is said to have remarked that he wished he could extend his life by 50 years in order to devote that entire time to studying the I Ching. The Taoist wise men believed it to hold great knowledge and valued the text.

It is said that the I Ching gauges the flow of yin and yang energies surrounding the querant and provides assistance on how to proceed in the future that is based on positive and negative forces.

According to historians, the I Ching was unknown in Europe until Marco Polo returned from China, and then it slowly spread through the continent, although it was already widely practiced throughout the Far East. James Legge, an Englishman, translated the I Ching into English in 1854 and was published as *The Yi-King*. Richard Wilhelm translated it into German, and his edition was translated into the English version that is most familiar today. Wilhelm's I Ching included a foreword by psychiatrist Carl Jung. Jung believed that through meditating on the symbols of the I Ching one could delve into the unconscious mind. He believed that the I Ching worked infallibly when one took the time to meditate and internalize the knowledge.

During the 1960s there was a resurgence of interest in the I Ching, and most Americans have at least an idea of the Chinese system. Those who use I Ching do so with three coins (typically, coins that resemble ancient Chinese currency) or yarrow sticks. Some practioners use I Ching cards, much like the ones used for the tarot. The faces on the I Ching cards are unique and include the hexagrams; however, these are a recent invention and not the traditional method of casting I Ching. Stones, dice or any two-sided coin with which the yin and yang symbols can be distinguished can be used.

Each hexagram has a complex meaning that provides more in the line of guidance than a divination of the future. It is recommended that

I CHING
Any two-sided coin can be tossed when using I Ching to predict the future.

the querant have a clear, simple question in mind, although he or she does not have to write it down or speak it aloud in order to receive an answer. Depending on the interpretation of the toss of coins or drawing of sticks or cards, many variations are possible. What seems like a random choice or luck in the toss is said to connect with the ethereal plane, providing advice and explaining the changes that occur at that moment in time.

Although the system is complex and one should refer to a book specifically on this topic, most practioners of I Ching believe that anyone who is willing to meditate and seriously consider the answer to their question can find the guidance needed in the I Ching and interpret the meaning in an I Ching manual.

The Book of Changes is believed by some to be the oldest book in the world. I Ching is used in the GEOMANCY practice of FENG SHUI.

See also SORTILEGE SYSTEMS.

Further reading

Drury, Nevill. *Dictionary of Mysticism and the Esoteric Traditions.* Dorset, England: Prism Press, 1992.

Fox, Judy; Karen Hughes; and John Tampion. *An Illuminated I Ching.* New York: Arch, 1984.

Legge, James. *The I Ching* (translation). New York: Dover, 1963.

Needham, Joseph. *Science and Civilisation in China.* London: Cambridge University Press, 1956.

Palmer, Martin; Joanne O'Brien; and Kwok Man Ho. *The Fortune Teller's I Ching.* London: Century, 1986.

Rossbach, Sarah. *Feng Shui: The Chinese Art of Placement.* New York: Arkana/Penguin, 1991.

Wilhelm, Richard, and Cary F. Baynes. *The I Ching* (translation). Bollingen series 19. Princeton, N.J.: Princeton University Press, 1969.

ICHTHYOMANCY *Divination by observing fish in and out of the water and by examining the internal organs of fish.*

Ichthyomancy is a variation of both HEPATOMANCY (divination by observing animal livers), and HARUSPICY (divination by observing the entrails and bones of animals).

Practiced by the ancient Greeks and other civilizations that put stock in omens, including early Scandinavian peoples, ichthyomancy did not always require the sacrifice of fish. Psychics of the time might meditate as they watched fish within a stream or lake, and then interpret their activity as the omen.

As with other chance meetings of animals, such as in ALECTRYOMANCY, practiced by the ancient Etruscans, depending on the kind of fish, the color, the behavior and even the amount of fish, the psychic makes a determination on everything from the success of a battle to the sex of a forthcoming noble child. With the early tribes in the Scandinavian countries, where much of life centered around fish and fishing, forms of

Ichthyomancy is an ancient practice whereby fish are observed both in and out of the water. Future events are forecast by the examination of their internal organs.

ichthyomancy were treated with great reverence. As with harispicy and divination with sheep and ox bones, fish bones and internal organs were often used as divination tools.

The symbol of the fish has had great significance since the beginning of time, referred to as the Great Mother (a pointed oval sign of the yoni goddess). Fish and the womb became synonymous in Greek times, and throughout Greek mythology, there are references to fertility and fish. Catholic faithfuls inherited the custom of eating fish on Friday from the myth of the fish goddess Aphrodite Salacia. The ancient Celts believed that fish eating could bring new life to a woman's womb.

The fish symbol considered to be part of Christian tradition today was once worshiped throughout the Roman Empire and then was accepted, revised and adopted by early Christians. The fish has come to represent Christ; the Greek word for fish is *ichthys,* which was an acronym for Jesus Christ, Son of God. In another instance, in Exodus 33:11, the promised Jewish messiah is referred to as "Joshua son of Nun." (*Nun* means fish in the sacred Hebrew alphabet.)

Omens derived from ichthyomancy are still accepted today. In some parts of Ireland, it is considered very bad luck to burn fish bones. According to an Irish book of folklore published in 1885, "Fisher-folks will on no account burn the bones of the fish they use as food and the shells of the mussels employed for bait. Hence the rhyme, 'Roast me weel, or boil me weel, Bit dinna burn ma behns, And e'll get plenty 'fish Aboot yir fire-stehns.' "

Further reading

Goldberg, B. Z. *The Sacred Fire.* New York: University Books, 1958.

Hook, S. H. *Middle Eastern Mythology.* Harmondsworth, England: Penguin, 1963.

Opie, Iona, and Moira Tatem. *A Dictionary of Superstitions.* Oxford: Oxford University Press, 1992.

Spence, Lewis. *The History and Origins of Druidism.* New York: Samuel Weiser, 1971.

Walker, Barbara G. *The Woman's Encyclopedia of Myths and Secrets.* New York: Harper Collins, 1983.

INDIAN MEDICINE BUNDLE *Sacred objects believed to have the power to make the wearer clairvoyant.*

In Native American culture and among the Navajo in particular, the Indian medicine bundle (called a "jish") contained specially selected objects chosen for their spiritual significance and were meant to conjure up various powers to help the tribe. They were carried and cared for in medicine bags, small skin pouches. It is unclear whether the bundles were specific to healing, a means of diagnosis (as with IATROMANCY) or were used to psychically call out game animals for the hunt. It was believed that if the bundle was mistreated, terrible misfortune would come to the tribe.

The Indian medicine bundles were rarely on display and were treated with reverence. They held the essence of the spirits and were used in ceremonies, along with preventive or curative religious practices.

The Indian medicine bag also may have held specific articles that the Navajo tribe member had visualized or seen in a dream. The objects were considered to have great power, even, perhaps, protective power, and were held with respect. These objects were also kept for medicinal purposes and to evoke power from the universe and/or native spirits and spirit guides.

Further reading

Bierhorst, John. *The Mythology of North America.* New York: Morrow, 1985.

Hirschfelder, Arlene, and Paulette Molin. *The Encyclopedia of Native American Religions.* New York: Facts on File, 1992.

Paper, Jordan. *Offering Smoke: The Sacred Pipe and Native American Religion.* Moscow: University of Idaho Press, 1988.

Underhill, Ruth M. *Red Man's Religion: Beliefs and Practices of the Indians North of Mexico.* Chicago: University of Chicago Press, 1965.

INFLUENCE LINES *In* PALMISTRY, *the major lines of the palm used to foretell coming events and interpret characteristics of the querant.*

The influence lines, also known as major lines and fundamental lines, consist of the heart, head and life lines. Minor lines, also called secondary lines, are said to include the FATE LINE, the line of Apollo, and the line of Mercury. Palmists differ in their use of terms when giving readings and also debate which lines are the most influential.

The HEART LINE indicates the temperament of the querant and his or her emotional health and satisfaction. The shape, depth and strength of the line are all considered when interpreting an individual's capacity to give and receive love.

The HEAD LINE indicates the ability to understand and reflects the level of reason and cerebral ability; it does not specifically reflect an IQ level. According to the palmist, the length of the line indicates the strength of the intellect, and the longer the better.

The LIFE LINE indicates the health and vitality of the querant. Contrary to what most people believe, a long life line does not indicate a long life but may mark physical well-being.

Further reading

Altman, Nathaniel. *Palmistry Workbook.* New York: Sterling, 1990.

Buckland, Raymond. *Secrets of Gypsy Fortune Telling.* St. Paul, Minn.: Llewellyn, 1988.

Cheiro. *Cheiro's Book of Numbers.* New York: Prentice-Hall, 1988.

———. *The Language of the Hand.* New York: Prentice-Hall, 1987.

Morgan, Chris. *Fortune Telling: How to Predict Your Own Future.* London: Quintet Publishing and Random House, 1992.

Robinson, Rita. *The Palm: A Guide to Your Hidden Potential.* North Hollywood, Calif.: Newcastle, 1988.

INTUITION *The knowing of something without prior knowledge or the use of reason.*

Intuition is a psychic gift accepted by most people, sometimes referred to as "gut feeling," "gut instinct," "hunch," "sixth sense" and "luck." Others see intuition as a blessing from God.

Intuition often defies what is logical and rational, and intuitive feelings are stronger in some people than others. Most parapsychologists believe it is a form of ESP yet have come to understand that it is even more powerful, since it is not simply knowing but affects the feelings, the emotions and the mental abilities. Most psychics believe that all babies are born with a keen sense of intuition. Slowly, typically by the end of the teenage years, individuals lose or quell the ability to connect with this right-brain function. Left-brain reason and logic replace intuition in most people by the time they reach their 20s.

Often physical sensations are combined with intuition. These are manifested in goose bumps, bits of unexplained apprehension, upset stomachs or tinglings of the skin. Sometimes there is a "little voice inside the head" that directs an individual to follow a certain course or play a hunch that seems totally illogical at that instant. These are attributed to clairvoyant messages from the higher self, the guidance of spirits or angels or a closeness with God, among other things.

Females are often said to have a "woman's intuition," that is, a more attuned ability to sense things and accept information without employing rigid forms of analysis. Additionally, those who begin to rely on intuitive guidance discover that the "voices" or "hunches" are correct most of the time, and they begin to trust this facility more often.

Psychiatrist Dr. Carl G. Jung, among others, believed in intuition, and in his book *Psychological Types* (1923) he explained that intuition was not just insight but a creative process that possessed the ability to motivate individuals. Psychics like to explain that anyone can become more intuitive. Through meditation, for example, it is possible to become attuned to the superconscious mind, the all-knowing mind of all things (sometimes called the soul-mind) and thus can unblock creative, inspired and intuitive powers.

See also CLAIRVOYANCE; DEJA VU; EXTRASENSORY PERCEPTION (ESP).

Further reading

Burns, Litany. *Develop Your Psychic Abilities.* New York: Pocket, 1985.

Butler, W. E. *How to Develop Clairvoyance.* 2d ed. New York: Samuel Weiser, 1979.

Gawain, Shakti. *Living in the Light*. San Raphael, Calif.: Whatever Publishing, 1986.

Popper, Karl. *Objective Knowledge*. Oxford: Oxford University, 1971.

Reed, Henry. *Edgar Cayce on the Mysteries of the Mind*. New York: Warner, 1989.

Rogo, D. Scott. *Our Psychic Potentials*. Englewood Cliffs, N.J.: Prentice-Hall, 1984.

Vaughan, Frances. *Awakening Intuition*. Garden City, N.Y.: Anchor/Doubleday, 1979.

IRIDOLOGY *Observance of the iris of the eye to discern personal characteristics or health aspects of the querant.*

Iridology is a variation of PHYSIOGNOMY, devised by the Swiss poet and theologian Johann Kaspar Levater in the late 1700s. It is also the blend of a more ancient Chinese mantic art called OCULO-MANCY, the study of the eyes, and it is one portion of the Five Vital Organs of Chinese face reading. Since most people in the Far East have dark eyes, iridology is commonly practiced only in the West. Various parts of the eye's iris are said to correspond with specific areas of the body and are used to diagnose illness.

In iridology, the color of the querant's iris is studied. Not a divination method in the sense that it does not foretell future events, it is similar to PALMISTRY. Those who practice this art believe that each color reflects specific personality traits. Some iridologists explain that the iris can reveal physical defects and illnesses, weaknesses in the body, and indicates how best to cure the querant; thus iridology can be a form of IATROMANCY (psychically diagnosing illness).

Recent scientific studies have discovered that eye color does seem to demonstrate specific traits. For example, those with dark-colored eyes have quicker reflexes. People with light-colored eyes tend to be more creative and to search for innovative solutions.

An iridologist is someone who practices this form of metaphysics. He or she often categorizes eye color as follows:

Dark blue eyes indicate someone who tends to be sensitive and enjoys cultural pursuits. He or she may also be too sensitive and an elitist, or snobbish.

Light blue eyes indicate a personality ready to commit to a cause, a relationship or a career. He or she may have trouble expressing emotion, although be deeply emotional.

Green eyes indicate someone with a keen sense of the whimsical and a good imagination but has the ability to be practical, too. The green-eyed person may be temperamental and have trouble communicating his or her imaginative ideas.

Hazel eyes indicate a person who has a high energy level, a quick mind and a balanced personality. However, he or she may be too stoic and/or dogmatic.

Brown eyes indicate a person who is faithful and steady, who enjoys being part of a team effort yet can be reserved, too.

Dark brown eyes indicate a person who is passionate about life, able to quickly make decisions, works well under pressure and manages people well. However, he or she may be too impetuous and rash.

Gray eyes indicate a person who can confidently lead others. He or she has a specific purpose and fulfills obligations well; however, this individual may hide talent or intelligence to stay a part of the group.

Those with two different-colored iris are thought to be extremely psychic. They use their abilities naturally, and those who have yet to delve into metaphysics are often encouraged to study it in order to honor their gifts.

See also LEVATER, JOHANN KASPAR.

Further reading

Bletzer, June G. *The Donning International Encyclopedic Psychic Dictionary*. West Chester, Pa.: Whitford Press, 1986.

Maven, Max. *Max Maven's Book of Fortunetelling*. New York: Prentice-Hall, 1992.

JAQUIN, NOEL *(1893–1974) English palmist.*

Jaquin studied with famous 19th-century palmist W. G. Behmam, author of one of the most respected palmistry books, *Hands.* Jaquin, however, did more than just give readings. He had a lifelong determination to see palmistry move from the realm of gypsies and seances into the field of science, as had been the case with GRA-PHOLOGY.

Jaquin theorized that the shape of the fingers, palms and nails and the texture of the skin were a reflection of the personality traits of the individual. According to him, one could detect any number of deviant personality characteristics in the hands. Jaquin worked with Scotland Yard on a number of investigations and is most likely the only palmist to have consulted with the national British police force.

Further reading

Benham, William G. *Hands.* Los Angeles: Newcastle, 1988.

Cheiro. *Cheiro's Book of Numbers.* New York: Prentice-Hall, 1988.

———. *The Language of the Hand.* New York: Prentice-Hall, 1987.

Wilson, Colin. *The Psychic Detectives.* San Francisco: Mercury House, 1985.

JIDDU *See* KRISHNAMURTI, JIDDU.

JONES, CHARLES STANSFELD *(1886–1950) Occultist and Kabbalist.*

Often referred to by his mystical name of Frater Achad, Jones was a student of Aleister Crowley and became Crowley's "mystical son." Jones became known and respected through his work interpreting the KABBALAH with the specific intention of deciphering its connections with tarot and the Tree of Life. Those who debate Jones's respectability say that the explanations he offered are confusing and misconstrue what the ancient works really mean.

Jones is said to have lost his mental acuity after devoting himself to the occult, when he accepted the magical grade of Ipsissimus as part of the HERMETIC ORDER OF THE GOLDEN DAWN. At this level of mystical consciousness, Jones believed that his every action held cosmic significance.

Jones also interpreted the numerical keys in Crowley's *Book of the Law.* He is best known for his books on QBL, which is the Hebrew word for "from mouth to ear." QBL signifies the knowledge of the secret oral tradition of the Kabbalah. Jones's books include *The Bride's Reception* and *Anatomy of the Body of God.*

See also CROWLEY, ALEISTER.

Further reading

Cavendish, Richard, ed. *The Encyclopedia of the Unexplained*. New York: McGraw-Hill, 1974.

Giles, Cynthia. *The Tarot: History, Mystery and Lore*. New York: Paragon House, 1992.

Guiley, Rosemary Ellen. *The Encyclopedia of Witches and Witchcraft*. New York: Facts On File, 1989.

MacKenzie, Norman. *Secret Societies*. New York: Holt, Rinehart & Winston, 1967.

Symonds, John, and Kenneth Grant, eds. *The Confessions of Aleister Crowley; An Autobiography*. London: Routledge & Kegan Paul, 1979.

JUDGE, WILLIAM QUAN *(1851–1896)*
Irish-American theologist and metaphysical scientist.

Judge is best remembered for his work as one of the co-founders of the THEOSOPHICAL SOCIETY, along with Madame Helena Blavatsky (known as H.P.B) and Colonel Henry Steel Olcott (1832–1907), who became the society's first president. He began publishing *The Path* in New York City in 1893, a monthly magazine on the Theosophical movement, and continued to do so until his death. Judge is the author of *The Ocean of Theosophy*, published in the United States in 1893, which some believed to be a consolidated rendition and a complementary volume of Madame Blavatsky's *The Secret Doctrine*.

Judge was trained as an attorney; however, his true vocation was metaphysics. He worked closely with H.P.B. and Colonel Olcott. The Theosophical Society was founded in New York in 1886 and then moved to London before finally finding a permanent home in India. In 1888, Judge assisted H.P.B. in establishing her Esoteric School, and after her death, Judge became joint administrator of the school with Dr. Annie Besant (1847–1933), a British theosophist and social reformer.

After the deaths of H.P.B., Olcott and Judge, the society's influence diminished. However, sections still thrive with adamant followers. The branch that Judge retained continues to distribute information around the world with headquarters based in Pasadena, California, as the Theosophical University Press. The society remains active today with astrologers, psychics and other students of metaphysics supporting the organization.

See also BLAVATSKY, HELENA P.

Further reading

Caldwell, Daniel H. *The Occult World of Madame Blavatsky*. Tucson, Ariz.: Impossible Dream Publications, 1991.

Cranston, Sylvia. *H.P.B.: The Extraordinary Life and Influence of Helena Blavatsky*. Los Angeles: Jeremy P. Tarcher, 1992.

Guiley, Rosemary Ellen. *Harper's Encyclopedia of Mystical and Paranormal Experience*. San Francisco: HarperSan Francisco, 1991.

Judge, William Q. *The Esoteric She: Articles on Madame Blavatsky's Life, Work and Teachings*. Compiled and edited by Daniel H. Caldwell. San Diego: Point Loma, 1991.

———. *Hidden Hints in the Secret Doctrine*. Los Angeles: Theosophy Company, n.d.

Ryan, Charles J. *H. P. Blavatsky and the Theosophical Movement*. Pasadena, Calif.: Point Loma, 1975.

Spence, Lewis. *The Encyclopedia of the Occult*. New York: Carol, 1984.

JUNG, DR. CARL G. *(1875–1961)* *Pioneer in mythic symbolism as it related to human consciousness; the father of analytical psychology.*

Complicated and complex, Jung's ideas and theories have shaped our time and provide a basis for modern-day acceptance of metaphysics. Jung spent his entire life studying people and human ability. More than analyzing the mind as did Freud, Jung's one-time mentor, Jung studied the collective unconsciousness. Jung theorized that through the collective unconsciousness (much like a large library of thoughts that are accessible to all, referred to by some as the AKASHIC RECORDS) thoughts can be passed from one individual to another, from one period of time to another or from a spiritual entity to a human. People who display the powers of CLAIRVOYANCE and TELEPATHY can supposedly connect with this library of thought.

Unlike Freud, who believed that all people were driven by sexual forces beyond their control, Jung felt that the spirit was the compelling power and that dreams were the private messages and languages of the spirit; he believed that dead spirits could communicate with the living. This philosophical division was but one that split mentor and pupil.

Jung was born in Switzerland; his mother and both his grandmothers were mediums, as were other members of his family. He studied medicine and other physical sciences and practiced medicine in Basel and Paris. Throughout his life, Jung had metaphysical experiences; for example, during one heated conversation with Freud, it is said that he exhibited psychokinetic powers. (Psychokinetic powers are energy that comes from the mind through profound concentration and give one the ability to change form, position and structure of an energy field. For example, this energy could be used to levitate objects.)

After his break with Freud, Jung experienced a long period of self-examination that is often referred to as his psychotic phase. During this time, he believed he could contact and connect with the world of the dead. This time period and his metaphysical experiences are detailed in his autobiographical account, *Memories, Dreams, Reflections.*

Jung was instrumental in explaining the two psychological types of introvert and extrovert, and he suggested that humans are the sum of the emotions, thoughts, feeling, sensation and intuition and the images of masculine and feminine, along with the collective unconsciousness. These thoughts were included in his *Psychological Types* (translated 1923). Quests for knowledge on mythology, GNOSIS, Taoism, the I CHING, the TAROT and other mystical systems and methods including alchemy and DREAM INTERPRETATIONS were interwoven throughout Jung's life.

Jung was a firm believer in reincarnation and felt his own life was not karma but a thirst for knowledge and a quest to piece together the mythical unknown. He believed that the confrontation of death and the selection of a life partner were reflections of past experiences, mythology and the collective unconsciousness. His analytical method reflected the belief that a patient can achieve a state of individuation or wholeness of self through understanding how one is a product or part of the universal unconscious, rather than a product of physical forces.

In the years before his death, Jung had a near-death experience. He reported that he saw his body floating through the air and got a bird's-eye view of the Middle East. After the experience, Jung's attitude changed remarkably and he became happy and satisfied.

In his last years, Jung became increasingly immersed in spiritual dimensions. Just before his death in 1961, he had a visionary dream of the end of his physical life. The dream included the symbol of a tree with roots interlaced with gold, which is the alchemist's symbol of completion. He died in Zurich, Switzerland, three days later.

Jung is known internationally for the way his principles apply to religion, mysticism and even quantum physics and the relationship between psychotherapy and metaphysical beliefs. His other works include *Aion; Man and His Symbols* and *Mysterium Coniunctionis.*

See also ASTRAL PLANE.

Further reading

Campbell, Joseph, ed. *The Portable Jung.* New York: Penguin, 1971.

Fodor, Nandor. *Between Two Worlds.* West Nyack, N.Y.: Parker, 1964.

Giles, Cynthia. *The Tarot: History, Mystery and Lore.* New York: Paragon House, 1992.

Guiley, Rosemary Ellen. *Harper's Encyclopedia of Mystical and Paranormal Experience.* San Francisco: HarperSan Francisco, 1991.

Jung, C. G. *Aion: Researches into the Phrenomenology.* Princeton, N.J.: Princeton University Press, 1968.

———. *Aspects of the Feminine.* Princeton, N.J.: First Princeton, 1982.

———. *Dreams.* Princeton, N.J.: Princeton University Press, 1974.

———. *Memories, Dreams, Reflections.* Recorded and edited by Anilea Jaffe. New York: Random House, 1961.

O'Connor, Peter. *Understanding Jung, Understanding Yourself.* New York/Mahwah, N.J.: Paulist Press, 1985.

KABBALAH   *The Hebrew system of medieval mysticism, magic and religion.*

The Kabbalah (with alternate spellings of Kabalah, Cabalah, Qabala and others) is said to be a blend of powerful God-inspired magic and mysticism combined with astrology, along with strong influences from the TAROT and NUMEROLOGY. The Kabbalah and the study of Kabbalistic teaching are shrouded with mystery and mysticism.

The word *Kabbalah* is Hebrew for "that which is received," implying a secret oral tradition passed from scholarly mentor to novitiate. It is said that God taught the Kabbalah to the angels, who in turn taught it to Adam after he and Eve were expelled from the Garden of Eden. Thus, through the knowledge secretly available and placed in Kabbalah, the angels provide all individuals (beginning with Adam and Eve) with a way to return to God.

· Some historians believe that the greatest work of the Kabbalah is the *Sefer Yetzirah*, the Book of Creation (also called the Book of Foundation), thought to have been written in the first century and attributed to a rabbi, Akiba ben Joseph. This former shepherd formed a school to study the Kabbalah and had more than 24,000 followers before his martyrdom by the Romans about A.D. 138. The Kabbalah was further investigated in the teachings of a Spanish philosopher, Ibn Gabirol, and evolved to encompass all Hebrew mystical teachings.

In the 13th century a Spanish religious scholar, Moses de Leon of Guadalajara, interpreted the *Sefer-ha-Zohar* or *Zohar* (known as the Book of Splendor or Books of Lights). De Leon claimed that the actual author was the mythical mystic Simeon ben Yoah. That claim has been disproved; it is believed that de Leon was the real author of this masterpiece of mystical thought. Medieval scholars studied the Hebrew teachings of the Old Testament hoping to discover hidden truths and messages concealed from the uninitiated. They devised a complex system that produced secret information from the text, with a relationship between words and numbers, a form of numerology known as GEMATRIA.

The Kabbalists do not follow a specific teaching order or religious dogma but believe instead in unity with family and friends and education. They do not believe one must separate oneself or become a religious scholar in order to be true to God. Rather, they recognize that through love of family and community one comes closer to God. Kabbalists also believe in reincarnation, and the Kabbalah is strongly aligned to the tarot and ASTROLOGY, along with magic and mysticism, as well as gematria.

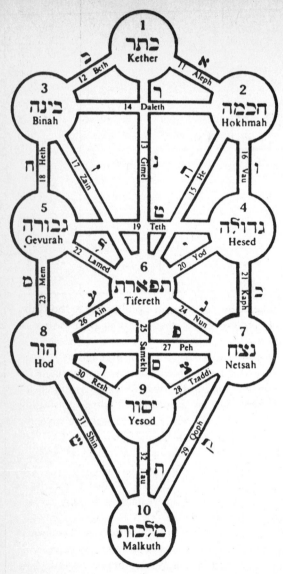

and hidden messages in the Old Testament, the Kabbalists believed that they could construct magical spaces and conjure powerful invocations. Unlike previous systems of magic, the Kabbalah incorporated another dimension, that of employing the power beyond astral influences, including the strength and spirit of angels, archangels and God's potency.

The Kabbalah has inspired New Age metaphysical investigation and many interpretations of the Tree of Life (the physical format of the Kabbalah). The Tree of Life is an inverted tree and is duplicated in many metaphysical philosophies. The Kabbalah's version is drawn to indicate how concepts of the world came into being and how the soul understood knowledge before accepting a body. The 10 circles of the Tree of

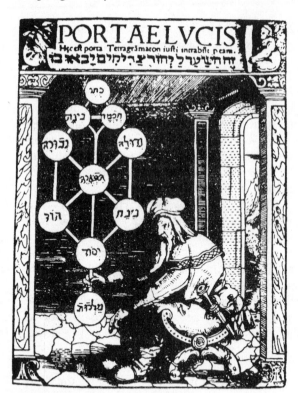

KABBALAH
An illustration from Paulus Riccius's 1515 manuscript "Porta Lucis" ("Gate of Light") symbolizes the sephirotic tree, or Tree of Life. The Kabbalah, with alternative spellings including Qabala, Kabalah and Cabalah, is said to be a blend of powerful God-inspired divination and mysticism.

KABBALAH
The Tree of Life is a mystical belief based in part on traditional Judaism. The Tree of Life is said to be the map so that when one's lessons are understood, one can return to God.

Kabbalists contend that numbers can have great hidden power. As in numerology, every letter of a name is assigned a number. The numbers are then added and the total is believed to be a reflection on the person's life. For example, one might be found to be a healer, an artist, or a teacher. When numbers were assigned to names

Life connect to show the flowing force of the spirit and the levels of mystical understanding. It is a map from which the learned can understand their life lesson and thus return to God. Eliphas Levi (1810–1875), a sometime magician and a full-time mystic, was the first to point out that the 22 cards of the tarot's MAJOR ARCANA appear to have a correlation with the Kabbalistic Tree of Life.

The Kabbalah is based on the doctrines of the Hebrew faith. However, strictly speaking it is not part of Jewish religious practices but rather a philosophical point of instruction included in the folklore and traditions of the religion.

See also LEON, MOSES BEN SHEM TOV DE; LEVI, ELIPHAS.

Further reading

Fortune, Dion. *The Mystical Qabalah*. 1935. Reprint. York Beach, Maine: Samuel Weiser, 1984.

Franck, Adolphe. *The Kabbalah*. New York: Bell, 1978.

Giles, Cynthia. *The Tarot: History, Mystery and Lore*. New York: Paragon House, 1992.

Ponce, Charles. *Kabbalah: An Introduction and Illumination for the World Today*. Wheaton, Ill.: Theosophical Publishing House, 1973.

Schmaker, Wayne. *The Occult Sciences in the Renaissance*. Berkeley and Los Angeles: University of California Press, 1972.

Scholem, Gershom. *Origins of the Kabbalah* (translation). Princeton, N.J.: Jewish Publication Society, 1987.

KAHUNAS *Practitioners of the ancient Hawaiian Huna religion; the Keepers of the Secret.*

Considered magical priests somewhat similar to the Native American shamans, the Kahunas believed that each person had three souls (often compared to Freud's theory of self). The three souls were the low self, located in the solar plexus; the middle soul, which was normal consciousness; and the high self, the all-knowing self that could be contacted through TELEPATHY and CLAIRVOYANCE. It was also believed that all living things could connect mentally through the *aka*, the pathway of universal knowledge. The energy that carries this knowledge is referred to as *Mana* and is directly tied to the various soul levels.

The Kahunas were said to have powerful psychic skills and extensive healing powers along with the ability to recall that which was known in previous lives. Max Freedom Long, a schoolteacher who spent 14 years in Hawaii, chronicled much about the Huna religion, devoting his life to deciphering the remnants of the fading order. Through his work and collections and interpretation of folklore, it is known that Huna is based on mythology and contains stories of the civilizations of Lemuria and Atlantis.

The Huna religion evolved from a point in which there were three levels of priests. The Intuitionists, or Order of Kane, was the highest order of priesthood. The Intellectuals, or the Order of Long, were thought to be the gods of medicine, meteorology and agriculture. And the Emotional, which became known as the Order of Ku, was the group associated with fertility, rain, war and the unconscious nature of all living things.

According to scholars, Huna, with Kahunas practicing the art of healing, psychic powers, prophetic dream interpretation and magic, was diluted over the centuries. By the time Captain Cook arrived in the islands, few Kahunas were able to tie into the psychic powers of their predecessors. However, the Order of Huna International was once more revived, through Long's work, and reorganized in 1973. Serge King can be thanked for revitalizing the traditional practices. He wrote about Huna and Kahunas in his book, *Kahuna Healing*. One of the new books on the subject, *Huna Awareness: The Wisdom of the Ancient Hawaiians*, was written by a certified Kahuna priest, Dr. Erika S. Nau, who holds a teaching certificate from the Una Research Associates. Dr. Nau and others stress that by using the techniques perfected by the Kahunas, one can be healed and heal others and use dreams as a source of guidance from the higher self.

Further reading

Hoffman, Enid. *Huna: A Beginner's Guide*. Gloucester, Mass.: Para Research, 1976.

King, Serge. *Kahuna Healing*. Wheaton, Ill.: Theosophical Publishing House, 1983.

Long, Max Freedom. *Recovering Ancient Magic.* London: Rider Publishers, 1936.

———. *The Secret Science behind Miracles.* Santa Monica, Calif.: De Vross, 1948.

Nau, Erika S. *Huna Awareness: The Wisdom of the Ancient Hawaiians.* York Beach, Maine: Samuel Weiser, 1990.

KARDEC, ALLAN (1804–1869) *French psychic and spiritualist.*

Allan Kardec was the pseudonym of the French psychic Hypolyte Leon Denizard Rivail; he believed that both Allan and Kardec were names he had had in past lives, and he adopted them as his magical name. Kardec strongly supported the concept of reincarnation, and his written work reflected the fact that spiritual progress is effected by a series of compulsory reincarnations. This was an innovative concept at the time.

Kardec was so adamant in his convictions that he refused to consider the opinions of others. He and his followers ignored advances in metaphysics, and because of his great influence, the French remained 20 years behind other countries in their investigation of the occult.

Kardec is best known for establishing the Parisian Society for Spiritualistic Studies and was the editor of *La Revue Spirite.* While Kardec's psychic gifts are often overlooked in England and the United States, his is almost a household name in France and Brazil.

Kardec is best known for his books, which include *The Spirit's Book, The Medium's Book* and *Spiritualist Initiation.*

Further reading

Brown, Slater. *The Heyday of Spiritualism.* New York: Hawthorn, 1970.

Fodor, Nandor. *Encyclopedia of Psychic Science.* New York: University Books, 1966.

Psychic Voyages. Mysteries of the Unknown. Alexandria, Va.: Time Life Books, 1990.

KARMA *Actions followed by consequences, according in Hinduism, Buddhism, New Age thinking, metaphysics and the Theosophy movements.*

Karma encompasses the sum of all past lives and so is the explanation of reincarnation. Everything that has happened in previous incarnations affects the challenges or accomplishments in the present life. Following the principle of karma, people are the result of their prior experiences, relationships and deeds; their birthplace, appearance, abilities and life are a consequence of these foregoing experiences.

Many believe that karma can be compared to lessons one might learn in school. In what may be considered a negative situation, the lesson is to grow and overcome the circumstance. Others believe that challenging situations or extremely good fortune are the result of a past-life (negative or positive) experience. Therefore, there is no good karma or bad karma but simply the laws of nature and the sum total of all actions. The ancient symbol for karma is the endless knot, referring to the fact that the intricacies of karma are profound and ongoing.

Karma is the Sanskrit word for "deed." It is the sum of one's accomplishments, successes, failures and positive and negative experiences, as well as familial, regional, national and global associations occurring in previous lives. In Buddhism and Zen Buddhism, it is the universal law of cause and effect. These philosophies hold that karma is caused by words, deeds, acts and thoughts and what comes from intent, even if the intended action is not carried out. In a Western view, karma is a law of causation. Simply put, our present actions will shape our future, and perhaps future lives. Those who believe in karma understand that while we may be a product of our past-life experiences, we can also alter and shape our present life and become architects of our present and our future. This is what is commonly referred to as free will. As metaphysical scholars point out, karma can be made to sound like fatalism only if there is an absolute belief of cause and effect that is rigid. But if the effect is dynamic, always shifting, then past causes and present effects can be changed.

According to traditional astrological teaching in India, karma is the progression and journey of one's soul through his or her various lives. It is the influence of the acts of previous lives, the influences in this present life and the acts or actions that have not yet been taken. The Christian equivalent is the old adage. "As ye shall sow, so shall ye reap." However, most Christian philosophies discount past-life conjecture and the theory of karma.

People who have undergone past-life regression—that is, been hypnotized in order to remember previous incarnations—often fail scientific and clinical tests. Scientists believe that heredity and environment are the only factors in personality and physical characteristics and do not accept the idea that there may be other variations that could be the result of previous lives.

See also AKASHIC RECORDS; REINCARNATION.

Further reading

The Encyclopedia of Eastern Philosophy and Religion. Boston: Shambhala, 1989.

Guiley, Rosemary Ellen. *Tales of Reincarnation.* New York: Pocket Books, 1989.

Hall, Manly P. *Reincarnation: The Cycle of Necessity.* Los Angeles: Philosophical Research Society, 1956.

Kapleau, Philip. *The Wheel of Life and Death: A Practical and Spiritual Guide.* New York: Doubleday, 1989.

Motoyama, Hiroshi, Ph.D. *Karma and Reincarnation.* Translated by Rande Brown Ouchi. New York: Avon, 1992.

Woodward, Mary Ann. *Edgar Cayce's Story of Karma: God's Book of Remembrance.* New York: Coward, McCann & Geoghegan/Edgar Cayce Foundation, 1971.

Woolfork, Joanna Martine. *The Only Astrology Book You'll Ever Need.* Landham, Mass.: Scarborough, 1992.

KELIDOMANCY
Divination using a suspended object in order to foretell the future and/or respond to a querant's questions.

Kelidomancy, as with CLEIDOMANCY, is another term meaning dowsing and penduluming. Uri Geller practices this mantic art.

See also DOWSING; PENDULUM PREDICTIONS.

Further reading

Fodor, Nandor. *Encyclopedia of Psychic Science.* New York: University Books, 1966.

Geller, Uri, and Guy Lyon Playfair. *The Geller Effect.* New York: Henry Holt, 1986.

Roberts, Kenneth. *Henry Gross and His Dowsing Rod.* Garden City, N.Y.: Doubleday, 1951.

KELLNER, KARL *(?–1935) German psychic.*

Kellner is said to have channeled three spirits, two of them Arabs and one a Hindu, who led to his understanding of the occult knowledge of the ages. Kellner is best remembered for organizing an occult association called the Ordo Templi Orientis (OTO), or order of Oriental Templars, in 1912. It was named after the medieval Knights Templar, who held great, some say magical, powers.

Kellner believed that through the sexual yoga he learned in the Middle East he possessed knowledge that could open up all Masonic and Hermetic secrets. Aleister Crowley was also a follower of sexual magic. Crowley eventually succeeded Kellner as head of OTO in 1922.

See also CROWLEY, ALEISTER; HERMETIC ORDER OF THE GOLDEN DAWN.

Further reading

Guiley, Rosemary Ellen. *The Encyclopedia of Witches and Witchcraft.* New York: Facts On File, 1989.

MacKenzie, Norman. *Secret Societies.* New York: Holt, Rinehart & Winston, 1967.

Symonds, John, and Kenneth Grant, eds. *The Confessions of Aleister Crowley: An Autobiography.* London: Routledge & Kegan Paul, 1979.

KEPHALONOMANCY
Ancient divination method of pouring lighted carbon on a baked goat's head to determine guilt or innocence.

Used during the time of the Lambards, an ancient Germanic people who lived in what is now Hungary and Austria (c. A.D. 547), kephalonomancy was routinely practiced to determine the guilt or innocence of those suspected of crimes.

Using the baked head of a goat (or donkey), lighted carbon was poured on the head while the names and alleged crimes of the accused were announced. If crackling was heard when the suspect's name was spoken, the accused was guilty. If there was no sound or the sound was interpreted to mean innocence, the accused would go free.

Kephalonomancy is somewhat similar to CAPNOMANCY, in which divination occurs through interpretation of smoke produced from various flammable objects, and PYROMANCY, in which the charred remains of objects are interpreted.

See also DAPHNOMANCY.

Further reading

Bletzer, June G. *The Donning International Encyclopedic Psychic Dictionary*. West Chester, Pa.: Whitford Press, 1986.

Goldberg, B. Z. *The Sacred Fire*. New York: University Books, 1958.

Opie, Iona, and Moira Tatem. *A Dictionary of Superstitions*. Oxford: Oxford University Press, 1992.

Visions and Prophecies. Mysteries of the Unknown. Alexandria, Va.: Time Life Books, 1990.

KING, FRANCIS (1904–1970) *English psychic and metaphysical historian.*

King is best known for his work recording theories of the magical side of metaphysics. As a psychic and historical writer, King has produced numerous books on the subject of magic, secret rituals and the occult. They include *Ritual Magic in England, 1887 to the Present Day* (1970), *Sexuality, Magic, and Perversion* (1971), and *The Secret Rituals of the O.T.O.* (1973). His newest and best book on the subject of ritual magic is *Techniques of High Magic* (1991).

With Israel Regardie, King revived the HERMETIC ORDER OF THE GOLDEN DAWN, originally founded in the late 1800s.

Further reading

Guiley, Rosemary Ellen. *Harper's Encyclopedia of Mystical and Paranormal Experience*. San Francisco: HarperSan Francisco, 1991.

Harper, George Mills. *Yeat's Golden Dawn*. Wellingborough, England: Aquarian Press, 1974.

King, Francis. *Ritual Magic in England, 1887 to the Present Day*. London: Neville Spearman, 1970.

King, Francis and Stephen Skinner. *Techniques of High Magic*. Rochester, Vt.: Destiny Books, 1991.

KINGSFORD, ANNA BONUS (1846–1888) *English psychic.*

Kingsford was a contemporary of Madame Helena Blavatsky, Macgregor Mathers and other mystics of the time. She specifically studied and practiced dream telepathy and prophetic DREAM INTERPRETATIONS along with a practice she termed "esoteric Christianity" that derived occult meaning in Bible teaching.

With Edward Maitland, Kingsford cofounded and organized the Hermetic Society at about the same time that the Hermetic Order of the Golden Dawn was started. She is best known for her work on mysticism and a book on the subject, published in 1882, called *The Perfect Way*.

Further reading

Brown, Slater. *The Heyday of Spiritualism*. New York: Hawthorn, 1970.

Drury, Nevill. *Dictionary of Mysticism and the Esoteric Traditions*. Dorset, England: Prism Press, 1992.

Ullman, M., ed. *Dream Telepathy*. New York: Macmillan, 1973.

KIRLIAN PHOTOGRAPHY *The art of photographing the auras of living and inanimate objects.*

The color vibrations seen in Kirlian photographs are said to coincide with the brilliant colors of auras seen by some psychics. Some people see Kirlian photography as a substantiation of the aura surrounding all things. The camera used in Kirlian photography is able to convert nonelectrical properties into electrical properties and thus capture images on film. They are technically called electrographic photographs.

Semyon D. Kirlian is credited with the discovery of the photography that bears his name. A Russian electrician, part-time inventor and photographer, he is said to have stumbled on the concept while fixing a piece of equipment in the 1930s. As with many great discoveries and inventions, others had previously been working on similar concepts. In 1898 Yakov Narkevich Yokdo displayed an early form of Kirlian photography at an exhibition of what he referred to as mystical energy coming from various objects.

Along with his wife, Valentina, who was a biologist, Kirlian devised a system to capture on film the aura emanating from all things, including plants, people and inanimate objects. The object that is to be photographed is placed on the film, which is a negative electrode. Then voltage is passed between two electrodes, and a corona (the aura) is produced. This corona is created when the electrons become excited and move about, and the electromagnetic activity inevitably affects the molecules in the photographic chemical. Scientists say that photos of any object taken in this way will have an aura, which does not indicate anything metaphysical at all.

Critics of Kirlian photography add that the aura energy fields photographed are merely changes in body temperature or the skin's surface chemistry.

Those who expound on the validity of Kirlian photography explain that the emanations and radiations are photographed by a high-energy system, with the images captured on film but not seen by the eye, and are a documentation of the ethereal or spiritual body. The energy field (or aura) changes depending on the stress level and health of the individual, and the colors are usually indigo, blue, aqua, pink and pale yellow. The energy field extends out from the object or body, and photos have shown that when an object (such as a plant) is moved, the Kirlian photo shows a change in the colors. If a leaf is removed from the plant, the energy sparks and changes color, and the shape of the leaf that is no longer there often continues to appear in the photograph.

Interestingly enough, when two people place their fingertips on the film, the Kirlian photograph shows that the auras push away from each other. However, when family members and, especially, married couples perform this experiment, the auras often merge.

In Russia's Moscow Institute of Normal Physiology, Kirlian photography is used as a device to indicate ailments such as cancer and tumors and is used to detect these disorders along with X rays, magnetic resonance imaging (MRI) and computerized axial tomography (CT) scans. Those who believe that the possibilities of Kirlian photography as a diagnostic tool have yet to be realized explain that electrographic photography is far safer than traditional X rays, since the system does not damage the tissues of the body. They believe that it will become the preferred examination method of the 21st century.

See also AURAS.

Further reading

Becker, Robert O., and Gary Selden. *The Body Electric: Electromagnetism and the Foundation of Life.* New York: Quill/Morrow, 1985.

Bowers, Barbara. *What Color Is Your Aura?* New York: Simon & Schuster, 1989.

Gerber, Richard. *Vibrational Medicine.* Santa Fe, N.Mex.: Bear & Co., 1988.

Guiley, Rosemary Ellen. *Harper's Encyclopedia of Mystical and Paranormal Experience.* San Francisco: HarperSan Francisco, 1991.

Kilner, Walter J. *The Aura.* New York: Samuel Weiser, 1973.

Krippner, Stanley, and Rubin, Daniel. *The Kirlian Aura.* New York: Doubleday, Anchor Press, 1974.

Ostrander, Sheila, and Lynn Schroeder. *Psychic Discoveries behind the Iron Curtain.* Englewood Cliffs, N.J.: Prentice-Hall, 1970.

Tomplins, Peter. *The Secret Life of Plants.* New York: Harper & Row, 1973.

KNIGHT, JZ *(1946–   ) American psychic and channeler.*

In the 1980s Knight came to fame in the United States by supposedly channeling an entity who is more than 35,000 years old, known as Ramtha, the Enlightened One. Part of the excitement regarding Knight's channeling abilities was her celebrity endorsements, including that of actress Shirley Maclaine.

Knight, who was born Judith Darlene Hampton on March 16, 1946, in Dexter, New Mexico, got her nickname by condensing the *J* for Judy and Z for "zebra," because of her love of wearing black-and-white clothing. She had no specific psychic talents as a child or teenager, and it was not until she had a psychic reading in the 1970s that Knight was told that "the most awesome power" was walking with her. However, the power did not speak or make itself known until 1977. Ramtha appeared to Knight as a glowing man while she and one of her sons were playing with toy pyramids in the kitchen of their modest home.

Ramtha is extremely egotistical and loves to chat about himself and his own accomplishments. When channeling the entity, Knight becomes a regal figure of nobility with a deep voice alteration. Critics have questioned the originality of Ramtha's sermons, saying that his lectures are filled with commonplace thoughts. According to them, Ramtha is simply repeating, albeit in a somewhat different fashion, the very same concepts and ideals professed by others of spiritual insight.

Knight's career as a channeler has been filled with spectacular ups and downs. The peaks have been dazzling; her reputation was flying high after the publication of Maclaine's book *Dancing in the Light* and the publicity brought about by the book's mention of Knight. JZ became a media darling after the actress proclaimed that in a past life she had been Ramtha's brother on Atlantis. But her reputation suffered when Knight bought an extensive Washington State ranch and lavishly decorated the 13,000-square-foot ranch house. Her plan was to raise Messiah Arabian horses, which were said to be housed in stables with exclusive appointments. With Ramtha's financial counseling, a number of Knight's disciples invested heavily in the ranch, hoping to make incredible amounts of money. However, when the investment money was reportedly lost, misused or mismanaged, many became extremely dissatisfied and resentful, resulting in a loss of credibility for Knight.

Knight no longer channels Ramtha to standing-room only crowds, though she continues to channel privately.

Further reading

Guiley, Rosemary Ellen. *Harper's Encyclopedia of Mystical and Paranormal Experience.* San Francisco: HarperSan Francisco, 1991.

Kautz, William H., and Melanie Branon. *Channeling: The Intuitive Connection.* San Francisco: Harper & Row, 1987.

Klimo, Jon. *Channeling: Investigations on Receiving Information from Paranormal Sources.* Los Angeles: Jeremy P. Tarcher, 1987.

Knight, JZ. *A State of Mind: My Story.* New York: Warner, 1984.

KRAFFT, KARL ERNEST (1900–1945)
Swiss astrologer and cosmologist.

Krafft is known as the astrologer who worked with the Nazi propaganda machine in an attempt to undermine the morale of the Allied troops and British citizens. The psychic skills of this pro-Fascist Swiss were brought to the attention of the Nazis when he correctly predicted an attempt on Hitler's life and was temporarily jailed for possessing this information. When the Nazis began searching for an expert in the prophecies of Nostradamus, which were to be interpreted to indicate Nazi supremacy and to use astrology in psychological warfare, Krafft was drummed into service. As a genuine expert on the great prophet's predictions, Krafft began working in Berlin in January 1940. At the same time, the Nazis banned all privately published occult material. Throughout a major portion of World War II, Krafft interpreted Nostradamus's prophecies only in ways that indicated Nazi dominance and the expectation that the Axis powers would rule the world.

While others doubted that these prophecies were correct, Krafft firmly believed that Germany's victory over all its enemies had been predicted in the obscure codes of Nostradamus. Hundreds of thousands of pamphlets detailing Krafft's deciphering of the medieval prophet's words were distributed throughout Europe and air-dropped over the British Isles.

It is believed that many of Germany's attacks were forecast through Krafft's calculations of the planets and their astrological influences. To defend itself against this astrological battle plan, the British Defence Department hired its own astrologer, Louis De Wohl, to interpret astrological charts to discover what Hitler would do. De Wohl was called the British "Secret Service" astrologer. The British government quietly reverted to more traditional types of warfare, but only after magazines, printed in German, were dropped over the German-occupied countries offering bogus astrological predictions to counteract any predictions made by the Nazis.

Krafft eventually fell out of favor with the Germans. Some say he had the audacity to claim that General Montgomery's astrological chart indicated that he was a better soldier, including many more favorable aspects than did that of Field Marshal Rommel. Or, another theory indicates, Krafft was found guilty of encouraging Rudolph Hess's defection to the English and his fleeing of the Third Reich. It was said that Hess deserted because he was "crazed by astrologers." Hundreds of astrologers, clairvoyants, radiesthetics, faith healers and other practitioners who were even remotely connected with metaphysics were arrested by the Gestapo, imprisoned and, in some cases, exterminated. Many military historians believe that the Nazi war machine simply had to blame Hess's defection on someone, since it was feared that it would demoralize the armed forces. Books on metaphysics were burned, occult literature was seized and private collections were destroyed. It became dangerous even to be seen looking at metaphysical material.

Like millions of others, Krafft was imprisoned by the Nazis. The exact time and place is unclear, but it has been reported that in 1945 Krafft died while being transported to (or while held in) the prison camp at Buchenwald, Germany.

Further reading

Cosmic Connections. Mysteries of the Unknown. Alexandria, Va.: Time Life Books, 1990.

Howe, Ellic. *Astrology: A Recent History Including the Untold Story of Its Role in World War II*. New York: Walter, 1967.

————. *Astrology and the Third Reich*. Wellingborough, England: Aquarian Press, 1984.

Woolfork, Joanna Martine. *The Only Astrology Book You'll Ever Need*. Landham, Mass.: Scarborough, 1992.

KRISHNAMURTI, JIDDU (1895–1986)
Spiritual teacher and metaphysical leader.

Krishnamurti was discovered in India by Dr. Annie Besant and the Reverend C. W. Leadbeater of the Theosophical Society. It was predicted by Besant (and Madame Blavatsky) that a World Teacher and Lord, termed a *bodhisattva*, would be found. Besant and Leadbeater knew that Krishnamurti was the future teacher because of his remarkable aura. Krishnamurti later denied his position as a chosen world leader.

Leadbeater, using clairvoyance and psychic skills, tapped into the AKASHIC RECORDS, and through past-life recollections discovered that Krishnamurti had been a healer and teacher for a number of lifetimes. Leadbeater also said that the young Krishnamurti was a follower of Buddha. In 1910, Krishnamurti was invited by the Theosophical Society to enter the Great White Brotherhood of which Jesus, the Comte de St. Germain, Serapis and other teachers were a part. According to notes in his book, *At the Feet of the Masters,* Krishnamurti explained that being accepted into the prestigious group was like a great sunshine to the soul.

A year later, Leadbeater established the Order of the Star of the East, with Krishnamurti as its leader. After the announcement, plans to build U.S. headquarters moved quickly, and Besant bought land in Ojai, California. The organization and the teaching prophet moved there, establishing the Krishnamurti Foundation.

After the painful and untimely death of his brother, Nityanada, with whom he shared a great closeness, Krishnamurti lost faith in the masters and reincarnation, admonishing his disciples to throw off the chains of previous teachings, books and doctrines. Krishnamurti formally broke ties with the Krishnamurti Foundation in 1930, setting humankind free of self-proclaimed authorities. He believed that he was simply a yogi master, rejecting the position of supreme guru. Krishnamurti toured extensively throughout the world, spending time lecturing on yogic philosophies.

He believed that the individual must proceed on his or her own pathway to enlightenment, without the dogma of authorities telling what should be learned. He gently suggested, among other instructions, use of the imagination, concentration on creative thought and awareness of past-life experiences as part of the instruction process to be used to move from this life to the next dimension. He taught that one must transform a system, not allow a system to transform the person. Krishnamurti is remembered as a great master and thoughtful human being, and his teachings live on in seven schools throughout the world, including one in Ojai, California called the Krishnamurti Foundation.

Accounts of his teachings are included in *Commentaries on Living, The First and Last Freedom, The Impossible Question* and *The Urgency of Change*.

Further reading

Campbell, Bruce F. *Ancient Wisdom Revived: A History of the Theosophical Movement.* Berkeley and Los Angeles: University of California Press, 1980.

Eastern Mysteries. Mysteries of the Unknown. Alexandria, Va.: Time Life Books, 1990.

Jayakar, Pupul. *Krishnamurti's Journal.* San Francisco: Harper & Row, 1982.

Ryan, Charles J. *H. P. Blavatsky and the Theosophical Movement.* Pasadena, Calif.: Point Loma, 1975.

LAMPADOMANCY *Divination through the observation of flames from a candle or torch.*

Sometimes referred to as lampandomancy, lampadomancy is a form of fire divination or PYROMANCY, the analysis of the shape of flames to foretell the future. It is quite logical that the interpretation of flames from a candle or a torch would become a prognostication method, since fire has played an integral role in human evolution; the first stage was the harnessing of flames for heat and then for cooking food; subsequently, flames were incorporated into mystical and ritualistic ceremonies, including religious services. Even today, most religious services involve the burning of candles; some, such as in the Catholic Church, have candles available for lighting when a special prayer is made.

The use of flames to foretell future events and interpret omens is thought to be one of the earliest methods of divination employed, perhaps, by cave dwellers in prehistoric times, who studied the patterns of flames in the campfire, as well as the shadows that bounced off the cave walls. It is believed that before written time, lampadomancy was used, along with other SCRYING methods. Candle prophecies are mentioned in the Old Testament of the Bible.

Lampadomancy and variations involving CANDLE PROPHECY, including LYNCHOMANCY, were used by the ancient Egyptians about 1,700 years ago. Specifically, the Egyptians studied the flame at the wick of the candle for divination and guidance. However, only children were allowed to make these forecasts.

Whereas the Egyptians used one candle, the Greeks took the ancient practices and devised a variation that required three or four specially blessed candles. Three candles were set in a triangle shape, and a fourth was placed in the center. All the candles were lighted; the three candles were used as a way to draw in the spirits, who would reveal through the fourth candle that which needed to be known.

In practicing lampadomancy, a question must be seriously considered and then asked, either aloud or silently. Then all the candles are lit. Interpretations are based on the fourth or middle candle's appearance and behavior:

If the candle burns small and bright and the wick glows, success will be forthcoming.

If the candle burns large and bright and the wick glows, there will be exceptional good luck.

If the candle burns dim and looks as though it will go out, there will be disillusionment, perhaps a setback in plans or a relationship.

If the candle leans to the side or the wick moves to the side, a significant change in circumstances will be experienced by the querant.

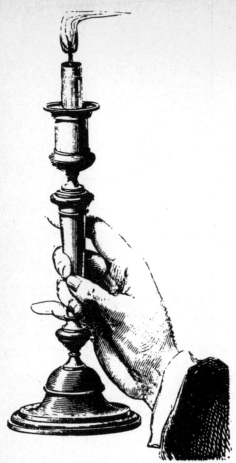

LAMPADOMANCY
Observation of the flames from a candle or torch is still used as a divination method.

If the candle flickers, there will definitely be a change, perhaps one in finances, career or business. This may be a good omen because change brings forth creativity.

If the candle sparkles, the querant should take special care with his or her health. The sparkling candle indicates a concern about health and safety.

If the candle twists and burns tall, it is an indication that there are those who are out to upset the querant, to foil plans and place obstacles in the road to a relationship or career or financial success.

If the candle flame dies without any outside wind source, this is a bad omen. It may also mean that the answer to the question is an absolute NO!

A variation of this method of candle prophecy long used by psychics requires only one candle. To use this method to its best advantage, all lights must be extinguished, although a flashlight may be used to help light the candle, in a room that is pleasant and inviting. The prophecy, as with the above, must be made with a serious determination to understand the future and a clear and open mind for what is to be revealed.

The following are some of the interpretations for the one-candle method:

If the candle burns brightly, the answer is yes.

If the candle seems to burn slowly or goes out by itself, the answer is no, or there will be a negative result of the action under consideration.

If sparks flicker from the candle flame or around the wick, caution should be taken. This is a warning to be careful.

If a brightly burning candle should suddenly extinguish, there is grave danger, perhaps disaster ahead.

Using one match to light all three candles, the following are interpretations of the three-candle method:

If one candle burns more brightly than the others, the portents are good. The answer to the question is affirmative.

Should any of the candles have an extrabright sparkle of color at the tip of the flame, this is a very lucky omen.

If the flames move from side to side, it means a change or a journey. If only one flame moves from side to side while the others are still, this means a singular endeavor, an unaccompanied journey or a project that must be undertaken alone.

If only one candle is extinguished while the others continue to burn, it means there is an obstacle approaching, perhaps a sign of danger; this is definitely a warning of caution.

If one of the flames spirals and twists, with or without smoke, there may be difficulties and/or plots against the querant.

After singing the "Happy Birthday" song, who hasn't leaned over, made a secret wish and attempted to blow out all the candles? It's a traditional way of celebrating a birthday. Just a whimsical birthday game? Actually, it is a form of candle prophecy that, like so many other charming customs, is actually a derivative of prognosticating the future using the candle as a tool.

In Tibet today, a form of lampadomancy is still very much in use. It is called *mar-me-tag-pa*, and divination is attempted with the use of lamps burning butter. The Tibetan form is thought to have originated around A.D. 1300.

According to tradition, this method must only be used on the 8th or 10th day of the month, or when the moon is in half or full position. *Mar-me-tag-pa* specifically prognosticates from the wick of the flame, and even after the flame is extinguished, the wick is scrutinized for consideration in the answer to the querant's question. Additionally, a butter lamp that produces a pleasant odor provides the basis for even better luck or good fortune for the one posing the question.

See also CAPNOMANCY.

Further reading

Dey, Charmaine. *The Magic Candle*. Bronx, N.Y.: Original Publications, 1989.

Maven, Max. *Max Maven's Book of Fortunetelling*. New York: Prentice-Hall, 1992.

Morgan, Chris. *Fortune Telling: How to Predict Your Own Future*. London: Quintet Publishing and Random House, 1992.

Opie, Iona, and Moira Tatem. *A Dictionary of Superstitions*. Oxford: Oxford University Press, 1992.

Pajeon, Kala, and Ketz Pajeon. *The Candle Magic Workbook*. New York: Citadel Press, 1992.

LAWS OF METAPHYSICS
The principles of psychic and mystical sciences that are known to occur time and again. Also known as Spiritual Laws.

The Laws of Metaphysics, functional and philosophical, are the doctrines and canons of esotericism, New Age teaching and philosophies, occultism, alchemy, psychic gifts and mysticism. Although they are complex and thought provoking, at the same time, initially, the descriptions seem too elementary. However, psychics encourage understanding of the laws through meditation, by reading and studying the laws and other principles of metaphysics and by making the laws part of one's personal philosophy.

For example, the Law of Absorption explains that all matter in the universe, regardless of type or vibration, assimilates vibrations from all other matter. The Law of Universal Law explains that principles are absolutely necessary for a universe to exist.

Some of the laws seem too scientific to be considered within the realm of metaphysics; however, all thoughts, whether occult, New Age or highly scientific, are combined in these universal laws. For example, the Law of Uncertainty (or the Uncertainty Principle) is attributed to Albert Einstein. The Law of Synchronicity is attributed to Carl Jung, and the Law of Readiness may have had its beginnings in the I Ching.

The following are a few of the Laws of Metaphysics:

The Law of Free Will states that every person has freedom of choice; therefore, not making a choice is actually making a choice. Additionally, free will allows men and women to use this present incarnation as a tool to continue learning life lessons for their personal evolution.

The Law of Good tells us that there is only good in the universe. There is no bad and no evil, only a system of polarity, of opposites and experiences that are converse.

The Law of Infinite Universes states that each person sees the universe in a different way. There is no right or wrong way to see the universe and universal order but that which is individual to each person.

The Law of Karma provides the principles to be responsible for all actions and acts and is the sum total of all past and present experiences and actions, perhaps even intentions. The Law of Karma explains that experiences, actions and intentions of one lifetime may be carried over into the next.

The Law of Omnipresence states that the universe is within every particle of the universe and it is within and without in the past, present and future. The universe is always with us.

The Law of Personal Return states that everything in the universe is cyclic. The Bible states that we should do unto others as we would like them to do for us: an example of the Christian Law of Personal Return.

The Law of Readiness, in Eastern philosophies, explains that "When the pupil is ready, the Master is ready. When the student is ready, the Teacher will come."

The Law of Uncertainty states that any realistic description of the universe must describe it in all possible states at the same instant of time; thus a person is unborn, alive and dead at the same moment.

Further reading

Bailey, Alice. *A Treatise on White Magic.* New York: Lucis, 1951.

Bletzer, June G. *The Donning International Encyclopedic Psychic Dictionary.* West Chester, Pa.: Whitford Press, 1986.

Cavendish, Richard, ed. *The Encyclopedia of the Unexplained.* New York: McGraw-Hill, 1974.

Cayce, Hugh Lynn, ed. *The Edgar Cayce Collection.* New York: Bonanza, 1986.

LAYING ON OF HANDS *A method of psychic healing.*

Traditionally considered a way of healing or releasing evil spirits from the querant, laying on of hands is used in many civilizations and continues to be utilized today in religious and New Age groups including the Mormons (Latter-Day Saints).

Healing is produced when the hands of the healer (or psychic) are used to channel and transmit energy from the universe or God source through his or her body to the person who is to be healed.

In this method, which is sometimes called magnetic healing, psychics or healers concentrate on the querant's problem (physical or mental) and use their hands to accelerate the power of the individual's cells to heal. It was thought that the magnetism of the healer's system was generated through the hands, palms and especially the fingertips, and the hands were placed on the specific area of illness. For example, in an internal illness involving the stomach, the hands of the healer would be placed on or close to the abdomen. Typically, hands do make contact with the skin, but they can also be held over the patient; laying on of hands can be practiced at a distance by imagining that hands are being held over the troubled physical area or visualizing a healing circle of light. Sometimes those who are to receive the healing are told to concentrate their thoughts on the specific area or to feel the heat of the healing.

Healing, sometimes immediately and sometimes over a period of time, is often accompanied by a feeling of warmth or relaxation. Some patients report feeling chilled, a tickling sensation or agitation during the experience. Doctors and scientists often believe that this form of healing is really the power of positive thinking; however, cells and tissues that have been examined after laying on of hands and mental healing have taken place reflect a change in cell activity. It would seem that cells are attempting to normalize and heal themselves.

Edgar Cayce (1877–1945) is said to have exhibited psychic abilities since childhood. He was consulted by thousands of people regarding health problems, often curing those whom doctors had reported to be terminally ill. Some of the healing was done in person; often it was done through meditation. Cayce claimed that he could review the AKASHIC RECORDS of the person who was ill to ascertain whether or not the illness was the result of a past-life experience or karma. Thus, he would be able to explain and specifically release a block in the patient's evolution and encourage healing. Transcripts of the healing readings are included in the book *Edgar Cayce on Healing.*

Other psychics who practice healing have also claimed to be able to heal the illness or infirmity of a previous incarnation of which a remnant is affecting the querant in his or her present lifetime. For instance, if the querant had a lung disease in a previous life, he or she may now have a breathing problem. Often just by knowing that this is a disease left over from the past and that the problem that caused the disease is no longer valid, the cure is manifest.

Many psychics practice healing; some charge fees while others do not. Some use the power of crystals, believing that certain gems vibrate especially strong healing powers. For example, the amethyst is considered to be a healing stone; it is recommended that those who are ill wear and/or meditate with the gem. Other psychics who heal do so through herbal or Native American practices. From the beginning of time right up to today, there also have been charlatans who take people's money promising cures but do not produce. As with all medical concerns and health issues, it is essential that querants also consult with medical professionals.

Andrew Jackson Davis (1826–1910) is known as one of the great American psychic healers. Harry Edwards is the best known of British psychic healers (1893–1976). At a "performance" in Kings Hall, Manchester, Edwards had a crowd of more than 7,000 people watching as he placed on hands and healed various ailments. He was said to be able to best heal arthritis, spinal lesions, paralysis and sometimes blindness and deafness. He claimed that the spirits of Pasteur and other great medical practitioners guided him from the ethereal world.

Those who practice laying on of hands often are using another method of mental healing, as did Cayce during his years of providing healing readings. Mental healing is said to be a variation of psychokinesis whereby natural electrical energy is transmitted from the brain of the psychic (or healer) to the patient. Psychics often see the need for healing when viewing the querant's aura and can see the change in the color emanating from the body after healing has been completed.

One can use this power to heal oneself or others; however, if the patient does not believe in the power of the mind to heal, the healing will not be effective. Healing can occur through visualization, meditation, mental telepathy and affirmations. The healing is often referred to as a miracle; there are references to laying on of hands in the Bible and other holy books, where the mental authority or charisma of a religious figure for his or her followers produces healing or health.

Also see CAYCE, EDGAR; CRYSTAL PREDICTIONS; DAVIS, ANDREW JACKSON; EDWARDS, HARRY; GEMS.

Further reading

Bravo, Brett. *Crystal Love Secrets*. New York: Warner, 1991.

[Cayce, Edgar.] *Edgar Cayce on Healing*. Virginia Beach, Va.: ARE Press, 1969.

Krippner, Stanley, and Alberto Villoldo. *The Realms of Healing*. 3d ed. Berkeley, Ca.: Celestial Arts, 1986.

Meek, George W., ed. *Healers and the Healing Process*. Wheaton, Ill.: Theosophical Publishing House, 1977.

Powers of Healing. Mysteries of the Unknown. Alexandria, Va.: Time Life Books, 1990.

West, D. J. *Eleven Lourdes Miracles*. New York: Helix, 1957.

Worral, A. *The Gift of Healing*. New York: Harper & Row, 1965.

LECONOMANCY *Divination by the sound or movement made when an object is thrown into water; sometimes the water is covered with a film of oil.*

This prognostication method is said to have begun with the ancient Assyrians, who answered querants' questions, interpreted omens and foretold the future using leconomancy. However, they preferred using a thin layer of yellowish oil (since chickens were also used regularly as a prediction tool, the oil may have actually been the fat produced when chicken was cooked). After the querant posed a question, the Assyrian psychics cast a pebble or gem into the dish and divination occurred. For example, if the querant (often of the nobility) questioned the outcome of a war, and the pebble dropped to the bottom of the bowl or dish without separating the pool of oil, it meant that the king would triumph. However, if the oil separated into tiny particles, the omen would have been interpreted to mean that the morale of the king's men would be dissipated and the effort foiled.

In the Bible, Joseph (Gen. 44:5, 15) used a variation of leconomancy, and Nostradamus

(1503–1566) is said to have practiced this method, too. The seer placed a bowl of water upon a brass tripod and interpreted the patterns in the water when viewed by an indirect light source.

Also spelled lecanomancy, leconomancy is a variation of HYDROMANCY, that is, divination by staring at water and interpreting what is seen. The visions seen in the patterns on the surface or through a mist or image sometimes offer a message in the water itself.

Sometimes divination occurred, in ancient Greek and Roman times, through the ripples on a lake or body of water, after a specific type of stone was tossed by the querant or by the psychic or when the wind moved the layer of water. Ripples made by raindrops and the drops poured from a vessel were also interpreted. When we've "skipped" a rock across water, unknowingly perhaps, we have practiced leconomancy.

See also CATOPTROMANCY; ENOPTROMANCY; SCRYING.

Further reading

Cavendish, Richard, ed. *The Encyclopedia of the Unexplained.* New York: McGraw-Hill, 1974.

Miller, Madeleine S., and J. Lane Miller, eds. *Harper's Encyclopedia of Bible Life.* San Francisco: Harper & Row, 1978.

Roberts, Henry C. *The Complete Prophecies of Nostradamus.* New York: American Book–Stratford Press, 1969.

LEE, ANN *(1736–1784) English religious leader and mystic.*

Lee, originally from Manchester, England, was instrumental in the formation of the religious group called the Shakers, formally known as the United Society of Believers in Christ's Second Coming, a sect first heard about in 1750 in England. It is said that after attending a service conducted by Jane Wardley (Wardley and her husband James were two of the first to practice the religion) and hearing that, according to Wardley, Christ would return to earth manifest as a woman, Lee joined Wardley's followers. Wardley had had a visionary dream telling her to leave the Friends (Quakers) and help form a new sect, the Shakers.

Shortly thereafter Lee was imprisoned for disturbing the peace, by preaching the gospel according to the Shaker doctrine. It was at this time that Lee had a dream (or vision) that she was in fact the "Bride of the Lamb." Since visionary dreams had changed the lives of many during Old Testament times, it was not unusual for this religious woman to believe she was the chosen one. From that time on, Lee was often referred to as "Mother Ann" or "Ann the Word." Her followers believed that she was the female counterpart of Jesus Christ.

In 1774, Lee immigrated to the American colonies, finding religious freedom not available in England at the time. Along with a handful of British followers, Lee founded a Shaker conclave in what is now Watervliet, near Albany, New York. Lee and other Shakers abided by the doctrine of pacifism and communism and were dedicated to celibacy and chastity. At the height of the movement, in about 1860, the number of flourishing Shaker communities was 18, with more than 6,000 members. Since that time, the communities have dwindled, with fewer than 50 members today.

Shakers, once thought of as original religious thinkers, are now best known as the craftspeople who specialize in designing and building sparse-looking, smoothly contoured furniture.

Further reading

Bethards, Betty. *The Dream Book: Symbols for Self-Understanding.* Petaluma, Calif.: Inner Light Press, 1992.

Drury, Nevill. *Dictionary of Mysticism and the Esoteric Traditions.* Dorset, England: Prism Press, 1992.

Glass, Justine. *The Story of Fulfilled Prophecy.* London: Cassell, 1969.

Loewe, Michael, and Carmen Blacker, eds. *Divination and Oracles.* London: Allen & Unwin, 1981.

Stern, Jess. *Edgar Cayce, the Sleeping Prophet.* New York: Bantam, 1968.

LE NORMAND, MADAME *(1772–1843) French psychic, astrologer and card reader.*

Le Normand may be one of the most gifted of all card readers, known as "the Sybil of the

Faubourg Saint Germain." She was renowned for foretelling the futures of such French revolutionary figures as Jean Paul Marat and Maximilien Robespierre.

Because of her psychic gift, Le Normand was embraced by the nobility, and she is said to have read Napoleon's horoscope. After this triumph and as her reputation spread among the wealthy, she moved to Paris, reading cards for affluent Parisians. While traveling, she was caught up in a war in Belgium and imprisoned. Whether she died in prison or died after losing favor with the aristocracy of the time is unclear. However, in the history of divination, Le Normand is still remembered today for powerful and disquietingly factual psychic gifts of predicting the future.

Further reading

Buckland, Raymond. *Secrets of Gypsy Fortune Telling.* St. Paul, Minn.: Llewellyn, 1988.
Giles, Cynthia. *The Tarot: History, Mystery and Lore.* New York. Paragon House, 1992.
Innes, Brian. *The Tarot: How to Use and Interpret the Cards.* London: Orbis, 1979.

LEO *One of the 12 astrological signs of the zodiac. The symbol is the lion.*

Those who are born between July 23 and August 22 are natives of the sign of Leo and have specific traits indicative of the time and date on which they were born. Divination of events can also be charted through this astrological sign.

Astrologers divine what is in store throughout life through the time, date and place in which an individual was born as they coordinate the

LEO

influences with other signs, the planets, the Sun, the Moon and other powers.

In traditional Western astrology, Leo is the fifth sign of the zodiac and is a fire sign. Those born during the period typically exhibit qualities that exemplify an extroverted nature, are outgoing and enjoy being in the spotlight; typically, most enjoy being alone on center stage.

According to astrologers, natives of the sign of Leo are proud, ambitious, generous and friendly. They have a strong practical streak in their nature that tends to surprise those who see Leo as a somewhat arrogant and magnificent individual. Of course, the Leo native can have a darker side, too, when twinges of a boastful, ironclad determination surface. The Leo may also be (often to an extreme and without knowing it) challenging, which can provoke others.

It is said that Leos most likable characteristic is vitality. Even if it has been a very long work week, and a very long Friday, one can count on Leo to go dancing or otherwise kick up his or her heels . . . even if it's two in the morning when the workday is ended. And when kicking those heels, if it just happens that Leo is the star, so much the better.

Leos are considered to be excellent managers with an extra measure of creativity and a sprinkling of drama. They can get employees motivated and brainstorming like no other sign. Whether it's good or bad, the Leo native knows no other way than to make a production out of everything. Small companies mushroom. Intimate parties turn into events. Nest eggs are invested and produce incredible returns, time and again, without the tedious planning required by those born in other signs. That's simply the Leo way.

The sign of the zodiac in which an individual is born is responsible for only one fragment of the qualities he or she receives at birth. Psychics are quick to point out that a general forecast solely on the stellar position of the Sun on the day an individual was born is unlikely to provide an accurate glimpse of the future.

While traditional astrologers use books to calculate a personal birth chart based on the position of the Sun, Moon and planets at a distinct time,

This ancient symbol represents the astrological sign of Leo.

computer software has replaced most of this time-consuming work. The correct term for calculating a birth chart is to "cast" it. In order to fully comprehend the extent of traits, potential and attributes, the exact time and place of birth must be known and interpreted.

See also ASTROLOGICAL SYMBOLS; ASTROLOGY.

Further reading

Cosmic Connections. Mysteries of the Unknown. Alexandria, Va.: Time Life Books, 1990.
Goodman, Linda. *Linda Goodman's Sun Signs.* New York: Fawcett/Columbine, 1978.
Morgan, Chris. *Fortune Telling: How to Predict Your Own Future.* London: Quintet Publishing and Random House, 1992.
Omarr, Sydney. *Leo.* New York: New American Library, 1992.
———. *My World of Astrology.* New York: Fleet, 1965.
Verlagsanstalt, Datura. *Leo Astro Analysis.* New York: Grosset & Dunlap, 1976.
Woolfork, Joanna Martine. *The Only Astrology Book You'll Ever Need.* Landham, Mass.: Scarborough, 1992.

LEO, ALAN *(1860–1917) British astrologer.*

Leo was one of the most influential astrologers of his time and was instrumental in publicizing astrology during the metaphysical revival in the late 1800s. Sometimes referred to as the "father of modern astrology," Leo worked to bring knowledge of astrology to the masses. In 1890, he became a member of Madame Blavatsky's group and joined the THEOSOPHICAL SOCIETY, eventually founding his own group, the Astrological Lodge of the Theosophical Society, in 1915.

Leo was one of the first to publish a monthly periodical on the use of the Sun and planets to prognosticate the future; it was called the *Astrologer's Magazine.* In 1914, Leo was arrested, accused of being a fortune-teller, which was against the law; however, the case against him was dismissed. Once more in 1917, he was prosecuted and fined a token sum of 25 pounds. Renaming his magazine *Modern Astrology,* he continued to spread astrology to the world. The magazine was extremely popular, as were his "shilling" horoscopes and inexpensive books on the subject.

Leo was an ardent and earnest astrologer, with strong leanings toward the serious side of the occult. He is also known for his many books on metaphysics. His most famous works include *Astrology for All, How to Judge a Nativity, The Progressive Horoscope* and *Esoteric Astrology.* These books are considered classics; they are often available through used-books stores and are used regularly as teaching manuals in astrology classes.

Further reading

Cosmic Connections. Mysteries of the Unknown. Alexandria, Va.: Time Life Books, 1990.
Drury, Nevill. *Dictionary of Mysticism and the Esoteric Traditions.* Dorset, England: Prism Press, 1992.
Meade, Marion. *Madame Blavatsky: The Woman behind the Myth.* New York: Putnam's, 1980.
Ryan, Charles J. *H. P. Blavatsky and the Theosophical Movement.* Pasadena, Calif.: Point Loma, 1975.
Woolfork, Joanna Martine. *The Only Astrology Book You'll Ever Need.* Landham, Mass.: Scarborough, 1992.

LEON, MOSES BEN SHEM TOV DE *(1240–1305) Spanish Jewish religious teacher and psychic.*

Moses de Leon is best known as a teacher of the KABBALAH, and, depending on the reference source used, he is thought to be the compiler or the author of the *Zohar,* one of the principal works of the Kabbalah.

The 13th-century religious scholar, born in Guadalajara, Spain, interpreted the *Sefer-ha-Zohar* (known as the Book of Splendor or Books of Lights). De Leon claimed that the real author was the mythical mystic Simeon ben Yoah. That, however, has subsequently been disproved, because there is no evidence that Simeon ben Yoah existed, and it is believed that de Leon is the actual author of this masterpiece of mystical thought.

Like other medieval scholars involved in religious investigation, de Leon studied the Hebrew teachings of the Old Testament hoping to discover hidden truths and messages concealed from the uninitiated. He worked on systems that produced secret information from the text, with a relationship between the words and numbers, a form of numerology known as GEMATRIA.

De Leon traveled throughout Europe, especially in the Spanish peninsula, teaching the Kabbalah and learning from other mystics. He wrote more than 20 books, many of which are now only fragments that can be viewed in museums.

See also TAROT.

Further reading

Drury, Nevill. *Dictionary of Mysticism and the Esoteric Traditions*. Dorset, England: Prism Press, 1992.

Schmaker, Wayne. *The Occult Sciences in the Renaissance*. Berkeley and Los Angeles: University of California Press, 1972.

Scholem, Gershom. *Origins of the Kabbalah* (translation). Princeton, N.J.: Jewish Publication Society, 1987.

LEONARD, GLADYS OSBORNE
(1882–1968) British psychic.

Leonard is remembered as one of the most gifted of trance mediums and psychics who channel entities. Leonard's entity was Feda, an Indian who supposedly had died circa 1800 but spoke through Leonard. It was through the encouragement of Feda that Leonard accepted her psychic gifts and used her clairvoyance to provide clients with metaphysical information, especially in the realm of past lives.

MOSES BEN SHEM TOV DE LEON
Moses Ben Shem Tov de Leon is best known as a teacher of the Kabbalah. He is thought by many to be the compiler or author of the Zohar, one of the principal works of the Kabbalah.

Leonard tried to warn the public about the advent of an upcoming war, World War I, years ahead of its beginning, among other prognostications. Leonard met Sir Oliver Lodge (the scientist, psychic researcher, investor and physicist), who investigated psychic phenomena, and he believed that her powers were genuine. At one time, Leonard worked with Lodge to contact the scientist's son, who had died in combat during the war.

Leonard was also tested for her abilities by Whately Carington, who, like Lodge, found that Leonard's channeled entity Feda was not merely a personification of the woman but a separate "being." *My Life in Two Worlds* is Leonard's autobiography. Throughout her life, she worked with the Society of Psychical Research and produced great amounts of testimony to substantiate the theory of reincarnation and life after death.

See also CHANNEL; REINCARNATION.

Further reading

Fodor, Nandor. *Encyclopedia of Psychic Science.* New York: University Books, 1966.

Guiley, Rosemary Ellen. *The Encyclopedia of Witches and Witchcraft.* New York: Facts On File, 1989.

Kautz, William H., and Melanie Branon. *Channeling: The Intuitive Connection.* San Francisco: Harper & Row, 1987.

Klimo, John. *Channeling: Investigations on Receiving Information from Paranormal Sources.* Los Angeles: Jeremy P. Tarcher, 1987.

Leonard, Gladys Osborne. *My Life in Two Worlds.* London: Two Worlds, 1931.

Psychics. Mysteries of the Unknown. Alexandria, Va.: Time Life Books, 1990.

Smith, Susy. *The Mediumship of Mrs. Leonard.* Hyde Park, N.Y.: University Books, 1964.

LEVATER, JOHANN KASPAR
(1741–1801) Swiss psychic and physiognomist.

Levater, whose name is sometimes spelled "Lavater," is remembered as a noted religious figure and poet and, in metaphysical circles, for his work establishing the science of PHYSIOGNOMY. As PALMISTRY relates personality traits to lines on the hand, physiognomy is the study of physical features and their relationship to characteristics. For an extremely simplified example, someone with a square-shaped face is said to have a practical nature. Someone with closely set eyes is said to have a devious or wily character.

Physiognomy had originated as a psychic science in the early 1500s in France, Austria and Italy. It was condemned by the British Parliament as sorcery in 1743; however, the study continued to take hold. Levater published a book in 1775 on the topic, promoting the concept that specific head shapes and facial features denoted particular personality characteristics and tendencies. A supporter of the Freemasons and a friend of Count Allesandro di Cagliostro, Levater is said to have done physiognomy readings for the aristocracy of Britain, France, Germany and Russia. One of his clients was Queen Victoria's father, Edward, duke of Kent.

Johann Goethe, the philosopher and a friend of Levater, helped him write a four-volume book on physiognomy called *Physiognomical Fragments for the Promotion of the Knowledge and Love of Man.* Published in 1775–1776, the book remains one of the best historical works on the topic.

See also ANTHROPOSOMANCY; IRIDOLOGY.

Further reading

Bletzer, June G. *The Donning International Encyclopedic Psychic Dictionary.* West Chester, Pa.: Whitford Press, 1986.

Knight, Stephen. *The Brotherhood: The Secret World of the Freemasons.* New York: Stein & Day, 1984.

Magical Arts. Mysteries of the Unknown. Alexandria, Va.: Time Life Books, 1990.

Maven, Max. *Max Maven's Book of Fortunetelling.* New York: Prentice-Hall, 1992.

LEVI, ELIPHAS *(1810–1875) Author, magician and psychic scholar.*

Levi's birth name was Alphonse-Louis Constant, but he changed it to Eliphas Levi Zahed, later deleting the final name. He took the identity of Eliphas Levi as a "magical name." The son of a French shoemaker, Levi was a flamboyant magician and the author of a number of important metaphysical volumes, including *The Mysteries of Magic* (edited by A. E. Waite) and *History of Magic.*

While Levi's books were called "sloppy" by occult scholars of his time, they have since become classics in the field of magic, Hermetic philosophy and the occult. (The world *occult* is reported to have been coined by Levi.) However, Levi is best remembered for his insightful determination that there was a strong symbolic connection between the 22 cards of the tarot's major arcana and the Kabbalah's Tree of Life, a connection that has been accepted to this day.

According to TAROT scholars, Levi saw the tarot not just as an intriguing deck of cards but as a practical tool through which the spirits could be contacted and revelations regarding the past and future could be made. Levi believed that through the merging of the Kabbalah and the tarot, he had finally discovered a powerful source of knowledge and magic. This discernment changed the course of the tarot, and through his work with divination, he created the basic structure of modern ritual magic.

So strong was his legacy that it is said that the leader of the HERMETIC ORDER OF THE GOLDEN DAWN, Aleister Crowley, believed that in his previous life, he had actually been Levi.

To Levi, the tarot was the entire world. He once told associates that if he was ever imprisoned, regardless of how many years, the only "book" he would require was a pack of tarot cards. He zealously believed that they were the key to the ultimate wisdom of the ages. Although it is often disputed whether or not Levi's later work helped or hindered students of metaphysics, it is agreed that his reputation and the legends about him have continued to be a fascinating part of the history and study of the occult.

See also CROWLEY, ALEISTER; KABBALAH.

Further reading

Drury, Nevill. *Inner Visions: Explorations in Magical Consciousness.* London: Routledge & Kegan Paul, 1979.

Giles, Cynthia. *The Tarot: History, Mystery and Lore.* New York: Paragon House, 1992.

Symonds, John, and Kenneth Grant, eds. *The Confessions of Aleister Crowley: An Autobiography.* London: Routledge & Kegan Paul, 1979.

LEVITATION *The lifting of an object or person into the air and holding it there without visible physical means.*

Levitation is made possible, according to psychics, through intense concentration and profound will power, both of which are said to be available to anyone. Though psychics are often in a trance state when levitation occurs, they always seem to be in control. Levitation was used by psychics and mediums in the spiritual resurgence of the late 1800s, and it was said to be a test of metaphysical powers. However, there were many who used so-called levitation in complicated hoaxes and schemes in order to defraud the public.

Scottish-American psychic Daniel Dunglas Home (1833–1886) is considered to be one of the most noted of all psychics because of his telepathic powers as well as his incredible ability to levitate objects and his body at will. His greatest feat was to transport himself out of a third-story window and, without touching the window ledge, return through another window.

The fakirs of India, the ninja of Japan and a great number of religious figures (including Saint Teresa of Avila and Simon Magus), in addition to others using psychic skills, are said to have had the ability to levitate. Saint Joseph of Cupertino (1603–1663) is said to have flown through the air, shrieking as he left the ground. Thirteenth-century Tibetan yogi Milarepa, considered by some to be the greatest yogi of all time, is supposed to have been able to levitate, in addition to his other psychic skills.

There are a number of varying theories of how levitation operates. One says that levitation works through the power of the psychic's mind to counteract the forces of gravity; thus, the psychic can rise or raise objects and keep them suspended in the air. Some psychics attribute the power to levitate objects to their guides and the way spirits can change the forces of gravity. Another school of metaphysical thought believes that through concentrating on the aura emanating from themselves or an object, psychics change the vibrational frequency and objects are not pulled toward the earth.

See also CLAIRVOYANCE; HOME, DANIEL DUN-
GLAS; GUPPY, AGNES.

Further reading

Belhayes, Iris, with Enid. *Spirit Guides.* San Diego:
ACS, 1985.
Bletzer, June G. *The Donning International Encyclo-
pedic Psychic Dictionary.* West Chester, Pa.: Whit-
ford Press, 1986.
Brown, Slater. *The Heyday of Spiritualism.* New
York: Hawthorn, 1970.
Edmonds, I. G. *D. D. Home: The Man Who Talked
with Ghosts.* Nashville: Thomas Nelson, 1978.
Ferguson, John. *An Illustrated Encyclopedia of Mysti-
cism and the Mystery Religions.* New York: Seabury
Press, 1976.
Fodor, Nandor. *Encyclopedia of Psychic Science.* New
York: University Books, 1966.
Rogo, D. Scott. *Our Psychic Potentials.* Englewood
Cliffs, N.J.: Prentice-Hall, 1984.

LIBANOMANCY *Divination through observing and interpreting the smoke rising from
incense.*

Libanomancy was first used by the ancient Babylonians. As with SCRYING, the interpretation of
smoke coming from objects is up to the psychic;
forms quickly vaporize and intuitive ability must
take over.

Libanomancy and other mantic arts, including
CAPNOMANCY, CRITOMANCY, DAPHNOMANCY and
SIDEROMANCY, are grouped under the main head-
ing of BOTANOMANCY.

Further reading

Bletzer, June G. *The Donning International Encyclopedic Psychic Dictionary.* West Chester, Pa.: Whitford Press, 1986.
Opie, Iona, and Moira Tatem. *A Dictionary of Superstitions.* Oxford: Oxford University Press, 1992.
Visions and Prophecies. Mysteries of the Unknown.
Alexandria, Va.: Time Life Books, 1990.

LIBRA *One of the 12 astrological signs of
the zodiac. The symbol is the scales.*

Those who are born between September 23 and
October 22 are said to be natives of the sign of
Libra and have specific traits indicative of the
time and date on which they were born. Divina-

LIBRA

tion of events can also be charted through this
astrological sign.

Astrologers divine what is in store throughout
life through the time, date and place in which
an individual was born as they coordinate the
influences with other signs, the planets, the Sun,
the Moon and other powers.

In traditional Western astrology, Libra is the
seventh sign of the zodiac. Those born during the
period typically exhibit qualities that exemplify a
charming, diplomatic and artistic nature.

Libra is the sign of balance, and Libras are
happiest when in relationships where everyone
knows the rules and what is expected of them.
Whether that relationship is a romantic one or a
business partnership, Libra has an astrological
gift to make things work, promote peace among
subordinates (and family members) and go to
almost any extent to inject harmony. Libra is like
a well-practiced juggler. When all is going right,
the world is perfect; however, one misstep and
Libra may have to step back to pick up the
pieces.

Men and women born during the time the Sun
is in Libra are often charismatic, loving, warm
hearted and even tempered. Their vitality seems
to draw people to them with magnetic power,
and they thrive in the social arena. Often, however, because their glossy outside is so attractive,
they draw superficial types who do not realize
that beneath that beautiful outside is a caring,
sensitive and sometimes tough individual.

The Libra native is said to be happiest when
life is running like clockwork. They love works
of art and culture and do extremely well in social
situations (and positions—with their tendency

This ancient symbol represents the astrological sign of Libra.

to possess highly polished skills of diplomacy). Sometimes, however, in trying to keep the peace, they forget that they must first be true to themselves and their own personal desires. Ruled by the planet Venus, Libra may find him- or herself in a romantic triangle (and enjoying the sparks, too).

The sign of the zodiac in which an individual is born is only one fragment of the qualities he or she receives at birth. Psychics are quick to point out that a general forecast solely on the stellar position of the Sun on the day an individual was born is unlikely to provide an accurate glimpse of the future.

While traditional astrologers use books to calculate a personal birth chart book based on the position of the Sun, Moon and planets at a distinct time, computer software has replaced most of this time-consuming work. The correct term for calculating a birth chart is to "cast" it. In order to fully comprehend the extent of traits, potential and attributes, the exact time and place of birth must be known and interpreted.

See also ASTROLOGICAL SYMBOLS; ASTROLOGY.

Further reading

Cosmic Connections. Mysteries of the Unknown. Alexandria, Va.: Time Life Books, 1990.
Goodman, Linda. *Linda Goodman's Sun Signs.* New York: Fawcett/Columbine, 1978.
Morgan, Chris. *Fortune Telling: How to Predict Your Own Future.* London: Quintet Publishing and Random House, 1992.
Omarr, Sydney. *Libra.* New York: New American Library, 1992.
————. *My World of Astrology.* New York: Fleet, 1965.
Verlagsanstalt, Datura. *Libra Astro Analysis.* New York: Grosset & Dunlap, 1976.
Woolfork, Joanna Martine. *The Only Astrology Book You'll Ever Need.* Landham, Mass.: Scarborough, 1992.

LIFE LINE *One of the many lines in the palm of the hand that are said to foretell specific characteristics.*

The life line is sometimes referred to as the line of life by palmists. Because there are many variations of the life line, and since palmistry is complex as well as intriguing, it is recommended that one should refer to a palmist or a book specifically on the subject for a complete examination and interpretation of the hand.

The life line is located in the lower portion of the hand, typically running from a point between the index finger and the place where the thumb is connected to the palm. Rather than indicating the length of an individual life in years, the life line is a barometer of the quality of that life. This line suggests the physical condition of the person whose palm is being read.

The length of the line indicates stamina, spunk and vigor, and palmists say that a long life line is one of the indications of an energetic disposition, with strong reserves of personal power. A line that moves downward toward the wrist indicates intense internal fortitude. If the line seems to be rather straight, without a downward curve, this is considered a measure of limited stamina. Lines that break off the life line may indicate that the querant will face challenges in the area of health or an illness followed by a recovery, or they may be a caution to take extra care with both physical and mental well-being, giving lifestyle choices additional reflection. A fork at the end of the life line, near the wrist, may indicate a journey of a long distance that will affect the life of the querant.

See also PALMISTRY.

Further reading

Altman, Nathaniel. *Palmistry Workbook.* New York: Sterling, 1990.

Cheiro. *Cheiro's Book of Numbers.* New York: Prentice-Hall, 1988.
———. *The Language of the Hand.* New York: Prentice-Hall, 1987.
Robinson, Rita. *The Palm: A Guide to Your Hidden
Potential.* North Hollywood, Calif.: Newcastle,
1988.

LIFE READING *Divination of future accomplishments and reverses and/or interpretation of past-life experiences; may also be used to
divine a child's future.*

The definition of a life reading, like other psychic
sessions, can vary depending on the specialty of
the psychic involved. Basically, there are three
main variants: future occurrences, past-life influences and the decoding of the scribblings of a
child to foretell the prospects during his or her
coming years. In addition, depending on the
psychic, there can be variations of the metaphysical tools used to connect with the spiritual forces
that can reveal what has or will transpire. For
example, one psychic may use tarot cards, the
second may study tea leaves, a third reads the
querant's palm and a fourth meditates on an
astrological chart or the color vibrations emanating from the querant's aura. Some psychics
use tools (such as cards, tea leaves or crystals);
others do not. If there is one standard, it is that
the psychic is using CLAIRVOYANCE and TE-
LEPATHY.

Some psychics are more dramatic, even theatrical, than others. For instance, a fortune-teller
at a charity benefit may dress the part, but when
meeting corporate clients at the office, he or she
wears the "costume" of business—a professional-
looking suit. Typically, a reading lasts between a
half hour and an hour, sometimes longer; depending on the area of the United States and the
reputation of the psychic, the fee varies from $10
to well over $300.

In a life reading, as with PSYCHIC READINGS,
the querant often poses precise questions; the
psychic meditates and then advises and consults
on the questions, providing spiritually acquired
information. He or she may go into a semi-
trancelike state, and a spiritual entity may be
channeled to share information, or the psychic

may simply talk to the querant as if they are
counselor and client. Again, as with psychic
readings, unless the life reading is conducted for
exhibition, only the psychic and the querant are
privy to the session, although most psychics tape
or allow the querant to tape the sitting.

In a life reading focusing on the present, the
psychic will often discuss relationships, career
and money, along with any specific spiritual information that the psychic's guides would like to
provide. Although psychics do not often advise
on what the future will hold in a life reading,
they sometimes explain that because of past influences, it is likely that specific things will happen in this life. As an illustration, if someone is
having a conflict with a stepchild or employee or
there's a knotty problem in the area of career
choices, the psychic may consider past-life happenings or the current placement of planets in
the astrological chart and then check the chart
for the individual in question before providing
recommendations.

Psychics who are able to connect with the
AKASHIC RECORDS, such as Edgar Cayce did,
often advise querants on the circumstances of
past lives, considering those that are the most
influential in this current life. The Akashic Records are thought to be a spiritual register of
experiences encountered in all ways throughout
every existence and experience and are located in
the storehouse of spiritual knowledge on the
ethereal plane. By understanding the events that
have occurred, most likely in no more than three
to six past lives, regarding personality traits,
talents, psychic gifts and the karma involved, the
querant can often untangle an incident that may
be impeding progress in this current lifetime.

A variation on life reading practiced by some
psychics uses the scribblings of a very young
child (before the age when he or she can write
the alphabet). In this form of life reading, a child
is given paper and a crayon or pencil, and the
psychic deciphers the scrawls to foretell the prospects during his or her coming years. The scrawls
are said to be a direct connection with the subconscious, because very young children have not
totally forgotten their life before birth and are
willing to use their intuition.

Those psychics who utilize this variation of life readings also may read auras, study the astrological birth chart and psychically connect with past-life experiences in order to understand the complete influences on a child. A child's life reading through the scribbling method may be only a portion of an extensive psychic reading that can help parents direct their offspring's talents, gifts and challenges. A life reading that reveals an aptitude for music and dance (perhaps seen as a past-life influence, when the spirit was an accomplished musician or dancer) may persuade parents to give their child piano or ballet lessons. Conversely, with a child whose energy is exhausting to channel, a life reading may reveal that he or she had a past-life involvement with athletics; once that vigor and strength is directed into sports or other strenuous activities, the talent can be fully utilized. A life reading with a child often provides clues to help children and their parents live happier lives.

See also KARMA; PAST LIFE.

Further reading

Altman, Nathaniel. *Palmistry Workbook.* New York: Sterling, 1990.

Bailey, Alice. *A Treatise on White Magic.* New York: Lucis, 1951.

Bowers, Barbara. *What Color Is Your Aura?* New York: Simon & Schuster, 1989.

Cavendish, Richard, ed. *The Encyclopedia of the Unexplained.* New York: McGraw-Hill, 1974.

Cayce, Hugh Lynn, ed. *The Edgar Cayce Collection.* New York: Bonanza, 1986.

Hall, Manly P. *Reincarnation: The Cycle of Necessity.* Los Angeles: Philosophical Research Society, 1956.

Kapleau, Philip. *The Wheel of Life and Death: A Practical and Spiritual Guide.* New York: Doubleday, 1989.

Woolfork, Joanna Martine. *The Only Astrology Book You'll Ever Need.* Landham, Mass.: Scarborough, 1992.

LILLY, WILLIAM (1602–1681) British astrologer and psychic.

Lilly is considered by many to be one of the most famous astrologers. Among Lilly's predictions, which were based on astrological forecasts and his psychic gifts, were the dispute between England's political foes (the Royalists and the Puritans), the death of Charles I, the Restoration and the Great Fire of London. Lilly was an adviser of Oliver Cromwell, the Lord Protector of England (1599–1658), who defeated Charles I in the English Civil War.

Lilly's reputation for reporting on events before they took place brought him under government scrutiny. When news reached the authorities that Lilly had predicted the Great Fire of London, he was accused of being the perpetrator, or, at the least, a co-conspirator. He was brought before Parliament and held on charges of arson, but he was later acquitted.

Lilly wrote a number of books on astrology; his most famous is *Merlinus Anglicanus*, written in 1641.

Further reading

Brau, Jean-Louis; Helen Weaver; and Allan Edmands. *Larousse Encyclopedia of Astrology.* New York: McGraw-Hill, 1980.

Drury, Nevill. *Dictionary of Mysticism and the Esoteric Traditions.* Dorset, England: Prism Press, 1992.

Woolfork, Joanna Martine. *The Only Astrology Book You'll Ever Need:* Landham, Mass.: Scarborough, 1992.

LINE OF HEALTH One of the many lines in the palm of the hand that are said to reveal specific characteristics.

The line of health is sometimes referred to as hepatica. It runs from where the little finger joins the hand down through the center of the palm.

If there is no line, as often is the case, the absence indicates a strong constitution and excellent health. A deep line shows one who may be susceptible to illness. A wavy line reveals intestinal problems, perhaps digestion concerns. A line that seems blurred or ragged may indicate the need to take extra care not to overextend one's endurance. Should the line of health touch the life line, it is said to indicate a warning that one should give a healthy lifestyle a top priority.

See also PALMISTRY.

Further reading

Altman, Nathaniel. *Palmistry Workbook*. New York: Sterling, 1990.

Cheiro. *Cheiro's Book of Numbers*. New York: Prentice-Hall, 1988.

———. *The Language of the Hand*. New York: Prentice-Hall, 1987.

Robinson, Rita. *The Palm: A Guide to Your Hidden Potential*. North Hollywood, Calif.: Newcastle, 1988.

LINE OF MARS *One of the many lines in the palm of the hand that are said to reveal specific characteristics.*

The line of Mars, or Mars line, is considered a secondary, or minor, line of the hand. The secondary lines do not reveal as much about personal characteristics; they back up the information revealed in other lines. The line of Mars, for example, may or may not appear in a querant's hand. When it is found, it indicates an extra measure of protection of the aspects of the health line. According to palmists, it is especially significant as a shield should there be a break in the health line. It's appearance is an indication that the querant will be able to thwart danger.

The line of Mars is found running parallel to the line of life between the wrist and the area of the palm between the index finger and the thumb.

See also PALMISTRY.

Further reading

Altman, Nathaniel. *Palmistry Workbook*. New York: Sterling, 1990.

Cheiro. *Cheiro's Book of Numbers*. New York: Prentice-Hall, 1988.

———. *The Language of the Hand*. New York: Prentice-Hall, 1987.

Robinson, Rita. *The Palm: A Guide to Your Hidden Potential*. North Hollywood, Calif.: Newcastle, 1988.

LINE OF THE SUN *One of the many minor lines in the palm of the hand that are said to reveal specific characteristics.*

The line of the Sun is sometimes referred to as the line of luck or the line of Apollo.

This minor line is not found in all palms. However, its absence does not indicate ill fortune. Those querants whose hands do not have a line of the Sun are often hard workers who make their own luck. They seek out opportunities, not relying on the good fortune of destiny.

Running vertically between the wrist area and up toward the ring finger, the line of the Sun is said to give clues about the querant's opportunities in life. Palmists say that the longer the line, the more chances there will be for lucky breaks, especially if the line begins near the wrist rings. Should the line begin in the middle of the palm, for example, it is said to indicate that luck will begin later in life.

See also PALMISTRY.

Further reading

Altman, Nathaniel. *Palmistry Workbook*. New York: Sterling, 1990.

Cheiro. *Cheiro's Book of Numbers*. New York: Prentice-Hall, 1988.

———. *The Language of the Hand*. New York, Prentice-Hall, 1987.

Robinson, Rita. *The Palm: A Guide to Your Hidden Potential*. North Hollywood, Calif.: Newcastle, 1988.

LINES OF CHILDREN *Minor lines in the palm of the hand that are said to foretell specific details of the future.*

Older books on palmistry place great stock in the lines of children; contemporary palmists enjoy pointing out that the lines are not found in as many palms today as in the past. Since people have options concerning the conception of children, the lines of children do not definitely indicate the size a querant's family will be.

The lines of children, sometimes called child lines, are found directly above the lines of marriage on the little-finger side of the palm. When found in the palm, they are vertical. Older books on the subject claimed that strong lines indicated male children and fainter lines female children. However, the palmists of today say that the strong lines show children who will be born with forceful, assertive personalities. The fainter lines indicate artistic, sensitive and generous offspring.

Further reading

Altman, Nathaniel. *Palmistry Workbook*. New York: Sterling, 1990.

Cheiro. *Cheiro's Book of Numbers*. New York: Prentice-Hall, 1988.

———. *The Language of the Hand*. New York: Prentice-Hall, 1987.

Robinson, Rita. *The Palm: A Guide to Your Hidden Potential*. North Hollywood, Calif.: Newcastle, 1988.

LINES OF MARRIAGE   *Minor lines in the palm of the hand that are said to foretell specific details of the future.*

The lines of marriage are found on the palm of the hand about one-half inch below where the little finger joins the palm. An absence of lines does not indicate a life without love or marriage; conversely, strong, deeply set marriage lines do not mean that one will find Ms. or Mr. Right. These lines are an indicator of things that will happen in a querant's life, but free will is always available to override what destiny has in store.

Strongly marked lines of marriage are said to indicate a fulfilling alliance or close relationship. The number of lines was traditionally thought to indicate the number of marriages, but contemporary palmists now feel that a committed relationship of some length often appears in the palm, while marriages that are ill-fated do not.

Lines of marriage that are broken are indicators of challenging intimate relationships, possibly divorce or separation; long, straight lines foretell lengthy, fortunate intimate alliances. Additionally, a line of marriage that begins on the palm with a fork shows there will be difficulties at the beginning of the relationship: a stormy start. If two lines of marriage run very close together, they may indicate two love relationships in which the querant is involved at the same time.

Further reading

Altman, Nathaniel. *Palmistry Workbook*. New York: Sterling, 1990.

Cheiro. *Cheiro's Book of Numbers*. New York: Prentice-Hall, 1988.

———. *The Language of the Hand*. New York: Prentice-Hall, 1987.

LITHOMANCY   *Divination by tossing colored stones, particularly crystals or gems, or other objects to foretell the future or interpret omens. May also refer to scrying with jewels and crystals.*

Lithomancy is thought by many to be one of the most ancient divination methods. It is a form of either SCRYING or CASTING OF LOTS, depending on the method used.

Using the casting of lots or sortilege method of lithomancy, specific crystals or gems are selected, often by the psychic who will interpret the reading, but sometimes by the querant. After careful consideration a question is posed, either spoken or unspoken, and the gems are tossed onto a circle and divided much like an astrological chart, with divisions for emotions and advice. The psychic deciphers the influence of the stone as well as its placement within the circle. Stones that land beyond the circle are sometimes considered, too.

The scrying form of lithomancy—that is, studying the gem or crystal and interpreting the visions or vibrations generated from the stone—was practiced well before biblical times. Many prophets and priests wore breastplates with a pocket that contained an Urim and a Thummin, shiny stones which were used as a prediction method, to divine the future or determine the innocence or guilt of an accused.

As with crystal balls, a specific gem is placed in a quiet area, and a light source is reflected off the natural sides or cut facets of the stone. Through studying and interpreting the plays of light, the visions seen in the stone or messages received telepathically, the psychic is able to answer a querant's question, advise on a specific concern or prognosticate future events.

See also CASTING OF LOTS; CRYSTAL PREDICTIONS; GEMS; SORTILEGE SYSTEMS.

Further reading

[Cayce, Edgar.] *Gems and Stones: Readings of Edgar Cayce*. Virginia Beach, Va.: ARE Press, 1976.

Markham, Ursula. *The Crystal Workbook: A Complete Guide to Working with Crystals.* Northamptonshire, England: Aquarian Press, 1988.

———. *Fortune-Telling by Crystals and Semiprecious Stones.* Northamptonshire, England: Aquarian Press, 1987.

Matteson, Barbara J. *Mystic Minerals.* Seattle: Cosmic Resources, 1985.

Mind over Matter. Mysteries of the Unknown. Alexandria, Va.: Time Life Books, 1990.

Tinney, Merrill C., ed. *The Zondervan Pictorial Encyclopedia of the Bible.* Grand Rapids, Mich.: Zondervan Publishing House, 1977.

Walker, Dael. *The Crystal Book.* Sunol, Calif.: Crystal Col, 1983.

LULLY, RAYMOND (1235?–1315?)
Spanish mystic and psychic.

Lully's early life seems more fitting for the hero of a romance novel than for a man remembered for his work in metaphysics. Also known as Ramon Lull, Lully was a great favorite in the courts of Europe, dazzling others with his charm and winning the love of countless ladies of the day. It is said that after an unhappy love affair, Lully committed his life to Christ and began to travel extensively, preaching and attempting to convert crowds of believers in Mohammed to Christ's teachings. He was often stoned and severely beaten, eventually dying of his wounds.

Lully is best known as a mystic and alchemist, and the legend is that he found the secret of turning base metals into gold at the request of England's King Edward III. However, the more modern theory is that this story was concocted or embellished by alchemist Sir George Ripley (d. 1490?), who enjoyed stretching a good tale in order to gain publicity and popularize the works of Lully. In fact, there is no record of Lully ever meeting the king of England or of his ever visiting the British Isles.

Further reading

de Camp, L. Sprague. *The Ancient Engineers.* New York: Ballantine, 1960.

Drury, Nevill. *Dictionary of Mysticism and the Esoteric Traditions.* Dorset, England: Prism Press, 1992.

Eastern Mysteries. Mysteries of the Unknown. Alexandria, Va.: Time Life Books, 1990.

Goodrich, Norma Lorre. *Medieval Myths.* New York: New American Library, 1977.

LYNCHOMANCY *Divination using the wick of a burning candle or lantern to interpret an omen or foretell the future.*

Lynchomancy is a variation of PYROMANCY, divination by burning an object and observing the flames, and of LAMPADOMANCY, observation of flames from a candle or torch for prognostication purposes.

An antiquated prognostication method, lynchomancy is thought to have begun about A.D. 200 in Egypt. Some believe it was used along with SCRYING by the prophets mentioned in the Old Testament. Using a candle, torch or lantern, they prophesied by meditating on a burning candle wick and interpreting the way the wick burned and/or what was seen in the part of the wick closest to the flame.

Unlike other methods that used flames and candles, only children in ancient Egypt were allowed to practice lynchomancy. It was thought that young minds were clearer than those of adults; their direct connection with the gods led to more valid predictions.

See also CANDLE PROPHECY; CAPNOMANCY; LAMPADOMANCY; PYROMANCY.

Further reading

Dey, Charmaine. *The Magic Candle.* Bronx, N.Y.: Original Publications, 1989.

Morgan, Chris. *Fortune Telling: How to Predict Your Own Future.* London: Quintet Publishing and Random House, 1992.

Pajeon, Kala, and Ketz Pajeon. *The Candle Magic Workbook.* New York: Citadel Press, 1992.

Walker, Barbara G. *The Woman's Encyclopedia of Myths and Secrets.* New York: Harper Collins, 1983.

MACHEN, ARTHUR (1863–1947) Welsh mystic, occult scholar and author.

Best remembered for his beautifully written novels and short stories, which reflected his personal philosophy of the metaphysical, pagan and mystical memories of reincarnation as well as a future world, Machen was also a conservationist. It is said that he was most comfortable and happiest in the Welsh countryside, and he spent considerable time there. He believed that in the outdoors he could come closest to his Celtic and Druid incarnations, which was his spiritual quest.

Published in 1900, *Hill of Dreams* is considered to be the most beautiful of Machen's novels. Among his best loved short stories are "The Happy Children," "The Great Return" and "A Fragment of Life." His personal, mystical convictions are outlined in *Far Off Things, Things Near and Far* and *The London Adventure* (published between 1915 and 1923). Many of his works are still in print and often are available at libraries and used-book stores.

For a short time, Machen belonged to the HERMETIC ORDER OF THE GOLDEN DAWN, the London-based magical society headed by various individuals, including Aleister Crowley. However, Machen withdrew from the group because his mystical beliefs did not coincide with the ritualistic magic that was the society's foundation.

Further reading

Drury, Nevill. *Dictionary of Mysticism and the Esoteric Traditions.* Dorset, England: Prism Press, 1992.

Nichols, Ross. *The Book of Druidry—History, Sites, Wisdom.* London: Aquarian Press, 1990.

MACULOMANCY Divination by the shape, placement and size of birthmarks on the human body.

It is thought that the study of birthmarks, also known as moleomancy, molesophy and molescopy, originated with the ancient Chinese. Maculomancy was practiced widely and then passed throughout Europe at a very early time. Greek scientist, teacher and doctor Hippocrates (460?–377? B.C.), called the "Father of Medicine" and considered to be the greatest physician of antiquity, is said to have investigated maculomancy to some length. Hippocrates came to the conclusion that birthmarks should be considered in reviewing the total health of his patients. This same belief is held by many physicians and healers today. The gypsies who traveled throughout Europe held great store in the size, color, shape and placement of moles, which they believed foretold personal fortune or misfortune as well as health.

The meanings of moles and other birthmarks vary as widely as the psychics who translate their message. Basically, the darker the mole or mark, the more significance they hold. Birthmarks that are round are considered fortuitous. Those that are long or oblong reveal a propensity for prosperity. Those marks that seem to have angles tell of a personality that has memorable qualities: a charismatic smile, a fiery temper.

According to those who practice maculomancy, the following are locations and meanings of marks found on the human body. To simplify the text, all moles, spots, freckles and birthmarks will be referred to as marks.

Forehead: A mark in the center of the forehead indicates an active, enterprising individual with the potential to be rich. He or she will be happy and successful in business as well as personal attachments, relationships and marriage. However, the aspects are not as promising if the mark is on the left side of the forehead; hard work and thrift will be the qualities needed to succeed. If the mark is on the right, the individual can count on happiness along with some toil; the mark might foretell of an extremely satisfying marriage and/or loving partnerships.

Eyebrow area: A mark near or on the right eyebrow denotes a vivacious personality and a wealth of courage. Those who have marks in this area can expect to have great wealth, as well as fulfillment in love and business. Someone with this mark will go through life with a successful love partnership, forming a lasting bond and producing healthy, well-adjusted offspring.

A mark on or near the left eyebrow is said to indicate a quick temper and a cantankerous disposition, perhaps with a predisposition to compulsiveness and alcohol or other addictions. Regarding romance and love, this individual may have disappointments in love and marriage, with children or career.

Eyes: A mark very near either eye is said to indicate someone who is confident and serious. He or she can see through the superficial to the heart of a person's motive.

Ears: Marks on either ear imply that one is destined for great wealth. But if the mark is on the lower portion of the lobe, the individual should be extremely careful around water, as there is the possibility of accidents.

Nose: When marks appear on the nose, it is thought to indicate a lustful and/or lively personality; he or she is a successful, goal-oriented individual, open to all friendships. This mark might foretell a brooding nature; this individual may also have a tendency to sulk, or to overindulge with food or alcohol.

Cheeks: Someone who has a mark on either cheek is industrious and kindhearted. If the mark is on the right cheek, there is a tendency to be flirtatious; on the left, the mark reveals a provocative nature.

Mouth: A mark near the mouth indicates a passionate, "life of the party" personality.

Lips: When a mark appears on or near the lips, one is said to empathize with the underdog, to be compassionate and love his or her fellow humans. The individual should continually monitor his or her health; this person may have a fragile constitution.

Chin: A mark on the chin means that the individual is generous and thoughtful. He or she will flourish regardless of career path.

Neck: A mark on the neck reveals an argumentative nature that may become more extreme with age. If the mark is in the front, the trait will be tempered with humor; if it is on the back, the trait will be more extreme.

Shoulders: A person who has a mark on the right shoulder is said to have a thirst for knowledge and often will be employed in academia. With a mark on the left shoulder, a person must beware of being too argumentative; yet great thinkers and successful entrepreneurs are often those who question the hows and whys of life, and those with marks on the left shoulder are often extremely successful in the world of business.

Arms: Marks on the upper left arm indicate a suspicious, sometimes anxious personality. Marks on the upper right arm indicate one who will be able to accomplish a great deal.

On either arm and in any position, a mark is indicative of one who may face many challenges in life but will overcome them in order to achieve lasting and meaningful success.

Armpits: In the left armpit, a mark may indicate that success is delayed but achievable. In the right armpit, one will deeply experience both the highs and lows of life.

Elbows: Marks on the elbows show a person who has great talent but with a tendency to be ambivalent.

Wrists: When there is a mark on the wrist, the individual has strong creative talents; this is someone who might be an inventor or an entrepreneur, with all the skills needed to turn ideas into million-dollar enterprises.

Hands: Marks on the hands tell of a person who understands that true affluence and personal achievement do not always mean wealth. Yet this person is far from complacent. He or she will continue to work hard, often in helping others to achieve their goals.

Fingers: Marks on the fingers are thought to indicate a shifty nature; here is someone who always thinks the grass is greener in someone else's field, business or life. He or she probably wants a half acre of that, too.

Back: The marks on the back below the shoulder blades indicate many obstacles and setbacks in life. Above the shoulder blades, the marks indicate that the obstacles will be surmounted quickly.

Buttocks: With their tendency toward laziness, those with marks on the buttocks may be destined to be poor. This poverty may be in an emotional, physical or spiritual sense, as well.

Chest: Marks on the right side of the chest indicate a tendency to be slothful and somewhat lacking in discipline. On the left side of the chest, marks indicate an enthusiastic, active personality. Marks anywhere on the chest also indicate an extremely amorous nature.

Breast: When a mark is on the right breast, it shows a tendency toward excesses in food or drink; this person may become overly passionate. Along with this comes a warning: Beware of false friendships and partnerships. On the left breast, a mark denotes one who is thrifty, helpful and caring. He or she may be a thoughtful, passionate lover and should have success in all areas of life.

Nipples: Marks on the nipples of women indicate they will have many children. On men, marks show they may spend too much time chasing women, ignoring long-term loving relationships.

Rib cage: On the right side of the rib cage, a mark reveals a heartless, cold personality. On the left side, a mark is indicative of an irascible nature.

Stomach: Marks on the stomach are thought to indicate a self-indulgent person who considers him- or herself to be above the common person. Such an individual may be able to convince others of anything. He or she may accumulate great wealth but little happiness.

Navel: This is a very fortuitous sign. A mark on the navel means that one has a nurturing personality; perhaps he or she will have many children or "birth" wonderful business or artistic concepts. This is a mark of success and genuine satisfaction in all undertakings.

Groin: A mark in this area is said to indicate a delicate disposition, perhaps someone who is easily hurt. On the right side, this person will have untold riches but disappointments in later life. On the left side, this person may experience the disappointments without the wealth.

Genitals: A mark on the genitals is said to indicate an unselfish nature. This person will have a long-term love relationship and will not want for anything. Someone with a mark in this area may become the parent of a genius.

Hips: When there is a mark on either hip, the individual is contented, loving and responsible. Here is a faithful lover and friend, a hardworking partner, a good provider.

Thighs: On the right thigh, a mark indicates someone who is able to achieve all he or she attempts. On the left thigh, a mark indicates challenges and the inability to commit wholeheartedly to a loving relationship.

Knees: When there is a mark on the right knee, it indicates a caring disposition and an even temper; this is a hardworking individual. A mark on the left knee is a sign of affluence.

Legs: A mark on either leg is a sign that motivation must come from within; the individual should depend on him- or herself more than on others. This is also a sign of a tendency toward capriciousness or of a liberal nature.

Ankles: Any mark on either ankle indicates strength of character, although the individual may be quiet and seem far too gentle. In women, a mark is a great sign of courage. In men, it may mean a streak of reticence that may be seen as cowardice.

Feet: On the upper foot, a mark is a sign of dishonesty or of one who entertains dishonest thoughts. Marks on the feet are said to indicate disappointment. A mark on the instep indicates a belligerent nature; this person strongly believes he or she is right. On the heel, a mark tells of an aggressive personality. Marks on the toes indicate that one may marry someone very rich but become disappointed with the absence of love in the relationship.

See also ANTHROPOSOMANCY.

Further reading

Bary, William Theodore de, ed. *Sources of Chinese Traditions.* New York: Columbia University Press, 1960.

Buckland, Raymond. *Secrets of Gypsy Fortune Telling.* St. Paul, Minn.: Llewellyn, 1988.

Leland, Charles Godfrey. *Gypsy Sorcery and Fortune Telling.* New York: University Books, 1962.

Maven, Max. *Max Maven's Book of Fortunetelling.* New York: Prentice-Hall, 1992.

Opie, Iona, and Moira Tatem. *A Dictionary of Superstitions.* Oxford: Oxford University Press, 1992.

Walker, Barbara G. *The Woman's Encyclopedia of Myths and Secrets.* New York: Harper Collins, 1983.

Visions and Prophecies. Mysteries of the Unknown. Alexandria, Va.: Time Life Books, 1990.

MAJOR ARCANA *Division of the most important cards in the tarot pack of divining cards.*

The major arcana, which is sometimes referred to as the greater trumps, includes 22 cards, typically numbered from 1 to 21—the Fool is often numbered with a 0 or else is unnumbered. The minor arcana has 56 cards.

Some contemporary, more artistically designed packs are not numbered. They can be beautifully crafted, appearing to be works of art rather than tools of prognostication. Antique tarot cards are sometimes worth considerable sums.

Psychics report that when most of the major arcana cards appear during a tarot reading, the querant is a seeker of spiritual knowledge; a preponderance of minor arcana cards often indicate that less consequential questions are being asked.

The Cards

The Fool Some readers believe that this card represents the querant, as in the broadest sense we are all fools and at times need to understand the children we are at heart. We can be tricked and misled and sometimes must be guided. Generally, this is a complex card that indicates things that the querant should be aware of or avoid. The Fool is said to reflect agitation and may indicate chaos of mind, personality or emotion. If the Fool card appears, it may mean that one will face a personal problem. The Fool also signifies someone (or something) who is lighthearted, pleasurable and warm, sometimes with little discipline or restraint.

If the card is reversed (i.e., appears upside down in a spread), it may indicate an inability to make a sound decision, or a wrong choice or excessive chaos. When a reversed Fool appears in a querant's spread, it may be that he or she needs to concentrate less on having fun and develop a more serious side in order to grow.

The Magician The Magician is said to reflect artistic and innovative endeavors or opportunities. The card indicates power, skill and secrets. When it appears in a tarot spread, the Magician may signify that the querant should finish what he or she has started, avoid fooling him- or herself and concentrate on the creative ability to proceed. If the card is reversed, it may indicate the misuse of power or force, an inability to complete work and/or bungling in personal or professional circumstances.

The High Priestess This card denotes great knowledge, shrewdness and perception. It is the symbol of intuition, mystery and psychic

THE FOOL.

THE MAGICIAN.

The Fool   *Typically, the Fool is unnumbered or is inscribed with a 0. Some readers believe that this card is the querant, as in the broadest sense, we are all fools and at times need to understand the children we are at heart. We can be tricked and misled and sometimes must be guided. Generally, this is a complex card and indicates things of which the querant should be aware or avoid. The Fool is said to reflect agitation and may indicate chaos of mind, personality or emotion. If it is in regard to the answer to the querant's question, there may be some upheaval that must be faced. The Fool also signifies someone (or something) who is lighthearted, pleasurable and warm, sometimes with little discipline or restraint.*

If the card is reversed, it may indicate the lack of ability to make a sound decision, a wrong choice or excessive chaos. When a reversed Fool is in a querant's spread, it may be considered that he or she needs to concentrate less on having fun and balance a more serious side in order to grow.

The Magician   *The Magician is a card said to reflect artistic and innovative endeavors. It indicates power, skill and secrets. When it appears in a tarot spread, the Magician may signify that the querant should finish what he or she has started, avoid fooling him- or herself and concentrate on one's creative ability to proceed. If the card is reversed, it may indicate the misuse of power or force, the inability to complete work or bungling of personal or professional circumstances.*

talents. It may signal that there is something hidden, something secret that is to be revealed. This card may indicate that there is great serenity in the situation or with the querant. The High Priestess can also signify that the querant is hiding from or avoiding emotional relationships. Reversed, this card is said to designate shallowness, ignorance or the choice to be ignorant and reflects poor judgment.

The Empress   This is the traditional "female" card and reflects the ideals of home and health. When the Empress appears in a tarot spread, it may signal marriage, children, fertility, evolution, creativity and nurturance of creative projects. For example, if the querant is a man asking about a specific work program, the Empress's position in the spread can reveal that he must nurture his work and/or seek out creative solutions rather than intellectual avenues in order to gain success.

Should the card be reversed, it may indicate inaction, problems in the areas of home and

THE EMPRESS.

The Empress *This is the traditional "female" card and reflects thoughts about conservative roles. When the Empress appears in a tarot spread, it may signal marriage, children, fertility, evolution, creativity and nurturing others or creative projects. For example, if the querant is a man asking about a specific work program, the Empress's position in the spread can reveal that he must nurture his work and/or seek out creative solutions rather than intellectual avenues in order to gain success.*

If the card is reversed, it may indicate inaction, problems in the areas of home and children and the squandering of creative and original energies.

THE HIGH PRIESTESS

The High Priestess *This card denotes great knowledge, shrewdness and perception. It is the symbol of intuition, mystery and psychic talents. It may signal that there is something hidden, something secret that is to be revealed. This card may show that there is great serenity in the situation or with the querant. The High Priestess can also express that the querant is hiding from or avoiding emotional relationships.*

Reversed, this card is said to designate shallowness, ignorance or the choice to be ignorant, and it reflects poor judgment.

children or the squandering of creative and original energies.

The Emperor The traditional "male" card, the Emperor signifies success, power, control and fatherhood. These qualities are exhibited, of course, in women, too. The Emperor card indicates a desire for strength and intelligence over emotion and love. If this card is reversed

THE EMPEROR.

THE HIEROPHANT.

to the querant's question has to do with an emotional decision, though not necessarily one relating to romantic issues. Often there is a conflict between emotion and intelligence, love and lust, earthly pursuits and spiritual desires. The card shows a quality of harmony and goodness.

When the card appears in a reversed position, the message is of hindrance. This stoppage may be the disintegration of a previously held opinion, philosophy or relationship. It may also draw the querant's attention to the need for reevaluation.

The Emperor   *The traditional "male" card, the Emperor signifies success, power, control and fatherhood. These qualities are exhibited, of course, in women, too. The Emperor card indicates a desire to have strength and intelligence over emotion and love.*

If this card is reversed in a spread, it is said to indicate a lack of power, dominance, strength or maturity.

in a spread, it indicates a lack of power, dominance, strength or maturity.

The Hierophant or High Priest   A spiritual card; this tarot symbol speaks of power and the power of rituals. The card indicates a kind, benevolent leader, but there is also a message that there is an unwillingness to change and/or an extremely conservative nature.

The reversed card indicates a zest for the unconventional that is shaded with the tendency to be naive and easily swayed.

The Lovers   When the Lovers appear in a tarot card reading, it is an indication that the answer

The Hierophant or High Priest   *A spiritual card, this tarot symbol tells of power and the power of rituals, indicating a kind, benevolent leader. However, there is also a message of a lack of willingness to change and/or the possession of an extremely conservative nature.*

A reversal of the card indicates a zest for the unconventional shaded with the tendency to be naive and easily swayed.

THE LOVERS.

she should accept a promotion. In the course of the conversation, it is brought out that she will have to move her family to another state and is concerned about the job and the move. When the reader considers other cards in a spread, it becomes evident that the move will be beneficial.

When the card is in the reverse position, the Chariot shows the tendency for defeat, failure or catastrophe. Thus, if a reversed Chariot appeared in the above example, it might indicate that the physician would do best to stay in her present location and not accept the new job.

The Lovers   When the Lovers appear in a tarot card reading, it is an indication that the answer to the querant's question has to do with an emotional decision (not necessarily one relating to romantic issues). Often there is conflict between emotion and intelligence, love and lust, earthly pursuits and spiritual desires. The card shows a quality of harmony and goodness.

When the card appears in a reversed position, the message is that there may be some hindrance. This stoppage may be the disintegration of a previously held opinion, philosophy or relationship. It may also draw the querant's attention to the need for reevaluation.

The Chariot   This card speaks of change, movement and transfiguration. It denotes some chaos but also that troubles will be overcome, and success is the final outcome. Often the Chariot indicates a journey. As an example, let's say this card appears in the spread of a doctor who is asking for counsel on whether

THE CHARIOT.

The Chariot   *This card indicates change, movement and transfiguration. It denotes some chaos but also asserts that troubles will be overcome and success will be the final outcome.*

When the card is in the reverse position, it indicates a tendency for defeat, failure, and catastrophe.

Justice As the name implies, Justice indicates balance, truth and equality. Temptation, while it might exist, will not entice the querant.

In the reversed position, Justice shows a proclivity for the abuse of power, discrimination and intolerance.

The Hermit This is the card that reveals wisdom, knowledge, spirituality and awareness of the universal message. It may also indicate a need to seek these lessons alone, perhaps even deserting previously held thoughts and ideas.

The reversed position indicates a naive, im-

THE HERMIT.

The Hermit *This is the card that tells of wisdom, knowledge, spirituality and awareness of the universal message. It may indicate a need to seek these lessons alone, perhaps even by deserting previously held thoughts and ideas.*

The reversed position tells of a naive, immature outlook on life and of a personality that acts before thinking.

JUSTICE .

Justice *As the name implies, Justice indicates balance, truth and equality. Temptation, while it might exist, will not tempt the querant.*

In the reversed position, Jutice shows a proclivity for the abuse of power, discrimination and intolerance.

mature outlook on life, a personality that acts before thinking.

The Wheel of Fortune An auspicious card, the Wheel of Fortune shows that there will be unexpected or abrupt prosperity. Prosperity, however, does not always mean money; it can also signify a wealth of friends, love, opportunities and experiences. The meaning of the Wheel of Fortune is, of course, dependent on the other cards in the spread. It may also suggest a transmutation, intellectually, emotionally and/or spiritually.

When the Wheel of Fortune appears in the

WHEEL of FORTUNE.

He or she may be easily swayed to negative thoughts and allows (real or imagined) barriers to inhibit progress.

The Hanged Man While this card looks deadly, tarot card readers claim that it simply means that a change is imminent. As with the Death card, all changes make action in one direction stop (sometimes for a while); then another energy guides us on a different course. The Hanged Man is fortuitous because it indicates a rebirth, a renewal of effort and great improvement coming to the querant.

STRENGTH.

The Wheel of Fortune *An auspicious card, the Wheel of Fortune predicts unexpected or abrupt prosperity. Besides money, prosperity can mean a wealth of friends, love, opportunities and experiences. The meaning of the Wheel of Fortune is, of course, dependent on the other cards in the spread. It may also tell of an intellectual, emotional and/or spiritual transmutation.*

When the Wheel of Fortune appears in the reversed position, there is a message to hold back until there is more information.

reversed position, the message is to hold back until there is more information and to interrupt a current course of behavior.

Strength A strong, favorable card in any reading, the Strength card indicates that through courage and conviction, good will triumph over evil; love will win. It also conveys the message that one should acknowledge and depend on physical ability. The Strength card says that through fortitude, all is possible.

In the reverse position, Strength signifies that the querant has frequent losses of hope.

Strength *A strong, favorable card in any reading, the Strength card tells that through courage and conviction, good will triumph over evil; love will win. There is also the message that one should acknowledge and count on physical ability. The Strength card says that through fortitude, all is possible.*

In the reverse position, Strength shows that the querant has frequent losses of hope. He or she may be easily swayed to negative thoughts and allows real or imagined barriers to inhibit progress.

When the card appears in the reversed position, there is an absence of effort, a need to find the "easy way out," rather than persevere, and perhaps a refusal to do what is necessary to accomplish goals.

Death This card shows unexpected changes, often abrupt, often exciting and definitely different. Though the illustration on the card looks foreboding, it is a good card. It tells the

DEATH.

Death *This card shows unexpected changes, often abrupt, often exciting and definitely different. Although the illustration on the card looks foreboding, it is a good card. It tells the querant that there is to be progress made. It explains new beginnings and transformations. For example, if a querant has asked if he or she should sell a house and buy a smaller residence, the appearance of this card is probably saying yes.*

However, in this same example, should the card be reversed, it would indicate that the querant needs to stay in that house for some time to come. In the reverse, Death indicates that this is not a time for change, perhaps not a time to take on new ventures.

THE HANGED MAN.

The Hanged Man *Though this card looks deadly, tarot card readers claim that it simply means that a change is imminent. As with the Death card, all changes make action in one direction stop (sometimes for a while); then another energy guides us on a different course. The Hanged Man is fortuitous because it indicates a rebirth, a renewal of effort and great improvement coming to the querant.*

When the card appears in the reversed position, it tells there is an absence of effort, a need to find the "easy way out," rather than through perseverance, and perhaps a refusal to do what is necessary to accomplish goals.

querant that there is to be progress made. It explains new beginnings and transformations. For example, if a querant has asked if he or she should sell a house and buy a smaller residence, the appearance of this card is probably saying yes.

However, in this same example, should the card be reversed, it would indicate that the querant needs to stay in that house for some time to come. In the reverse, Death indicates that this is not a time for change, perhaps not a time to take on new ventures.

Temperance   One of the most fortunate cards of the tarot, Temperance tells of the joy of patience and frugality. In a spread, its message is to learn of spiritual ideas and seek harmony through action and love.

In the reversed position, Temperance shows lack of harmony, lack of balance, conflicts and negative emotions.

The Devil   Even this ominous-looking card provides a worthy message to a querant, since the Devil reveals influences of evil sur-

rounding the querant. Should he or she choose not to alter present circumstances, there may be failure. This is a warning. Those who read tarot cards explain that the Devil's warning is much like a yellow traffic signal—there will be a change forthcoming. The card also indicates

THE DEVIL.

TEMPERANCE.

Temperance   One of the most fortuitous cards of the tarot, Temperance tells of the joy of patience and frugality. In a spread, its message is to learn of spiritual ideas and seek harmony through action and love.

In the reversed position, Temperance shows lack of harmony, lack of balance, conflicts and negative emotions.

The Devil   Even this ominous-looking card provides a worthy message to a querant, since the Devil reveals influences of evil surrounding the querant. Should he or she choose not to alter present circumstances, there may be failure. This is a warning. Those who read tarot cards explain that the Devil's warning is much like the yellow traffic signal—there will be a change forthcoming. The card also indicates sexual temptation. For instance, if the querant is considering having an affair and this card appears in an influential position, the likelihood of a happy future is small, regardless of the current indications.

When the Devil appears in the reversed position, this tells of a release from past burdens, illumination, an opportunity for freedom. Thus, it is a fortuitous card.

sexual temptation. For instance, if the querant is considering having an affair and this card appears in an influential position, the likelihood of a happy future is small, regardless of the current indications.

The Devil in the reversed position indicates a release from past burdens, illumination and an opportunity for freedom. Thus, it is a fortuitous card.

The Tower Change is the message of the Tower card; it signifies sudden disruption, unexpected alteration. What was hoped for may be

lost forever, yet through change there is time to rebuild, to reestablish and to become even stronger through the experience.

In the reversed position, the Tower means there will be a continuation of life as it is now. This can indicate boredom, an imprisonment or a need to have life stay the same.

The Star If one is looking for bright and beautiful opportunities, when the Star appears in a

THE TOWER.

THE STAR.

The Tower   *Change is the message of the Tower card; it signifies sudden disruption, unexpected alteration. What was hoped for may be lost forever, yet through change there is time to rebuild, to reestablish and to become even stronger through the experience.*

In the reversed position, the Tower means there will be a continuation of life as it is now. This can indicate boredom, an imprisonment or a need to have life stay the same.

The Star   *If one is looking for bright and beautiful opportunities, when the Star appears in a tarot card spread, there is a strong possibility that these goals will be manifest. The card indicates true success through hard work and perseverance, new opportunities, new creative ways to channel knowledge. When this card appears in a reading, it might indicate that it is a good time to embark on a new business or change careers and that strife will end.*

When the card is in the reversed position, there is the possibility of disappointment, little chance for success in the current position or place and a possible setback.

tarot card spread, there is a strong possibility that these goals will be manifest. The card indicates true success through hard work and perseverance, new opportunities, creative ways to channel knowledge. When this card appears in a reading, it might indicate that it is a good time to embark on a new business or change careers and that strife will end.

When the card is in the reversed position, there is the possibility of disappointment, little chance for success in the current position or place and a possible setback.

The Moon The message of this card is to be cautious of being deceived, particularly involving trickery. It may be telling the querant to beware of disloyal or false friends. All is not what it seems.

When the card appears in the reverse position, the querant is to be advised that problems or concerns are insignificant, although it might seem the opposite at that time. Mistakes or subterfuge will be overcome. The querant need not be afraid.

The Sun The theme of the Sun card is enlightenment, revelation, knowingness beyond expectation. There is also the news that success is forthcoming, there is love here, perhaps happiness in marriage or satisfaction and delight in the little events of life.

The Sun in the reverse position, however, may foretell disillusionment, failure, shattered alliances and relationships. Readers tell querants to keep in mind that even when the Sun appears upside down, it does not absolutely mean a romance will be ended. It is a warning that should events continue without change, a breakup may occur.

Judgment This card represents the culmination of spiritual growth. It indicates that the flowering of knowledge has taken place and that the querant is close to understanding the meaning of his or her life, or perhaps the meaning of the question at hand. Yet it comes with a warning: One must review past experiences and conduct in order to continue to move ahead.

When the card is reversed, it indicates that

THE MOON.

The Moon. *The message of this card is to be cautious of being deceived, particularly involving trickery. It may be telling the querant to beware of disloyal or false friends. All is not what it seems.*

When the card appears in the reverse position, the querant is to be advised that problems or concerns are insignificant, although it might seem the opposite at that time. Mistakes or subterfuge will be overcome. The querant need not be afraid.

there may be a holdup of some sort, perhaps a period of indecision. Again, here is a warning that one must review in order to move forward.

The World The focus of The World is change. One must look to change in order to succeed; by doing so success will be possible. The World shows the continuing cycle of life, of death and rebirth in the physical sense as well as emotionally and spiritually. Most readers believe that this is one of the most fortuitous of all cards.

Appearing in the reversed position, The World indicates the possibility for failure or the inability to complete projects or follow through with opportunities. Yet as with all cards, this may be just the counsel the querant needs in order to reverse trends and previous actions.

See also ARCANA; CARTOMANCY; TAROT.

Further reading

Buckland, Raymond. *Secrets of Gypsy Fortune Telling.* St. Paul, Minn.: Llewellyn, 1988.

Giles, Cynthia. *The Tarot: History, Mystery and Lore.* New York: Paragon House, 1992.

Morgan, Chris. *Fortune Telling: How to Predict Your Own Future.* London: Quintet Publishing and Random House, 1992.

THE SUN .

JUDGEMENT.

The Sun *The theme of the Sun card is enlightenment, revelation, and knowingness beyond expectation. There is also the news that success is forthcoming; there is love here, perhaps happiness in marriage or satisfaction and delight in the little events of life.*

The Sun in the reverse position, however, may foretell disillusionment, failure, shattered alliances and relationships. Readers tell querants to keep in mind that even when the Sun appears upside down, it does not absolutely mean a romance will be ended. It is a warning that should events continue without change, a breakup may occur.

Judgment *This card represents the culmination of spiritual growth. It indicates that the flowering of knowledge has taken place and that the querant is close to understanding the meaning of his or her life or perhaps the meaning of the question at hand. Yet it comes with a warning: One must review past experiences and conduct in order to continue to move ahead.*

When the card is reversed, it indicates that there may be a delay of some sort, perhaps a period of indecision. Again, here is a warning that one must review in order to move forward.

THE WORLD.

The World *The focus of The World is change. One must look to change in order to succeed; by doing so success will be possible. The World shows the continuing cycle of life, of death and rebirth in the physical sense as well as emotionally and spiritually. Most readers believe that this is one of the most fortuitous of all cards.*

Appearing in the reversed position, The World indicates the possibility for failure, the inability to complete projects or follow through with opportunities. Yet as with all cards, this may be just the counsel the querant needs in order to reverse trends and previous actions.

Secrets of the Alchemists. Mysteries of the Unknown. Alexandria, Va.: Time Life Books, 1990.
Visions and Prophecies. Mysteries of the Unknown. Alexandria, Va.: Time Life Books, 1990.

-MANCY *In divination, a suffix meaning to obtain knowledge from something or in a particular manner.*

For instance, in chiromancy or necromancy, one seeks metaphysical knowledge from the hand or from the dead.

The suffix comes from the Middle English and Old French *mancie,* derived in turn from the Late Latin *-mantia,* which is descended from the Greek *manteia,* meaning divination. *Manteia* came from the word *manteuesthia,* meaning to predict, and from *mantis,* meaning a prophet.

MANNING, MATTHEW *(1956–) British psychic.*

One of the most reclusive but important psychics of contemporary times, Manning lives in England and attempts to stay out of the public eye.

Manning, who prefers the term *mentalist* to psychic, is able to write and draw automatically. His paintings, according to art experts, often are in a strikingly accurate style, very close to that of Leonardo da Vinci, Beatrix Potter and Henri Matisse, to name a few. He communicates with their spirits telepathically. He can move objects and transports them around rooms, making them appear and disappear at will. He can bend metal with the same ability as Uri Geller, and he has correctly predicted the future.

Like many psychics, Manning realized his gifts at an early age but was plagued by visits from ghosts and poltergeists. During his school years, strange happenings continued; once he began trying to communicate with the spirits, the ghostly activities stopped. He believes he has communicated with a number of great people from the past, including Bertrand Russell, the British Nobel laureate, mathematician and philosopher who died in 1970.

Manning's books describe his initiation into the metaphysical realm. *The Link,* written in 1974, describes how he learned of his gifts at age 11. *In the Mind of Millions,* written in 1977, describes the startling events he has predicted, including a plane crash at Kennedy International Airport and a subway accident in London's underground.

As with many who possess psychic gifts, he has been accused of fraud and trickery and, as a result, Manning prefers to live in seclusion.

Further reading

Fodor, Nandor. *Encyclopedia of Psychic Science*. New York: University Books, 1966.

Guiley, Rosemary Ellen. *The Encyclopedia of Ghosts and Spirits*. New York: Facts On File, 1992.

———. *Harper's Encyclopedia of Mystical and Paranormal Experience*. San Francisco: HarperSan Francisco, 1991.

Manning, Matthew. *The Link*. New York: Ballantine, 1974.

MANTIC ART *To ask a question either silently or verbally and to immediately use a system in a manner that reveals the hidden answer.*

The mantic arts date from well before recorded time. There is reference to their use as far back as the Ice Age. Cave dwellers attempted to use available objects to foretell the future, settle disputes, reveal hidden answers, solve problems or explain events. Through myths and legends, we know that natural objects such as bones, sand, fire, rocks and clouds were all employed as prognostic methods by the earliest psychics.

Mantic arts refer specifically to the use of inert or nonhuman objects. Other forms of prognostication use telepathic qualities without the use of tools. The popularity of the mantic arts has waxed and waned throughout the centuries. At times those who practiced prediction methods hid their gifts for fear of being put to death, as did Nostradamus. During other periods those with psychic gifts have been lavished with wealth and riches. Mediums and psychics often became popular in the courts, ballrooms and parlors of the world, including during the resurgence of spiritualism that occurred in the late 1800s.

There have been entire centuries when mantic arts have been suppressed and those who practiced them persecuted. This has not been confined to the so-called Dark Ages. During Hitler's Third Reich psychics were hunted down, arrested and jailed, and many were put to death. Metaphysical books and other occult material, even those found in private libraries and museum collections, were destroyed regardless of their historical value.

In about 2000 B.C. in ancient China, the I Ching was used by the nobility as well as the common person to help forecast future events and open a window of understanding on situations currently troubling the querant. Some believe that all mantic arts were derived from the I Ching's *Book of Changes*, which says, "Symbols come into existence in precedence of substance."

During Old Testament times, determining the future and interpreting events through the use of MANTIC OBJECTS was accepted. Most people believed that the universe guided people through signs and symbols. For example, it is thought that priests and other psychics of the time used a method similar to TASSEOGRAPHY, the technique of divining the future that also used the patterns formed by oil poured on top of water in a bowl or cup. This skill was attributed to Joseph (Gen. 44:5, 15). Many prophets and priests wore breastplates with a pocket that contained shiny stones said to have been used as a sortilege method (see SORTILEGE SYSTEMS). With the spread of Christianity, the use of objects to foretell upcoming events or explain situations was considered dangerous and was outlawed in most of Europe.

Most mantic arts are technically known by their Greek or historical root word name, ending with *-mancy*. For instance, sciomancy (predicting the future through interpreting shadows) comes from the Greek word *skia*, which means shadow. Halomancy (predicting the future by casting salt and then interpreting the patterns formed) originated from the Greek word *hals*, for salt.

As with every "rule," the definition of mantic arts has exceptions; there are mantic arts that do employ human points of focus as tools. As an illustration, cheriomancy is divination and character analysis by studying the nails, lines and fingers of a person's hand. And ANTHROPOMANCY, an offshoot of hepatomancy practiced by the ancient Babylonians, Sumerians, Japanese, Greeks and Romans, utilizes the entrails, the inner organs (specifically the intestines) of human sacrifices.

See also BIBLICAL PROPHETS AND DIVINATION METHODS; DIVINATION; I CHING; MANTIC OBJECTS; PSYCHIC; TASSEOGRAPHY.

Further reading

Buckland, Raymond. *Doors to Other Worlds*. St. Paul, Minn.: Llewellyn, 1993.

King, Francis, and Stephen Skinner. *Techniques of High Magic*. Rochester, Vt.: Destiny Books, 1991.

Loewe, Michael, and Carmen Blacker, eds. *Divination and Oracles*. London: Allen & Unwin, 1981.

Logan, Jo, and Lindsey Hodson. *The Prediction Book of Divination*. Dorset, England: Blandford Press, 1984.

Miller, Madeleine S., and J. Lane Miller, eds. *Harper's Encyclopedia of Bible Life*. San Francisco: Harper & Row, 1978.

Wilhelm, Richard, and Cary F. Baynes. *The I Ching* (translation). Bollingen series 19, Princeton, N.J.: Princeton University Press, 1969.

Woods, R., ed. *Understanding Mysticism*. New York: Doubleday, 1980.

MANTIC OBJECTS *Articles used as a point of focus in a divination process.*

The following articles, objects, animals and items have been and/or are currently used to predict the future or to interpret omens and events:

Animals and animal behaviors: Alectryomancy, apantomancy, felidomancy, hippomancy, myomancy, ophimancy, ornithomancy, theriomancy, zoomancy.

Animals and chance encounters: Apantomancy.

Animal innards and livers: epatoscomancy, extispiciomancy, hapatromancy, hepatomancy.

Arrows: Belomancy.

Ashes: Tephramancy.

Atmospheric conditions: Aeromancy, alectromancy, nephelomancy, selenomancy.

Attire, dress: Stolisomancy.

Ax: Axinomancy.

Baby caul: Amniomancy.

Barley bread: Alphitomancy.

Barley flour: Critomancy.

Beans, bones, other small objects: Cleromancy.

Bible passages: Bibliomancy.

Birds: Ornithomancy.

Bones: Astragyromancy, cephalomancy, haruspicy, kephalonomancy, onomancy, scapulomancy.

Books and verses: Stichomancy.

Burned branches: Botanomancy.

Burning of objects or sacrifices: Anthropomancy, capnomancy, causimonancy, pyromancy.

Cakes: Critomancy.

Candles: Lapadomancy, lynchomancy, zoanthropy.

Cards: Cartomancy, tarot.

Casting of lots: Astragyromancy, sortilege.

Cats: Felidomancy.

Chance words and/or remarks overheard in a crowd: Cledonomancy, transatuaumancy.

Circles that revolve: Cyclomancy.

Circle trance: Aspidomancy.

Clouds: Aeromancy, nephelomancy.

Communication with the dead: Necromancy, nigromancy.

Cookies and cakes: Aleuromancy.

Crystal ball and crystal gazing: Crystalomancy, scrying.

Dice: Astragalomancy, astragyromancy, casting of lots, runes, sortilege.

Disease diagnosis: Iatromancy.

Dizziness from circling: Gyromancy.

Dowsing: Rhabdomancy.

Dreams: Oneiromancy.

Earth-based or earth-related and naturally found objects: Alectromancy, *feng shui*, geomancy, halomancy, nephelomancy, tasseography, pessomancy.

Eggs: Oomancy.

Entrails: Anthropomancy, epatoscomancy, extispiciomancy, hepatomancy, hapatromancy.

Excrement: Scatomancy.

Eyes: Anthroposomancy, iridology, oculomancy.

Facial features: Anthroposomancy.

Feces: Copromancy, scatomancy.

Fig leaves: Sycomancy.

Fingernails: Onychomancy.

Fire: Causimonancy, pyromancy.

Fire gazing: Pyromancy.

Fish: Ichthyomancy.

Flames and smoke: Capnomancy, pyromancy, spodomancy.

Flora: Botanomancy, geomancy.

Forehead: Anthroposomancy, metopomancy.

Gems and precious stones: Lithomancy.

Goats: Kephalonomancy.

Grain, tossed: Geomancy, sortilege.

Hands: Cheiromancy, chiromancy, palmistry.

Horses and horses hooves: Hippomancy.
Human shoulders: Armomancy.
Incense: Empyromancy, libanomancy.
Inspirational musings: Theomancy.
Keys: Clidomancy.
Laughter and laughing: Gelomancy, geloscomancy, geloscopy.
Laurel branches and leaves: Daphnomancy.
Lines on the hands: Cheiromancy, chiromancy, palmistry.
Mediumship and psychic abilities: Clairvoyance, psychomancy.
Melted lead: Molybdomancy.
Mirror gazing: Enoptromancy, scrying.
Moles: Maculomancy, moleomancy.
Moon phases: Selonomancy.
Names: Numerology, onomancy, onomamancy, onomatomancy.
Naturally occurring or thrown patterns: Geomancy.
Numbers: Arithmancy, gematria, numerology.
Oil: Leconomancy.
Olive oil: Onimancy.
Onions: Cromniomancy.
Ouija board: Dactylomancy.
Patterns of natural objects: Geomancy.
Pearls: Margaritomancy.
Pebbles: Pessomancy, psephomancy.
Pendulum: Cleidomancy, dactyomancy, kelidomancy, pallomancy.
Poetry and verses: Rhapsodomancy.
Poppy and other flower seeds: Capnomancy.
Poultry: Alectryomancy.
Priests' breastplates: Urimancy.
Psychometry: Hylomancy.
Rats: Myomancy.
Rose petals and leaves: Phyllorhodomancy.
Sacred names: Theomancy.
Sacred objects, books and/or things: Heiromancy, psychometry.
Salt: Halomancy.
Seeds: Capnomancy.
Shadows: Sciomancy.
Sieves: Coscinomancy.
Skulls: Cephalomancy, phrenology.
Smoke: Capnomancy, empyromancy, libanomancy, pyromancy, tephramancy.
Snakes: Ophimancy.

Soles of the feet: Podomancy.
Stars: Astrology, astromancy.
Straws: Sideromancy.
Swiss cheese: Tiromancy.
Tea leaves and coffee grounds: Tasseomancy, tasseography.
Trance: Aspidomancy, chresmonancy.
Urine: Uromancy.
Voice-altered trance: Gastromancy.
Water: Cylicomancy, hydromancy.
Water currents: Bletonomancy.
Water fountains or geysers: Pegomancy.
Wax: Ceromancy.
Wells: Captromancy.
Wind: Austromancy.
Wine: Oinomancy.
Wood: Xylomancy.
Words: Transatuaumancy.

Further reading

Bletzer, June G. *The Donning International Encyclopedic Psychic Dictionary.* West Chester, Pa.: Whitford Press, 1986.
Logan, Jo, and Lindsey Hodson. *The Prediction Book of Divination.* Dorset, England: Blandford Press, 1984.
Maven, Max. *Max Maven's Book of Fortunetelling.* New York: Prentice-Hall, 1992.
Opie, Iona, and Moira Tatem. *A Dictionary of Superstitions.* Oxford: Oxford University Press, 1992.

MARGARITOMANCY *Divination of guilt or innocence using pearls.*

In this ancient prognostication method, after a crime has been committed, those who are suspect are gathered around a fire. A pearl is placed in a vessel or vase and set near the blaze. The local magistrate slowly speaks the names of all the accused. When the name of the guilty party is spoken, the pearl is supposed to bounce around in the container, shooting upward. It should then change directions and shoot straight down, hitting or piercing the bottom of the container. Thus, the accused's guilt is proven without a doubt.

Pearls have long been held to have a mystical quality. The ancients believed that pearls should only be worn in the moonlight, because sunlight would destroy their luster. Until the last 200 years, brides avoided wearing pearls at their weddings because they were thought to signify tears of sorrow. In the countryside of Ireland, there are still people who believe pearls are unlucky. One Irish superstition says that should a couple desire to remain childless, all they had to do was sleep with a pearl beneath their pillows or mattress.

Further reading

Bletzer, June G. *The Donning International Encyclopedic Psychic Dictionary.* West Chester, Pa.: Whitford Press, 1986.

de Lys, Claudia. *The Giant Book of Superstitions.* Secaucus, N.J.: Citadel Press, 1979.

Opie, Iona, and Moira Tatem. *A Dictionary of Superstitions.* Oxford: Oxford University Press, 1992.

Visions and Prophecies. Mysteries of the Unknown. Alexandria, Va.: Time Life Books, 1990.

MATHERS, SAMUEL LIDDEL MACGREGOR (1854–1918) *English mystic and occultist.*

Mathers was a leading organizer and supporter of the Hermetic Order of the Dawn. With the London-based mystical group, Mathers translated and channeled ancient rites and rituals that were adapted and practiced by the members.

Attributed to Mathers are the English translations of many medieval magical works, including Knorr Von Rosenroth's *Kabbalah Denudata (The Kabbalah Unveiled)* and Solomon Trismosin's alchemical treatise known as *Splendor Solis.* Other works include the translation of various medieval books on magic, spells, rituals, incantations and hexes. These volumes are called grimoires and are believed to have been the work of Kabbalistic mystics of the Middle Ages. The best known of the grimoires that were translated by Mathers are *The Sacred Matic of Abra-melin* and *The Grimoire of Armadel.* He was also the translator of *The Key of Solomon,* which was published as two books: *The Greater Key of Solomon* and *The Lesser Key.* The former contains magical instructions, prayers and descriptions of the forces for each of the planets as they relate to the tarot and astrology. The latter explains ceremonial magic, the use of witchcraft and necromancy, along with ways to contact nature spirits.

A serious scholar of occult topics, Mathers accepted a top position with the Hermetic Order and began asserting that he alone had received inspiration and material from the Secret Chiefs (the highest-ranking spiritual leaders in the universe). He believed that those in the order should follow him without question.

Later, after moving to Paris with his wife, Moina Mathers, the academic occultist began to insist that the members of the Hermetic Order support and finance his life as he continued to study occult material. His demands were not readily accepted by the other members, and disagreement ensued.

Mathers died in 1918 from complications of the Spanish flu. His wife continued to claim that he had had a transcendental encounter with the Secret Chiefs that no human could survive. Mrs. Mathers asserted that this encounter was the real cause of her husband's death.

Other members of the Hermetic Order of the Golden Dawn, which was basically an occultist's society, included Aleister Crowley, the poet W. B. Yeats, Arthur Edward Waite (famous for his philosophy and study of tarot cards, including the Rider-Waite deck) and author Bram Stoker (*Dracula*).

See also CROWLEY, ALEISTER; HERMETIC ORDER OF THE GOLDEN DAWN; WAITE, ARTHUR EDWARD.

Further reading

Guiley, Rosemary Ellen. *Harper's Encyclopedia of Mystical and Paranormal Experience.* San Francisco: HarperSan Francisco, 1991.

Harper, George Mills. *Yeat's Golden Dawn.* Wellingborough, England: Aquarian Press, 1974.

King, Francis. *Ritual Magic in England, 1887 to the Present Day.* London: Neville Spearman, 1970.

MEDITATION *A state of higher awareness, typically achieved through a quiet period of concentration.*

Most people who practice meditation have no specific goals other than to achieve a state of awareness that is otherwise not available while living in this world.

Meditation is often thought of as clearing one's mind of mundane thoughts to concentrate on religious, metaphysical or spiritual topics. Meditation has been called concentrated mental activity. Some use it simply to relax. Actually, it is all those things. The end result is often a desire to focus in order to release other concepts, energies and abilities that are hidden in another portion of the mind.

One need not travel to Tibet and live with monks to meditate. Techniques vary. There are no rules, guidelines or standards. Those who practice meditation suggest that one should be comfortable and in a quiet area and not be disappointed if the first number of attempts to meditate are interrupted with everyday thoughts, worries and ideas.

During meditation, some people center their thoughts on one topic, word, idea. Some stare at or focus on an object such as a crystal, mirror or candle flame or an element of nature such as a flower, a tree or even the Moon. Others clear their minds of every thought, purposely trying to achieve a totally blank mind. Still others try to separate everyday thoughts in order to focus on one problem or concept in order to evaluate and review all the impressions and theories connected with it. And there are some people who do "active meditation"—that is, reciting positive affirmations (declarations of what they want or desire to achieve) while walking, running, resting or even falling asleep. This, too, is considered meditation.

People meditate to relax, to allow clairvoyant thoughts to be channeled into their minds and to heighten their awareness of past lives and their life lessons. Clairvoyants such as Edgar Cayce have reported that they use a form of meditation in order to allow images and thoughts to come through to them in a channeling experience. They often refer to this as relaxed awareness. Those who practice yoga meditate in various yoga positions in order to achieve a stronger balance of mind and body. T'ai chi and other martial arts experts combine meditation and mind exercises along with exercises for the body.

See also CAYCE, EDGAR; CHANNEL; PSYCHIC; and specific prognostication methods, including CANDLE PROPHECY.

Further reading

Cayce, Hugh Lynn, ed. *The Edgar Cayce Collection.* New York: Bonanza, 1986.

Da Liu. *T'ai Chi Ch'uan and Meditation.* New York: Schocken, 1986.

Goleman, Daniel. *The Meditative Mind: The Varieties of Meditative Experience.* Los Angeles: Jeremy P. Tarcher, 1988.

Guiley, Rosemary Ellen. *Harper's Encyclopedia of Mystical and Paranormal Experience.* San Francisco: HarperSan Francisco, 1991.

MEDIUM *One who translates spiritual information from the ethereal realm to others on this Earth plane.*

Typically, a medium (the term is somewhat old-fashioned) will call forth a spiritual entity during a seance. The querant or members of the audience ask the medium questions that are then transmitted by him or her to the entity for answers.

Sometimes the answers or revelations come through automatic writing, pendulums, table tipping or other manifestations. Sometimes the medium will release control of his or her body and the entity will talk through this person, often with a complete change in the sound of the medium's voice. This is known as channeling.

Nonhuman entities who speak to or through a psychic or to an individual may be angels, nature spirits, guardian spirits, deities, demons or spirits of the dead. Sometimes the messages are transmitted from the higher self or from other spirits who may not have been human in a past life; they often have exotic names.

The information is said to have come from outside the Earth plane. This is not an innovative concept first practiced by New Age metaphysicians. Throughout history, there has been documentation of channeled information. Mediumship was said to be a highly developed art among the priests of ancient Egypt. The Greeks, Tibetans, Japanese, Babylonians, Druids and Assyrians, along with early Christians, Muslims and Jews, all took part in the translation of information from another realm. Madame Helena P. Blavatsky, Alice Bailey, Eilene Garrett and JZ Knight are known for their ability to connect with the spiritual world and dispense information from it. The medium is also sometimes referred to as the control.

See also AUGUR; BAILEY, ALICE; BLAVATSKY, HELENA P.; CHANNEL; GARRETT, EILEEN; KNIGHT, JZ; PSYCHIC.

Further reading

Kautz, William H., and Melanie Branon. *Channeling: The Intuitive Connection.* San Francisco: Harper & Row, 1987.

Klimo, John. *Channeling: Investigations on Receiving Information from Paranormal Sources.* Los Angeles: Jeremy P. Tarcher, 1987.

Leonard, Gladys Osborne. *My Life in Two Worlds.* London: Two Worlds, 1931.

Rodegast, Pat, and Judith Stanton, comps. *Emmanuel's Book: A Manual for Living Comfortably in the Cosmos.* New York: Bantam, 1987.

Stewart, R. J. *The Elements of Prophecy.* Dorset, England: Element Books, 1990.

MESMER, FRIEDRICH ANTON

(1733–1815) German scholar, astrologer, healer and doctor best known as the developer of therapeutic hypnosis.

Also referred to as Franz Mesmer, he was the first to recognize the basics of hypnotism and investigate the healthful effects of the power of the mind. The term *mesmerize*, that is, to enchant, was coined when people believed that a hypnotist put a spell on the subjects; hypnotists have also been known as mesmerists. Both words are derived from Mesmer's name and reputation. Some considered him a flamboyant showman without real psychic powers, an accusation that was most likely justified; during his years in Paris, he liked to dress in long, colorful, flowing robes and carried a wand. However, he was one of the first to realize the potential of what he coined the theory of animal magnetism.

Mesmer believed for a time that waves of an unseen magnetic force were generated by the hypnotist's eyes, hands, motions and perhaps

MESMER
Friedrich Anton Mesmer was the first to recognize the basics and potential of hypnotism.

even the mind's concentrated thought patterns that hypnotized the subject. Mesmer came upon the use of hypnosis while studying for the priesthood. With a gift and curiosity for mathematics and science, he became obsessed with the then current theory that all things were controlled by a life force. This magnetic force was thought to be fluid and flowing, and was somehow attracted to the human nervous system. This wasn't really a new concept even at that time; practitioners of I Ching, *feng shui* and other Eastern methods of prognostication have believed for thousands of years, and continue to believe today, in this same ideology. In Chinese, this magnetic force is called *chi* (or Ch'i) and is considered to be the lifeblood of the earth, present in all living things, including plants, minerals and animals.

During Mesmer's study of the basics of the magnetic flow of life, he came upon the theories of J. B. van Helmont, a 16th-century scientist. Van Helmont believed that if one could control the magnetic flow, one could shape thoughts and have power over others. Basing his studies on this concept, Mesmer continued to study magnetism, gaining recognition from Father Maximilian Hehl, a Jesuit priest and court astrologer to Empress Maria Theresa. Mesmer adopted much of Hehl's philosophy that the planets held a magnetic power over humans. That power, he postulated, could be transferred to magnets placed on the body to bring it into balance (and thus cure ills or reshape diseased organs).

Because of his popularity as a healer and doctor, the public began to seek out Mesmer, paying well for his treatments. He set up a very fashionable clinic in Paris when he realized that he could cure patients without the help of magnets placed on the body. It was, of course, the power of suggestion under hypnosis that brought about the cure, rather than the power of the magnets. But Mesmer believed that the life force coming from his own body transferred healing energies to his patients.

Mesmer's Paris clinic was unlike any hospital known in his time. The music, paintings, flowers and general air of relaxation were similar to what one might find at an expensive health resort or spa today. The patients were sometimes grouped in a room for mass healings while Mesmer and his associates treated them by stroking their bodies, waving magnetic wands and making suggestions. There were many reported cures. Mesmer had a falling out with Father Hehl but continued to be popular with the public, becoming the darling of Paris society.

Regard for Mesmer weakened when Louis XVI, who had been a strong defender and advocate of the doctor, hesitantly agreed to have the hypnotist's theories secretly and then publically investigated. The committees found no basis to substantiate the existence of animal magnetism, and Mesmer was expelled from the French medical academy. Though he no longer treated the nobility of the time, Mesmer's reputation for healing was still celebrated by the masses, and he continued to practice in France. Somewhat later, Mesmer's reputation was further undermined after a physician, who had come to Mesmer to be treated for a nonexistent medical problem and was pronounced cured of it, accused Mesmer of swindling him and his other patients. He was publically and professionally ridiculed.

As with many who had formerly hobnobbed with the aristocracy, the French Revolution brought difficulties to Mesmer. He fled France for the small town of Karlsruhe, Austria. But once settled there, he was accused of being a French spy. After serving time in prison, Mesmer returned to his birthplace near Lake Constance, Germany, where he lived until his death at age 81.

Mesmer is best remembered today as being one of the first to understand the healing power of the mind through the therapeutic possibilities of hypnosis.

Further reading

Cuddon, Eric. *The Meaning and Practice of Hypnosis.* New York: Citadel Press, 1965.

Drury, Nevill. *Dictionary of Mysticism and the Esoteric Traditions.* Dorset, England: Prism Press, 1992.

Fodor, Nandor. *Encyclopedia of Psychic Science.* New York: University Books, 1966.

Powers of Healing. Mysteries of the Unknown. Alexandria, Va.: Time Life Books, 1990.

Seligmann, Kurt. *The History of Magic and the Occult.* New York: Pantheon Books, 1948.

METAPHYSICS *The study of that which is accepted as real without visible evidence of its existence.*

Metaphysics is an entire philosophy claiming that all things (which inhabit or take up space on the earth) originate from one source. It is the study of cosmic consciousness, the basis of energy and intelligence. It is the doctrine, investigation and analysis of truth and reality; it is the study of existence and the search for knowledge. A student of metaphysics might contemplate present, past and future lives in order to understand a life lesson or to answer specific questions regarding behavior. He or she may delve into the use of various prediction tools, such as I Ching, tarot and palmistry. Some experts believe metaphysics encompasses God, consciousness, cosmic origins and all that is truth to answer the question, What is life? One who studies metaphysics may do so with a slant toward conventional religion, whether that is Buddhism, Christianity or Judaism.

Metaphysics is a somewhat new term and encompasses all that was formerly referred to as occult, magical, religious or mystic. Today, we often hear the term *New Age*, indicating a study or interest in mystical knowledge or knowledge that cannot be proven by facts or figures. People have been studying metaphysics since the first cave dwellers read palms, studied light on crystals and deciphered natural and unexplained occurrences.

See also LAWS OF METAPHYSICS.

Further reading

Bailey, Alice. *A Treatise on White Magic.* New York: Lucis, 1951.

Besant, Annie. *The Ancient Wisdom.* London: Theosophical Publishing House, 1905.

Ferguson, John. *An Illustrated Encyclopedia of Mysticism and the Mystery Religions.* New York: Seabury Press, 1976.

Fodor, Nandor. *Encyclopedia of Psychic Science.* New York: University Books, 1966.

Hall, Manly P. *The Secret Teachings of All Ages.* 1928. Reprint. Los Angeles: Philosophic Research Society, 1977.

Sheldrake, Rupert. *A New Science of Life.* London: Blond & Briggs, 1981.

METOPOMANCY *Division and character analysis by studying the lines on a person's forehead.*

As with palmistry, metopomancy may have been one of the earliest forms of foretelling specific character traits and aspects of the future. It was first practiced in China, along with other methods of Chinese face reading, and is still popular today in many Asian cultures.

Published in the Sung dynasty, *Ma-Yee-Shang-Fa (The Simple Guide to Face Reading)* was the first book on the topic. It discusses the significance of all of the facial features. Reading foreheads as well as total faces was practiced during the Chou dynasty, more than 3,200 years ago. (The book is still used as the basic source of information on a skill that continues to be practiced in Asia and is held with far more credence than palmistry.)

METOPOMANCY
In 1658, Jerome Cardan published Metoposcopia, *a guide to face reading and divining the future by use of lines on the forehead.*

Aristotle commended the practice of metopomancy. He believed that there was a distinct relationship between human characteristics and features of the face. Hippocrates, the "Father of Medicine," also believed that there was some certainty to the belief that one's face revealed traits of future disease.

In the 16th century, facial interpretations proliferated and books on the subject increased. In 1658, in Paris, Jerome Cardan published *Metoposcopia*, a guide to face reading and specifically the divination of the future by studying the lines on the forehead. His comprehensive volume contained more than 800 illustrations to substantiate his thesis.

According to Cardan, the forehead can be divided into seven distinct positions between the brow and the hairline. These were given planetary names: the Moon, Mercury, Venus, Sun, Mars, Jupiter and Saturn.

To read the forehead one must consider the length, depth and prominence of the lines. The following are the basic principles of metoposcopy:

No matter where on the forehead they appear, long, unbroken horizontal lines are said to indicate a straightforward personality, an honest man or woman, a good partner. Three long and widely spaced lines crossing the forehead horizontally indicate a psychic and/or spiritual nature.

X lines or wrinkles denote a shifty personality; here is someone who doesn't necessarily mean what he or she says. These lines often show a dishonest bent.

Short vertical lines, according to Cardan and other face readers, tell of abrupt changes. They may indicate a personality type that changes opinions, perhaps even a wishy-washy person who cannot make up his or her own mind.

Short diagonal lines indicate the ability to overcome obstacles. However, if one of these lines touches the left eyebrow, that indicates future challenges and, perhaps, misfortune.

Wavy lines reveal a person who loves to travel, to learn and to move about, physically, mentally or emotionally.

Slight curves in the main lines of the forehead tell of a balanced personality, an easygoing nature, this person can go with the flow. However, if the curve turns sharply and angles back, this is a sign of instability.

One horizontal S-curve is considered an indication of someone with a Machiavellian personality.

Three horizontal S-curves that move across the forehead in a slight arch indicate a loving and generous nature.

See also ANTHROPOSOMANCY; PALMISTRY; PHRENOLOGY.

Further reading

Bary, William Theodore de, ed. *Sources of Chinese Traditions*. New York: Columbia University Press, 1960.

Leland, Charles Godfrey. *Gypsy Sorcery and Fortune Telling*. New York: University Books, 1962.

Maven, Max. *Max Maven's Book of Fortunetelling*. New York: Prentice-Hall, 1992.

Walker, Barbara G. *The Woman's Encyclopedia of Myths and Secrets*. New York: Harper Collins, 1983.

MILAREPA, JETSUN (1052–1135) *Tibetan mystic and scholar.*

Milarepa was considered to be one of the leading Tibetan mystics of all time. He is a Tibetan national hero, referred to as the "Fully Enlightened One" by his followers in other Asian countries. In his early life he practiced black magic; he was transformed into a religious mystic after meeting a lama named Marpa. From that point on, he became a hermit, meditating in the mountains of Tibet. Considered by many to have been the greatest yogi of all time, he is supposed to have been in contact with the Supreme Oneness, ruler and absolute spiritual leader.

Further reading

Bromage, Bernard. *Tibetan Yoga*. 1952. Wellingborough, England: Aquarian Press, 1979.

Evans-Wentz, W. Y. *Tibet's Great Yogi, Milarepa: A Biography from the Tibetan*. 2d ed. London: Oxford University Press, 1951.

Worthington, Vivian. *A History of Yoga*. London: Routledge & Kegan Paul, 1982.

MING (OR OTHER "FORTUNE") STICKS *Divination through the random selection of a numbered stick.*

Practiced in ancient China and often used today, ming sticks are numbered. The number corresponds with a listing of the answers for questions that are printed in an answer book. Here in the United States, ming sticks are often sold in Asian stores.

To prognosticate the future, one considers the question at hand and asks it silently or aloud.

Then one shakes the long cylinder containing the sticks. The cylinder is shaken so that only one stick falls forward or out. The number is read and then interpreted by the saying or "fortune" in the book. This practice is sometimes done daily, as one might read a sun sign horoscope in the newspaper.

Further reading

Heywood, R. *Beyond the Reach of Sense*. New York: Dutton, 1961.
Magickal Almanac. St. Paul, Minn.: Llewellyn, 1989.
Maven, Max. *Max Maven's Book of Fortunetelling*. New York: Prentice-Hall, 1992.
Morgan, Chris. *Fortune Telling: How to Predict Your Own Future*. London: Quintet Publishing and Random House, 1992.
Visions and Prophecies. Mysteries of the Unknown. Alexandria, Va.: Time Life Books, 1990.

MIRROR PROPHECY *Divination using a mirror to foretell the future or interpret omens and events.*

As with many older prognostication practices, mirror prophecy (called ENOPTROMANCY) has had a resurgence in popularity. One can sometimes buy "magic mirrors" or books discussing how to use a mirror to foretell the future.

In ancient times, a shiny surface was placed in water to predict an individual's recovery (or death). Enoptromancy is a form of catoptromancy, in which divination occurs by interpreting patterns or images produced by looking at a light source reflected in a shiny object, such as a mirror. The psychic or healer suspended a mirror into water with only the base of the mirror touching it. He or she would then gaze into the mirror, interpreting the vision that was revealed on the shiny surface.

The more contemporary method of mirror prophecy is to place a specially cleansed or blessed mirror in an indirect light source and to stare at the mirror while in a meditative state. After some practice, one should be able to understand the solution to problems, receive answers from the guides and/or learn the wisdom of the ethereal world. Those who practice this divination method suggest that one should not be disappointed if the first few sessions with a mirror reveal nothing. They claim that patience should be rewarded.

See also HYDROMANCY; SCRYING.

Further reading

Butler, W. E. *How to Develop Clairvoyance*. 2d ed. New York: Samuel Weiser, 1979.
Fodor, Nandor. *Encyclopedia of Psychic Science*. New York: University Books, 1966.
Krippner, Stanley, and Alberto Villoldo. *The Realms of Healing*. 3d ed. Berkeley, Calif.: Celestial Arts, 1986.

MOLEOMANCY *Divination by the shape, placement and size of moles on the human body.*

Also known as molescopy.

See also MACULOMANCY.

MOLYBDOMANCY *Divination by interpretation of the hisses and patterns made by dropping molten lead into water.*

A popular prognostication method, molybdomancy was most likely practiced first by the ancient Greeks, with the interpretation done by government-paid augurs (psychics). Just as the patterns of tea leaves are read in tasseography, the formation of the molten lead poured into water, and allowed to cool, revealed guilt or innocence and translated omens. The practice remained in fashion for centuries.

According to the book *Discoverie of Witchcraft* (1584), molybdomancy was still in use at that time. At this point it was utilized to discover whether someone was bewitched. The book advises, "To learne how to know whether a sicke man be betwitched or no . . . You must hold motlen lead over the sicke bodie, and powre it into a porrenger full of water; and then if there appeare upon the lead, anie image, you may then knowne the partie is bewitched."

During the early 19th-century Regency period in England, young girls dropped molten lead into cold water on Valentine's Day. The formation of the cooled metal was interpreted as specific letters of the alphabet; supposedly, a girl would marry a man whose first name began with the letter the lead resembled.

A variation of this practice was long reputed to be a variation of romantic divination systems. An account published in the English book *Everlasting Fortune-Teller* (1839) directed, "On Midsummer eve, take a small lump of lead . . . put it in your left stocking on going to bed, and place it under your pillow, the next day . . . take a pail of water, and . . . pour in your lead boiling hot. As soon as it is cold, take it out, and you will find emblems of his trade. If a ship, he is a sailor, if a book, he is a parson . . . and so on." By the early 20th century, a further modification was popular: *Folk-Lore of Wales* (c. 1909) instructed, "If a spinster on Christmas Eve pours melted lead into cold water, it will turn into the shape of the tools her future husband will use. A doctor will be represented by a lancet, and so on."

See also CEROMANCY; TASSEOGRAPHY

Further reading

Alleau, Rene. *History of Occult Sciences.* London: Leisure Arts, 1965.

Denning, Melita, and Osborne Phillips. *Voudou Fire: The Living Reality of Mystical Religion.* St. Paul, Minn.: Llewellyn, 1979.

Hazlitt, W. Carew. *Faiths and Folklore of the British Isles.* 2 vols. New York: Benjamin Blom, 1965.

MOUNT OF APOLLO *The muscled pad on the palm beneath the ring finger, which is used to predict character.*

The mount of Apollo, also referred to as the mount of the Sun, can be found on both palms, slightly below the place where the ring finger joins the hand. In palmistry, each significant mount of the hand is indicated by a specific name, along with the astrological sign of a planet.

Depending on the size and location, the mount of Apollo is said to indicate one's disposition and outlook on life.

A normal-size mount (about the size of a nickel) is said to indicate a personality that is bright and vivacious. This individual possesses a happy disposition, often with an innate ability to grasp opportunities, along with strong creative tendencies. A large mount (about the size of a quarter) indicates a self-indulgent personality, and a small one (the size of a dime) indicates a dull, unperceptive nature.

See also PALMISTRY.

Further reading

Altman, Nathaniel. *Palmistry Workbook.* New York: Sterling, 1990.

Benham, William G. *Hands.* Los Angeles: Newcastle, 1988.

Cheiro. *Cheiro's Book of Numbers.* New York: Prentice-Hall, 1988.

———. *The Language of the Hand.* New York: Prentice-Hall, 1987.

Fitzherbert, Andrew. *Hand Psychology.* Garden City, N.Y.: Avery, 1989.

Robinson, Rita. *The Palm: A Guide To Your Hidden Potential.* North Hollywood, Calif.: Newcastle, 1988.

MOUNT OF JUPITER *The muscled pad on the palm beneath the index finger, which is used to predict character.*

The mount of Jupiter, which can be found on both hands, is located slightly below the place where the index finger joins the hand. In palmistry, each significant mount of the hand is indicated by a specific name along with the astrological sign of a planet.

Depending on the size and location, the mount of Jupiter is said to indicate one's temperament and nature.

If the mount is of normal size, one is considered to be good tempered, determined, able to accept and work through any endeavor and possess an above-average ability to succeed.

If the mount of Jupiter is small, flat or underdeveloped, it is said to indicate one who is thoughtless, egocentric and lacking in confidence.

When the mount of Jupiter is large, puffy and prominent, it supposedly indicates a self-centered person who is highly motivated. This individual may have the proverbial "one-track mind" and be a classic workaholic.

Should the mount of Jupiter be connected to the mount of Saturn, this individual is probably somewhat of a loner, happy working apart from others. He or she may not do well in a team or partnership effort.

See also PALMISTRY.

Further reading

Altman, Nathaniel, *Palmistry Workbook*. New York: Sterling, 1990.

Benham, William G. *Hands*. Los Angeles: Newcastle, 1988.

Cheiro. *Cheiro's Book of Numbers*. New York: Prentice-Hall, 1988.

———. *The Language of the Hand*. New York: Prentice-Hall, 1987.

Fitzherbert, Andrew. *Hand Psychology*. Garden City, N.Y.: Avery, 1989.

Robinson, Rita. *The Palm: A Guide To Your Hidden Potential*. North Hollywood, Calif.: Newcastle, 1988.

MOUNT OF LOWER MARS *The muscled pad on the palm half way between the mount of Jupiter and the mount of Venus, which is used to predict character.*

The mount of lower Mars, which can be found on both hands, is located below the index finger before the thumb connects to the palm. In palmistry, each significant mount of the hand is indicated by a specific name along with the astrological sign of a planet.

A normal size mount of lower Mars is indicative of one who is physically brave, with a persistent streak.

A flat, small mount of lower Mars is supposed to reveal a person who lacks courage, is often fearful of physical pain and thus avoids bodily challenges like athletics.

A very large mount of lower Mars tells of an argumentative person who might be so strong willed, he or she is unable to concede even when obviously in error. This may also be the individual who is willing to take physical chances, the daredevil or the sports hero.

See also PALMISTRY.

Further reading

Altman, Nathaniel. *Palmistry Workbook*. New York: Sterling, 1990.

Benham, William G. *Hands*. Los Angeles: Newcastle, 1988.

Cheiro. *Cheiro's Book of Numbers*. New York: Prentice-Hall, 1988.

———. *The Language of the Hand*. New York: Prentice-Hall, 1987.

Fitzherbert, Andrew. *Hand Psychology*. Garden City, N.Y.: Avery, 1989.

Robinson, Rita. *The Palm: A Guide To Your Hidden Potential*. North Hollywood, Calif.: Newcastle, 1988.

MOUNT OF MERCURY *The muscled pad on the palm slightly below the little finger, which is used to predict character.*

The mount of Mercury, which can be found on both hands, is located below the little finger on the outside portion of the palm. In palmistry, each significant mount of the hand is indicated by a specific name along with the astrological sign of a planet.

A normal-size mount of Mercury is indicative of a clear-thinking individual, someone who can quickly explore and resolve problems. He or she is supposed to be hardworking and thrifty and enjoys working and being with others. This individual is a good team player.

When the mount of Mercury is large and puffy, the individual is said to have a keen sense of humor without a hint of sarcasm. He or she thrives on amusement and is often the life of the party.

When the mount of Mercury is extremely large, it is said to reveal a person who could sell anything to anyone. It may also indicate a tendency to avoid revealing all the details of any transaction involving money or property. Thus he or she may gain an unsavory reputation in business.

Should this mount be marked by short, straight lines, it may indicate a healing nature; perhaps the individual has a soothing personality or, in the very real sense of healing, is someone who is in a healing profession.

See also PALMISTRY.

Further reading

Altman, Nathaniel. *Palmistry Workbook*. New York: Sterling, 1990.

Benham, William G. *Hands.* Los Angeles: Newcastle, 1988.

Cheiro. *Cheiro's Book of Numbers.* New York: Prentice-Hall, 1988.

———. *The Language of the Hand.* New York: Prentice-Hall, 1987.

Fitzherbert, Andrew. *Hand Psychology.* Garden City, N.Y.: Avery, 1989.

Robinson, Rita. *The Palm: A Guide To Your Hidden Potential.* North Hollywood, Calif.: Newcastle, 1988.

MOUNT OF SATURN *The muscled pad on the palm slightly below the middle finger, which is used to predict character.*

The mount of Saturn, which can be found on both hands, is located below the middle finger. In palmistry, each significant mount of the hand is indicated by a specific name along with the astrological sign of a planet.

A normal-size mount of Saturn, speaks of an introspective personality. This person is most likely involved in some academic pursuit or would prefer to be. He or she is thrifty and is able to make sound decisions after a short period of contemplation.

A small or flat mount of Saturn is said to be indicative of one who favors the middle of the road and is content without high personal or professional aspirations.

A mount of Saturn that is large and puffy is supposed to show one who tends toward pessimism and is often melancholy for no apparent reason.

If the mount of Saturn is close to the mount of Jupiter (the muscled area beneath the index finger), the individual is thought to be quiet but with strong ideas and goals.

Should the mount of Saturn lean toward the mount of Apollo (the muscled area beneath the ring finger), this may indicate an intense love of beautiful things, artistic appreciation, and creativity, although possibly without the talent to produce.

See also PALMISTRY.

Further reading

Altman, Nathaniel. *Palmistry Workbook.* New York: Sterling, 1990.

Benham, William G. *Hands.* Los Angeles: Newcastle, 1988.

Cheiro. *Cheiro's Book of Numbers.* New York: Prentice-Hall, 1988.

———. *The Language of the Hand.* New York: Prentice-Hall, 1987.

Fitzherbert, Andrew. *Hand Psychology.* Garden City, N.Y.: Avery, 1989.

Robinson, Rita. *The Palm: A Guide To Your Hidden Potential.* North Hollywood Calif.: Newcastle, 1988.

MOUNT OF THE MOON *The muscled pad on the little finger side of the palm, which is used to predict character.*

The mount of the Moon, which can be found on both hands, is located below the little finger, next to the wrist. Each significant mount of the hand is indicated by a specific name along with the astrological sign of a planet.

When the mount of the Moon is of normal size, it indicates a nature that is creative, romantic, joyful and sensitive, often with psychic abilities. Some palmists believe a normal-size mount of the Moon tells of someone who has a deep love for the sea or ocean travel or is involved in an occupation that involves the ocean.

A very prominent mount of the Moon indicates an individual who may be hard, coarse, introspective and uncaring with his or her fellow humans.

When the mount of the Moon appears high on the palm and is well developed, the person often has powerful creative tendencies that cannot and should not be ignored. This individual may be involved in creative fields where imagination rules.

A well-developed but soft mount of the Moon is said to show someone who may be inconsistent and flighty. It is indicative of the dreamer.

When the mount reaches out toward the mount of Venus, one may have a passionate, lustful nature, not only in love and sex but toward life on a whole.

A mount of the Moon that is close to the wrist lines is believed to reveal a person with psychic gifts.

See also PALMISTRY.

Further reading

Altman, Nathaniel. *Palmistry Workbook*. New York: Sterling, 1990.

Benham, William G. *Hands*. Los Angeles: Newcastle, 1988.

Cheiro. *Cheiro's Book of Numbers*. New York: Prentice-Hall, 1988.

———. *The Language of the Hand*. New York: Prentice-Hall, 1987.

Fitzherbert, Andrew. *Hand Psychology*. Garden City, N.Y.: Avery, 1989.

Robinson, Rita. *The Palm: A Guide To Your Hidden Potential*. North Hollywood, Calif.: Newcastle, 1988.

MOUNT OF UPPER MARS
The muscled pad on the palm about half way between the mount of Mercury and the mount of the Moon, which is used to predict character.

The mount of upper Mars, which can be found on both hands, is located below the little finger before the final mount of the palm. In palmistry, each significant mount of the hand is indicated by a specific name along with the astrological sign of a planet.

A normal-size mount is supposed to indicate a strong moral disposition and a courageous personality.

A small, somewhat flat mount of upper Mars reveals a person who often thinks only of him- or herself, perhaps even a cowardly way of perceiving life and humanity.

An overly large mount of upper Mars is said to be indicative of one who may be a sharp-tongued cynic. This might be the pessimist who seems always to be walking around with a dark cloud over his or her head.

See also PALMISTRY.

Further reading

Altman, Nathaniel. *Palmistry Workbook*. New York: Sterling, 1990.

Benham, William G. *Hands*. Los Angeles: Newcastle, 1988.

Cheiro. *Cheiro's Book of Numbers*. New York: Prentice-Hall, 1988.

———. *The Language of the Hand*. New York: Prentice-Hall, 1987.

MOUNT OF VENUS
The muscled pad on the palm where the thumb connects to the hand, which is used to predict character.

The mount of Venus, which can be found on both hands, is located below the thumb and index finger, close to the wrist. Each significant mount of the hand is indicated by a specific name along with the astrological sign of a planet.

A mount of Venus that is wide, firm and puffy indicates a warm nature. This is an individual who joyfully embraces life, his or her family, children and, often, humanity. The compassionate disposition of this individual tends to lead him or her into public service, the healing arts or creative fields where one can take an idea and nurture it to fruition.

A mount of Venus that is extremely large is said to indicate a person with remarkable energy, vitality and enthusiasm.

A firm mount of Venus indicates a highly developed libido. One that is soft and pliable indicates an individual who may be overly agitated and possibly capricious.

When the mount of Venus falls closer to the lower portion of the palm, palmists say this reveals a tendency to use artistic skills and an ability to focus, concentrate and work toward completing projects and accomplishing goals.

See also PALMISTRY.

Further reading

Altman, Nathaniel. *Palmistry Workbook*. New York: Sterling, 1990.

Benham, William G. *Hands*. Los Angeles: Newcastle, 1988.

Cheiro. *Cheiro's Book of Numbers*. New York: Prentice-Hall, 1988.

———. *The Language of the Hand*. New York: Prentice-Hall, 1987.

Fitzherbert, Andrew. *Hand Psychology*. Garden City, N.Y.: Avery, 1989.

Robinson, Rita. *The Palm: A Guide To Your Hidden Potential*. North Hollywood, Calif.: Newcastle, 1988.

MURPHY, BRIDEY
Virginia Tighe, who claimed in 1952 to have been a woman named Bridey Murphy in a previous life.

Tighe was a housewife from Chicago who, during a hypnotic session involving past-life regression, began saying that she had been an Irish woman who had lived in the area of Belfast from 1789 to 1864. Bridey Murphy is also referred to as Bridget Murphy.

Chronicled in the book *The Search for Bridey Murphy,* Tighe's story was serialized by a leading Chicago newspaper and supposedly validated the authenticity of reincarnation. Tighe told the story of her life as Bridey Murphy while under hypnosis. She reported, in great detail, situations from her 19th-century world, including her relationship with her husband. The facts, dates and situations related were verified, but it was later discovered that the entire episode had been fabricated in order to sell newspapers. Tighe was involved in the hoax, and the case of Bridey Murphy was dismissed as a fraud.

Further reading

Bernstein, Morey. *The Search of Bridey Murphy.* New York: Doubleday, 1965.

Cavendish, Richard, ed. *The Encyclopedia of the Unexplained.* New York: McGraw-Hill, 1974.

Cayce, Hugh Lynn, ed. *The Edgar Cayce Collection.* New York: Bonanza, 1986.

Lenz, Frederick. *Lifetimes: True Accounts of Reincarnation.* New York: Fawcett Crest, 1977.

MYOMANCY
Divination by observing the behavior of rats or mice.

This form of prognostication had its origin in ancient Assyria, Egypt and Rome. According to the practice, when the cries or sounds of mice or rats were heard, great evil was thought to be present.

There is immense traditional superstition regarding rats and mice—none of it too savory. According to legend, when Assyrian king Sennacherib (705?–681 B.C.) and his armies stormed

Among other mantic arts that studied animal behavior, some ancient psychics used myomancy, whereby the future was divined by the observation of rodents.

Egypt, his soldiers awoke one morning to discover that their bows and quivers had been nibbled by rats. Believing this to be an inauspicious omen, they fled and were slain retreating from the battlefields.

In 319 B.C., Theophrastus said that one should always discuss the situation with an "expounder of sacred law" when a mouse or rat has nibbled any article. And should the wise man say that the visit of this rodent reveals a warning, one should "expiate the omen by a sacrifice."

In A.D. 77, Pliny explained, "By gnawing the silver shields at Lanuvium, mice had prognosticated the Marsian war; and the death of our general, Carbo, at Clusim, by gnawing the latches with which he fastened his shoes."

According to the 1793 *Every Lady's Fortune Teller,* "To dream you are attacked by rats shows that somebody will endeavour to injure you. Mice are pretty much of the same nature, but not in so high a degree."

Further reading

Bletzer, June G. *The Donning International Encyclopedic Psychic Dictionary.* West Chester, Pa.: Whitford Press, 1986.

de Lys, Claudia. *The Giant Book of Superstitions.* Secaucus, N.J.: Citadel Press, 1979.

Opie, Iona, and Moira Tatem. *A Dictionary of Superstitions.* Oxford: Oxford University Press, 1992.

Visions and Prophecies. Mysteries of the Unknown. Alexandria, Va.: Time Life Books, 1990.

MYSTIC *One who professes to know and be capable of delivering metaphysical knowledge in a new or innovative way.*

Mystics have been known since the beginning of time. The word *mystical* comes from the root word *mystico*, which is Greek for "hidden wisdom." The Old and New Testaments are filled with accounts of stories, warnings and knowledge dispensed and shared by mystics. Saint Paul is considered to be the greatest of Christian mystics. Many of the most revered of Christian mystics have been women, including Saint Hildegard, Saint Catherine of Siena and Saint Theresa of Avila.

However, mysticism is not the sole province of Christianity. Abraham ben Samuel Abulafia (1240–1291) was a Kabbalistic mystic. Jiddu Krishnamurti (1895–1986) was a mystic as well as a spiritual teacher, yogi and metaphysical leader who followed, for most of his life, the teachings of the Theosophical Society. And Madame Blavatsky (1831–1891) herself was considered to be a mystic by many, yet she lived in the materialistic world of New York and London for a good part of her life. Every civilization seems to have had its own mystics, who were able to impose order and translate knowledge from the unseen world.

Some people refer to mystics as gurus; in the Arab world they are known as fakirs. Some call them psychics, learned people or prophets. In ancient Rome, for example, mystics of the time were called augurs and were officially sanctioned and paid by Caesar's government. During one portion of Hitler's reign of terror, mystics were hunted down, imprisoned and sometimes put to death.

Mystics are often involved with psychic or faith healings, elucidating omens, dispensing religious advice and performing miraculous feats indicating their almost supernatural abilities. It is believed that mystics strive to be as one with their God or their higher self. As they move toward this goal, they become less centered in this world, less materialistic. Like Jetsun Milarepa, the Tibetan mystic and scholar (1052–1135), some mystics choose to seclude themselves and become hermits or study with recluses who are delving into their specific area of metaphysics.

Most mystics believe in and have a desire to move on to a higher order. They espouse peace, joy and serenity and encourage harmony with the natural world and union with their God. They often live to change people's attitudes to one of acceptance of the LAWS OF METAPHYSICS.

Most contemporary teachers and scholars do not call themselves mystics but rather counselors, psychics and channelers.

See also CLAIRVOYANCE; KAHUNAS; PSYCHICS.

Further reading

Encyclopedia of Religion. New York: Macmillan, 1987.

Fortune, Dion. *The Mystical Qabalah.* York Beach, Maine: Samuel Weiser, 1935.

Krippner, Stanley, and Alberto Villoldo. *The Realms of Healing.* 3d ed. Berkeley, Calif.: Celestial Arts, 1986.

Mind over Matter. Mysteries of the Unknown. Alexandria, Va.: Time Life Books, 1990.

Walker, Barbara G. *The Woman's Encyclopedia of Myths and Secrets.* New York: Harper Collins, 1983.

MYTHOLOGY *Study and interpretation of myths, the cultural phenomena that are symbolic of and often describe and explain the origins of the cosmos.*

Mythology combines folklore, fairy tales and Greek tales of Zeus and Apollo, among others, along with the deeds of mystics, faith healers and psychics. Greek philosophers Plato and Aristotle, among others, used mythology as a basis for their debates and arguments and as a proper method of truly knowing reality. They believed that myths hold the wisdom of the culture.

Often prognostication methods are based on strong mythological origins. For example, tarot cards are inscribed with Kabbalistic symbols from the Tree of Life, which had its start in ancient mythology and mystic philosophies. Astrology includes mythology-based attributes of the Greek gods. For example, if Jupiter is influential in an astrological chart, one may have the personality traits of generosity and social dexterity along with conceit and wastefulness.

Further reading

Campbell, Joseph. *The Masks of God: Creative Mythology.* New York: Viking, 1970.

———. *The Mythic Image.* Princeton, N.J.: Princeton University Press, 1974.

Guthrie, W. K. C. *The Greeks and Their Gods.* Boston: Beacon Press, 1955.

Jung, C. G., and C. Kerenyi. *Essays on a Science of Mythology.* New York: Doubleday, 1964.

Patai, Raphael. *Myth and Modern Man.* Englewood Cliffs, N.J.: Prentice-Hall, 1972.

Silberer, Herbert. *Hidden Symbolism of Alchemy and the Occult Arts.* New York: Dover, 1971.

NATAL HOROSCOPE *A chart used for divination purposes, indicating the placement of the planets, Moon and stars at the time of birth or a particular event.*

An astrologer who has been specially trained to cast a birth or event chart uses ancient and modern tables and psychic ability to format a natal horoscope. This is sometimes called a birth chart.

To format a complete and correct chart, one must know the exact time, date and place of birth, including whether daylight saving time was in effect. Using precise calculations, astrologers can predict future happenings and interpret the nature or character of an individual or event. Many psychics spend their entire lives studying astrology because there are so many nuances to consider, including his or her ability to decipher the information provided by the mathematical configurations that are required for the chart.

Unfortunately, there are no simple "how to" formulas that can teach someone to format a natal horoscope. In the past, an astrologer would need many tables and lists to calculate the specifics required in a natal horoscope. Today's astrologer uses a computer software program into which a time, date and place of birth are input. A complete personal chart is calculated and printed in minutes, rather than the hours it used to take. The cost of a computer-generated chart produced by a company that is in business to sell the charts is about $10. Personal astrologers charge from $40 to thousands of dollars to do a comprehensive horoscope or chart, including interpretations. Many books supply the manual method of calculating a natal horoscope.

An emphemeris, which can be purchased at most metaphysical book stores, is an almanac that gives the positions of the Sun, Moon and planets for every day of the year and is necessary to the calculating process. However, a basic class on astrology is probably the best method to learn most easily the techniques of casting a natal horoscope.

Further reading

Baigent, Campion, and Harvey Baigent. *Mundane Astrology: An Introduction to the Astrological Nations and Groups.* London: Aquarian Press, 1984.

Bosanko, Susan, ed. *Predicting Your Future.* New York: Ballantine Books/Diagram Group. Visual Information Limited, 1983.

Forrest, Steven. *The Changing Sky: The Dynamic New Astrology for Everyone.* New York: Bantam, 1984.

Goodman, Linda. *Linda Goodman's Sun Signs.* New York: Fawcett/Columbine, 1978.

Wilson, James. *The Dictionary of Astrology.* New York: Samuel Weiser, 1974.

Woolfork, Joanna Martine. *The Only Astrology Book You'll Ever Need.* Landham, Mass.: Scarborough, 1992.

NECROMANCY *Divination by beckoning and contacting the spirits of the dead to interpret omens and forecast future events.*

The term *necromancy* comes from the Greek *nekos* and *manteia*, which means corpse soothsaying. Necromancy was widely practiced by the early Greeks and was mentioned in the Old Testament. For example, the Witch of Endor summons the spirit of Samuel in order to answer Saul's questions. Eliphas Levi, the author, magician and psychic scholar (1810–1875), used necromancy to summon the spirit of Apollonius of Tyana, the Greek philosopher and psychic. Levi is said to have done this by calling forth the spirits of Hermes, Asklepios and Osiris. The procedure for rousing these long-dead souls was recorded in Levi's *Dogme et Rituel de la Haute Magic,* also known as *The Mysteries of Magic* and *The Histories of Magic:* "Three times and with closed eyes I invoked Apollonius. When I again looked forth there was a man in front of me, wrapped from head to foot in a species of shroud . . . he was lean, melancholy and beardless." The figure disappeared as the occultist wielded a ritualistic sword; however, it later returned: "The apparition did not speak to me, but it seemed that the questions I had designed to ask, answered themselves in my mind."

The term *necromancy* has another accepted definition; referring to the field of black magic and witchcraft, in which it is used to call forth the dead for ritualistic practices or to raise the dead or conjure up voodoo or curses against another.

See also LEVI, ELIPHAS.

Further reading

Drury, Nevill. *Inner Visions: Explorations in Magical Consciousness.* London: Routledge & Kegan Paul, 1979.

Ferguson, John. *An Illustrated Encyclopedia of Mysticism and the Mystery Religions.* New York: Seabury Press, 1976.

Giles, Cynthia. *The Tarot: History, Mystery and Lore.* New York: Paragon House, 1992.

NEPHELOMANCY *Divination using the patterns seen in cloud formations.*

A variation of the more commonly known practice of aeromancy, nephelomancy (from the Greek *nephele,* meaning cloud) focuses on the forms and shapes made by clouds. (Aeromancy is a broader category encompassing all weather and wind conditions.) Using nephelomancy, the psychic intuitively interprets cloud configurations to answer questions or predict events. As with many other prediction methods that use patterns and require the translation of the patterns by a psychic, including tasseography (teacup reading), the symbols in the sky can be interpreted in many ways.

Nephelomancy was practiced by the ancient Greeks; it is no longer a popular method of prognostication.

See also AEROMANCY; TASSEOGRAPHY.

Further reading

Bletzer, June G. *The Donning International Encyclopedic Psychic Dictionary.* West Chester, Pa.: Whitford Press, 1986.

Maven, Max. *Max Maven's Book of Fortunetelling.* New York: Prentice-Hall, 1992.

Opie, Iona, and Moira Tatem. *A Dictionary of Superstitions.* Oxford: Oxford University Press, 1992.

Stewart, R. J. *The Elements of Prophecy.* Dorset, England: Element Books, 1990.

NEWBROUGH, DR. JOHN BALLOU

(1828–1891) American psychic who practiced AUTOMATIC WRITING.

During what is now referred to as the "heyday of spiritualism" in the United States, the mid- to late 1800s and early 1900s, many people called themselves psychics and mediums. Although it is impossible to know how many of them actually were able to impart knowledge and use their psychic skills, there were a great many who were known to be frauds. Dr. Newbrough, however, a dentist from the New York area (some sources say Boston), seems to have been a true psychic and expert in the art of automatic writing.

Using a typewriter while sitting in a darkened room, Dr. Newbrough produced OAHSPE, also known as the Kosman Bible. It is the words of Jehovah and his angel ambassadors as told to the doctor. Published anonymously in New York in

1882, the bible consists of more than 900 pages providing details of spiritual rules of Earth during various periods of time. It criticizes and condemns various traditional religious doctrines, calling the Bible's saints false deities.

It is said that Dr. Newbrough originally intended to keep his role in the publication of the bible a secret; however, a unsigned letter to the Boston magazine the *Banner of Light* revealed that the doctor had been the vehicle through whom the back had been written. According to the report in the magazine, Newbrough said, "One morning I accidentally (seemed accidental to me) looked out of the window and beheld the line of light that rested on my hands extending heavenward like a telegraph wire toward the sky. Over my head were three pairs of hands, fully materialized; behind me stood another angel with her hands on my shoulders. My looking did not disturb the scene, my hands kept right on printing [typing] . . . printing. For fifty weeks this continued, every morning, half hour or so before sunrise, and then it ceased and I was told to read and publish the book OAHSPE. The peculiar drawings in OAHSPE were made with pencil in the same way."

Newbrough claimed that with his eyes closed he could "read" any page from any book or newspaper and lift and levitate enormous weights of even so much as a ton with little effort. He could also recall his own astral travels.

See also LEVITATION.

Further reading

Brown, Rosemary. *Immortals at My Elbow.* London: Bachman & Turner, 1974.
Fodor, Nandor. *Encyclopedia of Psychic Science.* New York: University Books, 1966.
Guiley, Rosemary Ellen. *Harper's Encyclopedia of Mystical and Paranormal Experience.* San Francisco: HarperSan Francisco, 1991.
Montgomery, Ruth. *A Search for the Truth.* New York: Bantam, 1968.
Psychic Powers. Mysteries of the Unknown. Alexandria, Va.: Time Life Books, 1990.
Search for the Soul. Mysteries of the Unknown. Alexandria, Va.: Time Life Books, 1990.
Watson, Donald. *The Dictionary of Mind and Spirit.* New York: Avon, 1991.

NIGROMANCY *An ancient method of communicating with the dead to interpret omens and provide information on future events.*

Whereas necromancy summons the dead to speak with the psychic, when a psychic uses nigromancy, he or she walks around a grave in order to contact the deceased. In a variation, a grave will be opened to allow a psychic to communicate with the one who has died.

The term *nigromancy* is sometimes misused to indicate black magic.

See also CLAIRVOYANCE; NECROMANCY; PSYCHIC.

Further reading

Drury, Nevill. *Dictionary of Mysticism and the Esoteric Traditions.* Dorset, England: Prism Press, 1992.
Psychic Voyages. Mysteries of the Unknown. Alexandria, Va.: Time Life Books, 1990.
Watson, Donald. *The Dictionary of Mind and Spirit.* New York: Avon, 1991.
———. *Far Journeys.* Garden City, N.Y.: Dolphin/Doubleday, 1985.

NOSTRADAMUS *(1503–1566) French physician and prophet.*

Nostradamus is the magical name of Michel de Nostre Dame, the author of the best-known book on future-casting and predictions, *The Centuries*, which was written in 1555. Written in archaic French and Latin, Italian, Portuguese and Spanish, the predictions were often couched in rhythm and were heavily symbolic (for example, a tree might mean the Kabbalah, or it might mean just a tree), their meaning disguised in anagrams. They were jumbled out of sequence of forthcoming events in order to camouflage their meaning to the masses. It is said that he wrote the book in this fashion because of his fear of ruthless and intense persecution from Christian leaders of his time. The book is still in print and referred to today.

Many believe Nostradamus was the greatest clairvoyant and psychic of all time. It is said that he correctly predicted the Napoleonic Wars, the rise of the Third Reich, the history of British rule from Elizabeth I to Elizabeth II, including

NOSTRADAMUS
Nostradamus is the magical name of Michel de Nostre Dame, author of the most well known book on future-casting and predictions, The Centuries *(written in 1555).*

the abdication of Edward VIII, and the American Revolution, as well as the American Civil War and the assassination of Presidents Lincoln and Kennedy. It is interesting to note that during World War II, both the Allied and the Axis powers used interpretations of Nostradamus's predictions to declare that each would overthrow the other.

According to his followers, Nostradamus is said to have correctly foretold the advent of air travel, atom and nuclear bombs, manned space travel and rockets and submarines. He also predicted great calamity and worldwide destruction that, according to his modern interpreters, will arrive sometime between 1994 and July 1999. Supposedly, the planet will be in chaos, with a global war that will last 25 years, after which

there will be a golden 1,000-year period of love and enlightenment. He made more than 1,000 predictions that covered well past the year A.D. 3797.

Nostradamus was a gifted clairvoyant who often practiced scrying. While some books say he used a shiny surface, such as a mirror, others assert that he scryed into a cup of water. Still other sources claim Nostradamus used a crystal ball for his predictions. Obviously, it is unclear as to the method he used, or if he, in fact, used many methods of prognostication.

Nostradamus's critics declare that the interpretation of his tangled prose is far too loose to be verified and considered valuable or reliable. Conversely, some metaphysical scholars insist that so far more than half of his predictions have come to pass; there have been many books claiming to validate his predictions.

From a well-educated and wealthy family in the St. Remy de Provence area of France, Nostradamus was born a Jew; his family later converted to Catholicism. He had many psychic visions as a child and adolescent that were attributed to a divine gift. A scholar of Hebrew, Latin, Greek, mathematics, medicine, astronomy, the Kabbalah and astrology, Nostradamus studied medicine at Montpellier University in France, where he earned a degree and obtained a license to practice. He began his climb to notoriety as a doctor and a healer during an outbreak of plague in southern France. His healing methods were unspeakably unconventional for the time—he refused to bleed patients who were dying of the plague and instead formulated his own healing cures. So many of his patients recovered that his fame spread throughout France. Beginning around 1534, Nostradamus married, fathered two children and met Julius Cesar Scalinger. This friendship with Scalinger, an astrologer and well-known philosopher of the day, had a strong impact on Nostradamus. He began to study metaphysics in earnest and embarked upon what would become his lifelong work—predicting future events.

When his entire family perished in another outbreak of the plague, Nostradamus's life fell apart and he began to travel throughout Europe, studying astrology, philosophy and metaphysical subjects. It is unclear whether he continued to have clairvoyant visions or if he predicted the death of his wife and children. About 1550, he married a rich widow and fathered six more children, settling in the area of Salon en Craux de Provence in France, and he began recording his visions.

His fame grew, and in 1555, when *The Centuries* was published, it caught the attention of the French nobility. Nostradamus became the court astrologer of Catherine de Medicis, the queen of France. She invited him to cast the horoscopes of her sons and when one of them, Charles IX, ascended the French throne, Nostradamus also became the court physician.

It is said that Nostradamus would retreat to his study and stare at a bowl of water placed on a brass tripod. He would touch a magic wand to the tripod, dip it in the water and then touch his robe. After this procedure, the clairvoyant visions would begin. The information was often conveyed in short, disjointed fragments by a voice. Nostradamus believed the words were coming from the "Divine Presence" that "sits close" to the shoulders of humanity.

Many students of metaphysics spend years, even a lifetime, studying the words of Nostradamus.

See also ASTROLOGY; CLAIRVOYANCE; CYLICOMANCY; DIVINATION; SCRYING.

Further reading

Cheetham, E. *The Prophecies of Nostradamus.* London: Corgi, 1981.

Cosmic Connections. Mysteries of the Unknown. Alexandria, Va.: Time Life Books, 1990.

Fodor, Nandor. *Encyclopedia of Psychic Science.* New York: University Books, 1966.

Fontbrune, Jean-Charles de. *Nostradamus: Countdown to Apocalypse.* New York: Holt, Rinehart & Winston, 1980.

McCann, Lee. *Nostradamus: The Man Who Saw through Time.* New York: Farrar, Straus & Giroux, 1984.

Psychic Powers. Mysteries of the Unknown. Alexandria, Va.: Time Life Books, 1990.

Roberts, Henry C. *The Complete Prophecies of Nostradamus.* New York: American Book–Stratford Press, 1969.

Stewart, R. J. *The Elements of Prophecy.* Dorset, England: Element Books, 1990.

NUMEROLOGY   *A divination system that uses the assignment of a number value to the letters of the alphabet.*

According to those who study and give readings in numerology, called numerologists, each single digit number (1–9) has a specific cosmic vibration rate. This rate can foretell details about a person's future, karma and characteristics. It can foretell details of places and events. Believed by many metaphysical scholars to be one of the most ancient forms of divination, numerology may have begun with the early Babylonians. It was widely used in ancient Egypt and continues as a present-day prognostication method.

Most civilizations have found a correlation between the mystic significance of a number and a letter of their alphabet. The relevance is closely connected in the Kabbalah, the Hebrew system of medieval mysticism, magic and religion, based on the importance of the 12 letters of the Hebrew alphabet and a blend of astrology, numerology, mysticism and magic. Every major arcana card in the tarot has a number that affects the message given in a reading.

Even though there have been many variations throughout the years in the way numerology is used to predict personality, interpret omens and forecast the future, it most reflects the work of Greek mathematician and philosopher Pythagoras (582?–500? B.C.). Known to any student of geometry, Pythagoras believed that numbers reflected the ultimate principles of order and harmony in the universe. Since everything could be explained and expressed through numbers, Pythagoras theorized that they were the key to understanding anything unknown.

Also known as numeromancy and arithomancy, numerology uses only the prime numbers. The system assigns a number to each letter; two-digit numbers are reduced to one digit by adding them together. The system continues until one digit is found that is reflective of the personality, potential and future potential of the querant. Some numerologists call this the "ruling number."

Various numbers and letters can be used for analysis and prediction purposes. Personality, potential and future of an individual can be calculated using birth name, married name and/or nicknames, and it can also be determined through the use of the numbers in birthdates. One can predict the outcome of an event through the use of that day's date. Some numerologists assign numbers to specific career names, such as "doctor" or "teacher." They compare the numerology meaning with the querant's name and birth number to ascertain whether the person will be successful and/or find satisfaction in this profession.

In order to find one's ruling number, sometimes called the "primary number," an individual would write out the letters of the birth name, or the name most commonly used (often two analyses will be done when those names are different). Then he or she would review the chart below to find which numbers are assigned to the names. There are a few different numerological systems that can be used to find the ruling number, including the Kabbalist system that was adopted by Cornelius Agrippa (1486–1535), which dropped the number 9 because it was considered divine and unattainable for humans. The more modern system includes the number 9. These two systems are charted below.

Using the Kabbalist system, attach a number to each letter of the querant's name.

The number 1: A, I, Q, J, Y.
The number 2: B, K, R.
The number 3: C, G, L, S.
The number 4: D, M, T.
The number 5: E, H, N.
The number 6: U, V, W, X.
The number 7: O, Z.
The number 8: F, P.

For example, Rose Smith's name would look like this when a numerologist analyzed it:

ROSE
$2+7+3+5=17=1+7=8$

SMITH
$3+4+1+4+5=17=1+7=8$

$8+8=16=1+6=7$

The number 7 as a ruling number indicates the strong creative qualities of Rose Smith, and a numerologist might recommend that she begin writing, keeping a journal or studying art. Because 7 is highly spiritual ruling number, it would not be unusual for Rose to be a psychic, a leader in a religious group or a student of philosophy. She probably has a gentle, encouraging nature that makes her a favorite among friends and associates.

Using the more contemporary method of numerology (which includes the number 9), the following numbers are assigned to letters:

The number 1: A, J, S.
The number 2: B, K, T.
The number 3: C, L, U.
The number 4: D, M, V.
The number 5: E, N, W.
The number 6: F, O, X.
The number 7: G, P, Y.
The number 8: H, Q, Z.
The number 9: I, R.

Using the more modern procedure John Bly's name would look like this when a numerologist analyzed it:

JOHN
$1+6+8+5=20=2+0=2$

BLY
$2+3+7=12=1+2=3$

$2+3=5$

With the ruling number of 5, John Bly has a personality that is quick witted. He's fun to be with, draws people to him and enjoys being the center of attention. He strives for success and can make decisions quickly. A numerologist might recommend that John study law—he would have an excellent courtroom style. Those with a ruling number of 5 make friends easily, so John would do well in sales or any business in which he can interact with the public.

The following are the ways in which numerologists generally interpret the meaning of the numbers. Numerologists often recommend studying the tarot card that equates to the ruling number, wearing the colors for each number and understanding the influence of the planet that exerts power over this individual in order to discover full potential. The numbers have the same meanings in both systems.

The Number 1

This ruling number indicates innate leadership abilities; these are take-charge people who effortlessly accept responsibility. This is the number of success, and those with the ruling number 1 are almost guaranteed to attain it. Every number comes with a caution, including the number 1. If this drive for power, leadership and success is carried too far, the querant can become a stern taskmaster, always wanting things his or her "right" way. If this is the querant's ruling number, he or she should be advised to use power carefully and with love. The number 1 equals the Magician in the tarot; 1s are ruled by the Sun, and their colors are brown and yellow.

The Number 2

This ruling number indicates great intuitive powers; 2s are gentle, helpful and empathetic. They tend to be wonderful partners and friends, giving the shirt off their back if necessary. They can be supremely and naturally artistic and creative, instantly visualizing concepts obscure to others. Conversely, 2s may be too wishy-washy, unable to make and/or stick with a decision. A 2 may have concerns about self-image and can become adept at weaving white lies to cover up insecurity. The number 2 equals the High Priestess in the tarot; 2s are ruled by the Moon, and their colors are jade, green, cream and white.

The Number 3

Like the number 2, the number 3 as a ruling number is highly creative. Unlike 2s, though, 3s will settle for nothing less than success in their creative encounters, whether that means winning a top prize at the quilting or crafts show or making millions on an advertising campaign. They are talented, vivacious, lovable and extremely disciplined. With this mixture of discipline, a drive for success and creativity, some 3s become intolerant of others who lack their mettle, and thus must put some boundaries on their desire to control. The number 3 equals the Empress in the tarot; 3s are ruled by Jupiter, and their colors are mauve, violet and all the pinks and purples.

The Number 4

This ruling number indicates a person who is earth oriented, balanced and practical. This is the feet-on-the-ground individual who knows where he or she is going and enjoys the trip getting there. These people often are the methodical folks who are accused of being dull, when it's just that they have their minds set to get the job (often an incredibly important and world-shaking one) done. Leave it to a 4, and it's sure to be finished. They tend to be loners, are rebellious and often have trouble making friends; thus they can feel isolated and may be lonely. The number 4 equals the Emperor in the tarot; the ruling planet is Uranus, and the colors are blue and gray.

The Number 5

This ruling number indicates a personality that is outgoing, fun and funny. These are quick-witted, lively, pleasure-seekers. They crave excitement and often have quick tempers to go along with their quick sense of humor. The number 5 personality may also have a tendency toward being highly excitable, with an abhorrence for any routine and mundane work. They love excitement, the more intense the better, and will make some if a situation, relationship or job seems too humdrum. Thus 5s may need to temper these characteristics in order to achieve their objectives. The number 5 equals the Hierophant in the tarot; the ruling planet is Mercury, and the colors are all of the lighter tones, such as pale gray and blue.

The Number 6

This ruling number indicates a balanced (sometimes considered perfect) personality type, since, as numerologists like to say, it is the sum of 1, 2 and 3. This personality has a love for harmony and order and family life; 6s are reliable, trustworthy individuals. They are true romantics and extremely sensual, with an expansive love of beauty. They are typically the most attractive people, yet they are far from self-centered. Conversely, they can be bullheaded, and when fighting for family (or the family of humanity), they will war to the end. The number 6 equals the

Lovers in the tarot; the ruling planet is Venus, and the colors are all shades and tones of pink and blue.

The Number 7

This ruling number indicates a personality with strong metaphysical gifts or the desire to learn about the unknown. He or she tends to see the world through spiritual or philosophical glasses. Often 7s are the psychics, the geniuses, the intuitive businesspeople and possess creative and intuitive powers in the arts, especially writing and painting. They love people and may have a great influence over others. Since 7s are so highly intuitive, they sometimes feel lost among others who are less psychic and become shy and withdrawn. The number 7 equals the Chariot in the tarot; the ruling planet is Neptune, and the colors are green, moss and silver.

The Number 8

This ruling number indicates individuals who are destined for worldly success. Numerologists explain that 8 is a strange, mysterious number; 8s seem to double the possibility for rebellion found in 4s. Number 8 people have incredible determination and willpower, but 8s are sometimes accused of being cold and callous, though they do feel deeply about others. This contradiction often confuses loved ones and associates, and 8s are considered the most misunderstood people. Because of their rebellious nature, 8s need to throttle their sometimes critical nature, and with age many mellow. The number 8 equals Strength in the tarot; the ruling planet is Saturn, and the colors are dark tones, including sapphire and black.

The Number 9

Found only in the modern guide to numerology, this ruling number indicates strong, self-reliant, determined fighters. They may have to struggle to achieve what they want, but 9s will do it. They have an incredible reserve of energy. They may be argumentative, and because they move so quickly and with so much determination, they tend to have accidents. They must slow their innate pace, double-check the route they plan to take and only then charge full speed ahead. The number 9 equals the Hermit in the tarot; the ruling planet is Mars, and the colors are shades of red and garnet.

It is interesting to note that numerologists recommend finding and analyzing other numbers in a person's life in order to compile a complete profile of abilities, tendencies and potential. Therefore, they suggest finding the numerological significance of a date-of-birth number, one's city or location and one's profession or business name.

Numerologist refer to numbers over 9 as "secondary numbers." All two-digit numbers have significance. They can be reduced by adding the numbers together, and these two-digit number sometimes contain special messages. For example, for one who is born on the 17th of the month, the number equals the Sun in the Tarot and indicates a most fortunate birth time.

As with astrology and other metaphysical sciences, some people spend their entire lives devoted to the study of a topic this size.

See also AGRIPPA; VON NETTESHEIM, HEINRICH CORNELIUS; ASTROLOGY; GEMATRIA; KABBALAH; TAROT.

Further reading

Hall, Manly P. *The Secret Teachings of All Ages.* 1928. Reprint Los Angeles: Philosophical Research Society, 1977.

Hitchcock, Helyn. *Helping Yourself with Numerology.* West Nyack, N.Y.: Parker, 1972.

Lawrence, Shirley Blackwell. *Behind Numerology.* San Bernardino, Calif.: Borgo, 1989.

Stewart, R. J. *The Elements of Prophecy.* Dorset, England: Element Books, 1990.

Woolfork, Joanna Martine. *The Only Astrology Book You'll Ever Need.* Landham, Mass.: Scarborough, 1992.

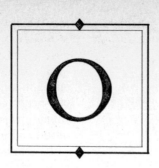

OCCULTISM *The synthesis of science, mysticism, philosophy, psychology and religion. Used to indicate that which is of a spiritual, hidden, mystical, traditional or secret nature.*

From the Latin *occulere*, meaning "to hide," occultism has acquired an unsavory reputation for superstition, black magic, deviant sexual rituals, devil worship and voodoo. Most psychics and metaphysical scholars and historians like to point out that occult teachings were once a valued part of all religions, as in the hidden meaning in the Hebrew alphabet. Some also like to explain that this negativity seems to have stemmed from contemporary religious beliefs that anything even vaguely unexplainable is objectionable and unclean. Thus, anyone and anything implicated with the unexplainable may be dangerous. The word *occult* now generally includes magic, spiritualism, mysticism and theosophy.

As noted above, *occultism* is a term formerly used in place of our modern-day metaphysical words, sometimes referred to as "New Age." Many people use the term *New Age* without thinking twice; however, they wouldn't use occult, which in fact has the same meaning. According to Cyril Scott, author of the classic book *An Outline of Modern Occultism*, written in 1935, occultism is "the synthesis of science, mysticism, philosophy, psychology and religion." He suggests that it accepts all of the proven theories of science and religions and rejects untenable dogmas and superstitions. Therefore, astrology and graphology would be included, but voodoo excluded.

Scott sums up the opinion of many in the occult fields: "The goal of practical occultism is an expansion of consciousness with its essential concomitant, unconditional happiness."

See also LAWS OF METAPHYSICS; METAPHYSICS.

Further reading

Buckland, Raymond. *Doors to Other Worlds*. St. Paul, Minn.: Llewellyn, 1993.

Drury, Nevill. *Dictionary of Mysticism and the Esoteric Traditions*. Dorset, England: Prism Press, 1992.

Fodor, Nandor. *Encyclopedia of Psychic Science*. New York: University Books, 1966.

Hall, Manly P. *The Secret Teachings of All Ages*. 1928. Reprint. Los Angeles: Philosophic Research Society, 1977.

Scott, Cyril. *An Outline of Modern Occultism*. 1935. Reprint. London: Routledge & Kegan Paul, 1950.

Sheldrake, Rupert. *A New Science of Life*. London: Blond & Briggs, 1981.

Wilson, Colin. *Beyond the Occult*. London: Bantam, 1988.

OCULOMANCY *Observance of the eye to discern the health aspects of the querant.*

A part of the ancient Chinese mantic art known as Chinese face reading, oculomancy is a variation of iridology and physiognomy, which was devised by the Swiss poet and theologian Johann Kaspar Levater in the late 1700s. Oculomancy concerns itself strictly with the health of the querant, whereas iridology and physiognomy are broader, more contemporary mantic arts in which physical as well as emotional health are interpreted. For example, a grayish color to the eye might mean a vitamin deficiency; a tiny mark near the edge might mean heart trouble.

See also IATROMANCY; IRIDOLOGY; LEVATER, JOHANN KASPAR; PHYSIOGNOMY.

Further reading

Achterberg, Jeanne. *Imagery in Healing: Shamanism and Modern Medicine.* Boston: Shambhala, 1985.

Bowers, Barbara. *What Color Is Your Aura?* New York: Simon & Schuster, 1989.

[Cayce, Edgar.] *Edgar Cayce on Healing.* Virginia Beach, Va.: ARE Press, 1969.

Hirschfelder, Arlene, and Paulette Molin. *The Encyclopedia of Native American Religions.* New York: Facts On File, 1992.

Sherman, Harold. *"Wonder" Healers of the Philippines.* Los Angeles: DeVross, 1967.

Stern, Jess. *Edgar Cayce, the Sleeping Prophet.* New York: Bantam, 1968.

Weil, Andrew. *Health and Healing: Understanding Conventional and Alternative Medicine.* Boston: Houghton Mifflin, 1983.

ODIN *Supreme spiritual guide who communicates with those in need of inspiration. Also known less commonly as Od or Odyle.*

In mythology (German and Scandinavian), Odin is the god of war, poetry, knowledge, wisdom and the dead. In metaphysical contexts, Odin is said to be a one-eyed ethereal world guide who works as a medium. He provides knowledge and guidance through astral projection and visions.

Odin is considered an ethereal world intelligence with great powers. It is said that he helps develop psychic powers in human beings and assists in understanding physical death. Specifically Icelandic mythology, Odin is known to have the ability to turn into various animal forms in order to assist people or provide information in the form of omens.

In mythology, Odin is considered the All-Father who lives in Valhalla, a resting place for fallen heroes. He is said to continue to travel among the elderly and the champions of the oppressed as a one-eyed old man.

Further reading

Bletzer, June G. *The Donning International Encyclopedic Psychic Dictionary.* West Chester, Pa.: Whitford Press, 1986.

Earth Energies. Mysteries of the Unknown. Alexandria, Va.: Time Life Books, 1990.

Fodor, Nandor. *Encyclopedia of Psychic Science.* New York: University Books, 1966.

Walker, Barbara G. *The Women's Encyclopedia of Myths and Secrets.* New York: Harper Collins, 1983.

OINOMANCY *Divination and omen interpretation through studying and evaluating the color, consistency and taste of wine.*

Sometimes referred to as oenomancy, oinomancy was practiced by the ancient Romans. Not only

OINOMANCY
In 13th-century Europe, red wine was used as the liquid in which to boil the skull of a cow, sheep or ox. The future was interpreted by the cracks in the skull bones, easily defined by the saturation of the red wine.

was the color and taste of wine scrutinized, but the tiny bits of sediment left in the bottom of an empty wine cup were read as well. Oinomancy was believed to have been practiced much as tea-leaf reading (tasseography) is today.

A variation of oinomancy is cephalomancy. In this variant, the head of a sheep, goat or donkey was placed in boiling liquid, after which the skull was examined for information in order to foretell the future. It is said that in 13th-century Europe, red wine was the preferred liquid for oinomancy. An animal skull was boiled in wine instead of water, and the future was interpreted through the remaining bones.

This ancient mantic art is no longer practiced today.

See also CEPHALOMANCY; HARUSPICY; PHRENOLOGY.

Further reading

Cumont, Franz. *Oriental Religions in Roman Paganism*. New York: Dover, 1956.
Opie, Iona, and Moira Tatem. *A Dictionary of Superstitions*. Oxford: Oxford University Press, 1992.

OLCOTT, COLONEL HENRY STEEL
(1832–1907) American theosophist.

Along with Madame Helena Blavatsky and William Q. Judge, Olcott co-founded the Theosophical Society. When the organization moved its headquarters to India, Olcott became intensely interested in Buddhism and Hinduism. The tenets of these religions strongly influenced theosophy.

Olcott was well-educated and an author of a number of books on the occult (many of which are still in print). These books include *People from the Other World* (1875), *Theosophy, Religion and Occult Languages* (1885), *A Buddhist Catechism* (1881) and a three-volume *Old Diary Leaves* (1895–1904). He was a member of the Royal Asiatic Society and the Bengal Academy of Music.

See also THEOSOPHICAL SOCIETY.

Further reading

Caldwell, Daniel H. *The Occult World of Madame Blavatsky*. Tucson, Ariz.: Impossible Dream, 1991.

Cranston, Sylvia. *H.P.B. The Extraordinary Life and Influence of Helena Blavatsky*. Los Angeles: Jeremy P. Tarcher, 1992.

OMARR, SYDNEY *(1926–) American astrologer.*

Omarr was born in Philadelphia, Pennsylvania, and is best known as one of the most widely read astrologers. Omarr is the only American ever given full-time duty in the U.S. Army as an astrologer. He has been well known and respected in his field since World War II.

Omarr's daily astrological predictions, by sun sign, are carried in a syndicated column read by countless Americans in well over 300 national newspapers. He has also appeared on numerous radio and television programs and has been called the most "knowledgeable astrologer since Evangeline Adams."

His forecasts of a fourth term for Franklin D. Roosevelt, the final days and events of World War II, the assassination of President John F. Kennedy, Richard Nixon's undoing and the associated circumstances of Watergate and many other recorded and documented predictions have made him the most legendary astrologer of contemporary times.

Further reading

Omarr, Sydney. *Astrological Guide for 1994*. New York: New American Library, 1994.
———. *Astrological Revelations about You*. New York: New American Library, 1969.
———. *Astrology: Off the Top*. New York: American Federation of Astrologers, 1975.
———. *Cooking with Astrology*. New York: New American Library, 1969.
———. *Henry Miller: His World of Urania*. London: Villiers Publications, 1960.

OMEN INTERPRETER *One who translates and clarifies omens.*

Used in many civilizations since the beginning of time, omen interpreters are psychics who are able to psychically translate the meaning of an event or activity. They are typically hired by the querant to decode the meaning of changes in the earth, weather or other acts of nature.

See also CLAIRVOYANT; PSYCHIC.

Further reading

Butler, W. E. *How to Develop Clairvoyance.* 2d ed. New York: Samuel Weiser, 1979.

Kautz, William H., and Melanie Branon. *Channeling: The Intuitive Connection.* San Francisco: Harper & Row, 1987.

Klimo, John. *Channeling: Investigations on Receiving Information from Paranormal Sources.* Los Angeles: Jeremy P. Tarcher, 1987.

Psychics. Mysteries of the Unknown. Alexandria, Va.: Time Life Books, 1990.

Seligmann, Kurt. *The History of Magic and the Occult.* New York: Pantheon, 1948.

Visions and Prophecies. Mysteries of the Unknown. Alexandria, Va.: Time Life Books, 1990.

OMENS *Unusual activities, occurrences or events used to prognosticate the future.*

Omens are typically nonhuman in origin and are thought to be impossible according to the normal laws of cause and effect. Omens are believed to be signs of opportunities to be taken, dangers to be avoided or impending news of an emotional change for oneself or others.

Omens can be spontaneous; a comet crossing the sky the day a baby is born might mean that he or she will achieve great success. Or the omen may be brought about through various divination methods such as seeing a message of prosperity in tea leaves during a tasseography session. People have been seeing events and occurrences as omens and seeking out the answer to the why, when, where and how of life since the first cave dweller set out an offering to provide good luck for the hunt.

Good omens are thought to be encouraged through the acquisition of lucky tools, spells, stones, tokens, coins or charms. Some people believe that if one sets out to find a good-luck charm or seeks a fortunate omen, bad luck will be the result. As with all superstitions and folk beliefs, the discovery of luck is most likely with the one who believes. A rabbit's foot is considered to be a lucky charm (alas, not for the rabbit), as are the rattlers of a rattlesnake.

Often, one culture will believe that a specific omen means terrible misfortune, while another will strongly assert the opposite. A rainbow is considered a good omen in some cultures (the end of a storm and clearing weather) and a bad omen in others. In England in the 1600s, a rainbow over the top of one's house was considered dreadful luck because it predicted the death of one of the inhabitants.

Folklore regarding prognostication is intriguing. The following are some fascinating omens.

Spiders are either considered a sign of good luck or an indication that something bad is about to happen. Thus, a spider in the morning is excellent, but a spider in one's bedroom in the afternoon may spell disaster.

Finding a horseshoe is an excellent omen. However, if the horseshoe is found with its points down, the luck will disappear.

If one's nose tickles, it means either love is forthcoming or one will kiss a fool.

OMENS
According to those who believe in omens, the discovery of a spider in the bedroom in the afternoon may spell disaster.

A ringing in the ear means that one is being gossiped or talked about, typically in an unkind manner.

If a baby cries at a baptism, he or she is possessed by evil spirits; the sacred water and ceremony are making the spirits leave the infant's body.

To have a photo fall is a sure indication that something dreadful will happen to the person in the picture.

Should a stone fall from a ring, beware of future tragedy.

Weather plays an important role in omens. A red sky in the morning is a warning to sailors of an upcoming storm, as in the New England rhyme "Red sky in the mornin', sailors take warnin'. Red sky at night, sailors delight."

Meeting the same person twice in one day is a most fortunate omen.

It's lucky to pick up a penny, pencil, pin or button from the street. However, one's luck will turn if the object is subsequently thrown down.

An open umbrella in the house will bring bad luck. However, simply carrying an umbrella may keep the rain away.

If one drops a spoon, a young person will visit. If one drops a fork, a woman will visit. If one drops a knife, a man will visit. Depending on the direction of the handle of the silverware, one can determine from which direction the visitor will come. For example, if a fork handle points north, a woman from the northern part of the city, county or country will arrive.

Seeing a white horse, a white butterfly or a white bird is always a sign of good fortune. Seeing a black sheep is a lucky omen, too.

Sleeping with wedding cake under the pillow is said to produce dreams of one's next lover.

Whistling in the theater is considered terrible luck, as is speaking the last line of a play at anytime during rehearsal.

Should a baby be born with his or her hands open, the child will have wealth or a generous life ahead.

Further reading

Bosanko, Susan, ed. *Predicting Your Future.* New York: Ballantine Books/Diagram Group. Visual Information Limited, 1983.

Cumont, Franz. *Oriental Religions in Roman Paganism.* New York: Dover, 1956.

Opie, Iona, and Moira Tatem. *A Dictionary of Superstitions.* Oxford: Oxford University Press, 1992.

Showers, Paul. *Fortune Telling.* Philadelphia: New Home Library, Blankiston Company, 1942.

ONE CARD READING
In tarot, a card selected from the deck to give a quick yes or no answer to a querant's question.

In this reading, the tarot cards are placed face down. They are then cut by the querant, who selects one card at random from the top of the cut. Sometimes the entire deck is spread out on a table in a fan shape and the querant draws a card from the deck.

This is a favorite reading for many who ask for spiritual guidance on a daily basis. Other spreads, such as the Twenty-one Tarot Card Spread, are said to be excellent for a more thorough reading.

See also TAROT.

Further reading

Buckland, Raymond. *Secrets of Gypsy Fortune Telling.* St. Paul, Minn.: Llewellyn, 1988.

Giles, Cynthia. *The Tarot: History, Mystery and Lore.* New York: Paragon House, 1992.

Secrets of the Alchemists. Mysteries of the Unknown. Alexandria, Va.: Time Life Books, 1990.

Visions and Prophecies. Mysteries of the Unknown. Alexandria, Va.: Time Life Books, 1990.

ONEIROMANCY
Divination by interpreting visions experienced during the deepest state of sleep.

Oneiromancy, practiced by the ancient Hebrews, is another term for dream interpretation and is better known by this phrase today. Many psychics, psychologists and scientists encourage clients and patients to recall their dreams in order to help clarify specific questions in their lives.

According to those who practice metaphysical beliefs, during the deepest phases of sleep the astral and mental bodies disconnect themselves from the physical and ethereal forms. We are free to move and consider past lives and intuitive information that our minds may censor during waking hours. Dream time may also fill a physical need. Psychologists and scientists, while still only guessing why people dream, often like to compare the brain to a computer that needs time to process all that is experienced during waking hours.

See also DREAM INTERPRETATIONS; JUNG, DR. CARL G.

Further reading

Bethards, Betty. *The Dream Book: Symbols for Self-Understanding*. Petaluma, Calif.: Inner Light Press, 1983.

Buckland, Raymond. *Secrets of Gypsy Dream Reading*. St. Paul, Minn.: Llewellyn, 1990.

Coxhead, David, and Susan Hiller. *Dreams: Visions of the Night*. New York: Thames & Hudson, 1976.

Garfield, Patricia. *Healing Power of Dreams*. New York: Fireside Books, 1991.

Jung, C. G. *Dreams*. Princeton, N.J.: Princeton University Press, 1974.

Maybrock, Patricia. *Romantic Dreams*. New York: Pocket Books, 1991.

Reed, Henry. *Dream Solution*. San Rafael, Calif.: New World Library, 1991.

Signell, Karen A. *Wisdom of the Heart*. New York: Bantam, 1990.

Ullman, M., ed. *Dream Telepathy*. New York: Macmillan, 1973.

ONIMANCY   *Divination using olive oil.*

Onimancy, like many other prognostication methods, was used widely until the Middle Ages, when it came to be considered witchcraft. There are two variations of the ancient mantic art, which was first practiced by the Romans, but neither is routinely practiced today.

Using one method, the querant mixes a small amount of olive oil and tallow in the palm of the hand. He or she considers the pressing question and poses it, out loud or silently. Then a special coin or token (special because of some metaphysical significance) is dropped on the palm. The direction in which it moves when dropped indicates the answer to the question. For example, if the token moves to the north, the answer is yes; to the south, the answer is no. Easterly and westerly directions indicate indecision or the need for the querant to ask again at another time.

In another variation of oniomancy, one pours a small amount of oil in a bowl half filled with water. The future can be foretold from the patterns on the water after one has meditated on the question at hand. This prediction method was often used during Old Testament times (Gen. 44:5, 15). Nostradamus (1503–1566) is supposed to have used a bowl of water set upon a brass tripod when predicting more than 1,000 future events, more than half of which are said to have come true.

See also BIBLICAL PROPHETS AND DIVINATION METHODS; HYDROMANCY; NOSTRADAMUS; SCRYING.

Further reading

Bletzer, June G. *The Donning International Encyclopedic Psychic Dictionary.* West Chester, Pa.: Whitford Press, 1986.

Cavendish, Richard, ed. *The Encyclopedia of the Unexplained.* New York: McGraw-Hill, 1974.

Miller, Madeleine S., and J. Lane Miller, eds. *Harper's Encyclopedia of Bible Life.* San Francisco: Harper & Row, 1978.

Roberts, Henry C. *The Complete Prophecies of Nostradamus.* New York: American Book–Stratford Press, 1969.

ONOMAMANCY
See ONOMANCY.

ONOMANCY   *Divination by the meaning of a person's name.*

Sometimes called onomamancy or onomatomancy, onomancy is a variation of numerology. This mantic art was used in ancient Greece to predict personality, interpret omens and forecast the future. In the use of onomancy, particular attention is paid to the number of vowels of a name, and there is special emphasis on the total number of letters in the name.

Onomancy reflects the work of Greek mathematician and philosopher Pythagoras (582?–500? B.C.). Pythagoras, known to any student of geometry, believed that numbers reflected the ultimate principles of order and harmony in the universe. Since everything could be explained and expressed through numbers, Pythagoras theorized that they were the key to understanding all that is unknown.

Onomancy is based on the concept that a person's name reflects and influences his or her personality and character. For some who practice this mantic art, it is the flow of energy and the sound of the name that has more influence than conversion through a mathematical system. Additionally, names have meanings, and these meanings transfer to the person who carries the name. Whether or not we agree with the concept, names such as Ernestine, Augustus, Clarence and Bertha all have different connotations than names such as Kathy, Matt, Jennifer and David. Some names promote a feeling of power: John, William, Katherine and Elizabeth are examples. Conversely, names such as Sissy, Shorty, Lefty and Red all reveal something personal about the individual.

Because one's name is so important to personality, some psychics believe that before being born into the earth plane, spirits select their own names. Many superstitions surround names and words. For example, in Ireland in the late 1500s, it was considered extremely unlucky to name a child after his or her living parent—a sure sign that a parent would die an untimely death. Naming a child after a religious figure, however, is often considered (even today) to provide a special blessing for the youngster.

See also NUMEROLOGY.

Further reading

Hall, Manly P. *The Secret Teachings of All Ages*. 1928. Reprint. Los Angeles: Philosophical Research Society, 1977.

Hitchcock, Helyn. *Helping Yourself with Numerology*. West Nyack, N.Y.: Parker, 1972.

Lawrence, Shirley Blackwell. *Behind Numerology*. San Bernardino, Calif.: Borgo, 1989.

Opie, Iona, and Moira Tatem. *A Dictionary of Superstitions*. Oxford: Oxford University Press, 1992.

Stewart, R. J. *The Elements of Prophecy*. Dorset, England: Element Books, 1990.

ONOMATOMANCY
See ONOMANCY.

ONYCHOMANCY *Divination by the study of the fingernails.*

There are two distinctly different methods of onychomancy, one as contemporary as modern palmistry and the other shrouded in the mystery of ancient Arabia. In the archaic method, a psychic scryed or stared into a child's thumbnail in order to foretell the future and/or questions regarding the child. The method, with a variation, is still practiced today in Brazil, where a psychic coats the querant's thumbnail with a mixture of specially anointed soot and oil. The coating is left to dry slightly; then the coating provides a reflective surface from which to scry.

The modern variation of onychomancy is typically considered part of palmistry, the divination of personality traits, potential and characteristics discerned by studying the hands. A palmist or an onychomanist divides fingernails into specific groups.

Long fingernails are believed to indicate talent, artistic gifts and abilities in the arts. The individual with long fingernails is supposed to have a serene disposition.

Short fingernails are an indication of one who is vivacious and highly energetic, who has a tendency toward self-righteousness or being overly critical. This individual may also be curious and scientifically minded.

Very short fingernails are considered to be indicative of one who is easily annoyed, who frets, who is a true worrywart and who also possesses a temper with a short fuse.

Broad, wide fingernails are indicative of an individual who is highly opinionated, strong in his or her beliefs, and often finds it a challenge to see the other sides of issues.

Fingernails that taper outward are believed to indicate people who are easily swayed by others' thoughts and opinions. They are the impressionable folks who often have trouble making firm decisions.

Fingernails that are wedge shaped are indicative of one who is sensitive; the more wedge shaped, the more sensitive.

Fingernails with vertical ridges are supposed to tell of one who is easily agitated; this individual is often angry and has an abundance of nervous energy.

Fingernails with horizontal ridges indicate an injury to the fingernail area or perhaps an illness in the body.

White spots on the nail, according to palmists, reveal someone who is about to have incredible luck—the more white spots the better.

Pale pink nails are believed to tell of a warm heart and a loving nature.

Whitish nails speak of a person who has a tendency to being closed minded and selfish.

A reddish blush to the fingernails supposedly indicates a strong temper or an outspoken nature.

A bluish blush tells of one who is unhealthy or is suffering from an illness.

See also PALMISTRY; SCRYING.

Further reading

Altman, Nathaniel. *Palmistry Workbook.* New York: Sterling, 1990.

Benham, William G. *Hands.* Los Angeles: Newcastle, 1988.

Cheiro. *Cheiro's Book of Numbers.* New York: Prentice-Hall, 1988.

———. *The Language of the Hand.* New York: Prentice-Hall, 1987.

Diagram Group. *Predicting Your Future.* New York: Ballantine, 1983.

Fitzherbert, Andrew. *Hand Psychology.* Garden City, N.Y.: Avery, 1989.

OOMANCY *Divination through the interpretation of the pattern made when egg white is mixed with water. Wine is also used in oomancy.*

Also referred to as ooscopy (from the Greek *oion,* meaning egg) and ovomancy (from the Latin *ovum,* also meaning egg), oomancy was performed in ancient times with a freshly laid egg. Although oomancy is no longer regularly practiced, to foretell the future using this method, one needs only a newly laid egg, a needle and a bowl of water. While concentrating on what one wants the universe to explain or predict, the eggshell is pierced with the needle. The egg is held over the bowl of water. When oomancy was practiced in ancient Rome, only three drops of egg white were used. The patterns of the egg white were then interpreted in much the same way as one would read tea leaves (in tasseography), patterns of clouds (aeromancy and nephelomancy) or the ripples in a stream (bletonomancy).

As with other scrying methods, to discern the patterns and interpret the meanings of the egg whites takes time. One should not be frustrated if at first only the liquids seem to be evident, because through concentration shapes will be visible.

A variation of oomancy is leconomancy; here, yellow oil is placed in water and the resulting patterns are read. Since leconomancy is related to the biochemical term *lecithin* (meaning egg yolk), it may have originally required the yolk of an egg. The prognostication method was practiced by the ancient Assyrians, who conceived an extensive system of interpretations for the oil or yolk water. Again, the patterns were probably read much like tea-leaf reading or oomancy.

See also GEOMANCY; MOLYBDOMANCY; TASSEOGRAPHY.

Further reading

Bletzer, June G. *The Donning International Encyclopedic Psychic Dictionary.* West Chester, Pa.: Whitford Press, 1986.

Feuchtwang, Stephen, *An Anthropological Analysis of Chinese Geomancy.* Taipei: Southern Materials Center, 1974.

Opie, Iona, and Moira Tatem. *A Dictionary of Superstitions.* Oxford: Oxford University Press, 1992.

OPHIMANCY *Divination by observing the behavior of snakes.*

A variation of alectryomancy and apantomancy, ophimancy derives its name from the Greek word *ophis,* meaning serpent. Practiced by many early civilizations, ophimancy was used to interpret omens. For example, a coiled snake might mean to wait and be patient. A snake ready to strike might mean to proceed immediately with the topic on the querant's mind.

Ophimancy may once have been the prognostication method of choice because in the ancient world people believed that, unlike other animals, snakes never died. Supposedly, they were renewed and reborn into another life (as a snake) and held great power. The evidence of this was

Ophimancy is divination by observing the behavior of snakes.

the shedding of the snake's skin. Snakes are mentioned often in the Old and New Testaments, including in Psalms 74:14 and 89:10 and Genesis 2:15, which referred to the serpent in Eden. Snakes were considered God-like creatures or purveyors of information and enlightenment.

Further reading

Bardens, Dennis. *Psychic Pets.* Boca Raton, Fla.: Globe Communications, 1992.

Green, Marian. *The Elements of Natural Magic.* Dorset, England: Element Books, 1989.

Malvern, Marjorie. *Venus in Sackcloth.* Carbondale: Southern Illinois University Press, 1975.

Miller, Madeleine S., and J. Lane Miller, eds. *Harper's Encyclopedia of Bible Life.* San Francisco: Harper & Row, 1978.

ORNITHOMANCY *Divination by the observance of flying birds or through birds' songs.*

Since birds could fly, it must have seemed to many early peoples that they had God-like abilities. Birds became a part of many ancient religions. The dove remains the bird of peace, having special significance in Christianity.

Practiced in ancient Greece and Rome, ornithomancy was a prognostication method of considerable importance. Often an augur and his or her apprentice would undertake to interpret an omen or foretell the future by traveling to a holy or inspirational place. The augur would sit blindfolded (or with closed eyes), and the apprentice would describe the flight of the birds passing overhead. It is unclear why the augur couldn't look himself.

Further reading

Maven, Max. *Max Maven's Book of Fortunetelling.* New York: Prentice-Hall, 1992.

Sinnigen, William G., and Arthur E. R. Boak. *A History of Rome to A.D. 565.* 6th ed. New York: Macmillan, 1977.

Visions and Prophecies. Mysteries of the Unknown. Alexandria, Va.: Time Life Books, 1990.

OUIJA BOARDS *Trade-marked products sold as toys but actually used in a form of dowsing.*

The Ouija board, used under the guidance of a psychic, dactyomancer, medium or someone practicing mediumship, taps into unconscious radiations to divine the future and answer questions. Instead of the pendulum used in other dowsing methods, the Ouija board employs a small wheeled device, called a planchette, that slides over the board to the letters, numbers and yes and no printed on the surface. On the lower

Ornithomancy is the mantic art of predicting the future by observing the behavior of birds.

portion of the board are the words "good bye," indicating that the spiritual session is over. The board measures 12 by 18 inches.

Some believe that when the Ouija board is in the hands of those who are not truly interested in the occult or who believe that the session is held strictly for fun, evil spirits can be conjured up and there may be danger.

The Ouija board was first produced by Baltimore cabinetmaker William Flud in 1892. It became immensely popular at that time, when a spiritual revival had many people believing that one could call back the spirits of dead relatives and friends through mediums and psychic seances. The rights to the original Ouija board were later sold to Parker Brothers. The toy manufacturer continues to sell more than 2 million boards a year.

The Ouija is often guided by a single person, but as many as six people can place their fingers on the planchette as it spells out the answers to questions. Those who use this method of prognostication report that it takes some time for the spirits to connect with the querants and that the more often one does it, the easier it becomes.

Critics of this system believe that the planchette is guided by the querant's subconscious. Those who regularly use the Ouija board state that it is guided by a spiritual entity who wants to impart knowledge or foretell the future to the querant. They say that one can use the board to produce messages in the same manner as automatic writing.

During a Ouija board session, the querant (or querants) usually asks out loud if any spirits are in the room. If there is a spiritual connection, the planchette will move to "yes" immediately. Sometimes, it takes a few minutes of concentration to connect with a spiritual entity. The next question posed is often, "What is your name?" The entity will sometimes give a name. The name may even be someone whom the querant knows who has died. This doesn't necessarily mean that the deceased is speaking through the Ouija board and planchette, although it might. It typically means that the spirit drawn to the session has made a connection with the deceased and is speaking for him or her. This is much the way a translator works.

Sometimes malicious spirits make themselves known through the Ouija board, playing spiritual tricks on the querant. For example, in a session the querant might ask the name of the spirit moving the planchette. The answer might be the devil. Psychics say that if one does connect with a malicious spirit and chooses not to talk with it, one should tell the spirit to go away. The querant can then ask for a benign spiritual entity to enter the room and direct the planchette.

This type of divination has been in service since about 540 B.C., when Pythagoras used it. According to a historical account of the philosopher's life, his sect held frequent seances or circles. Pythagoras and his followers used a mystical table that moved on wheels around the floor. The philosopher and his pupil, Philolaus, interpreted to the audience revelations from the unseen world.

Tertullian, the Roman Christian theologian (c. A.D. 160–230) also knew about table communications with the unseen world. Greek professional soldier, historian and prolific writer Ammianus Marcellinus (c. 330–390) describes a table with a slab engraved with letters of the alphabet above which a ring was held suspended by a thread. This is a direct reference to dactyomancy, the precursor of the Ouija board. Additionally, other similar devices were used to predict the future and interpret omens in ancient China and in the Mongol empires.

Further reading

Fodor, Nandor. *Encyclopedia of Psychic Science.* New York: University Books, 1966.

Geller, Uri, and Guy Lyon Playfair. *The Geller Effect.* New York: Henry Holt, 1986.

Guiley, Rosemary Ellen. *Harper's Encyclopedia of Mystical and Paranormal Experience.* San Francisco: HarperSan Francisco, 1991.

Ostrander, Sheila, and Lynn Schroeder. *Psychic Discoveries behind the Iron Curtain.* Englewood Cliffs, N.J.: Prentice-Hall, 1970.

Showers, Paul. *Fortune Telling.* Philadelphia: New Home Library, Blankiston Company, 1942.

OUT-OF-BODY EXPERIENCES

To spiritually leave one's physical body for a metaphysical experience.

Out-of-body experiences (sometimes referred to as OBE) occur typically during the dream state, but one does not have to be asleep to have an OBE. It sometimes happens during meditation. During an out-of-body experience, the dreamer will often explain that he or she felt the physical body flying or floating. Looking at the spirit/soul body in the air, the dreamer says that it resembles the physical body. Sometimes he or she will look down at the physical body as it reclines.

Great distances can be traveled, and many times psychics report that they have traveled high above the earth and looked down at minute details of life such as ants or bugs in a field during an OBE.

It is thought that when one is "flying," it is done through the astral plane. Typically in out-of-body experiences the spirit/soul is able to move into other dimensions. He or she can perceive events that have yet to occur. Thus, the astral plane and out-of-body experiences can be used to divine upcoming events or circumstances that foretell the future. A psychic may enter the state of deep meditation, have an out-of-body experience and then return with information on forthcoming events in response to a querant's question.

Carl Jung, the famous psychologist, reportedly and regularly accessed the astral plane during out-of-body experiences, with what he termed "active imagination," which is a point where reality and imagination combine to produce a new reality. He claimed that he spoke with a spirit named Philemon and that talking with this entity helped him to maintain objectivity in the psychic world. Jung was not alone in documenting communication concerning out-of-body experiences and the astral plane. Robert Monroe, in *Journeys out of the Body*, describes the astral plane as populated by a host of spiritual entities. These "inhabitants" include those who have strange appearances such as demons, goblins and bizarre "rubbery" entities, who supposedly possessed the ability to make Monroe's life miserable. Other psychics say that magical spirits like fairies and elves also inhabit the astral plane, and many psychics believe that humans must pass through the dominion before entering heaven or hell or an afterlife.

See also JUNG, DR. CARL G.

Further reading

Bletzer, June G. *The Donning International Encyclopedic Psychic Dictionary.* West Chester, Pa.: Whitford Press, 1986.

Campbell, Joseph, ed. *The Portable Jung.* New York: Penguin, 1971.

Fodor, Nandor. *Between Two Worlds.* West Nyack, N.Y.: Parker, 1964.

Guiley, Rosemary Ellen. *Harper's Encyclopedia of Mystical and Paranormal Experience.* San Francisco: HarperSan Francisco, 1991.

Monroe, Robert A. *Journeys out of the Body.* New York: Doubleday, 1971.

Psychic Voyages. Mysteries of the Unknown. Alexandria, Va.: Time Life Books, 1990.

Watson, Donald. *The Dictionary of Mind and Spirit.* New York: Avon, 1991.

———. *Far Journeys.* Garden City, N.Y.: Dolphin/Doubleday, 1985.

P

PALMIST *In palmistry, one who interprets the lines of the hand in order to divine an individual's future or analyze his or her character traits.*

More than simply studying the lines of the hand, the palmist examines the muscled areas, called "mounts," the rings around the wrists and other marks on the palms such as diamond shapes, circles or stars. A palmist also takes into account the size and shape of the hands, the palms, the fingers and the fingernails, along with the color and texture of the skin.

Most palmists use the palm as a basis for a psychic reading and often rely on their intuitive skills in other areas, such as clairvoyance, to provide additional information. One can learn to become a palmist by studying material regarding the hand. In ancient China and India, podomists studied the soles of the feet in the same way that palmists studied the hand, using the mantic art of podomancy.

CHEIRO (1866–1939), whose birth name was Louis le Warner de Hamond, is considered to have been the world's leading palmist.

See also PALMISTRY; PODOMANCY.

Further reading

Altman, Nathaniel. *Palmistry Workbook.* New York: Sterling, 1990.

Burns, Litany. *Develop Your Psychic Abilities.* 1985. Reprint. New York: Pocket Books, 1987.

Cheiro. *Cheiro's Book of Numbers.* New York: Prentice-Hall, 1988.

———. *The Language of the Hand.* New York: Prentice-Hall, 1987.

Fitzherbert, Andrew. *Hand Psychology.* Garden City, N.Y.: Avery, 1989.

Vaughn, Frances. *Awakening Intuition.* Garden City, N.Y.: Anchor/Doubleday, 1979.

PALMISTRY *Divination by studying the shape and size of the hand, along with analysis of the lines, mounts, skin color and finger length.*

Considered to be one of most ancient forms of prognostication, palmistry continues to have a strong following today. It is, also, less commonly, known as cheiromancy. During a palm reading, a PALMIST (one who reads palms) studies the shape and texture of the querant's skin, palm shape and size, hand flexibility, shape and flexibility of fingers, the shape of the nails and the lines on the palm's surface and the muscle areas known as mounts. Most palmists report that the left hand (or less prominent hand) indicates the potential and the right shows what has actually occurred in a person's character development. At first glance, it might look like the right palm is a mirror image of the left; however, scrutinizing as witchcraft, and those who practiced them, including palmistry, were killed, persecuted or went into hiding.

During the mid-1800s palmistry, like many other spiritual techniques, saw a revival. British palmist Cheiro (1866–1939) is probably the best known of all palmists, and his books are still widely used today.

In palmistry, all portions of the hand, including the length between joints and areas on the wrist, are considered when analyzing character and consulting about the future.

PALMIST
Reading the lines of the palm is a mantic art taken seriously by some but considered trivial by others.

the palms will reveal a number of differences. Sometimes lines are deeper on one hand than the other; sometimes there are lines on one palm that do not appear at all on the other hand.

Palmistry may have begun as humanity developed and began looking inward for a purpose to the rigors of daily life. It is believed to have been redefined by the Chinese around 1100 B.C., along with the art of face reading (physiognomy).

There are mentions of the use of palmistry in the Bible. In Isaiah 49:16, it is written, "Behold, I have graven thee on the palms of thy hands thy walls are continually before me." And in Job 27:7, "He sealeth up the hand of every man; that all men may know his work." In Proverbs 3:16, the Bible says, "Length of days in her right hand, and in her left hand riches and honor." Palmistry continued to be a popular prognostication method throughout the Middle Ages, especially so as traveling gypsies moved from the East and India to Europe and the British Isles. In the 15th century, many mystical arts were condemned

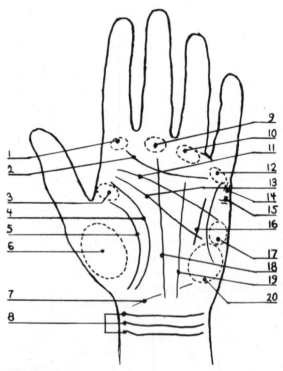

PALMISTRY

1 Mount of Jupiter	11 Heart Line
2 Girdle of Venus	12 Mount of Mercury
3 Mount of Lower Mars	13 Head Line
4 Life Line	14 Child Lines
5 Line of Mars	15 Marriage Lines
6 Mount of Venus	16 Hepatica
7 Via Lasciva	17 Mount of Upper Mars
8 Rascettes	18 Line of Fate
9 Mount of Saturn	19 Line of the Sun
10 Mount of Apollo	20 Mount of the Moon

The following is a brief list of the important lines and mounts of the palm. However, there is much more to the topic. Palmistry is complex as well as intriguing, with countless variations in fingers, hands and palms.

The LIFE LINE is located in the lower portion of the hand, typically running from a point between the index finger and the point where the thumb is connected to the palm.

The HEAD LINE is located beneath the fingers between the heart line and the life line; the head line's endings and beginnings are important.

The HEART LINE is one of the deepest lines of the palm. It begins at the mount of Jupiter (on the palm beneath the index finger) and crosses the palm.

The FATE LINE runs from a point just above the wrist across the palm vertically to a place just below where the middle finger is joined to the hand.

The LINE OF THE SUN, also known as line of Apollo or line of fate, runs vertically between the wrist area and up toward the ring finger.

The GIRDLE OF VENUS lies beneath the fingers and just above the heart line.

The LINE OF MARS is found running parallel to the life line between the wrist and the area of the palm between the index finger and the thumb.

The LINE OF HEALTH runs from where the little finger joins the palm down through the center of the palm.

The LINES OF MARRIAGE are found on the side of the palm of the hand about one-half inch below where the little finger joins the palm.

The LINES OF CHILDREN are found directly above the lines of marriage on the little-finger side of the palm. When found in the palm, they are vertical.

The VIA LASCIVA isn't found in all hands, but when present, it is located slightly above the wrist toward the fingers.

The RASCETTES, also known as bracelets, are found circling the palm side of the wrist.

The MOUNT OF APOLLO is located on both palms, slightly below where the ring finger joins the hand.

The MOUNT OF JUPITER is located on both hands and is slightly below where the index finger joins the hand.

The MOUNT OF LOWER MARS is located on the muscled pad on the palm halfway between the mount of Jupiter and the mount of Venus.

The MOUNT OF UPPER MARS is found in the muscled area on the palm about halfway between the mount of Mercury and the mount of the Moon.

The MOUNT OF MERCURY is located on the palm slightly below the little finger.

The MOUNT OF SATURN is located on the palm slightly below the middle finger.

The MOUNT OF THE MOON is located on both hands and is in the area below the little finger, next to the wrist.

The MOUNT OF VENUS is located on both hands, in the area of the palm below the thumb and index finger, close to the wrist.

Further reading

Altman, Nathaniel. *Palmistry Workbook*. New York: Sterling, 1990.

Asano, Michael. *Hands: The Complete Book of Palmistry.* New York: Japan Publications, 1985.

Buckland, Raymond. *Buckland's Complete Book of Witchcraft*. St. Paul, Minn.: Llewellyn, 1986.

Cheiro. *Cheiro's Book of Numbers*. New York: Prentice-Hall, 1988.

———. *The Language of the Hand*. New York: Prentice-Hall, 1987.

MacKenzie. *Palmistry for Women*. New York: Warner, 1973.

Robinson, Rita. *The Palm: A Guide to Your Hidden Potential*. North Hollywood, Calif.: Newcastle, 1988.

PAST LIFE *Existence in a previous incarnation.*

Those who believe in reincarnation say that when one experiences a physical death, one is reborn in a new physical body in order to learn a new lesson in life. This is considered to be spiritual evolution. Karma is the result of moral actions in previous lives. Thus, what has happened in previous incarnations affects what is to be challenged or accomplished in the present life.

Although considered Taoist and Buddhist concepts, past lives and reincarnation have been espoused by many great philosophers and psychics, including Pythagoras, Plato, Plotinus, Emerson, Blavatsky and Cayce. Contemporary metaphysical thinkers also embrace the belief in past lives. Internationally known physician, scientist and psychic the Reverend Hiroshi Motoyama, Ph.D., provides one of the most notable books on the topic—*Karma and Reincarnation*.

Some physics practice past-life regression with the use of hypnosis, during which a subject is said to be regressed beyond the point of their birth through various lives in order to provide information concerning a current problem or situation. This controversial technique supposedly gives information on specific crises in previous incarnations that is not available during waking hours.

See also CAYCE, EDGAR; REINCARNATION.

Further reading

Binder, Bettye B. *Past Lives Regression Guidebook.* Culver City, Calif.: Reincarnation Books, 1985.

Brennan, J. H. *The Reincarnation Workbook.* New York: Sterling, 1990.

Goldberg, Bruce. *Past Lives, Future Lives.* New York: Ballantine, 1982.

Guiley, Rosemary Ellen. *Tales of Reincarnation.* New York: Pocket Books, 1989.

Hall, Manly P. *Reincarnation: The Cycle of Necessity.* Los Angeles: Philosophical Research Society, 1956.

Kapleau, Philip. *The Wheel of Life and Death: A Practical and Spiritual Guide.* New York: Doubleday, 1989.

Motoyama, Hiroshi. *Karma and Reincarnation.* Translated by Rande Brown Ouchi. New York: Avon, 1992.

Woodward, Mary Ann. *Edgar Cayce's Story of Karma: God's Book of Remembrance.* New York: Coward, McCann & Geoghegan/Edgar Cayce Foundation, 1971.

PEGOMANCY *Divination by interpreting the images created when water is run from a fountain.*

Pegomancy is a variant of hydromancy. Like hydromancy, which encompasses all prognostica-tion using water, pegomancy was a popular divination method practiced in ancient Greece. It is no longer practiced today, nor are the details of the method now known. It is believed that the psychic watched the droplets and ripples in the fountain, although some psychics preferred to use raindrops or rainwater. It is thought that the psychic used the water's patterns as a basis for visions through scrying.

Other variations of hydromancy include divination by examining and deciphering the colors, waves or turbulence of the ocean, running water in a stream or river or the pattern of the current in a brook.

Further reading

Bletzer, June G. *The Donning International Encyclopedic Psychic Dictionary.* West Chester, Pa.: Whitford Press, 1986.

Cavendish, Richard, ed. *The Encyclopedia of the Unexplained.* New York: McGraw-Hill, 1974.

Miller, Madeleine S., and J. Lane Miller, eds. *Harper's Encyclopedia of Bible Life.* San Francisco: Harper & Row, 1978.

Roberts, Henry C. *The Complete Prophecies of Nostradamus.* New York: American Book–Stratford Press, 1969.

PENDULUM PREDICTIONS *Divination using an object suspended from a string in order to interpret omens and/or foretell the future.*

Regardless of the object suspended, it typically has a special significance to the psychic. Some use coins, ancient relics, crystals or gems. In ancient times, the object was strung on a gold-covered thread or a special golden chain.

Making predictions using a pendulum is a variation of dowsing, in which a stick or other suspended object is used to locate people, information and articles. The exact date of the first use of a pendulum to predict the future and contact the ethereal world is unknown; however, cave paintings found in the Sahara, from about 6000 B.C., depict a person holding a divining rod. Greek and Roman literature refers to rhabdomancy (dowsing with rods, arrows or wands).

Ancient myths and legends suggest magical rods and suspended objects used by Hermes and Aaron; however, these are often thought of as magician's wands rather than as pendulums or the dowser's forked stick or rod.

Pendulums are still widely used in the location of hidden objects (and at times missing people and bodies) and to uncover natural resources such as water and minerals. When searching for an object or person, the psychic generally walks around the area in question. Some psychics stay in their offices and spiritually connect with the help of guides or one's higher self. They study a map of the area, allowing the pendulum to direct the search party by moving the pendulum slowly over the map.

For those who are seeking a particular object, a representative of the object (a crystal, key, a significant rock or some other article) is suspended from a chain, thread or cord. The psychic covers the terrain either by walking or holding the pendulum over a map while concentrating on what is to be located. When the object or thing is located, the pendulum swings. Others consult with the pendulum for personal guidance of a spiritual nature.

For a psychic consultation, one would hold the pendulum while sitting quietly and meditating on the topic at hand. The querant poses a question, and the direction in which the pendulum swings provides the answer. Although the "correct" direction of the swinging pendulum may differ from one psychic to another, generally when the pendulum swings in circles to the right, the answer is affirmative. Circles to the left mean no. However, another theory is that movements to the north and south mean yes; east and west movements mean no.

Those who practice this prognostication method suggest that it takes practice and patience to use a pendulum, but with time guidance from the higher self or guides will come.

See also DOWSING; OUIJA BOARDS; RADIESTHESIA; RHABDOMANCY.

Further reading

Butler, W. E. *How to Develop Clairvoyance.* 2d ed. New York: Samuel Weiser, 1979.
Geller, Uri, and Guy Lyon Playfair. *The Geller Effect.* New York: Henry Holt, 1986.
Roberts, Kenneth. *Henry Gross and His Dowsing Rod.* Garden City, N.Y.: Doubleday, 1951.
Thomas, Keith. *Religion and the Decline of Magic.* New York: Macmillan, 1971.

PESSOMANCY *Divination through the use of pebbles.*

In pessomancy, the formation of the pebbles is deciphered when they are poured to the ground. This is a variation of halomancy, in which salt is used as the divination medium. Pessomancy was most likely practiced, along with halomancy, by the ancient Egyptians; it was more widely used by the ancient Greeks. The Greeks selected specific stones or pebbles for pessomancy, often shaking the pebbles up in a basket or bowl that held some significance or was considered to be blessed.

After the querant asked a question, or once confusion regarding an omen was discussed, the pebbles were shaken and then tossed out on the temple floor or on the ground. As with tasseography, patterns could be seen in the way in which small stones landed—at least in the eye and mind of the psychic.

There is a variation of pessomancy still practiced today by the Masai of East Africa. They cast stones from a buffalo horn to foretell the future of crops and the prosperity of their tribe. Those who practice a variation of this mantic art today do so with semiprecious and precious stones. This is a mantic art that in a contemporary sense often combines both pessomancy and scrying or even casting of lots.

See also CASTING OF LOTS; CRYSTALOMANCY; GEMS; LITHOMANCY; SCRYING.

Further reading

[Cayce, Edgar.] *Gems and Stones: Readings of Edgar Cayce.* Virginia Beach, Va.: ARE Press, 1976.
Markham, Ursula. *The Crystal Workbook: A Complete Guide to Working with Crystals.* Northamptonshire, England: Aquarian Press, 1988.
———. *Fortune-Telling by Crystals and Semiprecious Stones.* Northamptonshire, England: Aquarian Press, 1987.

Matteson, Barbara J. *Mystic Minerals.* Seattle: Cosmic Resources, 1985.

PHRENOLOGY *Divination of physical, mental and spiritual characteristics through the interpretation of bumps on the head.*

Credit for the use of phrenology as a prognostication method is given to Dr. Franz Joseph Gall (1756–1828), a Viennese physician. Along with a colleague, Dr. J. G. Spurzheim, he authored a definitive volume on phrenology called *The Physiognomical System*, which included charts. Dr. Gall theorized that one's talents and attributes were associated with specific parts of the brain that could be felt through a raised area on the scalp. This area is commonly known as a bump and is officially referred to as a "faculty."

Thus, if the head was examined, one could determine the strong points and weaknesses of an individual by the faculty. Dr. Gall's book was a systematic plan, with head areas outlined, to identify various characteristics. For example, a bump on the top of the head in line with the top of the ear was said to mean that one had high self-esteem.

Dr. Spurzheim continued the work of his associate and brought phrenology to the British Isles and America. By the early 1800s, its popularity had grown, and it was supported by many notable people of the time. Horace Mann, Clara Barton (who founded the American Red Cross), Mark Twain, Ralph Waldo Emerson, Walt Whitman and Edgar Allan Poe, among others, believed in this prognostication method. It also had its adversaries, including former president John Quincy Adams, who, although retired from public life, was extremely outspoken against the method. At one time there were more than 50 phrenology organizations in the United States espousing Spurzheim's theory. When he died, his autopsy was held open to the public at Harvard University, so that people could view the lobes of the great man's brain.

George Combe accepted the phrenology "torch" and continued to advocate its accuracy. Combe examined such notable heads as Daniel Webster and President Martin Van Buren. The *American Phrenology Journal* began publication in 1839 by Orson Fowler and his siblings Lorenzo and Charlotte. Published monthly, it had more than 50,000 subscribers. In 1842, the Museum of Phrenology was established in New York City, displaying wax heads of famous people.

In 1896, Nelson Sizer and Dr. H. S. Drayton published *Heads and Faces and How to Study Them: A Manual of Phrenology and Physiognomy for the People*, which encouraged business owners to practice this art. They said, "This knowledge will enable employers to meet the requirements of peculiar people whom they may be required to please." Sizer and Drayton's analysis included ways to discover if prospective employees were lazy, criminals, immoral or moral. Want-ads in the classified section of the newspaper at this time often informed job applicants that they would have to submit to a mandatory phrenology exam before being considered for a position.

As with other fads, phrenology lost favor as the public began considering other theories, including those of Dr. Sigmund Freud. Phrenology, a variation of physiognomy, divination of the future and analysis of one's character by studying the face, is practiced infrequently today, although current phrenologists explain that there is a strong relationship between head bumps and personal attributes.

To "read" a head, phrenologists suggest first reviewing the size and shape of the skull. A round head is supposed to be indicative of a strong, self-assured personality. A square head tells of a stable individual. A wide head is said to show one who is vivacious and extroverted, whereas the reverse is believed of one with a narrow skull. The "egg head," a slang term for one who is intellectual or academic, is oblong and looks much like an egg.

To determine the placement of the faculties, a phrenologist runs his or her hands over the querant's head. People can, of course, do a phrenology analysis on themselves. Notice should be taken of the placement of the bumps, size and firmness. Phrenologists say that both hemispheres of the brain should be taken into consideration, but most likely they coincide in the placement and size of the faculties.

The following are the faculties, often still referred to by antiquated terms, that help one read the personality map of the head. The numbers indicated in the illustration coincide with the number preceding the description.

1. Amativeness: Sexuality.
2. Conjugality: Faithfulness, faithful love.
3. Philoprogenitiveness: Strong parental love, love of family.
4. Adhesiveness: Gift for friendship and forming strong bonds with others.
5. Inhabitiveness: Love of home and country.
6. Continuity: Powerful abilities of concentration.
7. Vitativeness: Vivaciousness, love of living, resilience.
8. Combativeness: Strong inner fortitude, courageous nature.
9. Execution: Ability to persist.
10. Alimentiveness: A love and appreciation for food, drink.
11. Acquisitiveness: Talent with money, ability to accumulate it.
12. Secretiveness: Confidential nature.
13. Cautiousness: Prudent and discreet personality.

14. Approbativeness: Concern regarding others' opinions.
15. Self-esteem: Confidence, craves leadership.
16. Firmness: Persistence, staying power.
17. Conscientiousness: Moral integrity.
18. Hopefulness: High degree of enthusiasm and optimism.
19. Spirituality: Strong powers of intuition, religious leanings.
20. Vernation: Respect for traditional rules and rites.
21. Benevolence: Empathy.
22. Constructiveness: Mechanical aptitude.
23. Idealy: Artistic leanings and wisdom.
24. Sublimity: Cultured tastes.
25. Imitativeness: Talents for acting, drama.
26. Mirthfulness: Joyful sense of humor.
27. Casualty: Ability to clearly think through situations, powers of deduction.
28. Comparison: Ability to analyze.
29. Humanity: Keen judge of humanity.
30. Agreeableness: Dexterity with words.
31. Eventuality: Strong memory.
32. Time: Ability with music, powerful sense of rhythm.
33. Tune: Musical talent or leanings.
34. Language: Communication skills, especially in foreign languages.
35. Individuality: Questioning mind and able to discern the truth in situations.
36. Form: Strong sense of artistic design.
37. Size: Ability to understand and measure objects.
38. Weight: Ability to understand proportion.
39. Chromaticity: Ability to understand and use color.
40. Order: Organizational talents.
41. Calculation: Ability and gift for numbers.
42. Locality: Love and appreciation of travel.

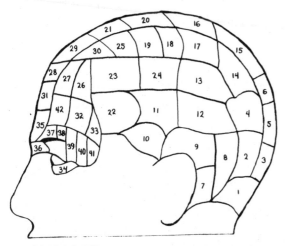

PHRENOLOGY
The numbers indicated in the illustration coincide with the numbers preceding the description.

A faculty that is large and firm indicates a strong attribute in this character area. A nonexistent or small, soft area indicates the opposite. Phrenologists explain that learning to perform a phrenology examination accurately takes time and patience and often requires the assistance of a phrenology master, should a student be serious about learning this art.

Further reading

Bletzer, June G. *The Donning International Encyclopedic Psychic Dictionary*. West Chester, Pa.: Whitford Press, 1986.

Drury, Nevill. *Dictionary of Mysticism and the Esoteric Traditions*. Dorset, England: Prism Press, 1992.

Magical Arts. Mysteries of the Unknown. Alexandria, Va.: Time Life Books, 1990.

Maven, Max. *Max Maven's Book of Fortunetelling*. New York: Prentice-Hall, 1992.

PHYLLOMANCY *Divination by studying the shape, patterns, veins and color of leaves.*

A variation of botanomancy, phyllomancy was practiced by many groups, including the ancient Greeks and the Druids. It was used as a method of foretelling the future and interpreting omens.

It is interesting to note that scientists and environmentalists now study the shapes and patterns of leaves to ascertain the health of soil and environmental conditions in an area. Some even believe that, as in folklore, one can anticipate the intensity of an upcoming season by studying the behavior, color and health of leaves.

Further reading

Ancient Wisdom, Ancient Sects. Mysteries of the Unknown. Alexandria, Va.: Time Life Books, 1990.

Carr-Gomm, Philip. *The Elements of the Druid Tradition*. Dorset, England: Element Books, 1991.

Maven, Max. *Max Maven's Book of Fortunetelling*. New York: Prentice-Hall, 1992.

PHYLLORHODOMANCY *Divination by slapping a rose petal between the hands.*

This ancient Greek method most likely used *Rosa gallica*, commonly known today as autumn damask. Using phyllorhodomancy, the psychic would select a rose petal with a concave form. After meditation and/or asking a question out loud, the querant would take the petal and place it in the palm of the right hand and then firmly slap his or her hands together. A burst petal meant that the answer was yes. If the petal did not burst, the answer was no.

Phyllorhodomancy is a variation of BOTANO-MANCY.

PHYLLORHODOMANCY
Rose leaves and petals were used by ancient Greeks to calculate the success of various causes.

Further reading

Christopher, Thomas. *In Search of Lost Roses*. New York: Avon, 1989.

Cumont, Franz. *Oriental Religions in Roman Paganism*. New York: Dover, 1956.

Maven, Max. *Max Maven's Book of Fortunetelling*. New York: Prentice-Hall, 1992.

PHYSIOGNOMY *Divination of the future and analysis of one's character by studying the face.*

Also know as anthroposomancy, physiognomy may include the reading of moles, lines on the face and the definition of a profile. Chinese face reading, palmistry, phrenology and body-typing are sometimes included in this category.

Published in the Sung dynasty, *Ma-Yee-Shang-Fa (The Simple Guide to Face Reading)* was the first book on the topic of physiognomy, although it had been practiced during the Chou dynasty, more than 3,200 years before. The book is still used as the basic source of information on a skill that continues to be practiced today in Asia and is given far more credence than palmistry.

See also ANTHROPOSOMANCY; LEVATER, JOHANN KASPAR; MACULOMANCY; PALMISTRY; PHRENOLOGY.

Further reading

Bray, Theodore de, ed. *Sources of Chinese Traditions.* New York: Columbia University Press, 1960.

Leland, Charles Godfrey. *Gypsy Sorcery and Fortune Telling.* New York: University Books, 1962.

Maven, Max. *Max Maven's Book of Fortunetelling.* New York: Prentice-Hall, 1992.

Walker, Barbara G. *The Woman's Encyclopedia of Myths and Secrets.* New York: Harper Collins, 1983.

PIPER, LEONORE E. *(1859–1950) American psychic.*

Piper is considered to be one of the most talented of contemporary American psychics. She was a healer and began giving readings when she was in her early 20s.

In one trance, Piper wrote a complex message for one of the clients sitting in the seance. The client was a judge from the Boston area, and the message was supposedly from the magistrate's deceased son. The judge was astonished at the accuracy and seeming validity of the message, which cited little known facts about his child. After this point, Piper channeled a succession of SPIRITUAL GUIDES. Rather than working with other mediums, Piper began giving readings on her own. In a session, she would enter a trance with teeth grinding and physical spasms, as if she was in intense pain. When the spiritual energy took over her body and mind, her persona and voice would change dramatically.

Although there were many so-called psychics at this time who were exposed as frauds, Piper's abilities were never disproved, nor was it ever proved that she was involved in a hoax of any type. Most people were in awe of her ability to go into a trance and give detailed accounts of dead friends and relatives, but her critics included American psychical researcher Richard Hodgson (secretary to the American branch of the Society for Psychical Research). During hundreds of readings, many with people unknown to Piper, her information was always found to be accurate. The method by which she derived her information could never be explained by anyone who did not believe in psychic abilities. Critics thought she read the thoughts of the strangers, but she insisted that she was in contact with their departed relatives.

At one time, Piper was hounded by private detectives who were trying to discover where she obtained the information she gave in her readings. They never discovered any fraud. The English Society for Psychical Research and the American branch of the organization found that her psychic skills were truly genuine. They credited her gifts to telepathy.

Piper channeled a spirit known as Dr. Phinuit until 1892, then one called George Pellew, nicknamed GP. Later, she began channeling other spirits and doing a greater amount of AUTOMATIC WRITING.

See also CHANNEL; CLAIRVOYANCE.

Further reading

Kautz, William H., and Melanie Branon. *Channeling: The Intuitive Connection.* San Francisco: Harper & Row, 1987.

Klimo, John. *Channeling: Investigations on Receiving Information from Paranormal Sources.* Los Angeles: Jeremy P. Tarcher, 1987.

Leonard, Gladys Osborne. *My Life in Two Worlds.* London: Two Worlds, 1931.

Piper, Alta L. *The Life and Work of Mrs. Piper.* London: Kegan Paul, Trench, Trubner & Co., 1929.

Stewart, R. J. *The Elements of Prophecy.* Dorset, England: Element Books, 1990.

PISCES *One of the 12 astrological signs of the zodiac. The symbol is the fish.*

Those who are born between February 20 and March 20 are natives of the sign of Pisces and are supposed to have specific traits indicative of the time and date on which they were born. Divination of events can also be charted through this astrological sign.

Astrologers divine what is in store throughout life through the time, date and place in which an individual was born as they coordinate the influences with other signs, the planets, the Sun, the Moon and other powers.

In traditional Western astrology, Pisces is the 12th sign of the zodiac. Those born during the

PISCES

period typically exhibit qualities that exemplify a patient, humanistic and sensitive nature.

Pisces natives are considered to be one of the gentler types of the zodiac. They are emotional and imaginative, with a strong intuitive sense. They are wonderfully romantic and adapt well to almost any situation. These are team players who can also work alone. They like support but often from a distance. They are loyal and should be able to attain high academic honors and provide the basis for great achievements.

The Pisces man or woman, while being able to adapt even to hardship, is believed to be quite impressionable. He or she may seem too easily swayed by the opinions of others, especially so when communicating with strong-willed types like Scorpio and Taurus natives. However, the Pisces man or woman knows that listening with the heart is the only way he or she can live.

This description may make Pisces natives sound too abstract and illusive, but on the contrary, they are practical and hardworking. They also have a strong materialistic side. Pisces natives also worry about the future, both personal and global, and seek spiritual answers.

The sign of the zodiac in which an individual is born is responsible for only one fragment of the qualities he or she receives at birth. Psychics are quick to point out that a general forecast solely on the stellar position of the Sun on the day an individual was born is unlikely to provide an accurate glimpse of the future.

While traditional astrologers use books to calculate a personal birth chart based on the position of the Sun, Moon and planets at a distinct time, computer software has replaced most of this time-consuming work. The correct term for calculating a birth chart is to "cast" it. In order to fully comprehend the extent of traits, potential and attributes, the exact time and place of birth must be known and interpreted.

See also ASTROLOGICAL SYMBOLS; ASTROLOGY.

Further reading

Cosmic Connections. Mysteries of the Unknown. Alexandria, Va.: Time Life Books, 1990.

Goodman, Linda. *Linda Goodman's Sun Signs.* New York: Fawcett/Columbine, 1978.

Morgan, Chris. *Fortune Telling: How to Predict Your Own Future.* London: Quintet Publishing and Random House, 1992.

Omarr, Sydney. *My World of Astrology.* New York: Fleet, 1965.

————. *Pisces.* New York: New American Library, 1992.

Verlagsanstalt, Datura. *Pisces Astro Analysis.* New York: Grosset & Dunlap, 1976.

Woolfork, Joanna Martine. *The Only Astrology Book You'll Ever Need.* Landham, Mass.: Scarborough, 1992.

PODOMANCY *Analyzing character or prognosticating the future through the study of the lines on the feet.*

No longer practiced, podomancy was used in ancient China and India much as palmistry is used today. Podomancy, like palmistry, is a variation of PHYSIOGNOMY, divination by studying the human body.

See also PALMISTRY.

This ancient symbol represents the astrological sign of Pisces.

Further reading

Maven, Max. *Max Maven's Book of Fortunetelling*. New York: Prentice-Hall, 1992.

Visions and Prophecies. Mysteries of the Unknown. Alexandria, Va.: Time Life Books, 1990.

PRANA *Sanskrit for "life force."*

The prana is often considered the spirit of life within each person, along with the principle of all life. It can be the God of all, the sum total of the laws of the universe or the force of life-producing fluids within the human body.

Many religions and civilizations believe in a life force. The Chinese call it *ch'i;* ancient Egyptians called it *sa.* The Iroquois refer to it as *orenda.* And the Polynesians call it *mana.*

The Taoists believe, as do other groups, that any imbalance or negativity can damage the life force and bring about sickness, disease and, ultimately, death.

See also LAWS OF METAPHYSICS.

Further reading

Drury, Nevill. *Dictionary of Mysticism and the Esoteric Traditions*. Dorset, England: Prism Press, 1992.

Fodor, Nandor. *Encyclopedia of Psychic Science*. New York: University Books, 1966.

Mather, George A., and Larry A. Nichols. *Dictionary of Cults, Sects, Religions and the Occult*. Grand Rapids, Mich.: Zondervan Publishing House, 1993.

PRECOGNITION *Divination through the interpretation of an internal feeling.*

Precognition stems from the same source as intuition. It is the knowledge of an event or situation before that event or situation transpires, without the use of reason.

Precognition is considered a psychic gift. It is sometimes referred to as a "gut feeling," a "hunch" or a "sixth sense." Some interpret it as part of being close to God and understanding and using his blessings.

As with intuition, precognition defies analysis. It is often illogical and irrational. Most parapsychologists believe it is a form of ESP, yet they have come to understand that it is even more powerful since it is not only knowledge; it affects feelings, emotions and mental abilities. Most psychics believe that all babies are born with a keen sense of their own intuitive powers. Slowly, typically by the end of the teenage years, children lose or quell the ability to connect with this right-brain function. Left-brain functions of reason and logic replace intuition in most people by the time they reach their 20s. Psychics explain that the more we use our ability, the stronger it becomes.

Often physical sensations are combined with precognition. These are the goose bumps, the bits of unexplained apprehension, the upset stomach or the tingling of the skin. Sometimes there's a "little voice inside the head" that directs an individual to follow another course or to play a hunch that seems totally illogical at that instant. These are attributed to clairvoyant messages from the higher self, guidance from spirits or angels or a closeness with God, among other things.

Females are often said to have a "woman's intuition"—that is, a more attuned ability to sense things and accept information without using rigid forms of analysis. Additionally, those who begin to rely on intuitive guidance discover that the "voices" or "hunches" are correct most of the time, and so they begin to trust this faculty more.

Psychiatrist Carl G. Jung, among others, believed in precognition. In his *Psychological Types* (1923), he explained that it was not just an insight but a creative process that possessed the ability to motivate individuals. In the metaphysical world, psychics like to explain that anyone can use the gift of precognition. Through meditation, they believe one can become attuned to the superconscious mind, the all-knowing mind of all things (sometimes called the soul-mind) and thus unblock creative, inspired and intuitive powers.

See also CLAIRVOYANCE; DEJA VU; EXTRASENSORY PERCEPTION (ESP); INTUITION.

Further reading

Burns, Litany. *Develop Your Psychic Abilities*. New York: Pocket Books, 1985.

Butler, W. E. *How to Develop Clairvoyance*. 2d ed. New York: Samuel Weiser, 1979.

Gawain, Shakti. *Living in the Light.* San Raphael, Calif.: Whatever Publishing, 1986.

Popper, Karl. *Objective Knowledge.* Oxford: Oxford University Press, 1971.

Rogo, D. Scott. *Our Psychic Potentials.* Englewood Cliffs, N.J.: Prentice-Hall, 1984.

Vaughan, Frances. *Awakening Intuition.* Garden City, N.Y.: Anchor/Doubleday, 1979.

PREDICTIONS *Psychically obtained information prognosticating the future.*

When we think of predictions, we often consider only foretelling information about things in one's personal future and of a personal nature. A querant may ask a psychic to predict: Will I find true love? When will I get a promotion? When will I be able to buy a house? Predictions can also be global, as seen in the predictions of astrologers Jeane Dixon and Sydney Omarr, for example, who foretell changes in government, assassinations and even tragic accidents and natural disasters.

Predictions often come without notice or when a psychic is given information by his or her guides or the higher self. Sometimes predictions come through clairvoyance and automatic writing, sometimes through the assistance of mantic objects and tools, such as tea leaves and tarot cards. At other times, as with Edgar Cayce, the psychic goes into a trancelike state. Predictions can also come through when information is channeled from a spirit in the ethereal realm.

The early Egyptians believed that they could contact and be guided by the gods through their dreams and regularly used this method of prognostication. Dream predictions and interpretation are mentioned in the Bible in many places, including Numbers 12:5–6 and Daniel 2:2 and 4:7. Greek psychics used arrows and rods as dowsing instruments. In ancient Rome, augurs were court-appointed psychics who helped the empire in prognosticating the future using such methods as scrying, casting of lots, iatromancy and rhabdomancy.

Contemporary predictions are often made through the use of palmistry, tarot card readings, astrological forecasts and aura readings; ancient methods, including I Ching and pyromancy, also continue to be employed today.

Further reading

Aylesworth, Thomas G. *Astrology and Foretelling the Future.* New York: Franklin Watts, 1973.

Bethards, Betty. *The Dream Book: Symbols for Self-Understanding.* 9th ed. Petaluma, Calif.: Inner Light Press, 1992.

Glass, Justine. *The Story of Fulfilled Prophecy.* London: Cassell, 1969.

King, Francis, and Stephen Skinner. *Techniques of High Magic.* Rochester, Vt.: Destiny Books, 1991.

Loewe, Michael, and Carmen Blacker, eds. *Divination and Oracles.* London: Allen & Unwin, 1981.

Logan, Jo, and Lindsey Hodson. *The Prediction Book of Divination.* Dorset, England: Blandford Press, 1984.

Stern, Jess. *Edgar Cayce, the Sleeping Prophet.* New York: Bantam, 1968.

Stewart, R. J. *The Elements of Prophecy.* Dorset, England: Element Books, 1990.

Woods, R., ed. *Understanding Mysticism.* New York: Doubleday, 1980.

PREMONITION *A forewarning regarding a future event.*

According to psychics, the use of premonition, also known as INTUITION and PRECOGNITION, is available to all. It is a gift all babies are born with, and only through deprogramming do we lose the ability to foretell future events and situations using this "sixth sense."

See also EXTRASENSORY PERCEPTION (ESP).

Further reading

Burns, Litany. *Develop Your Psychic Abilities.* New York: Pocket Books, 1985.

Gawain, Shakti. *Living in the Light.* San Raphael, Calif.: Whatever Publishing, 1986.

Reed, Henry. *Edgar Cayce on the Mysteries of the Mind.* New York: Warner, 1989.

PSEPHOMANCY *Divination by selecting at random small stones from a pile.*

Details of this ancient, perhaps pre-Egyptian, mantic art are lost in time. However, it may have been used as one draws specific cards from a deck to foretell the future, with certain stones having specific significance.

Further reading

Ancient Wisdom and Secrets Sects. Mysteries of the Unknown. Alexandria, Va.: Time Life Books, 1990.

Bletzer, June G. *The Donning International Encyclopedic Psychic Dictionary*. West Chester, Pa.: Whitford Press, 1986.

PSI *The 23d letter of the Greek alphabet, selected at random to represent the X factor, an unknown quantity that cannot be explained.*

Psychic researcher J. B. Rhine was the first to refer to psychic phenomena as PSI. He called it a "general term to identify a person's extra sensory motor communication with the environment."

Often people who possess and use psychic abilities are referred to as having PSI skills. PSI includes telepathy, precognition, ESP, clairvoyance and other abilities that cannot be explained by known scientific laws.

See also CLAIRVOYANCE; EXTRASENSORY PERCEPTION (ESP); INTUITION; RHINE, JOSEPH BANKS, M.D.

Further reading

Cavendish, Richard, ed. *Man, Myth and Magic: An Illustrated Encyclopedia of the Supernatural*. Vol. 7. New York: Marshal Cavendish Corporation, 1970.

Feyer, Dr. Ernest C. *The Call of the Soul: A Scientific Explanation of Telepathy and Psychic Phenomena*. San Francisco: Auto-Science Institute, 1926.

Halbourne, Max. *Mental Telepathy and ESP Powers for the Millions*. Los Angeles: Sherbourne Press, 1967.

Hintze, Naomi A., and J. Gaither Pratt. *The Psychic Realm: What Can You Believe?* New York: Random House, 1975.

Rhine, Louisa E. *ESP in Life and Lab*. New York: Collier-Macmillan, 1967.

Richet, Charles. *Thirty Years of Psychical Research*. London: William Collins Publishers, 1923.

Scott, Cyril. *An Outline of Modern Occultism*. London: Routledge & Kegan Paul, 1950.

Thouless, R. H. *Experimental Psychical Research*. New York: Penguin, 1963.

Tyrrell, G. N. M. *Science and Psychical Phenomena*. London, 1938. Reprint. New York: University Books, 1961.

PSYCHIC *One who has the ability to sense something without prior knowledge or the use of reason.*

A psychic is said to be able to translate spiritual information from the ethereal realm to others on this earth plane. He or she may ask for assistance or contact a spiritual entity during a seance. The querant or members of the audience will ask the psychic questions, which he or she then transmits to the universe or the entity for answers.

Sometimes the answers or revelations come through automatic writing, pendulums, table tipping or other manifestations. Sometimes the psychic releases his or her body and the entity talks through him or her, often with a complete change in the sound of the medium's voice.

The nonhuman entities may be angels, nature spirits, guardian spirits, deities, demons or spirits of the dead. Sometimes the messages are transmitted from the higher self or from other entities that often have exotic names (exotic names are often considered mystical).

One of the world's most famous psychics, but relatively unknown in the United States, was the Russian, Wolf Messing (1899–1972). In Messing's autobiography, published in the official Soviet press (and never officially denied), Soviet leader Joseph Stalin acted as a psychical researcher and put Messing's powers to the test. According to the reports, through his mental power to control other people's minds and direct their actions, Messing (under Stalin's request) persuaded a bank clerk that a blank piece of paper was a check for 100,000 rubles. The clerk then walked through the high-security area leading to the dictator's offices, right past the secret police. Messing had also controlled the police officers' minds, making them believe that the clerk was actually the head of security, Lavrenty Beria. Messing was never allowed to travel to the West, but continued to thrill and baffle Russian audiences with his clairvoyant powers. He explained that others' thoughts provided colorful images; he saw pictures rather than words.

Some people who have the ability to use their psychic skills say that when they first recognized this power, it scared them tremendously. It is said that the father of the great psychic Daniel Dunglas Home (1833–1886) was so distressed by young Daniel's visions and behavior that he hired an exorcist to rid the teenager of the devils within.

A psychic is sometimes called a medium, a sensitive or a control. The term *spiritualist* is rarely used today, although it was popular at one time.

See also AUGUR; BAILEY, ALICE; BLAVATSKY, HELENA P.; CHANNEL; HOME, DANIEL DUNGLAS; INTUITION; KNIGHT, JZ; PSYCHIC READINGS.

Further reading

Jones, Lloyd K. *Development of Mediumship.* Chicago: Lormar, 1919.

Kardec, Allan. *The Book of Mediums.* York Beach, Maine: Samuel Weiser, 1970.

Klimo, John. *Channeling: Investigations on Receiving Information from Paranormal Sources.* Los Angeles: Jeremy P. Tarcher, 1987.

Lungin, Tatiana. *Wolf Messing: The True Story of Russia's Greatest Psychic.* New York: Paragon House, 1989.

Rodegast, Pat, and Judith Stanton, comps. *Emmanuel's Book: A Manual for Living Comfortably in the Cosmos.* New York: Bantam, 1987.

Zolar. *Zolar's Book of the Spirits.* New York: Prentice-Hall, 1987.

PSYCHIC HEALER   *One who is able to heal the sick using unorthodox methods and therapies that employ psychic principles.*

Psychic healing continues to be frowned upon by the medical establishment. Yet most doctors agree that the belief in any medicine can often cure the patient, even when that medicine is a placebo. Often alternative cures have been found to work as well as those produced by high-tech medical firms.

American psychic Edgar Cayce (1877–1945) is one of the contemporary world's best-known practitioners of psychic healing.

Those psychics who read auras are said to be able to see when someone is ill because of specific color changes in the halo that surrounds the body. Psychic healing is sometimes practiced by clairvoyants who are able to psychically see and know about the health of a querant or someone about whom the querant has questions. Astrologers who use medical astrology interpret a birth chart to learn the influences on health and illness regarding a querant. From the birth chart, they are often able to tell what specific inclination a querant has to develop a particular disorder. For example, if one is born in Taurus, he or she has a tendency for disorders of the throat. Libra tends to experience lower-back disorders. Palmists look at a querant's life line to point out health challenges. Faith healers refer to psychic healing as "laying on of hands." Those who practice voodoo also perform psychic healing.

See also AKASHIC RECORDS; ASTROLOGY; AURAS; CAYCE, EDGAR; CLAIRVOYANCE; IATROMANCY; LAYING ON OF HANDS; LIFE LINE; PALMISTRY.

Further reading

Achterberg, Jeanne. *Imagery in Healing: Shamanism and Modern Medicine.* Boston: Shambhala, 1985.

Bowers, Barbara. *What Color Is Your Aura?* New York: Simon & Schuster, 1989.

[Cayce, Edgar.] *Edgar Cayce on Healing.* Virginia Beach, Va.: ARE Press, 1969.

Cornell, H. L. *Encyclopedia of Medical Astrology.* St. Paul, Minn.: Llewellyn, 1972.

Hirschfelder, Arlene, and Paulette Molin. *The Encyclopedia of Native American Religions.* New York: Facts On File, 1992.

Sherman, Harold. *"Wonder" Healers of the Philippines.* Los Angeles: DeVross, 1967.

Stern, Jess. *Edgar Cayce, the Sleeping Prophet.* New York: Bantam, 1968.

Weil, Andrew. *Health and Healing: Understanding Conventional and Alternative Medicine.* Boston: Houghton Mifflin, 1983.

PSYCHIC READINGS   *Information given by a psychic to a querant regarding that person's past, present and/or future, and/or as an answer to the questions on a querant's mind.*

Psychic reading is an umbrella phrase for all information provided in an intuitive, clairvoyant or telepathic way. Often psychics use various mantic objects and tools, such as palmistry or tarot cards, to provide information. There is usually a charge for the reading, which can last from 15 minutes to an entire day.

Those who provide psychic readings recommend that a querant use his or her best consumer skills when seeking a counselor or adviser. Consulting with someone who advertises psychic services at a fair or carnival may not provide quality or even truthful information. There are even psychics who provide readings at local shopping malls. Additionally, as with all consulting services, reputable psychics say that there are some in the field who prey on a querant's vulnerability. Many people consult psychics when other avenues of assistance seem to be exhausted or during a time of life-altering crisis, such as the death of a loved one. Thus, unscrupulous psychics continue to string along the unsuspecting and naive querant, coaxing him or her into a number of sessions to solve a particular problem, to discover troubling information about a past life or to contact a dead loved one. This is done, of course, for money.

Reputable psychics encourage the public to contact them through referrals and by attending a group session. One can often contact a psychic from a referral at a metaphysical bookstore or teaching center. Taking a beginner's class in a specific psychic skill or mantic art is often a good way to get to know a psychic before contacting him or her for a reading.

As with any other personal service, it is acceptable to talk with the psychic before a session. This can be done in person just before the session begins or over the telephone. The psychic will talk about his or her specialty (cards, astrology, crystals, etc.), along with the method used, but will most likely not provide personal information without charging for the session. Some psychics provide information during a telephone session; others will do it through the mail.

The psychic who uses dominoes, I Ching or tasseography should not be discounted; typically, the psychic is also employing telepathy and clairvoyance for the reading. Most people, explain psychics, prefer a psychic who utilizes predictive tools or articles. Cards, tea leaves or an astrological chart makes the spiritual work that the psychic does tangible. The information he or she dispenses becomes visible and, in a sense, touchable to the uninitiated.

Before a psychic reading, a querant should find out the cost. Most psychics charge by the hour, as do other service people, but some also have half-hour rates. Metaphysical teaching centers and bookstores dealing in the occult sometimes have "psychic fairs" where various psychics come together on a specific day and provide short readings for a lesser fee. This is a good time to meet a number of psychics and to determine which individual a querant is most comfortable with. It's also a good time to sample various methods.

Fees range from $15.00 an hour to the hundreds, depending on the experience and reputation of the psychic and the length of the reading. Some psychics do not charge for their services. While it might seem to be an awkward question, it is essential that one know the fee for the reading before the session begins. Many psychics take checks, charge cards and cash, but one must ask before the session starts. Fees are usually expected after the session.

The information provided during a psychic reading is often quite personal. Psychics report that most people ask about two things: Money and love are continually on clients' minds. When dealing with these sensitive areas, it's necessary to have a good rapport with a psychic. If one feels awkward for any reason, the reading will not be as successful.

The sessions should be held in private. When a psychic visits a party and every partygoer takes a turn, the individual readings may not be as reliable as when the meeting is on a one-to-one basis. Psychics often audiotape the session; however, there's no guarantee that this will be done. Some clients bring their own tape recorder or take notes during the session. Since one sometimes misses fragments of conversation while concentrating on the next question, a tape provides more insight because it can be listened to over again.

According to psychics, if at any time during a session the client doesn't like what he or she is being told or the approach being taken, the session should stop. In addition, if the information being provided doesn't feel correct intuitively, the session should be stopped by the querant. One can say, "That's not at all like me," or, "That's not true." Psychics do have "off" days, and there are unscrupulous people who pretend they have psychic abilities to take money from innocent people.

Sometimes querants go to a psychic expecting the man or woman to provide information without the querant saying anything, as if to test the psychic's skills. This can work well, and there are psychics who prefer to get a querant's attention by providing some little-known fact. However, in most cases, it is best to provide the psychic with the essential information and to be truthful in your quest. One might say, "I've been very unhappy in my job and in my career for quite some time. Could you tell me about this concern?" This ought to be done, rather than saying, "I'm unhappy."

It is always a good idea to come into a session prepared with questions. It is perfectly acceptable to have the questions written on a piece of paper. With a tarot card reading, for example, after the traditional spread and reading of the cards, some psychics ask that a querant concentrate on a specific question, then select a card from the deck. This can offer a final bit of information that can be most helpful.

Some querants become addicted to readings and travel from one psychic to another. Since many people consult with psychics during difficult periods in life, it is logical that one could become dependent on the advice offered. Typically, professional psychics recommend that one have a reading not more than once every six months; some say not more than once a year. Often a psychic will recommend that the querant study a metaphysical field or read metaphysical books for more information rather than consulting too often. Unlike ancient methods of prognostication, today's psychic usually advises on how to come to one's own decision, rather than telling the querant what decision to make.

A psychic reading is not fortune-telling, and it is not a game. A reputable psychic should be sensitive to the querant's problems and thoughts, be nonjudgmental and always have a positive outlook on the situation. Most psychics would never reveal an imminent personal tragedy. If the psychic sees or is given a spiritual warning, he or she will normally phrase it with helpful information. Thus, instead of saying, "You'll lose your job and get really angry," one might hear, "You'll be changing jobs shortly and find new challenges." Just because a psychic tells a querant something, it doesn't guarantee that this situation will occur. Human beings function with free will and, once information is made available, can make personal choices as to the best direction to take. For instance, if it seems as if a person is about to lose his or her job, it might be advisable to begin looking for a better job before this situation occurs. Thus he or she will not be fired. Was the psychic information correct? Since the information provided a new course of action, one cannot be sure.

See also CLAIRVOYANCE; DEJA VU; EXTRASENSORY PERCEPTION (ESP); INTUITION.

Further reading

Burns, Litany. *Develop Your Psychic Abilities*. New York: Pocket Books, 1985.

Butler, W. E. *How to Develop Clairvoyance*. 2d ed. New York: Samuel Weiser, 1979.

Nelson, Robert. *Secret Methods of Private Readers!* Columbus, Ohio: Nelson, 1964.

Northgate, Ivy. *Mediumship Made Easy*. London: Psychic Press, 1986.

Popper, Karl. *Objective Knowledge*. Oxford: Oxford University Press, 1971.

Vaughan, Frances. *Awakening Intuition*. Garden City, N.Y.: Anchor/Doubleday, 1979.

PSYCHIC SURGERY *A healing technique practiced in the Philippines and Brazil in which the psychic surgeon uses no instruments but claims to make incisions in the body.*

Psychic surgeons are alleged to operate on the body, whereas psychic healers perform healing acts that do not require incisions; nor do they require that the individual be in the same room as the healer.

There is much controversy surrounding the practice of psychic surgery. Those who support it say that God opens the body without the use of surgical instruments. Sometimes "surgery" is performed with scissors, knives, forks and tweezers. The practioner locates the diseased or affected organ and removes the ailing portion. Then the surgeon miraculously heals the incision. People travel from all parts of the world to the known psychic surgeons, and many such surgeons practice their arts in hotel rooms or lobbies, with the patient bookings for the healing arranged through international travel agencies.

One of the most famous psychic surgeons was Jose Pedro de Freitas (1935?–1971). A Brazilian, de Fretias claimed to have been the reincarnation of a famous German doctor who was killed during World War I. Edivaldo Silva, also a native of Brazil, uses his bare hands to perform the operations.

There are many who criticize psychic surgery, including the American judge Daniel H. Hanscom. In 1974, Judge Hanscom completed a lengthy, in-depth investigation into the validity of the practice. It was discovered that most "surgeons" practiced some trickery to indicate that the surgery had been performed. It was found that they actually used concealed sacks of blood and animal or vegetable matter covered with blood to indicate the organ or diseased area that had been removed. During the "surgery" the patient often claims to feel his or her organs being manipulated, but when the "surgery" is finished there is no mark from the incision.

It is interesting to note that although psychic surgery continues to be attacked and berated by the press and the medical establishment, it continues to be performed. Why does it work when such procedures are said to be successful? As with other placebo cures, it may be an example of the power of positive thinking and the will of a spirit to survive that has made the healing possible.

Further reading

Krippner, Stanley, and Alberto Villoldo. *The Realms of Healing*. 3d ed. Berkeley, Calif.: Celestial Arts, 1986.

Meek, George W., ed. *Healers and the Healing Process*. Wheaton, Ill.: Theosophical Publishing House, 1977.

Powers of Healing. Mysteries of the Unknown. Alexandria, Va.: Time Life Books, 1990.

PSYCHOMETRY *Prognostication through the use of objects or articles belonging to someone who is not present and who is unknown to the psychic.*

People, places and events are perceived through clairvoyance, telepathy and recognition. The term *psychometry* was coined by psychical researcher D. J. R. Buchanan about 1840. A psychic who practices this skill is referred to as a psychometrist. The objects used are often jewelry but may also be articles of clothing or other things of a personal nature. The more often the object has been in use, the more information will be available. Jewelry or other metal objects are supposed to be the best conductors of information for those who practice psychometry. In the case of antique jewelry, or something that has been owned by many people, conflicting information is often received. When an object has been touched by many people, a number of stories will be available to the psychometrist.

According to psychometry, whenever one touches an object, vibrations of that encounter become attached to it. When someone wears a ring for instance, the ring comes to acquire a psychic connection to the wearer, even when it is not on his or her finger.

Psychometry is very much in practice today. Psychics who use other divination methods often work with psychometry, too. In practice, an article or object is presented to the psychic. He or she handles it, often going into a trance during which information is received from the spiritual realm. The psychic will sometimes touch the object to his or her forehead, chest or another area of the body. The information may come through the palms of the psychic's hands or be seen as a vision or a voice, heard only by the psychic. Police have been known to employ psychics who practice psychometry to find missing persons and murder victims.

See also CLAIRVOYANCE; EXTRASENSORY PERCEPTION (ESP); GELLER, URI; INTUITION.

Further reading

Butler, W. E. *How to Develop Psychometry.* London: Aquarian Press, 1971.

Popper, Karl. *Objective Knowledge.* Oxford: Oxford University Press, 1971.

Rogo, D. Scott. *Our Psychic Potentials.* Englewood Cliffs, N.J.: Prentice-Hall, 1984.

Wolman, Benjamin B., ed. *Handbook of Parapsychology.* New York: Van Nostrand Reinhold, 1977.

PSYCHOTHERAPEUTIC CHIROMANCY *Psychic character analysis made by studying the nails, lines and fingers of the hands.*

Psychotherapeutic chiromancy is said to analyze the past life or hidden causes of a querant's current actions or life plan.

See also PALMISTRY.

Further reading

Altman, Nathaniel. *Palmistry Workbook.* New York: Sterling, 1990.

PYROMANCY *Divination by analyzing the flames of a combustible object.*

An ancient practice, pyromancy is sometimes referred to as lampadomancy, or pyroscopy. When considering primitive cultures, it is quite logical that the interpretation of flames from a candle, a torch or a campfire would become a prognostication method, since fire has played an integral role in human evolution. Flames and fire were used in rites and rituals long before recorded time.

The use of flames to foretell future events and interpret omens is thought to be one of the first methods used. A form of scrying, pyromancy may have begun with prehistoric psychics studying the patterns of the flames in a fire or perhaps the shadows of a fire as the movements made phantom forms against cave walls.

Depending on the ancient civilization, sometimes only firewood was used during the divination process. Other groups threw a wide variety of combustible materials and articles on the fire, from laurel branches and leaves (daphnomancy) and incense (empyromancy, libanomancy) to sacrifices, such as those rituals practiced by some groups of Druids. As early as 550 B.C., the Greek prophet, mystic and philosopher Pythagoras (582?–500? B.C.) is said to have used pyromancy as a means to answer questions. In Roman times, pyromancy was used to divine the future and answer a querant's questions, specifically those about reincarnation.

In pyromancy, the intensity of the flames, as well as the shape and form they took, was considered when divining the future or interpreting omens. Today, many people practice a form of pyromancy using candles. The wick, as well as the behavior of the flames of burning candles, is studied for advice and guidance.

There are many variations of pyromancy, including pyroscopy, in which divination is accomplished by studying the shape of the flames, as opposed to staring at the flames and observing visions within the fire or the smoke generated.

See also CRITOMANCY; DAPHNOMANCY; LIBANOMANCY; SIDEROMANCY.

Further reading

Dey, Charmaine. *The Magic Candle.* Bronx, N.Y.: Original Publications, 1989.

Kittredge, George. *Witchcraft in Old and New England.* Cambridge: Harvard University Press, 1929. Reprint. New York: Atheneum, 1972.

Maven, Max. *Max Maven's Book of Fortunetelling.* New York: Prentice-Hall, 1992.

Nichols, Ross. *The Book of Druidry—History, Sites, Wisdom.* London: Aquarian Press, 1990.

Opie, Iona, and Moira Tatem. *A Dictionary of Superstitions.* Oxford: Oxford University Press, 1992.

Pajeon, Kala, and Ketz Pajeon. *The Candle Magic Workbook.* New York: Citadel Press, 1992.

PYTHAGORAS *(582?–500? B.C.) Greek mathematician, philosopher and numerologist.*

Pythagoras, known to any student of geometry, believed that numbers reflected the ultimate principles of order and harmony in the universe. Most remember him as the creator of the Pythagorean theorem: The sum of the two sides of a

PYTHAGORAS
Pythagoras and his followers believed that each number from one to nine had its own psychic or spiritual significance.

right triangle squared equals the hypotenuse squared.

Pythagoras was born in Samos, Greece, and traveled widely, including trips to Egypt and perhaps other areas in Africa and into India. Later in life, he took up residence in Croton, in southern Italy, establishing a religious school and brotherhood. He believed in and taught a number of mystical principles unheard of at that

time, including the mortality of the soul and reincarnation (which was then referred to as transmigration). He believed that after physical death one could return as an animal or a human, depending on the lesson to be learned.

Pythagoras believed that everything could be explained and expressed through numbers. He theorized that numbers were the key to understanding all that is unknown. Although he was not the first to conceptualize numerology (that goes back to ancient Babylon), he was the most influential. He and his followers believed that each number, from one to nine, had its own psychic or spiritual significance. According to legend, he was the first to call himself a philosopher and believed in a contemplative life.

Pythagoras's theories have persuaded mystical thinkers and students of metaphysics throughout the centuries, including Socrates, Plato, Euclid and Aristotle.

See also NUMEROLOGY; REINCARNATION.

Further reading

Dacier, Andre. *The Life of Pythagoras*. York Beach, Maine: Samuel Weiser, 1981.
Gorman, Peter. *Pythagoras: A Life*. Boston: Routledge & Kegan Paul, 1978.
Hall, Manly P. *The Secret Teachings of All Ages*. 1928. Reprint. Los Angeles: Philosophical Research Society, 1977.
Hitchcock, Helyn. *Helping Yourself with Numerology*. West Nyack, N.Y.: Parker, 1972.
Rutherford, Ward. *Pythagoras: Lover of Wisdom*. York Beach, Maine: Samuel Weiser, 1984.

QABALA
See KABBALAH.

QUERANT *One who asks.*

Typically, an individual who is receiving a psychic reading is referred to as the querant. From the word *query,* it means to ask or to seek.

Those who search for inspirational advice and enlightenment are constantly asking questions. When applied to prognostication, a querant is one who specifically asks for knowledge or advice through the use of a prognostication method or with the help of a psychic. Various tools may be used, including an astrological reading, counsel from the I Ching or a palmistry or tarot card consultation. In ancient times, a querant would have employed other predictive methods in order to obtain information or interpret an omen, including bibliomancy, felidomancy and triomancy.

See also MANTIC OBJECTS.

Further reading

Buckland, Raymond. *Secrets of Gypsy Fortune Telling.* St. Paul, Minn.: Llewellyn, 1988.

Butler, W. E. *How to Develop Clairvoyance.* 2d ed. New York: Samuel Weiser, 1979.

Morgan, Chris. *Fortune Telling: How to Predict Your Own Future.* London: Quintet Publishing and Random House, 1992.

Stewart, R. J. *The Elements of Prophecy.* Dorset, England: Element Books, 1990.

R

RADIESTHESIA
Divination using the vibrations from an object, article or site to locate that object, article or site.

A variation of DOWSING, radiesthesia is used in much the same way. As with dowsing, one holds an instrument, concentrating on whatever is to be found. When one is close to the object, the vibrations or radiations move the instrument. A technique called radionics, used as a system of alternative medicine but uncommonly used today, employed a psychic holding his or her hands above the patient and interpreting the vibrations coming from the body.

George De La Warr (1904–1969), an Englishman and practitioner of radiesthesia, believed that one could locate diseased organs and the sites of illnesses using this method. His mentor, Dr. Albert Abrams, developed a "black box" for this purpose. This piece of electronic equipment was said to be able to pick up vibrations transmitted from the diseased portion of the body.

De La Warr continued Abrams's work. It is said that he found more than 4,000 dysfunctions that could be located through this method. Although De La Warr is remembered for being sincere in his quest to help the infirm, his techniques using radiesthesia are now termed *quasimedical* at best.

Further reading

Fodor, Nandor. *Encyclopedia of Psychic Science.* New York: University Books, 1966.

Geller, Uri, and Guy Lyon Playfair. *The Geller Effect.* New York: Henry Holt, 1986.

Guiley, Rosemary Ellen. *Harper's Encyclopedia of Mystical and Paranormal Experience.* San Francisco: HarperSan Francisco, 1991.

Krippner, Stanley, and Alberto Villoldo. *The Realms of Healing.* 3d ed. Berkeley, Calif.: Celestial Arts, 1986.

Meek, George W., ed. *Healers and the Healing Process.* Wheaton, Ill.: Theosophical Publishing House, 1977.

Ostrander, Sheila, and Lynn Schroeder. *Psychic Discoveries behind the Iron Curtain.* Englewood Cliffs, N.J.: Prentice-Hall, 1970.

RAJNEESH, BHAGWAN SHREE
(1931–1990) Indian teacher and mystic.

Rajneesh controlled and headed large metaphysical teaching centers in India and Oregon with more than 250,000 followers worldwide at one time. The movement connected with the Indian mystic was called Rajneeshism.

Because he taught that one need not be confined by traditional moral codes, he was nicknamed the "sex guru" by the media. In the 1960s his praise of permissiveness led many to embrace his theories of free sex and the dismantling of the fibers of the family unit and his denunciation of the pope, Mother Teresa and other religious figures. But some metaphysical scholars claim that behind the gossip, Rajneesh's works are as important as Krishnamurti's.

Rajneesh was a scholar and speaker on many religious practices including Zen, Taoism and Tibetan Buddhism, Christianity and many ancient philosophies. Some believe that he was the most important thinker of the 20th century. Others believe he was a power-hungry pseudo-prophet, more deceitful than the politicians and public figures he attacked.

Some books list Rajneesh as the teacher's last name; others list this mystic under his first name: Bhagwan Shree Rajneesh. He is best remembered for his books, including *The Book of Secrets, The Empty Boat, The Hidden Harmony* and *Meditation and the Art of Ecstasy,* which continue to be popular today.

Further reading

Bhagwan Shree Rajneesh. *Words like Fire.* San Francisco: Harper & Row, 1976.
Gorgon, James S. *The Golden Guru.* Lexington, Mass.: Stephen Green Press, 1987.
Mather, George A., and Larry A. Nichols. *Dictionary of Cults, Sects, Religions and the Occult.* Grand Rapids, Mich.: Zondervan Publishing House, 1993.

RAMAKRISHNA, PARAMAHAMSA
(1836–1886) Indian mystic and Hindu guru.

Ramakrishna was born in Bengal. As a child, he often fell into trances and foretold future events. At 20, he became a chief priest in a temple dedicated to the goddess Kali, whose worship continued throughout his lifetime. The Swami Vivekananda, who spread Ramakrishna's words and thoughts, was one of his most influential followers.

"Many paths lead to the same God" is one of the lessons Ramakrishna taught. Like other great thinkers, he believed that religion was best served in experience and not in repeating a prescribed dogma.

Further reading

Drury, Nevill. *Dictionary of Mysticism and the Esoteric Traditions.* Dorset, England: Prism Press, 1992.
Eastern Mysteries. Mysteries of the Unknown. Alexandria, Va.: Time Life Books, 1990.
Mather, George A., and Larry A. Nichols. *Dictionary of Cults, Sects, Religions and the Occult.* Grand Rapids, Mich.: Zondervan Publishing House, 1993.

RASCETTES *One of the many lines of the hand considered in* PALMISTRY.

Also known as bracelets, these lines can be found circling the palm side of the wrist. Strongly marked rascettes indicate a peaceful life filled with wealth and happiness. Chained lines are an indicator of challenging times early on and then joy later in life.

Further reading

Altman, Nathaniel. *Palmistry Workbook.* New York: Sterling, 1990.
Asano, Michael. *Hands: The Complete Book of Palmistry.* New York: Japan Publications, 1985.
Buckland, Raymond. *Buckland's Complete Book of Witchcraft.* St. Paul, Minn.: Llewellyn, 1986.
Cheiro. *Cheiro's Book of Numbers.* New York: Prentice-Hall, 1988.
———. *The Language of the Hand.* New York: Prentice-Hall, 1987.

REGRESSION *Delving into the unconscious mind to learn about experiences in a person's past lives.*

A querant may request regression in order to understand and release an experience that is troublesome in this lifetime. For example, if one has a fear of cats, a regression session might reveal that in a past life while living in India, he or she was attacked and killed by a Bengal tiger. Knowing the significance of cats, he or she no longer needs to be afraid, since it is highly unlikely that the fear needs to be continued into a present life. The karmic lesson is understood.

Many people hold the belief that our brain does not retain these past-life experiences but that they are stored in the AKASHIC RECORDS.

REGRESSION
If one has a fear of cats, a regression session might reveal that in a past life, he or she was attacked and killed by a Bengal tiger while living in India.

Regression was a popular fad during the 1980s and early 1990s. Querants sought to explain all their current problems through knowledge of past-life experiences.

During a regression session, often performed under hypnosis, a querant sometimes sees him- or herself as a bystander observing the events of previous lives. In other instances, he or she will feel the effects of the trauma as if it were happening once more. Many metaphysical followers believe that caution should be taken in regression sessions, as they may prove to be too traumatic for the querant.

Some psychics believe that if one can regress and experience what has occurred in a past life, one should be able to progress and see what the future holds. However, progression sessions have yet to catch the interest of many people involved in metaphysical philosophies.

See also AKASHIC RECORDS; KARMA; PAST LIFE; REINCARNATION.

Further reading

Binder, Bettye B. *Past Lives Regression Guidebook.* Culver City, Calif.: Reincarnation Books, 1985.

Cayce, Hugh Lynn, ed. *The Edgar Cayce Collection.* New York: Bonanza, 1986.

Cerminara, Gina. *Many Lives, Many Loves.* Marina Del Rey, Calif.: DeVross, 1963.

Goldberg, Bruce. *Past Lives, Future Lives.* New York: Ballantine, 1982.

Hall, Manly P. *Reincarnation: The Cycle of Necessity.* Los Angeles: Philosophical Research Society, 1956.

Motoyama, Hiroshi. *Karma and Reincarnation.* Translated by Rande Brown Ouchi. New York: Avon, 1992.

Stern, Jess. *Immortality: Startling Evidence for Human Survival of Physical Death.* Virginia Beach, Va.: Donning, 1976.

REINCARNATION *The theory that one has lived previously, in various forms, and that one's identity survives through physical death.*

People from all nationalities, religious beliefs and cultures accept reincarnation as part of the life-and-death cycle. Practically all religious movements with a basis in Hinduism teach a form of this concept. It is acknowledged that at physical death, the soul does not enter into a final state but is reborn into another body, and the cycle continues. Although for many Americans the thought of reincarnation is new or "New Age," this is not true. The ancient Sicilian Greek philosopher Empedocles (490?–430 B.C.) explained that he had had previous lives: "I have already been a boy and a girl, a bush, a bird, and a dumb sea fish." Pythagoras, Plato and Aristotle, among others, believed in reincarnation. Psychic and healer Edgar Cayce said, "You have inherited most from yourself, not from your family."

The Druids also believed in reincarnation, which is sometimes referred to as transmigration or metempsychosis. A few theological scholars believe there are references to reincarnation in the Bible, though this is disputed. For example, in Matthew 10, Christ distinctly marks John the Baptist as Elijah reborn. And in John 9:1–3 there are questions about a blind man asking if this blindness has been caused by his own sin (in a previous life). Some psychics point out another area that concerns reincarnation and the Bible. In Revelation 13:10 there is the statement "He that leadeth into captivity shall go into captivity: he that killeth with the sword must be killed with the sword." While there are those who would contradict that this is the ancient theory of an "eye for an eye," others believe that it clearly suggests the valid point of karma and reincarnation. This is also the Hindu and Buddhist system of cosmic balance.

Those who accept the concept of reincarnation believe that the spiritual essence of the soul, sometimes referred to as the soul-mind, lives many years between incarnations. It takes many lives to learn and understand all the experiences of life to make the soul mind perfect. Thus, the soul-mind, according to psychic scholars, assumes a number of personalities both male and female, in various cultures, social positions and geographical areas. Many books teach those interested in reincarnation how to tap into past-life memories. This may also be done through past-life regression and with the help of hypnosis.

See also AKASHIC RECORDS; BIBLICAL PROPHETS AND DIVINATION METHODS; KARMA; PAST LIFE; REGRESSION.

Further reading

Binder, Bettye B. *Past Lives Regression Guidebook.* Culver City, Calif.: Reincarnation Books, 1985.

Brennan, J. H. *The Reincarnation Workbook.* New York: Sterling, 1990.

The Encyclopedia of Eastern Philosophy and Religion. Boston: Shambhala, 1989.

Hall, Manly P. *Reincarnation: The Cycle of Necessity.* Los Angeles: Philosophical Research Society, 1956.

Kapleau, Philip. *The Wheel of Life and Death: A Practical and Spiritual Guide.* New York: Doubleday, 1989.

Motoyama, Hiroshi. *Karma and Reincarnation.* Translated by Rande Brown Ouchi. New York: Avon, 1992.

Woodward, Mary Ann. *Edgar Cayce's Story of Karma: God's Book of Remembrance.* New York: Coward, McCann & Geoghegan/Edgar Cayce Foundation, 1971.

RETROCOGNITION *Discovering knowledge of past events and past-lives through psychic means.*

Retrocognition is the opposite of precognition, knowing by psychic means about events that will happen in the future. The details received through retrocognition can be either of a personal or more general nature.

Further reading

Binder, Bettye B. *Past Lives Regression Guidebook.* Culver City, Calif.: Reincarnation Books, 1985.

Brennan, J. H. *The Reincarnation Workbook.* New York: Sterling, 1990.

Woodward, Mary Ann. *Edgar Cayce's Story of Karma: God's Book of Remembrance.* New York: Coward, McCann & Geoghegan/Edgar Cayce Foundation, 1971.

RHABDOMANCY *Divination for water or precious gems and metals using rods or wands.*

The word comes from the Greek *rhabdos*, meaning rod or wands. This method was used in ancient Greece to locate springs, areas where water and precious metals might be found.

Rhabdomancy is a less common term for dowsing. It is also known as radiesthesia and cleidomancy. As with other forms of dowsing, the origin of this art is unknown. However, it is interesting to note that there are paintings in caves hidden in the Sahara, thought to have been created about 6000 B.C., that show a person holding a divining rod. Greek and Roman literature refers to the practice, too, specifically by the name of rhabdomancy, but there is speculation as to whether this is dowsing in the contemporary sense. Ancient myths and legends suggest that magical rods were used by Hermes and Aaron; however, these are often considered something like magician's wands rather than the dowser's forked stick or rod.

See also DOWSING.

Further reading

Cayce, Hugh Lynn, ed. *The Edgar Cayce Collection.* New York: Bonanza, 1986.

Fodor, Nandor. *Encyclopedia of Psychic Science.* New York: University Books, 1966.

Geller, Uri, and Guy Lyon Playfair. *The Geller Effect.* New York: Henry Holt, 1986.

Roberts, Kenneth. *Henry Gross and His Dowsing Rod.* Garden City, N.Y.: Doubleday, 1951.

RHAPSODOMANCY *The use of literature or a sacred book to forecast the future or provide answers to a querant's question.*

This is a variation of bibliomancy, used by the ancient Romans and Greeks and also at other times throughout history. Some psychics specifically refer to rhapsodomancy as a method of divination to be performed only with works of poetry. Others believe that books of metaphysical wisdom, the translated works of Nostradamus, the I Ching or any volume by Edgar Cayce will suffice.

With the querant or psychic's eyes closed, a book is opened at random or wherever fate or a spiritual force intercedes. Either a finger is run down the page and stopped before the eyes are opened or, when the eyes are opened, they are directed to a certain passage (a psychic force tells the psychic where to look). The paragraph or verse is the one that answers the question at hand.

See also BIBLIOMANCY.

Further reading

Baring-Gould, Sabine. *Curious Myths of the Middle Ages*. New York: University Books, 1967.

Bevan, E. *Sibyls and Seers: A Survey of Some Ancient Theories of Revelation and Inspiration*. London: Allen & Unwin, 1982.

Cheetham, E. *The Prophecies of Nostradamus*. London: Corgi, 1981.

Fox, Judy; Karen Hughes; and John Tampion. *An Illuminated I Ching*. New York: Arch, 1984.

Hazlitt, W. Carew. *Faiths and Folklore of the British Isles*. 2 vols. New York: Benjamin Blom, 1965.

Opie, Iona, and Moira Tatem. *A Dictionary of Superstitions*. Oxford: Oxford University Press, 1992.

RHINE, JOSEPH BANKS, M.D.

(1895–1980) American scientist, called the "father of modern parapsychology."

The term EXTRASENSORY PERCEPTION (ESP) was coined by Rhine. He told friends that when selecting the name for telepathy, he wanted to make it sound as normal as possible so that the study would be accepted in the scientific community. *Perception* was an established psychology term, and Rhine hoped ESP would be considered an offshoot of a branch of perception, not something occult or mystical.

Rhine studied ESP throughout his life, through carefully documented experiments. He co-produced five of the shapes on the Zener cards to test ESP ability that are still in use today. The 25 Zener cards are similar to playing cards but with five unique shapes on the "picture" side. Rhine and other researchers have found that when the subject being tested for ESP is told that he or she is doing well, the result is often the same as for those who do not profess to have ESP. Additionally, the fear of failure in ESP tests has been shown to lower scores in tests in clinical surroundings. Boredom causes test scores to drop; caffeine tends to increase test scores. Children are more receptive and perceptive than adults in testing.

Rhine co-founded the Parapsychology Laboratory at Duke University with colleague Dr. William McDougall. Throughout his life, Rhine studied clairvoyance, telepathy and precognition among other psychic skills. He is best remembered for his books on ESP and the psychic disciplines, including *Extra-Sensory Perception* (1935), *The Reach of the Mind* (1947) and *Parapsychology, Frontier Science of the Mind* (1957).

Further reading

Cavendish, Richard, ed. *Man, Myth and Magic: An Illustrated Encyclopedia of the Supernatural*. Vol. 7. New York: Marshal Cavendish Corporation, 1970.

Halbourne, Max. *Mental Telepathy and ESP Powers for the Millions*. Los Angeles: Sherbourne Press, 1967.

Rhine, Louisa E. *ESP in Life and Lab*. New York: Collier-Macmillan, 1967.

Richet, Charles. *Thirty Years of Psychical Research*. London: William Collins, 1923.

Thouless, R. H. *Experimental Psychical Research*. New York: Penguin, 1963.

Tyrrell, G. N. M. *Science and Psychical Phenomena*. London, 1938. Reprint. New York: University Books, 1961.

ROSICRUCIANS *International order devoted to the pursuit of esoteric wisdom.*

There are two groups both commonly known as the Rosicrucians in the United States, and their teachings continue to be controversial. They are the Rosicrucian Fellowship (headquartered in Oceanside, California) and the Ancient Mystical Order Rosae Crucis (AMORC) with a main office in San Jose, California. Both groups believe that they are the oldest secret society in the Western world. According to the Rosicrucian literature, the groups began in ancient Egypt and the mystical schools of the Greeks. The AMORC states that Egyptian pharaoh Thutmose III established various mystery schools and may have been the first Rosicrucian. The society has remained in existence through years of deliberate secrecy and persecution, including a period of 108 years between the time when Benjamin Franklin and Thomas Jefferson were members and 1909 when Dr. H. Spencer Lewis rejuvenated the organization. This period was called the "outer silence" and was a self-proclaimed time of covert activity by the group.

The Rosicrucians believe and teach theories of Egyptian Hermetism, Gnosticism, Kabbalism, and other mystical practices. Although AMORC groups prefer to overlook the connection, many of the ritualistic practices have been borrowed from those originally embraced by Aleister Crowley and the Ordo Templi Orientis and the Hermetic Order of the Golden Dawn.

Some occult historians believe that the order actually began in Germany after the publication of two pamphlets, the *Fama Fraternitatis* and the *Confessio Rosae Crucis* (dated about 1615 and translated about 1652, they are *The Fame* and *The Confessions of the Fraternity of the Rosy Cross*). This material offers the account of a fabled journey to the Far East by Christian Rosenkreuz. It is claimed that the order is based on Rosenkreuz's teachings acquired on that journey. Some Rosicrucians, especially those associated with AMORC, believe that Rosenkreuz was merely a symbolic figure, perhaps a composite of many leaders in the group.

Modern Rosicrucian beliefs are a blending of religious tenets, paranormal and psychic interests and alchemy. The group members attempt astral projection, develop psychic skills including mind control, study dowsing and conduct chemical experiments. Training to become a member is normally done through a mail-order correspondence course called Mandamus. The courses are secret, each introducing more Rosicrucian theology, and novitiates are warned never to reveal the contents of the doctrine or discuss the secret rituals and ceremonies. Bible scholars explain that though Rosicrucian leaders claim that the order is not a religion, in fact the prayers, teachings, altars and affirmations all point to a religious group. Officially the AMORC denies that it is a spiritualist group, yet in its teachings it encourages members to contact their dearly departed and the spirits of the Rosicrucian masters.

Both groups have a wide international appeal through the use of exhaustive advertising. The ads tell consumers that through the course work one can "develop . . . psychic power of attraction."

Christian scholars believe that the esoteric ceremonies of the Rosicrucians lead followers into secret rites and rituals that have a demonic basis, including possession and spirit conjuration. They explain that the Rosicrucian initiation ritual has novitiates affirm "So mote it be," pointing out that this is a standard oral oath of witchcraft cults.

Many historical figures have claimed to be members of the organization, including Francis Bacon, Isaac Newton, Gottfried Leibniz, Benjamin Franklin and Claude Debussy. It would seem, from the variety of notable people who have been members that the movement appeals to the intellect.

The symbol of the order is a rose and a cross, or "Rosy Cross." Rosicrucians assert that Christians chose the cross as an "arbitrary symbol," whereas the order chose the cross to symbolize the body of man, and the rose to symbolize "man's soul unfolding and evolving."

See also HERMETIC ORDER OF THE GOLDEN DAWN; LAWS OF METAPHYSICS; SAINT GERMAIN, COMTE DE.

Further reading

Ahlstrom, Sydney. *A Religious History of the American People.* Garden City, N.Y.: Image Books, 1975.

Larson, Bob. *Larson's New Book of Cults.* Wheaton, Ill.: Tyndale House, 1989.

Matthews, Caitlin, and John Matthews. *The Western Way.* London: Arkana, 1986.

Schmidt, Alvin J. *The Greenwood Encyclopedia of American Institutions.* London: Greenwood Press, 1980.

RUNE STONES
Divination tool used to predict the future or answer a querant's question.

Rune stones, or more commonly simply runes, derive their name from the German word *raunen,* a secret or mystery. These stones, each marked with a mystical symbol, are used in the practice of CASTING OF LOTS, much the way dice are used to foretell the future, or they are selected randomly from the group of stones that are presented with symbols facedown.

Runes were in use in Europe long before recorded history. Runic symbols were carved into caves by the tribes that settled in northern Italy in the Neolithic period (c. 8000 B.C.–2000 B.C.). Rock carvings by Swedish tribes date from 1300 B.C. The use of runes was spread throughout the Germanic and Nordic peoples, and they were in regular use as a prognostic tool by A.D. 100.

One legend has it that ODIN, the Scandinavian, Viking and Germanic spiritual guide who communicates with those in need of inspiration, hung in torturous pain in the World Tree for nine days and nights. (The World Tree is said to connect the upper and lower worlds and to provide all knowledge. It is comparable to the Tree of Life in the Kabbalah.) This sacrifice, along with that of one of Odin's eyes, was said to be worth the price—knowledge of the runes. Another tale says that the knowledge of the runes was closely guarded by the masters, who may have been the Druids and other Celtic tribes. The last lived in Iceland in the 17th century.

In the 1900s, European mystics and occultists became increasingly interested in these tools. Germanic groups, including the secret chiefs of the Germanen Order, a runic society established in 1912, believed that the runes indicated Teutonic and racial superiority of this German group. Herman Pohl Magdeburg, the Germanen Order's first chancellor, manufactured and sold runic bronze rings to soldiers in World War I to protect them in battle. During another period of rune mania, Siegfried Adolf Krunner developed rune exercises, which were similar to the movements one might find in yoga exercises, said to reflect the symbols on the stones. There has been a resurgence in interest in rune stones in the last 10 years.

Those who practice prognostication through the use of runes believe that the etching or inscription of the symbols brings forth knowledge from the spirits.

Most sets of runes contain 25 stones or dice. A few of the sets have only 22 stones, but some contain 26 and others 40. There are some newer sets currently on the market that have from five to nine stones and are advertised as "Love Runes," believed to answer questions of the heart. In the traditional sets, all the dice or stones are marked with historical symbols (with symbol and spelling variations), except one, which is blank. The symbols have been derived from the pictographic language of early Nordic peoples that may have been the first written alphabet in Europe.

To divine the future using runes, it is not necessary to buy an expensive set. (Most sets start at about $20 and run into the hundreds of dollars, depending on the types of stones on which the letters are carved.) A set of runes can be made by selecting small stones with flat sides, such as those found at the beach or at a river's edge, and marking them with the proper symbols or letters.

Some who use the runes use layouts similar to the tarot spreads; others have devised their own specific methods. There are four common methods for reading runes. All begin by placing all the stones facedown, with the letters toward the table or a cloth. The stones are then shuffled or moved around. Stones are read exactly as they are drawn, as there is a change in the message if the stone is drawn upside down.

In the first method, 13 stones are selected and placed in a circle, like a clock face, starting in the nine o'clock position. The 13th stone drawn is placed in the center.

Each position on this "clock" of stones has a meaning.

1. Personality, character
2. Prosperity, material concerns
3. Family
4. Home
5. Self-expression
6. Health, stamina, the care of the world
7. Love, marriage, relationship
8. Heritage
9. Education
10. Career, rank
11. Pleasure, companions
12. Intuition, psychic knowledge
13. The questioner

Using a second method, three stones are selected. The first represents the past, the second indicates the present and the third is the future. All the symbols are then combined to provide a complete message regarding the querant's question.

A third method is called the Three Lifetimes spread. Stones are selected and placed in a diamond shape, with one stone in the center. The first stone selected is placed in the right point of the diamond. It reflects the birth and childhood conditions of the querant. The second is placed in the center of the diamond and deals with the present conditions. The third, set at the left point of the diamond, predicts possibilities for the future. The fourth stone is placed at the point closest to the querant and reveals past incarnations. The fifth stone is placed at the top point of the diamond and tells about future incarnations.

A fourth method of predicting the future uses only one stone. Here the querant asks for counsel or an answer to a question. He or she selects one rune from the bag of runes or takes one from the shuffled pile. Again all symbols are face-down. The stone is then read to provide guidance.

The stones in all methods should be selected by the querant. He or she may want to concentrate on the question for which answers are being sought. It is advisable not to read the runes more than once a week, and many psychics advise not more than once every six months. However, some people choose to read one rune a day, much like one reads the astrological forecast in the newspaper.

The following are the contemporary and most routinely accepted meanings to the symbols found on the runes. The key words come immediately after the name, with the message of the rune following. Sometimes the spelling of the rune letters varies. For example, in some reference manuals *Gyfu* is spelled *Gifu* and *Peorth* is spelled *Peord*. Although the spellings and sometimes the pictographs differ slightly, the meanings are the same. The "R" next to the description indicates that the rune was selected in the reverse position.

Feoh (Property, wealth, fulfillment, personal growth. R loss.) This is the rune of fulfillment. Success in love, business and personal achievements can be obtained. The rune provides the promise of satisfaction and fruition in endeavors. The querant must not simply accept these riches but reflect on the cycle of profit and loss. One must understand that true wealth often has little to do with possessions and money. This rune also instructs the querant to share his or her wealth and the wisdom that wealth may bring.

In the reversed position, the rune advises the querant to look within for the reason that this loss has happened. It instructs to look for ways to personally nourish the body and soul.

Ur (Strength, stamina, masculinity. R weakness.) This rune speaks of termination, endings, finalization and, ultimately, new beginnings. It is a time of growth and change, although some change is disquieting, and self-change is often the hardest to understand. The stone tells the querant to prepare for a period of transformation because this rune provides an opportunity for evolution and new strength.

In the reversed position, it says that the querant is refusing to accept the change that is imminent. It is a warning that the minor failures and disappointment, unless contemplated, will become more frequent. It calls for serious thought concerning the relationship one has with oneself.

Thorn (Protection. R jealousy, incorrect decisions.) This rune brings a message of protection.

There is still much knowledge to be sought and work to be accomplished. This may be in a personal way, with a relationship or with a career. The Thorn is a symbol of protection while the journey continues. It tells of strength and understanding. Sometimes strength is found in adversity; sometimes understanding is discovered in deprivation.

In the reversed position, this rune advises that one must be careful as a growth process is about to begin. The rune says that wonderful lessons can be learned in a difficult period. The querant should not make any hasty decisions when this rune is drawn. This is not the time to allow temptation to overrule thoughtful consideration.

Os (Mastery. R problems with those in charge.) The querant will receive messages or a gift of great worth. The gift can also be a warning, telling that an event or situation must be avoided. This rune brings the message to explore one's spirituals roots and study the foundations of the universe.

In the reverse position, this rune says that a breakdown in communication is actually a message to become alert and consider alternative pathways. This rune cautions one to become aware and careful, while being more creative in all dealings.

Rad (Movement, change, transformations. R problems with changes.) This is the rune of change, journeys, motion and a time to recognize the consequences of a change. Sometimes that journey must be undertaken alone, and a journey does not always speak of physical travel but may be a spiritual trip. The rune tells the querant to consider inner worth, to ask for guidance and be patient, to keep a watchful eye on excess. Obstacles will dissolve.

In the reversed position, the rune says to pay close attention to relationships. This may be a time of argument and disorder. The rune says to use humor to defuse anger in oneself and others.

Ken (Warmth, love, clarity. R lack of direction, love.) This rune presents enormous possibilities for renewed clarity in one's life. It tells of moving from the darkness (of frustration, anger, loneliness) into joy and reunion. It speaks to the querant of the possibility for new relationships and an awareness of light and happiness in life.

In the reversed position, it tells the querant to expect a period of darkness, a lack of insight and a change or the death of a partnership or a goal. This rune in the reversed position brings a wonderful message: Be aware and ready for a change; with change there are always new opportunities.

Gyfu (Gift, opportunities, openings.) This is the rune of partnership; however, there is a warning that one should not become too involved in the union and neglect oneself. This union may be personal, business related or a new partnership with one's metaphysical understanding. The union will require work; nothing is free.

There is no reverse to this rune.

Wyn (Joy, love, luck, happiness. R unstable emotions, depression, self-doubt.) This rune tells the querant to rejoice. The time of disorder and trouble are nearly at the end, and the message is that love, luck, joy and happiness are forthcoming. This rune explains that the time of trouble has been important in the querant's evolution because strength, insight and patience are now a part of his or her being.

The reverse of this rune tells that one should expect a time of slowing, a time to contemplate before action and a time to deliberate.

Hagal (Sudden changes, good and bad. R detainment, disaster.) This is the rune of freedom and liberation, all through sudden change. A querant who draws this rune is asking for advice on moving forward or receiving a message that that movement is imminent.

This is the rune of disruption and only has one position. Even in disruption, one must consider the lessons at hand. Each creates his or her own challenges and opportunities, and with each change comes growth. This rune says that the universe is demanding that the querant experience growth.

Nyd (Needs, continuance of self. R tension, stress, anxiety.) This rune tells the querant to understand the ramifications of need; need is a great lesson in life. Drawing this rune indicates that one is ready to understand that hard times, frustrations and setbacks are actually great teachers in life. These are the master forces to allow one to become strong.

In the reversed position, this rune brings a message of initiation. After collapse, there is a time to rebuild. The lesson learned from destruction is to strengthen the foundation of self. The message also tells to contain anger and impulses. Take time to appreciate an even disposition and modesty.

Is (Obstacles, stagnation, delays, fear, hopelessness.) This is the rune of obstacles, a time to reflect on these holdups and look toward the stagnation as a lesson in patience. Patience is the key, for drawing this rune indicates that there is a period of gestation that the querant must experience. After the birth (of a new idea, philosophy, understanding), there will be growth.

As with other runes, this stone has no reversed position. Thus the rune tells the querant not simply to rely on others or rely on hope but to take action and take control. Honor the isolation and fear, move with the feelings and then move forward into the light of renewal and rebirth.

Ger (Completion of a sequence, renewal.) This rune tells the querant that there will be good news ahead. It is a time for celebration and renewal. However, this joy will only come after a period of rest and patience. By drawing this rune, the querant knows the benefits of diligence and he or she must continue with persistence, ever knowing that the outcome will be joyful.

Do not try to push or pull for finality. It will come. Look within to study the changes. Honor the path that has been stony at times and see the progress made.

Eoh (Flexibility, cunning, shrewdness, retraction.) In times of self-examination or personal tests, this rune often appears in a spread. It tells the querant to accept the obstacle, to become more flexible and cunning. It is a time for creativity and invention. The message is to organize one's personal and professional business. Move on from clutter into clarity. It is a time of patience and work.

This rune examines the balance when new changes have been accepted. It assures the querant that even in periods of inconvenience and hardship, he or she will survive and prosper.

Sygel (Forces of life, healing, success, overindulgence of success, fame.) This is the rune for wholeness. The querant has reached a goal of fulfillment and personal understanding in his or her quest. The message is to become comfortable with self and embrace oneself for the lessons learned.

This rune also speaks of caution. While the feeling is "I've made it," success is too soon forgotten if one isn't successful in a spiritual sense. This is not the time to retreat, however, but perhaps learn to let go, to heal old wounds, and honor the forces of the universe.

Peorth (Mystical knowledge. R fear of the unknown.) The message of this rune to the querant is that he or she will begin a quest for knowledge of the self and the universe. It will at times be difficult, but the rune comes as a powerful talisman saying that the querant has the abilities to succeed. There may be some sacrifice, a giving away of possessions, but a cleansing will be accomplished too. There will be surprises ahead, and yet through all, one will feel satisfied, joyful and awakened.

In the reversed position, this rune tells to expect an end to the old ways. Its message is to focus on the journey, not the journey's end. See the choices in every new avenue taken; consider them wisely for each has possibilities.

Eolhs (Artistic talents or aptitude, pleasure. R fear or absence of these.) This rune tells the querant to control his or her emotions, accept creativity and pleasure and follow through with analytical actions. New opportunities and challenges are forthcoming. The rune counsels to guard against inappropriate behavior. The rune is the symbol of the spiritual warrior, and there may be a contradiction in one's feelings as one approaches each new challenge.

In the reversed position, this rune tells the querant to be gentle and careful. There may be a fear or even the absence of fear with change. Care should be given to personal health and the health of relationships.

Tir (Potency, bravery, romance. R loss of these.) This rune tells the querant the universe will provide, money is on its way, funding will be accomplished. The rune cautions that with money comes responsibility and new challenges. There is romance in the making too, perhaps the long-awaited love the querant has been waiting to meet.

In the reversed position, this rune warns that hasty actions or thoughtless acts will impede progress. Examining motives, actions and the results of actions is the only way to avoid a breakdown in effectiveness. Find the answer to all questions within.

Beorc (Fertility, abundance, continuance, beginnings. R delay, sickness, barrenness.) This is the rune of abundance, good omens, new beginnings. The rune celebrates success, a blossoming and ripening of ideas and concepts. It calls for gentle, loving actions, not power or strength. There may be a small amount of opposition, but through love, it will disappear and the querant can move ahead. The rune tells the querant to be patient, modest, loving and understanding.

In the reversed position, the rune advises that this period of frustration and dismay are a lesson. With this time of delay, consider carefully the options at hand, look toward illness as a time to reflect on wholeness and honor barrenness for helping to present windows of opportunity.

Eow (Travel, animals, theories. R problems with these.) This is the rune of transition, movement, shifts in position and residence. It tells the querant that now is the time to move, to change attitudes, residences, jobs, philosophies. Travel and animals are involved in the message of this rune, perhaps only with a deepening appreciation of nature. When this rune appears in a spread, it means one should examine his or her motives, reflect on ethics and prepare to move forward with a pure heart.

When this rune is drawn in the reversed position, it tells the querant to take heed. Movement is blocked, and perhaps that is a positive message to examine what one is getting into before action happens. Sometimes doing nothing is actually the best course of action, but this is only realized through examination and analysis.

Man (Authority, professionals. R problems with these.) This rune tells the querant to accept the clarity he or she is experiencing. It is time to

clearly see relationships, changes and personal theories for what they are, not what we wish they would be. This is a powerful rune and tells the querant that now is also the period to assert his or her power, especially in a business or creative project. Be modest but wise, and share that knowledge with others.

In the reversed position, the rune tells the querant not to allow others to decide the future. It is a time to look within and examine one's own motives. This rune acknowledges that there is a blockage of progress, but it says to reflect and perhaps take another direction to accomplish the same goal.

Lagu (Intuition, clairvoyance, change, fertility. R fear, avoidance.) This is the rune of intuition, mystical knowing, change in philosophy and creativity. It is a powerful rune, and one who draws this stone should be aware that a time to learn about the unseen has arrived. There is no fear in this rune, however, for the universe cares for each spirit, and the journey will be blessed and exciting.

In the reversed position, it tells the querant to examine what he or she is avoiding. Often we avoid what we must learn; often we fear the unknown. This rune tells the querant to honor the unknown and learn from fear.

Ing (Fertility, solution, rebirth. R illness, constraint.) This rune tells the querant that the solution to a problem, the end of a challenge and the joy of knowledge are at hand. It is a time of creativity and rebirth of self, a time to look within and be joyful of what one can share.

In the reversed position, this rune explains that the querant may be entering a period of limitation. It is a time to examine the meaning of existence, of work, of relationships. There may be a period of illness. Look at these impediments as lessons. Map a direction to walk toward success, health and happiness.

Daeg (Clarity, success, realization of qualities.) This rune marks a major success in the querant's life. It is a gift from the universe to tell the querant that he or she is traveling on the right pathway. There will be continued clarity of purpose and the feeling that everything is right. This may be a transition period too, when clarity brings disappointment, but the rune says that one must move ahead if one is to succeed.

This rune also tells that after a period of darkness, physically, mentally or spiritually, light is forthcoming. A major achievement is about to be realized. The rune tells the querant to continue to be thoughtful, humble and loving. Success often turns quickly to disappointment, unless one is successful on one's spiritual journey.

Ethel (Gifts, assistance. R problems with these areas.) This the rune of gifts, help, aid and acknowledgment. Drawing this rune tells the querant that he or she will be given something of great value. Often knowledge is of greater value than money. In difficult times, this rune tells the querant that aid and love will be arriving.

In the reversed position, this rune says that one should consider his or her movement carefully. Do not be selfish; consider relationships and the relationship to humankind before moving forward. There may be a problem with money, or someone may offer help but then back away. See this as a lesson to become more self-reliant.

The Blank Rune (Fate, hidden messages or agendas.) The message of the blank rune is an amplification of the messages found on adjacent runes. For example, if there is a blank rune next to the rune Ethel, it may mean that one will receive an abundant gift or be overwhelmed with assistance. Depending on the circumstances and the other runes, this may or may not be a time to celebrate.

The blank rune also tells the querant that he or she is in charge of destiny. Study the other runes and move forward with a focus on spiritual knowledge.

See also CASTING OF LOTS; DICE; KABBALAH; ODIN.

Further reading

Blum, Ralph. *The Book of Runes.* New York: St. Martin's, 1982.

Maven, Max. *Max Maven's Book of Fortunetelling.* New York: Prentice-Hall, 1992.

Tyson, Donald. *Rune Magic.* St. Paul, Minn.: Llewellyn, 1989.

Visions and Prophecies. Mysteries of the Unknown. Alexandria, Va.: Time Life Books, 1990.

Walker, Barbara G. *The Woman's Encyclopedia of Myths and Secrets.* New York: Harper Collins, 1983.

SACRED PATH WHEEL   *Method for interpreting one's life lesson.*

The Sacred Path Wheel system was channeled and formulated through exhaustive study of ancient metaphysics by Katherine Torres, Msc.D., Ph.D., a leading tarot card reader and psychic. It is one of the newest prognostication and occult methods to assist in better knowing oneself. While it is very up to date, it combines ancient beliefs including those of the Kabbalah, tarot and Tibetan numerology.

Dr. Torres explains that the information on the Sacred Path Wheel was provided to her from the spirit world, as a gift from the guardian angels.

The life lesson is the reason why, according to metaphysical scholars and those who believe in reincarnation and karma, we have incarnated into this specific physical plane. For example, one life lesson may be to balance. This can be accomplished through the harmony of family, work and love of self. Thus, if one is not following this life lesson of balance, he or she would feel out of control in areas of family, work and self. To look at this in another way, if one is to learn patience as a life lesson, he or she might incarnate as a strong-willed Scorpio. If one is to learn forgiveness, one might incarnate as a disabled individual.

The Sacred Path Wheel is a guide for spiritual growth and knowledge. It combines the arts and philosophies of Native American teachings, soul-mind connection, archetypal numerology, Kabbalah, astrology, colorology, angelology, symbology, herbology and other mystical schools, including the tarot. These are organized and blended in a circular chart, divided into 12 parts or spokes of the wheel. Each spoke is believed to represent an alignment with the whole self. It is through study and meditation that psychics can relate the life lesson information that combines these arts to assist on the journey on this earth plane.

According to Torres, the wheel represents the elements of power that walk with each individual as he or she aligns the soul. When these elements are in balance, one becomes aware of inner power and begins to walk in love, strength, integrity and creativity.

The Secret Path Wheel reveals that the soul is connected to the elements of the universe (fire, water, air and earth) that are manifest in the forms of guardians, animals, plants and minerals. These elements provide individuals with the energies of intuition, instinct, growth and stability in order to pursue their journey in the physical world.

See also ASTROLOGY; CHANNEL; KARMA; TAROT.

Further reading

Hirschfelder, Arlene, and Paulette Molin. *The Encyclopedia of Native American Religions*. New York: Facts On File, 1992.

Paper, Jordan. *Offering Smoke: The Sacred Pipe and Native American Religion*. Moscow: University of Idaho Press, 1988.

Torres, Katherine. *The Sacred Path Wheel*. Carlsbad, Calif.: Two Feathers Soaring Lightly, 1991.

Underhill, Ruth M. *Red Man's Religion: Beliefs and Practices of the Indians North of Mexico*. Chicago: University of Chicago Press, 1965.

This ancient symbol represents the astrological sign of Sagittarius.

SAGITTARIUS *One of the 12 astrological signs of the zodiac. The symbol is the archer.*

Those who are born between November 22 and December 21 are natives of the sign of Sagittarius and have specific traits indicative of the time and date on which they were born. Divination of events can also be charted through this astrological sign.

Astrologers divine what is in store throughout life through the time, date and place in which the individual was born as they coordinate the influences with other signs, the planets, the Sun, the Moon and other powers.

In traditional Western astrology, Sagittarius is the ninth sign of the zodiac. Those born during the period typically exhibit qualities that exemplify a fun-loving, enthusiastic nature.

Those born during this period are said to be perfect friends, always ready to join into any activity. They are team players and are vivacious and adventurous. They love new ideas, concepts, clothes and material possessions and are always

SAGITTARIUS

hungry for knowledge. They also are filled with wanderlust—it is excitement that keeps them going, whether it's a trip to Paris, France, or Paris, Texas. They don't just love travel, they lust after it. Planning a challenging adventure gets their blood pumping with pleasure and passion. Where there's fun, you'll usually find a Sagittarius native leading the laughter.

Sagittarius natives are considered to be the most likable people of all. They are honest to a fault, and if you're looking for a candid opinion, come to this man or woman. However, be warned: What you'll get is forthright, straight talk. If you want a more compassionate or gentle opinion, ask someone born under another sun sign. This attribute can get Sagittarius natives in hot water; their feet can get stuck in their mouths through their zeal to be honest. Those who appreciate honesty know that Sagittarius expects frankness right back.

Their sense of humor is renowned. They can tell a story that will have an audience in tears from laughter or melancholy, and they need to be in the spotlight. This showmanship sometimes makes them too independent. They don't want to be tied down or roped into anything. Thus, romantic relationships have to have a great deal of breathing room to keep Sagittarius happy and satisfied.

While traditional astrologers use books to calculate a personal birth chart based on the position of the Sun, Moon and planets at a distinct time, computer software has replaced most of this time-consuming work. The correct term for calculating a birth chart is to "cast" it . In order to fully comprehend the extent of traits, potential and attributes, the exact time and place of birth must be known and interpreted.

See also ASTROLOGICAL SYMBOLS; ASTROLOGY.

Further reading

Cosmic Connections. Mysteries of the Unknown. Alexandria, Va.: Time Life Books, 1990.

Goodman, Linda. *Linda Goodman's Sun Signs.* New York: Fawcett/Columbine, 1978.

Morgan, Chris. *Fortune Telling: How to Predict Your Own Future.* London: Quintet Publishing and Random House, 1992.

Omarr, Sydney. *My World of Astrology.* New York: Fleet, 1965.

———. *Sagittarius.* New York: New American Library, 1992.

Verlagsanstalt, Datura. *Sagittarius Astro Analysis.* New York: Grossett & Dunlap, 1976.

Woolfork, Joanna Martine. *The Only Astrology Book You'll Ever Need.* Landham, Mass.: Scarborough, 1992.

SAINT GERMAIN, COMTE DE
(1710–1780) Rosicrucian master.

Saint Germain was a charismatic religious and occult leader and extremely well-educated for his time. He claimed to be immortal. Among his other claims was that he was the son of Prince Rakoszy of Transylvania. He became a favorite at many European courts. He took on such glamorous titles as Marquis de Montferrat, Chevalier Schoening and Comte Bellamarre. He delighted aristocrats with stories that he had received Moses' magical wand and that he had obtained his wealth by turning base metals into gold (a process known as the philosophers' stone and accomplished through various rituals of alchemy).

Metaphysical historians point out that while Saint Germain's claims may have been extravagant, he was one of the most influential occult writers of his time. He is best remembered for his book *The Most Holy Trinosophia.*

See also ROSICRUCIANS.

Further reading

Drury, Nevill. *Dictionary of Mysticism and the Esoteric Traditions.* Dorset, England: Prism Press, 1992.

MacKenzie, Norman. *Secret Societies.* New York: Holt, Rinehart & Winston, 1967.

Matthews, Caitlin, and John Matthews. *The Western Way.* London: Arkana, 1986.

Secrets of the Alchemists. Mysteries of the Unknown. Alexandria, Va.: Time Life Books, 1990.

SCAPULOMANCY *Divination by interpreting the cracks in the shoulder bone of an animal, typically a sheep.*

Scapulomancy is believed to have been the most widely used prognostication method of ancient times. The practice involved roasting a shoulder bone from an animal, often a sacrificial animal. When the bone was completely dry, the cracks, caused by the heat of the roasting process, were deciphered by a psychic.

The Chinese began using scapulomancy more than 5,000 years ago, perhaps beginning when the charred remains of sacrificial animals were inspected to ensure that they would meet with the approval of the gods. The Romans also used the practice, as did the Druids, who are said to have preferred to use the shoulder blade of a pig. The bones of other animals have been used in similar divination processes. For example, the native tribes in Labrador are said to have used caribou, and in Japan, around 2,000 years ago, a deer's shoulder bone was prescribed for the process.

A variation of scapulomancy is CEPHALOMANCY, which requires a methodical boiling of the head of a sheep, goat or donkey. In 13th-century Europe, a variation known as OINOMANCY was developed, in which an animal skull was boiled in wine rather than water.

See also MANTIC OBJECTS.

Further reading

Bary, William Theodore de, ed. *Sources of Chinese Traditions.* New York: Columbia University Press, 1960.

Carr-Gomm, Philip. *The Elements of the Druid Tradition.* Dorset, England: Element Books, 1991.

Maven, Max. *Max Maven's Book of Fortunetelling.* New York: Prentice-Hall, 1992.

SCATOMANCY *Divination by interpreting the patterns in one's own feces.*

Also known as copromancy, from the Greek word *kopros*, meaning feces, scatomancy is no longer practiced and the premise is lost in time. Some believe that feces were "read" as one would interpret tea leaves in tasseography or smoke in capnomancy.

A modification of scatomancy is uromancy, once practiced by the ancient Greeks, in which one would gaze into urine to see visions or divine the future. This is actually a variation of scrying.

See also SCRYING; TASSEOGRAPHY.

Further reading

Bletzer, June G. *The Donning International Encyclopedic Psychic Dictionary.* West Chester, Pa.: Whitford Press, 1986.

Logan, Jo, and Lindsey Hodson. *The Prediction Book of Divination.* Dorset, England: Blandford Press, 1984.

Maven, Max. *Max Maven's Book of Fortunetelling.* New York: Prentice-Hall, 1992.

Opie, Iona, and Moira Tatem. *A Dictionary of Superstitions.* Oxford: Oxford University Press, 1992.

SCHNEIDER BROTHERS *Willy (1903–1971) and Rudi (1908–1957), Austrian mediums.*

While other psychics have been criticized as fakes, the Schneider brothers are considered to have been genuine. They succeeded in testing positive through rigorous trials by the British Society for Psychical Research in London and were carefully investigated by a number of psychical researchers, including Harry Price and Baron Schrenck-Notzing.

In addition to proving their psychic gifts in the research lab, the Schneider brothers are best remembered for being capable of producing an invisible substance that was said to be able to absorb infrared rays and set off camera flashbulbs.

Further reading

Drury, Nevill. *Dictionary of Mysticism and the Esoteric Traditions.* Dorset, England: Prism Press, 1992.

Mind over Matter. Mysteries of the Unknown. Alexandria, Va.: Time Life Books, 1990.

Richet, Charles. *Thirty Years of Psychical Research.* London: William Collins Publishers, 1923.

Thouless, R. H. *Experimental Psychical Research.* New York: Penguin, 1963.

SCIOMANCY *Divination by the size and shape of a shadow.*

In sciomancy, most likely used by early tribal peoples, and continuing with the Persians and Greeks, shadows were interpreted by tribal leaders and psychics. In ancient Greece the shadows used were those of corpses. Exactly how the future was determined with a shadow has now been lost in time.

It is interesting to note that there is still considerable superstition regarding shadows. In a book called *Yorkshire Customs* (c. 1898), older folks are recommended to look around a room before going to bed. If there is a shadowless head thrown on the wall from the light of the fire, it means that the one who has cast the shadow will die before the new year. It is still a Hebrew custom that the absence of a shadow altogether or a headless shadow on the night of Rosh Hashanah (Jewish New Year) is an omen of ill luck. It is said to foretell death in the course of the coming year.

Further reading

Bletzer, June G. *The Donning International Encyclopedic Psychic Dictionary.* West Chester, Pa.: Whitford Press, 1986.

Maven, Max. *Max Maven's Book of Fortunetelling.* New York: Prentice-Hall, 1992.

Opie, Iona, and Moira Tatem. *A Dictionary of Superstitions.* Oxford: Oxford University Press, 1992.

-SCOPY *To view, see or observe.*

This suffix added to a term indicates that one uses the method to view, see or observe. This is a common addition to many mantic arts. In ceraunoscopy, for example, predictions were made by observing the patterns of lightning during thunderstorms.

The suffix *-scopy* is from the Greek *-skopia* and *skopein*, meaning to look into, to behold.

SCORPIO *One of the 12 astrological signs of the zodiac. The symbol is the scorpion.*

Those who are born between October 23 and November 22 are natives of the sign of Scorpio and have specific traits indicative of the time and date on which they were born. Divination of events can also be charted through this astrological sign.

Astrologers divine what is in store throughout life through the time, date and place in which the individual was born as they coordinate the influences with other signs, the planets, the Sun, the Moon and other powers.

In traditional Western astrology, Scorpio is the eighth sign of the zodiac. Those born during the period typically exhibit qualities that exemplify a passionate, persistent, imaginative nature.

A native of this sign is quickwitted, highly confident and bold. These are people who have no problem with self-esteem; they exude it. Those who know little about astrology like to typecast Scorpio as the sexual giant of the zodiac. However, though Scorpio is the ultimate passionate individual, that passion is sometimes channeled into humanistic causes, into the arts, into business and government. Scorpios have an intense passion for life that others may envy.

Scorpio, as with other signs, has two sides. He or she may be so hotheaded, so unyielding, so recalcitrant that friends, family and co-workers shake their heads in dismay. However, put this same dynamic energy into a task and it is completed in a blaze of glory for all involved. Yes, Scorpio will be the leader, but he or she leads well, and shares the spotlight, too.

Scorpio is not often thought of as a sensitive

This ancient symbol represents the astrological sign of Scorpio.

and emotional sign, but the scorpion is, nonetheless. Those emotions are hidden sometimes, appearing to produce a person who is jealous or shifty, but deep within the Scorpio mind is a touchy-feely individual who wants to give and receive love. Misunderstood? Scorpio reveals him- or herself when the time is right . . . right for Scorpio, that is.

While traditional astrologers use books to calculate a personal birth chart based on the position of the Sun, Moon and planets at a distinct time, computer software has replaced most of this time-consuming work. The correct term for calculating a birth chart is to "cast" it. In order to fully comprehend the extent of traits, potential and attributes, the exact time and place of birth must be known and interpreted.

See also ASTROLOGICAL SYMBOLS; ASTROLOGY.

Further reading

Cosmic Connections. Mysteries of the Unknown. Alexandria, Va.: Time Life Books, 1990.

Goodman, Linda. *Linda Goodman's Sun Signs.* New York: Fawcett/Columbine, 1978.

Morgan, Chris. *Fortune Telling: How to Predict Your Own Future.* London: Quintet Publishing and Random House, 1992.

Omarr, Sydney. *My World of Astrology.* New York: Fleet, 1965.

———. *Scorpio.* New York: New American Library, 1992.

Verlagsanstalt, Datura. *Scorpio Astro Analysis.* New York: Grossett & Dunlap, 1976.

Woolfork, Joanna Martine. *The Only Astrology Book*

SCORPIO

You'll Ever Need. Landham, Mass.: Scarborough, 1992.

SCRYING *Divination by meditation with, staring at or interpreting the play of light on a shiny object or surface.*

Also, but less commonly, spelled skrying, this mantic art may be one of the oldest forms of divination. This ancient practice was developed about or before 1000 B.C. as a means of foretelling the future or forthcoming events.

With all applications of scrying, psychics stare into a shiny surface, sometimes a crystal ball, sometimes a natural crystal or even a surface such as a bowl of water on which a film of oil has been poured. It is the psychic who translates the vision that appears. Typically, the querant cannot see the vision. The vision or message is then translated to answer the querant's question.

Meditation should occur before the shiny object is studied. Consultation is usually done in a darkened room with a light source bouncing off the surface. Initially, the surface may appear clear and flat or simply reflect the available light, but as the psychic stares at the ball, it may become misty or foggy.

In ancient times polished surfaces were used to foretell the future. This practice is called catoptromancy. In catoptromancy, the psychic does not look directly at his or her image; the mirror is tilted to catch a light source and the patterns the light provides. Long before mirrors as we know them were invented, the Persians or perhaps the Chinese used this method of divining the future. The Greeks used polished plates made of bronze. Hebrew Kabbalists used a system that required seven highly polished mirrors made of a range of metals. More so, depending on the day of the week and the season, a specific polished metal surface was used.

The Thessalonians and Pythagorans scryed by moonlight. Some Bible scholars suggest that Joseph was using scrying to interpret the pharaoh's dreams with the silver cup filled with liquid referred to in Genesis 44:15. When glass mirrors were developed in Venice, Italy, about 1200, they were quickly selected as the best instrument to forecast the future.

Dr. John Dee, adviser to Queen Elizabeth I of England, used a scrying method to assist her majesty. Some believe it was a black mirror of obsidian. Others say Dee also used a crystal ball. Dee called the instrument a "shew-stone," and, along with other metaphysical objects and tools, his is housed in the British Museum. Scrying mirrors appear in many paintings of Rembrandt's and Leonardo da Vinci's. Nostradamus, the great psychic, is said to have used a bowl of water placed on a brass tripod.

To practice scrying without the assistance of a professional psychic, one needs only a mirror, a crystal, a bowl of water or any other shiny surface. After a period of quiet meditation, questions are asked (either out loud or silently) with the shiny surface stationed in front of the querant. The answers are clairvoyantly perceived. Some psychics perceive past-life information, see auras and are able to speak to the souls of the deceased through this gazing technique. Students of scrying may use the surface to see visions of their spirit guides or as a medium through which their spirit guides speak to them. Those who are learning how to become more clairvoyant sometimes are encouraged to use mirrors for practice in connecting with the spirit realm, particularly mirrors painted black on the raised side.

See also CATOPTROMANCY; ENOPTROMANCY; HYDROMANCY; LECONOMANCY.

Further reading

Butler, W. E. *How to Develop Clairvoyance.* 2d ed. New York: Samuel Weiser, 1979.

Dixon, Jeane, and Rene Noorbergen. *Jeane Dixon: My Life and Prophecies.* New York: Morrow, 1969.

Encyclopedia of Religion. New York: Macmillian, 1987.

Fontbrune, Jean-Charles de. *Nostradamus: Countdown to Apocalypse.* New York: Holt, Rinehart & Winston, 1980.

King, Frances, and Stephen Skinner. *Techniques of High Magic.* Rochester, Vt.: Destiny Books, 1991.

Magickal Almanac. St. Paul, Minn.: Llewellyn, 1989.

Visions and Prophecies. Mysteries of the Unknown. Alexandria, Va.: Time Life Books, 1990.

Walker, Dael. *The Crystal Book.* Sunol, Calif.: Crystal Col, 1983.

SEANCE *A serious meeting of individuals interested in psychic occurrences at which a psychic calls forth spiritual energies.*

Seances typically involve from 3 to 10 participants. Usually, the psychic who is leading the seance will proceed into a trance or a conscious level where he or she is able to communicate with a spirit, guardian angel or other entity. The psychic may communicate silently with this spiritual entity or use his or her body as a channel for information. In the case of channeled information, often the psychic does not remember what has occurred while the body has been taken over by an entity.

In some seances, participants will sit in a circle and hold hands, although this is not necessary. Most psychics who are involved in seances insist that those in attendance must take the same chair week after week.

There is often a prayer given or a period of meditation before the meeting begins and sometimes another such period at the end of the session. Typically, no one can leave the room during the seance because that would disrupt the spiritual communication.

Sometimes there is a religious lesson or knowledge that comes forth from the ethereal world to those in attendance, but this is not always the case. Meetings usually last from one to three hours and are held on a regular basis in a place where those in attendance feel comfortable. Psychics point out that there must be harmony between those who are sitters (participants) at the seance. Some sitters are thought to be used much like batteries; their energy is used by the spirits called forth to the seance.

Psychics and sitters often report feeling the touch of an entity against their arms or cheeks. For many this proves that the spirits are present in the room with the participants. These are called seance hands. Seance lights are small, glowing circles of light that have been known to visit seances occurring in a darkened room. These are said to be entities who wish to attend the seance. Some of them are the guides or guardians of those in attendance; others may be disincarnate spirits.

During the mid-1800s to the early 1900s, spiritualism and the study of metaphysics were beginning to blossom. It was also a period plagued with frauds and schemes involving parapsychology. Often those who had recently lost a family member paid handsomely to talk with the dearly departed. The "spiritualist" or "psychic" tricked the innocent out of money, bilking the unsuspecting with a host of deceptions. As the process of holding seances evolved, the practice of holding hands became popular in order to keep the psychic from performing any sleight-of-hand mischief. The psychic might also have his or her hands and legs tied to the chair to avoid the possibility of a hoax.

Today, the word *seance* has been replaced with phrases such as spiritual gathering, spiritual evening, circle of friends and other terminology indicating that a spiritual experience will be forthcoming.

See also CHANNEL; CLAIRVOYANCE; GUIDE; PSYCHIC.

Further reading

Brown, Slater. *The Heyday of Spiritualism*. New York: Hawthorn, 1970.
Fielding, Everard. *Sitting with Eusapia Palladino*. New York: University Books, 1963.
Hall, Manley P. *Solving Psychic Problems*. Los Angeles: Philosophical Research, 1956.
Leonard, John C. *The Higher Spiritualism*. Washington, D.C.: Philosophical Book Co., 1927.
Sherman, Harold. *You Can Communicate with the Unseen World*. New York: Fawcett, 1974.

SECOND SIGHT *Psychic abilities.*

Second sight is an old-fashioned term for receiving knowledge without the use of reason. Second sight refers to the fact that those with psychic gifts can see visions or "know" information that will occur in the future or has happened in the past without the use of their eyes. It is the same as the psychic gifts of clairvoyance, telepathy and ESP, among others.

Those famous for this gift include Madame Blavatsky, Edgar Cayce and JZ Knight.

See also CLAIRVOYANCE; EXTRA SENSORY PERCEPTION (ESP); TELEPATHY.

Further reading

Buckland, Raymond. *Doors to Other Worlds*. St. Paul, Minn.: Llewellyn, 1993.

Fodor, Nandor. *Encyclopedia of Psychic Science*. New York: University Books, 1966.

Psychics. Mysteries of the Unknown. Alexandria, Va.: Time Life Books, 1990.

SELENOMANCY *Divination by studying celestial conditions, especially the phases of the Moon.*

Selenomancy is a variation of alectromancy, forecasting the future through atmospheric or celestial conditions. Used in ancient Egypt, this mantic art might be employed by a psychic to foretell what the future might hold for a noble person at his or her birth. It was also used to prognosticate the downfall of an enemy after an eclipse of the Moon.

In Pliny's *Natural History* (c. A.D. 77), he stated that the Moon was the all-important force in life; thus it made sense that psychics would use it to prognosticate the future. Pliny said, "This it is that replenishes the earth; when she approaches it, she fills all bodies, while when she recedes, she empties them. For this cause it is that shell-fish grow with her increase, also that the blood of man is increased or diminished in proportion to the quantity of her light."

At one time (about A.D. 1050) it was believed that if a male child was born on the first day of the new moon, he would be wealthy and live a long life. Yet by 1878 (according to Thomas Hardy's *Return of the Native*), "No moon, no man" was a popular saying. It meant that a boy born during the new moon would never amount to much.

According to a folktale from Scotland (c. 1795), no couple should marry unless there was a growing moon if they wanted to prosper and be happy for all their days. It was, conversely, thought to be very unlucky to marry during a waning moon. Additionally, it was unlucky to point at the Moon: According to *Household Tales* (1895), if one pointed at the Moon, one would not go to heaven.

Other celestial occurrences have historically been used as predictive tools. The Roman historian Cornelius Tacitus (A.D. 55?–117?) wrote that "a comet blazed—a phenomenon which, according to the persuasion of the vulgar [plebeian], portended change of kingdoms." He was not alone. In A.D. 727, Bede wrote in *De Natura Rerum* that comets are "long-haired stars with flames, appearing suddenly, and presaging a change in sovereignty, or plague, or war, or winds, or floods."

The heavens were constantly watched for signs, and during ancient Roman times, government-sponsored augurs interpreted any unique or controversial occurrence. In 1583, Henry Howard wrote in *Poyson of Supposed Prophecies* that the appearance of a comet streaking across the night sky so upset Elizabeth I of England that she believed her empire was about to be overthrown. He wrote, "With a courage aunswerable to the greatnesse of her [Queen Elizabeth] state, shee caused the windowe to be sette open, and cast out thys word *lacta est alia*. The dyce are throwne, affirming that her stedfast hope . . . was too firmly planted to the prouidence of God, to be affrighted with those beams."

Further reading

Cavendish, Richard, ed. *The Encyclopedia of the Unexplained*. New York: McGraw-Hill, 1974.

Daniels, Cora Linn, and Prof. C. M. Stevans, eds. *Encyclopedia of Superstitions, Folklore and the Occult Sciences of the World*. Detroit: Gale Research, 1971.

Opie, Iona, and Moira Tatem. *A Dictionary of Superstitions*. Oxford: Oxford University Press, 1992.

SENSITIVE *One who is psychic and has the ability to know things without prior knowledge or the use of reason.*

See also AUGUR; BAILEY, ALICE; BLAVATSKY, HELENA P.; CHANNEL; HOME, DANIEL DUNGLAS; INTUITION; KNIGHT, JZ; PSYCHIC; PSYCHIC READINGS.

Further reading

Jones, Lloyd K. *Development of Mediumship*. Chicago: Lormar, 1919.

Kardec, Allan. *The Book of Mediums.* York Beach, Maine: Samuel Weiser, 1970.

Klimo, John. *Channeling: Investigations on Receiving Information from Paranormal Sources.* Los Angeles: Jeremy P. Tarcher, 1987.

Lungin, Tatiana. *Wolf Messing: The True Story of Russia's Greatest Psychic.* New York: Paragon House, 1989.

Rodegast, Pat, and Judith Stanton, comps. *Emmanuel's Book: A Manual for Living Comfortably in the Cosmos.* New York: Bantam, 1987.

Zolar. *Zolar's Book of the Spirits.* New York: Prentice-Hall, 1987.

SEVEN-POINT STAR
In tarot, one of the card layouts or spreads used to divine the future.

Typically, the Seven-Point Star can be used weekly (unlike other spreads that are best used once or twice a year). Each card is said to foretell the events or influences that will occur on specific days of the forthcoming week.

To use this spread, the cards are shuffled by the querant. He or she is asked to select a significator, a card that has some attraction to the querant or seems to reflect him or her. The shuffling process and selection of the significator is done while the querant considers what information is to be revealed or a specific question.

The significator is placed faceup in the center of the table. Then the querant draws seven cards from the deck and places them in a circle around the significator. They can be selected as the first seven cards from the top of the deck or any cards that seem to attract the querant in any way. They are placed in a circle facedown.

The first card is placed in the lower left-hand area of the circle, or in the "7 o'clock" position, if one thinks of the circle as the face of a clock. The second card is in the "8 o'clock" position, the third at "10," the fourth at "12," the fifth at "1," the sixth at "4" and the seventh at "5." (Some tarot card readers prefer to draw the cards for the querant. As with all prognostication practices, there are unlimited variations to each mantic art.) The cards are turned over one at a time as they are interpreted.

The first card is said to represent Monday, the second Tuesday, the third Wednesday, and so on. For example, if one draws the Moon as the first card, this might indicate that he or she will have a dreamy, mystical and perhaps indecisive week ahead. However, if the Death card is in the first position, it indicates a major change is about to occur. (Psychic readers point out that the Death card does not specifically indicate the physical end of life but rather the end of a phase or philosophy or the end of a relationship.)

In order to interpret the cards, many readers and psychics suggest referring to a book specifically for tarot; others suggest using one's own psychic skills and doing an intuitive reading. In an intuitive reading, the psychic looks at the pictures on the cards and those objects or figures or colors that come into his or her mind first are discussed.

See also CARTOMANCY; MAJOR ARCANA; SUIT OF CUPS; SUIT OF PENTACLES; SUIT OF SWORDS; SUIT OF WANDS; TAROT.

Further reading
Buckland, Raymond. *Secrets of Gypsy Fortune Telling.* St. Paul, Minn.: Llewellyn, 1988.

Cavendish, Richard. *The Tarot.* New York: Putnam's, 1967.

Giles, Cynthia. *The Tarot: History, Mystery and Lore.* New York: Paragon House, 1992.

Innes, Brian. *The Tarot: How to Use and Interpret the Cards.* London: Orbis, 1979.

King, Francis, and Stephen Skinner. *Techniques of High Magic.* Rochester, Vt.: Destiny Books, 1991.

Thierens, A. E. *Astrology and the Tarot.* Los Angeles: Newcastle, 1975.

Waite, Arthur Edward. *The Pictorial Key to the Tarot.* New York: Samuel Weiser, 1973.

SHAMAN
One who is able to share psychic gifts, especially in tribal groups.

The shaman is a natural-born psychic and highly respected among his or her group. The term *shaman* may also mean psychic, medium, mystic, magician, sensitive or clairvoyant. He or she may take on the shape, form and appearance of other animals, such as a bird, tiger, or fish. This individual is typically able to diagnose illness and often is able to heal the sick through the use of psychic cleansing and herbal cures.

In most cultures the role of the shaman is usually filled by a male, with females assigned other duties. However, there are a number of groups that have women shamans. In the Igorot tribe of the Luzon mountains in the Philippines, female shamans are called *aniteras*, intermediaries between this world and the next.

The shaman considers the mind, body and spirit to be one. Unlike modern physicians, he or she may not try to prolong life but to protect the soul or spirit of the individual.

The shaman is characteristically clairvoyant, and interpretation of dreams is an essential aspect of his or her work. The shaman may have the ability to levitate objects, bring forth and channel spiritual entities, interpret omens and prognosticate the future through observance of natural occurrences. A shaman may use water, smoke, fire or found objects to foretell the future or instruct students. The shaman may be called upon to protect a community or individual from evil spirits or natural disaster.

The role of the shaman may have begun more than 20,000 years ago in prehistoric times. He or she may have been the first storyteller, healer and mystic. Some believe that the Old Testament prophets can be regarded as shamans. During the Middle Ages in Europe, the role of the shaman may have fragmented into other functions, from magicians and astrologers to poets and priests. The shaman of that period may also have become an alchemist, searching for the philosophers' stone (the mystical method by which base metal may be turned into gold).

Even though most Americans think of the shaman as the psychic counselor, guardian, herbalist and prognosticator of Native American tribes, the role of the shaman is universal, found, in one form or another, in most cultures, and it continues to be important today. The shaman is said to act as a "middleman" between earth and the gods or spirits. He or she may use music, rituals and sleight-of-hand tricks and often falls into a trance during a ceremony.

In Siberia the shaman is considered the religious leader, a holy individual who uses his or her abilities to continue the theological underpinnings of the group. In the various Asian cultures, a shaman is a respected religious leader who acts as a teacher and guide for his or her flock and students. In the Navajo culture, the shaman is a tribal leader, extremely respected and believed to be able to search for the cause and cure illness. In the Algonquin culture, the shaman is more of a herbalist and healer than a religious leader.

See also KAHUNAS.

Further reading

Achterberg, Jeanne. *Imagery in Healing: Shamanism and Modern Medicine*. Boston: Shambhala, 1985.

Bierhorst, John. *The Mythology of North America*. New York: Morrow, 1985.

Halifax, Joan. *Shaman: The Wounded Healer*. New York: Crossroads Press, 1982.

Hirschfelder, Arlene, and Paulette Molin. *The Encyclopedia of Native American Religions*. New York: Facts On File, 1992.

King, Serge. *Kahuna Healing*. Wheaton, Ill.: Theosophical Publishing House, 1983.

Long, Max Freedom. *Recovering Ancient Magic*. London: Rider Publishers, 1936.

Paper, Jordan. *Offering Smoke: The Sacred Pipe and Native American Religion*. Moscow: University of Idaho Press, 1988.

Underhill, Ruth M. *Red Man's Religion: Beliefs and Practices of the Indians North of Mexico*. Chicago: University of Chicago Press, 1965.

SHIPTON, MOTHER *(1488?–1540?) English psychic.*

Stories of Mother Shipton's prophecies and psychic powers have been handed down through the centuries, but it is unclear whether or not she was an actual person. Stories have continued to circulate about her predictions of horseless carriages (cars), accidents that will defile the world (pollution and nuclear accidents), thoughts flying around the world (telephone, radio, satellite transmissions, etc.) and the end of the world. The final event, according to legend, was to happen in 1881.

A contemporary of Nostradamus, if she actually existed, Mother Shipton is often said to have been one of England's most intuitive seers.

Further reading

Cosmic Connections. Mysteries of the Unknown. Alexandria, Va.: Time Life Books, 1990.

Visions and Prophecies. Mysteries of the Unknown. Alexandria, Va.: Time Life Books, 1990.

SIDEROMANCY *Divination by the interpretation of the twisting and smoldering of pieces of straw placed on a red-hot surface.*

This divination practice was used in ancient Rome. The twirling, "dancing" motions of the sticks of straw were interpreted to foretell the future or interpret omens. Crushed beans and peas were also used.

Variations of sideromancy are capnomancy (patterns of smoke made by burning various objects and/or sacrifices, sometimes known as causimonancy), critomancy (burning of barleycorn), daphnomancy (divination by the crackle of burning laurel leaves), libanomancy (divination through incense smoke) and pyromancy (analyzing the flames of a combustible object).

See also ANTHROPOMANCY; BOTANOMANCY; CAPNOMANCY, CAUSIMONANCY; PYROMANCY.

Further reading

Dey, Charmaine. *The Magic Candle.* Bronx, N.Y.: Original Publications, 1989.

Kittredge, George. *Witchcraft in Old and New England.* Cambridge: Harvard University Press, 1929. Reprint. New York: Atheneum, 1972.

Maven, Max. *Max Maven's Book of Fortunetelling.* New York: Prentice-Hall, 1992.

Nichols, Ross. *The Book of Druidry—History, Sites, Wisdom.* London: Aquarian Press, 1990.

Opie, Iona, and Moira Tatem. *A Dictionary of Superstitions.* Oxford: Oxford University Press, 1992.

SITTER *One who is a participant at a* SEANCE.

A sitter has been compared to a lightning rod or a battery, in that the universe needs something to attract and hold energy so that the psychic can release it. Sometimes sitters are members of a group that meet regularly at a specific time. They have been referred to as part of a psychic development circle, often realizing their own psychic gifts as they assist others.

Additionally, "sittings" may refer to PSYCHIC READINGS.

Further reading

Buckland, Raymond. *Doors to Other Worlds.* St. Paul, Minn.: Llewellyn, 1993.

Burns, Litany. *Develop Your Psychic Abilities.* New York: Pocket Books, 1985.

Butler, W. E. *How to Develop Clairvoyance.* 2d ed. New York: Samuel Weiser, 1979.

SKINNER, STEPHEN *(1948–)*
Australian psychic.

Skinner, who now lives in London, is considered to be a modern authority on medieval rituals, magic and geomancy. In 1972, he founded Askin Publishers, which reprints contemporary versions of classic metaphysical literature, including works by Dr. John Dee, Cornelius Agrippa and others.

Skinner's *Techniques of High Magic* (1971) is considered to be the best contemporary book on the topic of modern magic. His other books include *The Search for Abraxas* (1972), *The Oracle of Geomancy* (1977) and *The Living Earth Manual of Feng-Shui* (1982). He has also interpreted, and Askin has republished, books by Aleister Crowley and the Hermetic Order of the Golden Dawn.

Further reading

Drury, Nevill. *Dictionary of Mysticism and the Esoteric Traditions.* Dorset, England: Prism Press, 1992.

King, Francis and Stephen Skinner. *Techniques of High Magic.* Rochester, Vt.: Destiny Books, 1991.

SOCIETY FOR PSYCHICAL RESEARCH *First organization to study metaphysics seriously.*

Founded in 1882 in Cambridge, England, the Society for Psychical Research (SPR) was founded in order to investigate paranormal experiences and unexplained phenomena through a rigorous system of laboratory tests. It was also started to explore the processes used by psychics.

More than 100 years since its conception, the SPR's aims are still much the same: to study

SOCIETY FOR PSYCHICAL RESEARCH
Like the Society for Psychical Research in England,
the American Society for Psychical Research (ASPR)
was founded to investigate paranormal activity—
including levitation, as illustrated here.

the unexplained functions of the mind including clairvoyance, ghostly visitations and apparitions, levitation, hypnotism and telepathy. Headquartered in London, the SPR's members have included the archbishop of Canterbury, E. W. Benson, Prime Ministers William Ewart Gladstone and Arthur Balfour, William Crookes, Sir Oliver Lodge and Sir William Barrett, among others.

In 1884, the American Society for Psychical Research (ASPR) was founded. Organized along

the same lines, it too has studied and continues to explore all facets of the paranormal. Like the British organization, ASPR maintains a highly respected library, said to be one of the best in the world on topics pertaining to metaphysics.

Further reading

Fodor, Nandor. *Encyclopedia of Psychic Science*. New York: University Books, 1966.

Gauld, Alan. *The Founders of Psychical Research*. London: Routledge & Kegan Paul, 1968.

Guiley, Rosemary Ellen. *Harper's Encyclopedia of Mystical and Paranormal Experience*. San Francisco: HarperSan Francisco, 1991.

Haynes, Renee. *The Society for Psychical Research, 1882–1982: A History*. London: Macdonald & Co., 1982.

SORTILEGE
See SORTILEGE SYSTEMS.

SORTILEGE SYSTEMS *Any prognostication methods that employ objects with sides that are cast or drawn.*

Sortilege systems originated more than 5,000 years ago, when the first pebbles or animal bones were tossed and a tribal shaman began to interpret how they fell. All forms of sortilege take place when an object is thrown into the air, dropped to the ground or selected from a bag or box, as with ming sticks, rune stones, tarot cards and other divination with playing cards and dice are considered by some to be sortilege systems because of the random selection. Sortilege systems are utilized to determine future happenings or interpret omens, and they cross all geographical and cultural lines.

The use of bones for sortilege can be traced back over 3,500 years ago to ancient Egypt and to Greece more than 3,000 years ago. The system of casting of lots to foretell the future is still based on the placement or the inscription on the objects, which psychics then interpret to answer a querant's question.

According to psychics, the fact that sortilege systems can predict the future is attributed to a metaphysical concept called the readiness wave, the esoteric belief that there is a portion of the brain in the frontal cortex that emits a signal into the surrounding area of the thinker. These signals relate to thought and experience, before the actual occurrence of the thought or experience itself.

Many systems, such as dominoes, are still common divination methods today, whereas those that employed animals bones have been adapted. Thus, people today prognosticate with dice rather than knucklebones. However, dice of various shapes and sizes are still used by the Zulu and the West African tribe of the Bantu. Sortilege has been and continues to be one of the most popular divination methods used to foretell future events and obtain spiritual guidance. Although the systems appear quick and easy to learn, interpreting and understanding the numerous nuances of a given system can take years. Many people spend their lives studying rune stones, tarot cards and ming sticks yet continue to state that they are still students of a particular system. For a complete course on a specific sortilege system, it is recommended that one take a class on the topic or locate a book to provide as much information as possible.

Objects used in sortilege systems vary in terms of the material from which they are made and the number of sides they have; at the minimum they have two, as with coins. In the Chinese method of *chiao-pai*, the objects have two sides. The ancient Egyptians used dice with eight sides; in medieval times, dice with 12 sides were used. It is said that the Romans predicted the future using dice with as many as 14 sides. The most commonly used dice to forecast the future are six-sided dice available throughout the United States; sides are arranged so that any pair of opposite surfaces add up to the number seven.

As with other prognostication methods, sortilege systems have sometimes been considered demonic tools. Because rune stones, for example, were inscribed with mystical symbols (the runic alphabet), early Christians believed that the runes were the work of the devil. They believed that witches could cause death or cast an evil spell through the casting of the runes. There are several references to the use of sortilege systems in the Old Testament. Some historians explain that

a variation of the Hebrew term for "diviner" can be translated to "witch."

In 785, the Catholic Church prohibited the use of "sorcery systems" to settle disputes. However, consulting with diviners, like the village wise man or woman, was not banned. During the Middle Ages and the Renaissance, those who used sortilege systems and other methods of prognostication were punished by fines, humiliation, torture and/or loss of property. Those who were accused and found guilty of practicing witchcraft were put to death. Therefore, runes and other sortilege systems became taboo, and their use was regarded with extreme disfavor among religious groups. The prejudice against students of metaphysics, including gypsies, continued into this century. The Nazis declared those who prognosticated the future to be "subhumans," along with Jews, Slavs and other "non-Aryans." More than 400,000 gypsies, psychics and occultists were killed in the German concentration camps.

Despite the occasional censure of sortilege and prognostication systems, employment of the methods has never been eradicated. People continue to want to know what the future holds, why specific occurrences have transpired and if their course of action is valid.

Along with simple sortilege systems, there are more intricate methods, including those that divide a 12-inch circle into 12 segments onto which objects are tossed. The placement of the object as it lands in one of the segments provides a more detailed answer to the querant's question. Other items that can be thrown in addition to dice and cards, are shells, stones, crystals, rocks, coins and pieces of bark. The divination of flipping a coin to determine an answer or to see which sports teams will go first is actually sortilege.

See also ASTRAGYROMANCY; BELOMANCY; CARTOMANCY; CASTING OF LOTS; CLEROMANCY; DICE; DOMINOES; GEMS; I CHING; MANTIC OBJECTS; MING STICKS; RUNE STONES; TAROT.

Further reading

Blum, Ralph. *The Book of Runes*. New York: St. Martin's, 1982.

Boulding, Elise. *The Underside of History.* Boulder, Colo.: Westview Press, 1976.

Buckland, Ray. *Secrets of Gypsy Fortune Telling.* St. Paul, Minn.: Llewellyn, 1988.

Fox, Judy; Karen Hughes; and John Tampion. *An Illuminated I Ching.* New York: Arch, 1984.

Heywood, R. *Beyond the Reach of Sense.* New York: Dutton, 1961.

Magickal Almanac. St. Paul, Minn.: Llewellyn, 1989.

Markham, Ursula. *The Crystal Workbook: A Complete Guide to Working with Crystals.* Northamptonshire, England: Aquarian Press, 1988.

Maven, Max. *Max Maven's Book of Fortunetelling.* New York: Prentice-Hall, 1992.

Morgan, Chris. *Fortune Telling: How to Predict Your Own Future.* London: Quintet Publishing and Random House, 1992.

Pajeon, Kala, and Ketz Pajeon. *The Candle Magic Workbook.* New York: Citadel Press, 1992.

Visions and Prophecies. Mysteries of the Unknown. Alexandria, Va.: Time Life Books, 1990.

Walker, Barbara G. *The Woman's Encyclopedia of Myths and Secrets.* New York: Harper Collins, 1983.

SOUL   *The essence of ethereal intelligence.*

The soul is believed to possess the knowledge of the entity. The soul gives instructions to the entity in order to enable it function. It is considered to be the energy of all substances, and all substances have a soul. It is the principle of life, and it is life.

Plato believed that the soul was made up of four substances: reason, understanding, faith and perfection. Carl Jung said that the soul had four faculties: thinking, sensation, feeling and intuition. Eliphas Levi theorized that the soul is and has no ending; it is a thought of God, and the soul holds all the attributes of God. Albert Einstein believed that the human soul is an electromagnetic force that holds together the protoplasmic energy in the body prior to death. This substance is then duplicated in a life after death.

In Western religious traditions, the soul is an immaterial element that is combined with the human form of blood, tissue and skin to make up the human body. It is conceived of inner, vital and spiritual essences and governs the body as well as the mind. In the Hindu religion and in other schools of thought, it is believed that the soul does not die but is reincarnated into other beings in order to learn various lessons.

Some cultural beliefs include healing the soul through ritual practices, often with the assistance of a shaman. In out-of-body experiences, it is the soul that travels to see and experience other dimensions. Edgar Cayce's "travels" to read the AKASHIC RECORDS were done through this soul journey.

See also CAYCE, EDGAR; REINCARNATION.

Further reading

Brenann, J. H. *The Reincarnation Workbook.* New York: Sterling, 1990.

The Encyclopedia of Eastern Philosophy and Religion. Boston: Shambhala, 1989.

Kapleau, Philip. *The Wheel of Life and Death: A Practical and Spiritual Guide.* New York: Doubleday, 1989.

Motoyama, Hiroshi. *Karma and Reincarnation.* Translated by Rande Brown Ouchi. New York: Avon, 1992.

Woodward, Mary Ann. *Edgar Cayce's Story of Karma: God's Book of Remembrance.* New York: Coward, McCann & Geoghegan/Edgar Cayce Foundation, 1971.

SPARE, AUSTIN OSMAN   *(1886–1956)*
English artist and psychic.

At age 16, while a student at the Royal College of Art in England, Spare was introduced to mysticism. He became intensely interested and intrigued by Egyptian mythology and witchcraft and was a follower of Aleister Crowley, known for his association with ritualistic magic.

A believer in reincarnation, Spare believed that our past lives may be accessed through a trance state. In a trance, Spare channeled a symbolic language, sigils. (Sigils are symbols that represent specific supernatural entities. In the Middle Ages they were often used to represent and summon spirits, angels and guardians and in magical rituals.) He used the sigils in his artwork and to help understand lessons from his past lives.

Spare is considered to be one of Britain's finest illustrators and is remembered for his *Book of*

Pleasure (1913; reissued 1975). Spare's work has been compared to Aubrey Beardsley's paintings; however, he is less known in the United States.

See also CROWLEY, ALEISTER; HERMETIC ORDER OF THE GOLDEN DAWN.

Further reading

Cavendish, Richard, ed. *The Encyclopedia of the Unexplained.* New York: McGraw-Hill, 1974.

King, Francis. *Ritual Magic in England, 1887 to the Present Day.* London: Neville Spearman, 1970.

MacKenzie, Norman. *Secret Societies.* New York: Holt, Rinehart & Winston, 1967.

Symonds, John, and Kenneth Grant, eds. *The Confessions of Aleister Crowley: An Autobiography.* London: Routledge & Kegan Paul, 1979.

SPIRIT *General term meaning an imperishable life force.*

The spirit is the "divine spark" that is within everyone and is said to be housed in the soul. It is said to connect the mental body to the physical body while being in touch with ethereal energy. Those who believe in metaphysics explain that the spirit is connected to the God force.

When asking for guidance from the spiritual world, one may be seeking advice from God, guardian angels, spiritual guides or other entities. These, too, are referred to as spirits.

Further reading

Belhayes, Iris, with Enid. *Spirit Guides.* San Diego: ACS, 1985.

Bletzer, June G., *The Donning International Encyclopedic Psychic Dictionary.* West Chester, Pa.: Whitford Press, 1986.

Miller, Madeleine S., and J. Lane Miller, eds. *Harper's Encyclopedia of Bible Life.* San Francisco: Harper & Row, 1978.

Watson, Donald. *The Dictionary of Mind and Spirit.* New York: Avon, 1991.

SPIRITUAL GUIDE
See GUIDE.

SPIRITUALISM *The belief that spirits of the dead can communicate with the living.*

Spiritualism is the belief that there is life after physical death and that there is the possibility of conversing with the spirits who exist in the nonphysical plane. This communication can be on a personal level, often through meditation, or with the assistance of a psychic. The information is then channeled through the psychic or by any variations of clairvoyance or automatic writing.

The word *spiritualist* is an outdated name for a psychic, although it is sometimes still used.

See also AUGUR; BAILEY, ALICE; BLAVATSKY, HELENA P.; CHANNEL: HOME, DANIEL DUNGLAS; INTUITION; KNIGHT, JZ; PSYCHIC; PSYCHIC READINGS.

Further reading

Barbanell, Maurice. *This Is Spiritualism.* London: Jenkins, 1959.

Bludson, Norman. *A Popular Dictionary of Spiritualism.* London: Arco, 1961.

Jones, Lloyd K. *Development of Mediumship.* Chicago: Lormar, 1919.

Kardec, Allan. *The Book of Mediums.* York Beach, Maine: Samuel Weiser, 1970.

Klimo, John. *Channeling: Investigations on Receiving Information from Paranormal Sources.* Los Angeles: Jeremy P. Tarcher, 1987.

Lungin, Tatiana. *Wolf Messing: The True Story of Russia's Greatest Psychic.* New York: Paragon House, 1989.

Rodegast, Pat, and Judith Stanton, comps. *Emmanuel's Book: A Manual for Living Comfortably in the Cosmos.* New York: Bantam, 1987.

Zolar. *Zolar's Book of the Spirits.* New York: Prentice-Hall, 1987.

SPIRITUALITY *In metaphysics, the potential within each person to grow more mentally aware.*

The word *spirituality* does not reflect a specific religious belief. Rather, it emcompasses an acceptance of a higher form of intelligence, the Laws of Metaphysics, and a belief in the concept of a universe. It is the desire to understand, learn and ultimately accept these laws and assimilate them into one's daily life.

Although most who believe in the spirituality of the universe also believe in reincarnation, guides and the use of predictive methods, this is not mandatory. One is allowed to seek his or her own spirituality at the rate and intensity necessary for personal illumination.

See also AKASHIC RECORDS; CHANNEL; and specific tools and mantic arts used to connect with guides.

Further reading

Belhayes, Iris, with Enid. *Spirit Guides*. San Diego: ACS, 1985.

Bletzer, June G. *The Donning International Encyclopedic Psychic Dictionary*. West Chester, Pa.: Whitford Press, 1986.

Buckland, Raymond. *Doors to Other Worlds*. St. Paul, Minn.: Llewellyn, 1993.

Butler, W. E. *How to Develop Clairvoyance*. 2d ed. New York: Samuel Weiser, 1979.

Hirschfelder, Arlene, and Paulette Molin. *The Encyclopedia of Native American Religions*. New York: Facts On File, 1992.

King, Francis, and Stephen Skinner. *Techniques of High Magic*. Rochester, Vt.: Destiny Books, 1991.

SPODOMANCY   *Divination by fire.*

Spodomancy is practiced by placing a message on a paper, setting it afire and examining and interpreting the smoke or flames that are consuming the paper.

When spodomancy was used in ancient Greece, it was the ashes of the combustible material that were interpreted, much in the same way tea leaves are "read." Spodomancy continues to have a following even today. This interesting prediction method is a variation of tephramancy and is grouped under the umbrella term *pyromancy*, with other fire and smoke prediction methods.

See also ANTHROPOMANCY; CAPNOMANCY; CAUSIMONANCY; PYROMANCY; TEPHRAMANCY.

Further reading

Kittredge, George. *Witchcraft in Old and New England*. Cambridge: Harvard University Press, 1929. Reprint. New York: Atheneum, 1972.

Maven, Max. *Max Maven's Book of Fortunetelling*. New York: Prentice-Hall, 1992.

Nichols, Ross. *The Book of Druidry—History, Sites, Wisdom*. London: Aquarian Press, 1990.

Opie, Iona, and Moira Tatem. *A Dictionary of Superstitions*. Oxford: Oxford University Press, 1992.

Pajeon, Kala, and Ketz Pajeon. *The Candle Magic Workbook*. New York: Citadel Press, 1992.

SPOTOMANCY   *Divination through the casting of spot cards and sortes to foretell the future.*

Spotomancy is technically a variation of sortilege (see SORTILEGE SYSTEMS). In this method, practiced in ancient Egypt, the psychic uses a set of spot cards, which bear symbols representing the possibilities of future events. Sortes (from the Latin *serere*, meaning to string) are a string of disks on which there are inscriptions delineating the conditions (often extremely trying) that a person (or place) must experience and ways that the experiences can be made less difficult. They are made by psychics. After the spot cards are cast and interpreted, the psychic refers to sortes and intuitively selects those that will assist in the reading.

Spotomancy is sometimes incorrectly used to refer to sortilege in general.

Further reading

Heywood, R. *Beyond the Reach of Sense*. New York: Dutton, 1961.

Magickal Almanac. St. Paul, Minn.: Llewellyn, 1989.

Morgan, Chris. *Fortune Telling: How to Predict Your Own Future*. London: Quintet Publishing and Random House, 1992.

Visions and Prophecies. Mysteries of the Unknown. Alexandria, Va.: Time Life Books, 1990.

STEINER, RUDOLPH   *(1861–1925) German clairvoyant, researcher and Theosophist.*

Steiner was a scholar whose work is still studied and discussed at Steiner Schools throughout the world. He was a prolific writer, and his many books, including *Occult Science, Christianity of Mystical Fact* and *The Knowledge of Higher Worlds and Its Attainment*, are still respected.

A member of Madame Helena P. Blavatsky's Theosophical Society, he became disillusioned with the way the group was building a religion based on the opinions of Krishnamurti (the society believed Krishnamurti to be the next messiah). In 1913 Steiner formed the Anthroposophical Society, based near Basel, Switzerland. There he founded the Goetheaplum School for esoteric research. Steiner's organization is now called the General Anthroposophical Society (organized in 1923). It has branches throughout the world but is most active in Europe.

A gifted clairvoyant and researcher, Steiner studied Atlantis and Lemuria and other metaphysical myths. He claimed to be able to access the AKASHIC RECORDS, thus learning and writing about the true evolution of knowledge and humanity. He was a member of the Ordo Templi Orientis and the Order of the Illuminati.

Steiner is considered a "futurist" by many, and his ideas of chemical-free agriculture, education that encompasses the spirit as well as the mind and eurythmy (moving the body to music to express language) are now considered part of many visionary ideas.

Further reading

Guiley, Rosemary Ellen. *Harper's Encyclopedia of Mystical and Paranormal Experience.* San Francisco: HarperSan Francisco, 1991.

McDermott, Robert A., ed. *The Essential Steiner.* San Francisco: Harper & Row, 1984.

Shepherd, A. P. *Rudolf Steiner: Scientists of the Invisible.* 1954. Reprint. Rochester, Vt.: Inner Traditions International, 1983.

STICHOMANCY *Divination through the reading of random selections of passages or verses from books.*

Stichomancy is sometimes grouped with BIBLIOMANCY; however, bibliomancy uses only a holy book. *Sortes sanctorium* is a variation of stichomancy that specifically employs a Bible.

Stichomancy, practiced in ancient Greece and Rome, required the querant to ask a question; then a book was opened at random. The querant (or sometimes the psychic) read the first verse on which the eye fell. A variation was to close one's eyes and run a finger down a page of literature. When the finger stopped, the verse was read. This was supposed to give advice or answer the querant's question as directed by fate or the spiritual guides. Works by Homer, Virgil,

Shakespeare and Nostradamus have been used in stichomancy.

Though stichomancy is no longer commonly practiced, contemporary psychics often remark that it is amazing that the method works so well. Even today, those who seek guidance from the I Ching spiritual book sometimes use this method to locate a passage that will assist or bring comfort during a time of trouble.

A variation is RHAPSODOMANCY, divination using the same method but with poetic verse.

Further reading

Baring-Gould, Sabine. *Curious Myths of the Middle Ages.* New York: University Books, 1967.

Bevan, E. *Sibyls and Seers: A Survey of Some Ancient Theories of Revelation and Inspiration.* London: Allen & Unwin, 1982.

Cheetham, E. *The Prophecies of Nostradamus.* London: Corgi, 1981.

Hazlitt, W. Carew. *Faiths and Folklore of the British Isles.* 2 vols. New York: Benjamin Blom, 1965.

Maple, Eric. *The Dark World of Witches.* Cranbury, N.J.: A. S. Barnes & Co., 1964.

STOLISOMANCY *Divination according to the way a person dresses.*

Stolisomancy concerns the significance of the way in which one dons clothing. For example, one might put on one sock and then a shoe on the same foot before repeating the practice on the other foot. Such behavior might mean that the individual is methodical and thorough. The person who puts on a shirt, then socks, then a watch, and only then slips into his or her shoes might be considered a creative thinker. Those who practiced this prognostication technique in the Middle Ages were very curious about mistakes in dressing, that is, not tying a shoe or tucking in a shirt. Each mistake was said to indicate a specific thing, although the significance of each has been lost in time.

According to Scottish folklore, if one inadvertently puts on his or her shirt inside out, it means trouble ahead or a turn of bad luck. The same holds true with caps and jackets. However, in the 1800s in England, people thought just the opposite. Sailors and fishermen, along with their wives and lovers, encouraged one another to wear clothing inside out to bid success for the voyage and a fair wind. Wearing the clothing of the dead has always been considered chancy. For instance, during World War I it was believed that it was unlucky to wear a dead man's boots; the new wearer might be the next to die.

Further reading

Bletzer, June G. *The Donning International Encyclopedic Psychic Dictionary.* West Chester, Pa.: Whitford Press, 1986.

Hazlitt, W. Carew. *Faiths and Folklore of the British Isles.* 2 vols. New York: Benjamin Blom, 1965.

Opie, Iona, and Moira Tatem. *A Dictionary of Superstitions.* Oxford: Oxford University Press, 1992.

SUIT OF CUPS
In TAROT, one of the four groups of cards, which also include the SUIT OF PENTACLES, the SUIT OF SWORDS and the SUIT OF WANDS.

The Suit of Cups is said to reflect the element of water and also creative enterprises and emotional matters. It is said that the Cups flow with love. Each of the 14 cards in this suit features a different illustration.

The cards are interpreted as follows:

Ace of Cups: Fertility, love and plenty.
Two of Cups: Love, relationships, loving connections.
Three of Cups: Joy from love, gratification.
Four of Cups: Emotional pleasure, delight.
Five of Cups: Pleasure turned to sadness, reconsideration.
Six of Cups: Past pleasure and joy remembered, memories.
Seven of Cups: Ambitions, dreams, faith.
Eight of Cups: Disillusionment, rebirth.
Nine of Cups: Peace and completion.
Ten of Cups: Peace and contentment.
Knave of Cups: A helpful adolescent.
Knight of Cups: A youth with joyful feelings, a lover.
Queen of Cups: A loving, fair-haired, creative female.

King of Cups: An articulate, intelligent, perhaps worldly male.

See also CARTOMANCY; MAJOR ARCANA.

Further reading

Bosanko, Susan, ed. *Predicting Your Future.* New York: Ballantine Books/Diagram Group. Visual Information Limited, 1983.

Buckland, Raymond. *Secrets of Gypsy Fortune Telling.* St. Paul, Minn.: Llewellyn, 1988.

Giles, Cynthia. *The Tarot: History, Mystery and Lore.* New York: Paragon House, 1992.

Visions and Prophecies. Mysteries of the Unknown. Alexandria, Va.: Time Life Books, 1990.

SUIT OF PENTACLES
In TAROT, one of the four groups of cards, which also include the SUIT OF CUPS, the SUIT OF SWORDS and the SUIT OF WANDS.

The Suit of Pentacles is said to reflect the element of earth and exhibits expressions of money, work, material possessions and success. Each of the 14 cards in this suit features a different illustration.

The cards are interpreted as follows:

Ace of Pentacles: Material possessions and wealth.
Two of Pentacles: Interruption in the search for wealth.
Three of Pentacles: Achievement in one's profession.
Four of Pentacles: Reaching the height of success.
Five of Pentacles: Ruin, collapse.
Six of Pentacles: Security and balance.
Seven of Pentacles: Progress, with a warning to be observant.
Eight of Pentacles: Rewards, celebrations, success.
Nine of Pentacles: Achievement, goals reached.
Ten of Pentacles: Wealth.
Knave of Pentacles: A logical, thoughtful youth.
Knight of Pentacles: An upstanding young male.
Queen of Pentacles: A sensible, affluent, beneficent female.
King of Pentacles: A practical, logical, successful male.

See also CARTOMANCY; MAJOR ARCANA.

Further reading

Bosanko, Susan, ed. *Predicting Your Future*. New York: Ballantine Books/Diagram Group. Visual Information Limited, 1983.

Buckland, Raymond. *Secrets of Gypsy Fortune Telling*. St. Paul, Minn.: Llewellyn, 1988.

Giles, Cynthia. *The Tarot: History, Mystery and Lore*. New York: Paragon House, 1992.

Visions and Prophecies. Mysteries of the Unknown. Alexandria, Va.: Time Life Books, 1990.

SUIT OF SWORDS

In TAROT, one of the four groups of cards, which also include the SUIT OF CUPS, the SUIT OF PENTACLES and the SUIT OF WANDS.

The Suit of Swords is said to reflect the element of air. It expresses logical choices, the search for truth and the need for sound decisions and decisive actions. It also has to do with struggles and challenges. Each of the 14 cards in this suit features a different illustration.

The cards are interpreted as follows:

Ace of Swords: Success, achievement of objectives.
Two of Swords: Good luck, excellent fortune.
Three of Swords: Obstacles are removed.
Four of Swords: Calmness, a break from challenges.
Five of Swords: Struggle, possible setback and disappointment.
Six of Swords: Travel, beneficial news, challenges overcome.
Seven of Swords: The need to be cautious and courageous.
Eight of Swords: Patience.
Nine of Swords: In disaster, stay strong, unwavering.
Ten of Swords: The situation will brighten soon.
Knave of Swords: A clever, witty youth.
Knight of Swords: A strong, dark young male.
Queen of Swords: A clever, dark woman, perhaps a widow.
King of Swords: A dark, imposing, masterful male.

See also CARTOMANCY; MAJOR ARCANA.

Further reading

Bosanko, Susan, ed. *Predicting Your Future*. New York: Ballantine Books/Diagram Group. Visual Information Limited, 1983.

Buckland, Raymond. *Secrets of Gypsy Fortune Telling*. St. Paul, Minn.: Llewellyn, 1988.

Giles, Cynthia. *The Tarot: History, Mystery and Lore*. New York: Paragon House, 1992.

Visions and Prophecies. Mysteries of the Unknown. Alexandria, Va.: Time Life Books, 1990.

SUIT OF WANDS

In TAROT, one of the four groups of cards, which also include the SUIT OF CUPS, the SUIT OF PENTACLES and the SUIT OF SWORDS.

The Suit of Wands is said to reflect the element of fire. It expresses the essence of the growth of ethereal spirit, self-improvement, creativity, energy, impression and intensity. Each of the 14 cards in this suit features a different illustration.

The cards are interpreted as follows:

Ace of Wands: New, fresh starts.
Two of Wands: Well-earned success.
Three of Wands: Benefit from challenges.
Four of Wands: Success, approval.
Five of Wands: Challenges, setbacks, reversals, the quality to overcome these.
Six of Wands: Encouraging information.
Seven of Wands: Dilemma or crisis, but hopefulness.
Eight of Wands: Progress, confidence.
Nine of Wands: Resistance, be steadfast.
Ten of Wands: Obstacles, challenges, strife.
Knave of Wands: A dark, funny youth.
Knight of Wands: A dark, energetic male. May mean travel or an expedition or a change in residence.
Queen of Wands: A dominant, practical female.
King of Wands: A powerful, self-assured male.

See also CARTOMANCY; MAJOR ARCANA.

Further reading

Bosanko, Susan, ed. *Predicting Your Future*. New York: Ballantine Books/Diagram Group. Visual Information Limited, 1983.

Buckland, Raymond. *Secrets of Gypsy Fortune Telling*. St. Paul, Minn.: Llewellyn, 1988.

Giles, Cynthia. *The Tarot: History, Mystery and Lore*. New York: Paragon House, 1992.

Visions and Prophecies. Mysteries of the Unknown. Alexandria, Va.: Time Life Books, 1990.

SUN SIGN
In astrology, the astrological sign through which the Sun was moving at a specific period of time or at the time of birth.

The sun signs are Aries, the Ram; Taurus, the Bull; Gemini, the Twins; Cancer, the Crab; Leo, the Lion; Virgo, the Virgin; Libra, the Scales; Scorpio, the Scorpion; Sagittarius, the Archer; Capricorn, the Goat; Aquarius, the Waterbearer; and Pisces, the Fish.

See also ASTROLOGICAL SYMBOLS; HOROSCOPE; ZODIAC.

Further reading

Forrest, Steven. *The Changing Sky: The Dynamic New Astrology for Everyone*. New York: Bantam, 1984.

Goodman, Linda. *Linda Goodman's Star Signs*. New York: St. Martin's, 1987.

———. *Linda Goodman's Sun Signs*. New York: Fawcett/Columbine, 1978.

Luce, Robert de. *The Complete Method of Prediction*. New York: ASI, 1978.

Wilson, James. *The Dictionary of Astrology*. New York: Samuel Weiser, 1974.

Woolfork, Joanna Martine. *The Only Astrology Book You'll Ever Need*. Landham, Mass.: Scarborough, 1992.

SYCOMANCY
Divination by the rate at which fig leaves dry.

Practiced in ancient China and through Roman times, sycomancy is a variation of other natural divination methods, often grouped with BOTANOMANCY and GEOMANCY.

Using sycomancy, one considers the question at hand, either silently or aloud. A fig leaf is then selected (right from the tree or from a receptacle holding many leaves). The question is written on the leaf, which is placed in the sun to dry. If the leaf begins to shrivel and dry immediately, the answer is no. If the leaf continues to look fresh for a number of hours, the answer is positive.

Further reading

Bary, William Theodore de, ed. *Sources of Chinese Tradition*. New York: Columbia University Press, 1960.

Cumont, Franz. *Oriental Religions in Roman Paganism*. New York: Dover, 1956.

Opie, Iona, and Moira Tatem. *A Dictionary of Superstitions*. Oxford: Oxford University Press, 1992.

SYNASTRY
In astrology, a technique of comparing horoscopes.

This method is used to match the result of two or more horoscopes from individuals to see the compatibility of their personalities. If the individuals are found to be compatible, they are considered to have the possibility of a good relationship. For example, one might have his or her horoscope compared with that of a future business partner to ascertain the probability of a sound working relationship.

According to astrologers, synastry is also employed to compare political running mates and the destiny of trade and relations between countries and in international affairs, as well as affairs of the heart.

Further reading

Adams, Evangeline. *Astrology: Your Place among the Stars*. New York: Dodd, Mead & Co., 1930.

———. *Astrology for Everyone*. 1931. Reprint. New York: Permabooks, 1943.

Woolfork, Joanna Martine. *The Only Astrology Book You'll Ever Need*. Landham, Mass.: Scarborough, 1992.

SYNCHRONICITY
Term created by Dr. Carl G. Jung (1875–1961) in 1930 to denote two separate and dissimilar events that occur at the very same instant and are, in fact, related.

It is said that Jung was fascinated by the correlation of patterns and divination systems of I CHING as compared with astrology and numerology. In later years, he used the term to discuss Tao.

Jung theorized that in synchronicity there is a blending together of incidents that cannot be explained rationally but is significant and meaningful.

For example, he reported an incident that concerned the wife of one of his patients. After the death of the woman's mother and grandmother, a flock of birds gathered directly outside the window of the death chamber. Jung said that there was a connection between the birds' appearance and the souls of the dead women or between the birds as messengers of the gods as noted in various myths.

Jung credited the work of Albert Einstein as the inspiration of his work in synchronicity. Jung first used the word *synchronicity* at a memorial address for Richard Wilhelm, who had translated the I Ching into German.

Further reading

Campbell, Joseph, ed. *The Portable Jung*. New York: Penguin, 1971.

Fodor, Nandor. *Between Two Worlds*. West Nyack, N.Y.: Parker, 1964.

Guiley, Rosemary Ellen. *Harper's Encyclopedia of Mystical and Paranormal Experience*. San Francisco: HarperSan Francisco, 1991.

Jung, C. G. *Aion: Researches into the Phrenomenology*. Princeton, N.J.: Princeton University Press, 1968.

———. *Aspects of the Feminine*. Princeton, N.J.: First Princeton, 1982.

———. *Dreams*. Princeton, N.J.: Princeton University Press, 1974.

———. *Memories, Dreams, Reflections*. Recorded and edited by Anilea Jaffe. New York: Random House, 1961.

O'Connor, Peter. *Understanding Jung, Understanding Yourself*. New York/Mahwah, N.J.: Paulist Press, 1985.

TABLES OF FATE   *Various sortilege methods, used as parlor games, to divine the future.*

Also known as magic tables, these are variations of casting or placing objects, which are then interpreted to answer a querant's question or explain an omen. The tables of fate often include diagrams on which objects, such as cards, dice or other articles, are tossed or placed in a specific pattern. The tables come with a listing of the meanings for each placement.

The tables of fate, considered merely party games in the early part of the 20th century, have a basis in actual prognostication methods. For example, one of the tables, called the Tree of Life, has its foundation in the Kabbalah. Another is a variation of a tarot card spread.

The tables of fate, while interesting, have lost favor with those who consider metaphysics more than a game. Thus they are rarely used today.

See also MANTIC OBJECTS; SORTILEGE SYSTEMS.

Further reading

Buckland, Raymond. *Secrets of Gypsy Fortune Telling.* St. Paul, Minn.: Llewellyn, 1988.
Butler, W. E. *How to Develop Clairvoyance.* 2d ed. New York: Samuel Weiser, 1979.
Innes, Brian. *The Tarot: How to Use and Interpret the Cards.* London: Orbis, 1979.
Showers, Paul. *Fortune Telling for Fun and Popularity.* Philadelphia: New Home Library, 1942.

TABLE TIPPING   *A technique used to communicate with spirits, by which a table would be tipped, turned or lifted.*

In this method, communication was received through a sitter who recites the alphabet, noting at which letter the table moves. It was also used to prove that spiritual entities were actually visiting a group.

During a seance, participants place the palms of their hands on a table. The "proof" that a spiritual entity has come into the room is that the table (or other objects) moves. The movement is often just a quiver, or there may be rapping sounds made on the table. In the mid- to late 1800s, when spiritual interest was in its heyday, the field was riddled with fake psychics. Unfortunately, table tipping was a favorite ploy used by unscrupulous individuals to indicate that the spirit of a dearly departed relative was present. A phony psychic would arrange for the movement of the table by corporeal means, charging for his or her services in enabling the grieving relative to communicate with the spirit.

There are a number of theories of how levitation or movement of the table operates. One says that it works through the power of the psychic's mind to counteract the forces of gravity. Some psychics attribute the power to levitate objects to their guides and explain that the spirits can change the forces of gravity. Another school of metaphysical thought asserts that through concentrating on the aura emanating from themselves or an object, psychics change the vibrational frequency of objects so they are not pulled toward the earth.

See also HOME, DANIEL DUNGLAS; LEVITATION.

Further reading

Belhayes, Iris, with Enid. *Spirit Guides.* San Diego: ACS, 1985.

Brown, Slater. *The Heyday of Spiritualism.* New York: Hawthorn, 1970.

Edmonds, I. G. *D. D. Home: The Man Who Talked with Ghosts.* Nashville: Thomas Nelson, 1978.

Ferguson, John. *An Illustrated Encyclopedia of Mysticism and the Mystery Religions.* New York: Seabury Press, 1976.

Fodor, Nandor. *Encyclopedia of Psychic Science.* New York: University Books, 1966.

Rogo, D. Scott. *Our Psychic Potentials.* Englewood Cliffs, N.J.: Prentice-Hall, 1984.

TAROT *Seventy-eight specially marked cards used in divination.*

It is believed that use of the tarot began more than 6,000 years ago in ancient Egypt. Some historians believe that tarot received its name from the archaic Book of Thoth (the Egyptian god of knowledge). The Egyptian words for Book of Thoth are believed to be *Tar Ro,* or "royal pathway," although in Hindustani the word *taru* means cards.

Regardless of its beginnings, the tarot seems to have been hidden by the mystic masters for more than 3,000 years. One story explains that the tarot resurfaced to be read and interpreted by the Rom, a nomadic tribe of Persia and Egypt. The Rom traveled widely and are better known as gypsies. (*Gypsies* is a slightly garbled term for those coming from Egypt.) Whether this is a colorful but bogus anecdote or the truth may never be clear. Some dispute the theory of the gypsy tribes. They insist that the cards originated in China, or Germany, or Spain. It is known

that the gypsies traveled through Europe in the Middle Ages, using a very fundamental set of tarot cards. The cards were also regularly used for playing cards.

The son of a French shoemaker, Eliphas Levi was a flamboyant magician and the author of a number of important metaphysical volumes including *The Mysteries of Magic* (edited by A. E. Waite) and *History of Magic.* He is considered by many to have produced the most important writings on the tarot of all time. Levi is best remembered for his insightful determination, controversial at that time, that there was a strong symbolic connection between the 22 cards of the tarot's MAJOR ARCANA and the Kabbalah's Tree of Life that has continued to the present.

According to tarot scholars, Levi saw the tarot not just as intriguing wisdom used by the gypsies to foretell the future or a bewitching deck of cards. Rather, he believed them to be a practical tool through which the spirits could be contacted and revelations regarding the past and future could be made. Levi believed that through the merging of the Kabbalah and the tarot, he had finally discovered a powerful source of knowledge and magic. This discernment changed the course of the history of the tarot.

In 1889, *The Tarot of the Bohemians,* written by Dr. Gerard Encausse, the first book devoted entirely to the tarot, was published. Also known as Papus, Encausse was a leading figure in the French occult spiritualist movement from the mid-1880s through 1900.

Papus was a devotee and follower of Levi, and while his book did not introduce new philosophy, it elaborated and refined the ideas that by that time had become almost mainstream in their acceptance. Rather than producing a how-to book, Papus discussed the magical principles of the tarot and his belief that the tarot encompassed occult science. Tarot historians says that Papus's work is lavishly romantic but provided the first documentation of Levi's revolutionary metaphysical concepts.

Other than astrology, the tarot is the most universally known divination system. Since each card has a deeply significant and symbolic meaning, many students of the tarot and metaphysical scholars dedicate their entire lives to the study and comprehension of the cards. Thus, should one desire to know more about the tarot, it is advised to take a class from a knowledgeable tarot reader, review some of the books mentioned below and obtain a deck of tarot cards for self-education.

Today, there are hundreds of different tarot card decks and books on the subject available to the consumer. The most thorough book is the *Encyclopedia of Tarot* by Stuart Kaplan, owner of U.S. Games Systems, Inc. It includes a thorough study of tarot history and illustrates more than 3,200 different cards, from 250 various tarot decks. The most popular is the Rider-Waite deck (sometimes called the Rider tarot), also manufactured by U.S. Games, Inc. There are decks with more modern likenesses, illustrations reflecting children, crystals, flowers, cats and people in medieval attire. These are often available at stores that sell metaphysical materials and through mail-order catalogs featuring metaphysical products.

The Aquarian tarot is almost identical to the Rider-Waite deck. The Thoth tarot deck includes swirling backgrounds and impressionistic images, often referred to as haunting recollections of another plane. The illustrations of Tarot Marscilles have a slightly grotesque appearance; this is the oldest of the popular decks. The Classic deck features an iconographic style.

Esoteric decks are said to produce special occult experiences. Whether that is true or not depends on the psychic and the querant. These decks include the Royal Fez Moroccan tarot deck, The Golden Dawn tarot, Gareth Knight tarot deck, the Magickal Tarot, and the Masonic tarot deck (not connected to the Freemason organization).

Other variations include historical decks such as the Visconti-Sforza Tarocchi deck (mid-15th century), Tarot de Paris (early 17th century), I Tarocchi del Mantegna (mid-15th century), the Tarot Vieville deck (mid-17th century), Vandenborre Bacchus tarot (late 18th century), Etteilla tarot deck (early 19th century), the Epinal tarot deck (early 19th century), the Oswald Wirth tarot deck (late 19th century), Papus tarot deck (late 19th century) and Knapp-Hall tarot (early 20th century).

There are Merlin decks, pop-art decks, medicine cards and even Wonderland tarot, which features Alice's adventurers underground with suits of Flamingos, Peppermills, Hats and Oysters.

The tarot is divided into two groups of cards. The major arcana, consisting of 22 cards, includes the Fool, the Magician, the High Priestess, the Empress, the Emperor, the Hierophant or High Priest, the Lovers, the Chariot, Justice, the Hermit, the Wheel of Fortune, Strength, The Hanged Man, Temperance, the Devil, the Tower, the Star, the Moon, the Sun, Judgment and The World.

The MINOR ARCANA has four suits: The SUIT OF CUPS, the SUIT OF PENTACLES, the SUIT OF SWORDS and the SUIT OF WANDS. The minor arcana can be compared to a pack of playing cards; the major arcana is said to reflect archetypal qualities. These cards have traditionally been regarded as possessing symbolic meditative concepts that are directly tied to the Kabbalistic Tree of Life.

To use the tarot, a reader employs a specific system, often in a ritualistic manner, to select the cards. Sometimes the querant is asked to select cards for the reading. The way the cards are selected and placed on a table to be interpreted is called a spread. Some of the spreads are the GYPSY 7 (said to be a favorite among gypsy readers), the HORSESHOE SPREAD, the SEVEN-POINT STAR, the TWENTY-ONE TAROT CARD SPREAD and the One-Card Reading. In the One-Card, a card is selected randomly from the deck. As with other sortilege methods, it is believed that the universe has directed the querant to the information on the card in response to the question that he or she posed.

Tarot card teachers instruct their students to interpret the cards through the traditional methods, such as those included in various spreads, and to decipher them intuitively. They suggest that for beginning students, a learning deck in which the meanings and key words are inscribed on the cards is the most effectual. Any deck can become a learning deck if the meaning and/or a key word is written on the card.

Tarot teachers tell students to record (either in writing or on tape) the results of their readings, to make a tarot notebook regarding the experiences with readings and even to create a personalized deck of cards. To become more in touch with the mystical meaning of the tarot, teachers instruct their students and clients to select a tarot figure and have this figure spiritually accompany them throughout the day or week. This activity, they believe, helps give personality and dimension to the figure on the card. They also suggest meditating on the images that appear on the cards, holding the image as long as possible in order to make a clear spiritual connection.

See also ARCANA; CARTOMANCY; LEVI, ELIPHAS.

Further reading

Buckland, Raymond. *Secrets of Gypsy Fortune Telling.* St. Paul, Minn.: Llewellyn, 1988.

Carlson, Laura E. *The Tarot Unveiled: The Method to Its Magic.* Stamford, Conn.: U.S. Games Systems, 1988.

Cavendish, Richard. *The Tarot.* New York: Cresent, 1975.

Crowley, Aleister. *The Book of Thoth.* Stamford, Conn.: U.S. Games Systems, 1977.

D'Agostino, Joseph. *The Tarot, the Royal Path to Wisdom.* York Beach, Maine: Samuel Weiser, 1976.

Giles, Cynthia. *The Tarot: History, Mystery and Lore.* New York: Paragon House, 1992.

Golowin, Sergius. *The World of the Tarot: The Secret Teachings of the 78 Cards of the Gypsies.* York Beach, Maine: Samuel Weiser, 1988.

Laurence, Theodor. *The Sexual Key to the Tarot.* New York: New American Library, 1973.

Nichols, Sallie. *Jung and Tarot: An Archetypical Journey.* York Beach, Maine: Samuel Weiser, 1980.

Torres, Katherine. *Tarot: A Pathway to the Spirit Within.* Carlsbad, Calif.: Earth People Medicine Publishers, 1994.

Waite, Arthur Edward. *The Pictorial Key to the Tarot.* York Beach, Maine: Samuel Weiser, 1973.

Woudhuysen, Jan. *Tarot Therapy: A Guide to the Subconscious.* Los Angeles: Jeremy P. Tarcher, 1979.

TASSEOGRAPHY *Divination of the future or answering a querant's questions through a ritual practice of telepathically reading tea leaves.*

More commonly known as tea-leaf reading or teacup reading, the practice is sometimes referred to as tasseomancy. Tasseography began with the ancient Chinese, who watched for omens from the residue, patterns and shapes left after drinking tea. The art of teacup reading is supposed to have been spread by nomadic gypsies, who foretold the future for the price of a coin; eventually, teacup reading was practiced throughout Europe. Teacup reading—in fact, reading the residue of any liquid, from coffee to wine—was extremely popular during the 1800s. In some societies molten lead was poured into water, with the results interpreted in much the same way. This practice is called molybdomancy. When melted wax is used, the technique is called ceromancy, and it is still used today by some voodoo priests to predict the future or interpret omens.

Historically, a psychic often has a special cup that he or she uses only for readings. It is usually plain inside, because a pattern would conflict with the interpretation of the leaves in a reading.

TEACUP READING
Tea leaves are read by the tasseographer, or tea-leaf reader. The reading includes size, placement and symbols formed by the loose tea that clings to the sides and bottom of the cup.

Today, some companies sell, and some psychics use, specially detailed teacups with the signs of the zodiac imprinted inside the cup. This cup not only gives reading from the tea leaves but also provides messages based on one's astrological sign.

It is best to use loose tea for a reading. As with all prediction methods, the exact nature of the ritual for reading tea leaves is in the hands of the individual psychic; typically, readers choose not to use the tiny leaves found in commercially prepared tea bags. Often the querant will select the tea he or she favors, from jasmine to Earl Grey, thus making the reading more personal.

The tasseographer, a teacup reader or psychic specializing in teacup reading, will ask the querant to spoon a measure of tea into a heated pot or directly into a china cup. The querant may be asked to stir the dried tea before selecting the leaves to be placed in the cup or pot. This can be compared to shuffling cards before a tarot card reading.

Sometimes a special spoon is used to give the reading a feeling of ritual magic. Teacup readers say this will ensure that true information will appear to the teacup reader. And most psychics cleanse the cup first (washing with soap and hot water and often rinsing cup, saucer and spoon with cold water before the next reading). Boiling water is poured over the tea as the querant stirs the pot or cup, concentrating on the information that is desired or a specific question to be answered.

A small teapot is swirled, and tea is poured into a cup. The cup should have a wide brim, and no design inside, and the saucer should be wide as well. When the tea is cool, the querant sips the liquid, focusing on his or her question. The querant leaves enough tea in the cup so that the leaves can be swirled around the edge of the cup (about one tablespoon of liquid).

Holding the cup with the left hand, the querant swirls the leaves three times clockwise and then flips the cup quickly facedown onto a napkin, which has been placed in the saucer. Some teacup readers ask that the querant count to seven before turning the cup rightside up. Not only are the leaf patterns read by the psychic,

TASSEOGRAPHY
Various shapes seen in tea leaves indicate special meanings. Others are exactly as they appear. For example, the appearance of an airplane and a heart in the cup could indicate a journey to a place one longs to visit.

but the pattern of leaves on the napkin add significance to the entire cup, too. This detail is not usually provided to the querant. The leaves in the cup combine with those found in the saucer for a complete reading.

Reading the cup clockwise, the handle represents the day of the teacup reading and the cup is divided into a year's time, with the side directly across from the handle indicating six months into the future. The leaves near the brim of the cup have more importance than those near the bottom, although some readers state that the opposite is true. Some psychics believe that the leaf patterns on the bottom of the cup spell tragedy; others regard this area with the same interest as leaves near the cup's brim. Often leaf symbols facing counterclockwise mean the significance of the shape is departing, and those facing clockwise mean the querant is moving toward this occurrence. Teacup reading should be accomplished with the entire cup and saucer.

The design and shapes formed by the leaves, including the size, placement and repetition of the symbols, are read by the tasseographer or psychic. Various shapes indicate special meanings, but some are exactly as they appear. For example, if a reader sees an airplane and a heart, this may indicate that the querant will journey to a place to which he or she has been longing to go.

It is important to note that, as with other prognostication methods, it is up to the reader to use all his or her intuitive powers to decipher the code of the leaves. And most psychics agree, as with any metaphysical skill, that the more one reads the leaves, the better one becomes at it. Thus, it is not unusual to see only vague shapes during a first reading.

Coffee grounds can be read using the same symbols and shapes mentioned below, as can other patterns from sand to clouds. This is called COFFEE GROUND READING or, less commonly, coffeeography.

The following are some of the symbols and interpretations used by those who read tea leaves:

Ace of Spades: Pointing up, an argument that will be short-lived. Pointing down, a difficult problem will ease. Lying across the bottom of the cup, a danger is diminishing.

Acorn: Become busy, create, accomplish. There will be success in a chosen field.

Airplane: Traveling great distances without risk. If the plane is broken, an accident or danger.

Alligator: News after a long wait.

Anchor: A hanging anchor, displeasure or an unsuitable situation. An anchor lying on its side, achieving one's aspirations or dreams will be accomplished shortly. If near the top of the cup, success in business or romance is indicated.

Angel: Guardian angel or guide. A blessing is coming.

Ant: A hardworking person, one with persistence, or a message to work industriously to obtain something.

Anvil: Hard work ahead.

Ape: A mimic, a copy cat, or trying to fit into a mode that is impossible.

Apple: Prosperity in business.

Apron: A new friend, perhaps someone with domestic skills or who loves to cook.

Arc: Great happiness.

Arm: Upward, begging. Forward, to receive assistance. Downward, needing help or discouragement.

Arrow: News will be received shortly, perhaps a letter or an important message.

Ax: There is a threat, possible trouble, one may be in jeopardy.

Baby: A series of small worries or interruptions. May be the creation of new ideas or a creative business venture.

Bag: Acquisition, attainment, to acquire something one has been working toward.

Banana: News from another country.

Barn: Great abundance in material goods.

Basket: Empty, money worries. Half full, continued concerns, but depression is short-lived. Full, abundance or receiving a present or gift (may be a gift of knowledge).

Bat: Danger, dangerous news.

Bed: A sensible, quiet agreement. A message that it is time to rest.

Bee: A busy time ahead. Great success through hard work.

Beehive: Requested meeting.

Bell: Unexpected announcement, marriage or engagement or smooth progress. Great news.

Bible: Spiritual guidance, may not be in the traditional religious sense.

Bird: Always indicative of good news. Perched, waiting for word, in a letter or over the telephone. Flying, word is on the way. In a nest, security is realized. In a cage, conflicts or the feeling of being trapped. May be a trapped idea or philosophy.

Bird Types: A crow, a perplexing person. A dove, a sign of love, a loving individual. A duck, gossip, a false rumor. A hen, a chatty individual. An owl, a learned friend. A parrot, a conversationalist, a show-off with no secrets. A penguin, one who is neat, well groomed, but may be somewhat self-centered. A turkey, one who is egocentric. A vulture, indicative of a corrupt individual, perhaps denoting serious business relationships.

Book: A message to seek more knowledge or information regarding a specific question.

Bottle: Fascination, allurement.

Box: A present, gift, a possession.

Bracelet: A charmed circle, a joyful union, perhaps a wedding.

Branch: Addition to family or to business.

Bread: A message to avoid wasting time or energy.

Bride: A new start, may mean a marriage.

Bridge: If unbroken, the problem at hand is being solved or will be solved shortly. If collapsed or broken, it may not be possible to overcome this problem; seek a variation or different route.

Broom: A new home.

Bull: One who is stubborn, or a stubborn problem.

Butterfly: Innocent pleasures.

Cabbage: Jealousy, envy from a business associate or false friend. Beware.

Cage: A proposition, perhaps business or marriage.

Cake: A celebration, often one that has been long awaited.

Camel: Useful news is forthcoming, may be slow to be understood.

Candle: A light in the pathway of the future.

Casket: A change in one's situation, perhaps a death.

Cat: Take care with one who seems like a friend. Dishonesty may be in store. Cat with a mouse, people playing emotional games or being untruthful with one's feelings.

Chair: Filled, a new person entering one's life during the time period indicated by the placement in the cup. Empty, a person of importance will leave during the time indicated by the placement in the cup.

Child: A fresh, innovative beginning or idea.

Chimney: Prosperity.

Circle: Empty, good news about business, a wish come true. Full of dots, success in one's chosen field. Half filled with dots, a wish come true, objective is reached.

Claw: A hidden enemy.

Clock: Message to act now.

Clover: Luck.

Clown: Happiness, or someone pretending to be happy.

Cobweb: Something is guarded or secured. May be a message that what was lost is safe and secure.

Coffee Mug: Too much idle chatter.

Coin: Abundance, prosperity, money worries will end.

Column: Success in all endeavors.

Compass: A change in professional direction, a change in residence.

Cow: A change in career, increased abundance.

Cross: Problems will be surmounted. A sacrifice may be demanded in the future, but the outcome will be positive.

Cup: One may find fault with another.

Dagger: Impetuousness, some danger ahead, others are plotting.

Daisy: Great love, a new love interest.

Dandelion: Project may be shattered.

Deer: A shy person, beautiful soul, friends will be supportive.

Desk: News will be received shortly regarding business projects.

Diamond: A message to reach for perfection.

Dice: A loss, a change, a gamble that may not be worth one's while or may have adverse effects.

Dish: An invitation.

Dog: A faithful friend.

Doll: Time for fun, looking for a mate.

Dollar Sign: Money.

Donkey: Wait for a better time.

Dots: Money coming to the querant during the time indicated by the placement in the cup. Many dots indicate considerable money.

Dove: Peace, forgiveness.

Dragon: Self-deception.

Drinking Glass: Clear thoughts. A time for honesty and openness in all dealings.

Drum: Meddling, chatter.

Ear: Excellent news.

Earring: Caution, a loss of some type, business or personal.

Easel: Creativity in an art field.

Eggs: Unbroken, success is assured, make plans for the future. Broken, plans for work or career may have to be revised, a setback.

Elephant: Loyalty, a good friend.

Envelope: News through the mail.

Eye: Strong psychic powers, a message to study metaphysics.

Eyeglasses: Study the situation thoroughly, look closer at details, analyze the proposition.

Face: Looking forward, stop dreaming and make plans. Looking backward, reflecting too much on the past or past accomplishments. Looking outward, a good balance.

Fairy: Light, joyful thoughts. Time to relax and play.

Fan: A flirtation, a feeling of satisfaction.

Feather: Someone who is insincere.

Fence: Restrictions or limitations. Success may be found by overcoming obstacles.

Fern: Old-fashioned ideas or ceremony.

Finger: A warning. Listen to what others are saying. Pay attention to the way the finger points regarding the placement in the cup.

Fish: Gains in possessions, material growth, spiritual progress. A wonderful symbol, fortunate.

Fishing Pole: Time to inquire. Ask questions.

Fist: Persistence pay's off.

Flag: Stay fast. Do not lose integrity.

Flowers: A series of compliments, praise, honors, tributes.

Fly: Illness, a warning to take care of one's health or change health habits.

Foot: Walk away from the past. Walk into a new experience.

Forest: A message to understand the entire situation. One's concepts may be too congested to see all the possibilities.

Fork: Receive aid and help gracefully. A forked line, a decision that must be made.

Frog: Someone who jumps to conclusions. A warning to move carefully to a decision; do not move too quickly.

Fruit: Any fruit signifies that one's hopes and objects will be fruitful.

Frying Pan: Someone may be untruthful; there may be trouble.

Funeral (People carrying a coffin): A lesson to learn; change.

Gallows: A warning, proceed with caution, especially in business. There may be trouble ahead.

Garden: A joyful occasion, a party, a celebration.

Gate: Problems will be overcome shortly. Proceed with confidence. All will be well.

Ghost: Someone who is trusted is unworthy of that respect. A friend may take unfair advantage of a situation or friendship.

Giant: One with great power.

Girl: Increased prosperity, happiness, a new beginning.

Globe: Travel in the future.

Goat: A stubborn person.

Gorilla: Someone with low self-esteem will try to say an opinion.

Guitar: Love, song, celebration.

Gun: A warning. One must take responsibility for personal actions. There may be a hidden agenda or something concealed.

Halo: Heavenly-angelic presence or visitor

Hammer: A complainer, a person who whines.

Hand: Assistance. Do not be too stubborn to ask for help.

Hanging Body: Delay.

Hat: A change in career, a promotion.

Heart: Caring, love, passion.

Heavenly Bodies (planets, Sun, Moon, stars): Good luck in all aspects. A very fortunate sign.

Helmet: Sign of protection.

Hills: Spiritual growth, personal awareness.

Hive: Satisfaction, a joyful home, good friends.

Holster: The danger has passed.

Hook: One who is eager for knowledge, education. A time to share one's gifts.

Horn: Self-appreciation; success.

Horse: A male friend, a true friend.

Horseshoe: A good-luck symbol, regardless of position. The larger in the cup, the more fortunate.

House: Home.

Hurdles: Obstacles.

Iceberg: Message not to hide behind a cold exterior. Allow the personality to come through.

Initials: Initials of people with whom one will come in contact or with whom one has relationships.

Insect: Pesky problems that will be conquered.

Iris: A spiritual message. There are still lessons to be learned and challenges ahead.

Iron: Problems will be resolved, "ironed out," be patient.

Ivy: A garden, garden of love.

Jar: Strength.

Jaw: A long discussion.

Jester: One who seems silly, a clown, a hidden agenda.

Jug: Good health, may indicate a party or festival.

Kangaroo: Movement, a trip.

Keg: Time to store supplies, store energy.

Kerchief: News will be received from another country or from one whose native language is not English.

Kettle: A forthcoming meeting in a relaxed atmosphere.

Key: Success. Doors will be opened.

King: A strong-willed individual who wants control.

Kite: Celebrate self-esteem, aim goals high.

Knapsack: Save for the future.

Knife: Fear. A warning, something will be "cut" apart, a friendship, a love relationship.

Knitting Needle(s): Time to create or exert more strength.

Knot: An argument.

Knots in a Row: A series of disagreements.

Lace: Old-fashioned ideas or philosophies. A formal meeting or relationship.

Ladder: Pathway toward success. Promotional opportunity.

Ladle: News will be delivered, abundance.

Lamb: A gentle, thoughtful individual.

Lamp: A way to be lead from the "dark," guidance.

Lantern: The pathway to a new beginning will be possible. A fortunate spiritual journey.

Lasso: Marital bliss, happiness in a love relationship.

Leaf: A fortunate sign. Good health, both mental and physical.

Lemon: Person with a sour disposition.

Letter: Initial of a person with whom one will come in contact or with whom one has relationships. Look at other symbols in the leaves to indicate the correlation.

Letter (mail): Look for an initial in the cup to ascertain from whom the letter will be received or for another indication on this symbol. A letter indicates receiving news. May be electronic mail or a computer message.

Lighthouse: "Stormy seas" ahead, or a good friend is available in times of trouble.

Lily: Stability, lasting love.

Lines: Journey. Wavy lines indicate uncertainty about a trip, perhaps disappointment.

Lion: One with a hot temper, a fiery relationship.

Lizard: A mistake.

Lock: Obstacles, a riddle to be solved.

Log: A spectacular gift.

Lollipop: Fun, happiness, light-hearted person.

Mail: See Letter, above.

Mail Box: Another is awaiting communication.

Man: A visitor, not necessarily a male.

Mask: A secret is hidden from view, or a message not to tell secrets.

Match: Time for action.

Medal: An honor bestowed.

Mermaid: Flirtation. Time for a flirtation or fun.

Money: Including the dollar sign ($), indicative of money coming to the querant. If there are a number of money signs or the sign is large, it means an abundance of money.

Monkey: One who likes to make mischief.

Moon: Change in life, change in situation.

Mountain: A major demand, but one that will be possible.

Mouse: Theft of object or idea.

Mushroom: A time to grow.

Musical Instruments: Piano, creativity. Guitar, love. Trumpet, an announcement of exciting news. Clarinet, a group player. Violin, do not be mislead, prepare for the future.

Musical Note: Compatibility, harmony, fortunate relationship.

Nail: Be careful. Watch over belongings and possessions.

Necklace: A group is in much admiration.

Needle: With thread, objective or dream will be realized. Without thread, a major decision is forthcoming.

Nest: A place or need for security.

Net: A warning, be careful of traps.

Nose: Acceptance of accomplishments.

Numbers: Read as numbers. See other symbols in the leaves to interpret their meaning. They may be months of the year, days of a month, time of the day or the number of days one must wait for a specific incident to occur.

Oar: A small worry, but success and achievement shortly.

Ostrich: Travel.

Owl: A symbols of the greatest knowledge. A fortunate, spiritual sign.

Ox: One who is strong-willed but gentle in his or her heart.

Oyster: Love, an engagement.

Palm Tree: A journey to a tropical place. Many surprises on the journey of life.

Pan: A desire for acceptance.

Pancake: Small amount of money coming.

Paper: Important papers will need consideration.

Path: A journey, perhaps through spiritual awareness and within the realm of the spiritual world.

Pear: Improvement in money matters. Have faith.

Pen: An analytical job opening.

Person: Another has a message, or an important stranger will enter one's life.

Piano: Creativity in music.

Pig: Greed and selfish behavior or someone with these characteristics.

Pipe: A relationship will be mended.

Pot: One in need of help. If full, one in need of significant help.

Purse: Matters relating to money.

Pretzel: Complex situation.

Pyramid: A solid foundation to success.

Question Mark: Look to the other symbols in the cup. May indicate an inquisitive individual or a child who is questioning morals.

Quill: Return to simpler philosophies or lifestyle.

Rabbit: Fun-loving friend.

Racket: A perfect love match.

Radio: Important news.

Rainbow: The worst is over, happiness from now on.

Rake: Give a decision thought.

Ram: A leader, leadership qualities.

Rat: One who is dishonest, unfaithful, devious.

Ring: Look forward to a special time. There will be a change for the better.

Road: New changes coming quickly.

Rock: Fear, concerns, problems, yet they will be resolved without undue stress.

Rope: That which one has been awaiting will arrive.

Rose: Popularity.

Rug: Traveling.

Ruler: Keep to timetables, watch deadlines.

Safe: One who is self-reliant, or a message that one will be self-reliant for the rest of one's life.

Saw: An obstacle that must be overcome in order to continue.

Scales: If balanced, one is leading a balanced life. If unbalanced, a decision must be made.

Scissors: Disappointment, failure, perhaps a quarrel.

Shark: Loss of material wealth.

Ship: A journey, a sea voyage.

Shoe: Time to increase productivity.

Skates: You're on your own.

Snake: Coiled, treachery and betrayal. Uncoiled, knowledge, power, spiritual reasoning, success.

Square: Message to guard against being locked into antiquated thinking. Do not become too comfortable in a situation.

Spoon: Series of events.

Star: Fortunate sign. Excellent outcome of projects. One will receive public credit for a job well done.

Stick: Abundance of money.

Storm: Difficult times, calm forthcoming.

Sword: A minor mishap. This is a warning message of possible stress or anxiety in the family or workplace.

Table: A very social message, good friends, good food, much to be thankful for.

Tall Building(s): Achievement realized, but through work. The more buildings seen in the leaf, the more acclaim one will receive when the work is complete.

Teapot: Warm, loving friends.

Tear Drop: Disappointment.

Telephone: Important message forthcoming.

Throne: Authority, may mean authority is in question.

Tiger: One who is unable to cope, or may seem to be unable to cope with a situation.

Toilet: Physical problem.

Train: Wishes will come true.

Trees: A new start, then success. Wishes and dreams will come true—and shortly. A pine tree, great success. An oak, strength. A palm, a tropical journey or relaxation of a troubled situation.

Triangle: Success, excitement, personal reward. If there is a symbol within the triangle, indicative of a hidden meaning.

Turtle: A message not to take shortcuts. Slow, thorough work will ultimately lead to success.

Typewriter/Computer: Creative ability.

UFO: See beyond the ordinary.

Umbrella: A fortunate sign. A symbol of protection.

Urn: May indicate the loss of a friend or animal, or a change in a personal relationship.

Valley: Stay calm, good fortune is ahead.

Vase: One has an unknown admirer who is greatly attracted.

Violets: One with a quiet nature. May mean one has a tender, emotional side that is concealed.

Vise: Hold on.

Volcano: A situation is about to erupt, or one with an unsettled emotional personality.

Wagon: There are hard times head, but a great deal of work. A message to adopt a pioneer spirit, accept a challenge, make plans for the future.

Wall: Misunderstanding.

Waterfall: A fortunate sign, abundance.

Web: Be cautious with advice from a friend, it is erroneous.

Whale: Too much is being made from too little. Concern is unjustified.

Wheel: Regardless of the situation or challenges, life continues.

Wig: Something hidden.

Window: Spiritual sign. There are many new spiritual experiences if one looks for them.

Wineglass: Celebration.

Wishbone: Unbroken, success and what has been wished for will be realized. Broken or with missing pieces, not all is granted in life.

Witch: Strange happening.

Woman: Happiness, love, friendship. Not necessarily a female.

Worms: Scandal.

Wreath: Disappointment possible, a time for reflection and grief. When conclusions are reached, a time for celebration.

Xylophone: Musical event.

Yoke: One who is tied to his or her work or in a relationship that needs a change.

Zebra: A move, from one city to another, one home to another, one relationship to another.

This is merely a sampling of the symbols and interpretions of tasseography. Psychics recommend honing one's skills in the art by further study. Since many psychics spend their entire lives learning to interpret and read the leaves in a teacup, among other metaphysical skills, it is recommended that one review the books listed below and others on this topic. One may also wish to have a personal tea-leaf reading and study the mantic art by attending a class on the subject.

See also AEROMANCY; GEOMANCY; LYNCHOMANCY; MANTIC OBJECTS; PYROMANCY.

Further reading

Bary, William Theodore de, ed. *Sources of Chinese Traditions.* New York: Columbia University Press, 1960.

Buckland, Raymond. *Secrets of Gypsy Fortune Telling.* St. Paul, Minn.: Llewellyn, 1988.

Leland, Charles Godfrey. *Gypsy Sorcery and Fortune Telling.* New York: University Books, 1962.

Maven, Max. *Max Maven's Book of Fortunetelling.* New York: Prentice-Hall, 1992.

McCrite, Harriet Mercedes. *Tea Leaf Reading Symbols.* Carlsbad, Calif.: McCrite, 1991.

TAURUS *One of the 12 astrological signs of the zodiac. The symbol is the bull.*

Those who are born between April 20 and May 20 are natives of the sign of Taurus and have specific traits indicative of the time and date on which they were born. Divination of events can also be charted through this astrological sign.

Astrologers divine what is in store throughout life by the time, date and place in which the individual was born as they coordinate the influ-

TAURUS

ences with other signs, the planets, the Sun, the Moon and other powers.

In traditional Western astrology, Taurus is the second sign of the zodiac. Those born during the period typically exhibit qualities that exemplify an affectionate nature. They are stable, stubborn, quiet, patient and intensely practical.

Taurus is said to be the sign of money, and collecting and keeping money is often at the forefront of a native's efforts. Money is extremely important to Taurus. It's not that he or she flaunts it, but what it means: a comfortable home, a few investments, a rosy retirement. Home and family are important to Taurus, and he or she wants everything running like clockwork—all the time. In today's world that is not always possible, and chaos of daily living sometimes puts Taurus on edge.

Ruled by Venus, Taurus loves beauty and luxury—beautiful homes, cars, romantic partners. Yet he or she is inordinately realistic and understands that often beauty, especially the superficial kind, does not last. Thus, his or her

This ancient symbol represents the astrological sign of Taurus.

gorgeous, sleek and brightly colored sports car will probably be ultra fuel-efficient and have won honors for reliability.

It is said that living with a Taurus isn't one of the easiest things in life. Taurus can be a tyrant, although he or she often hides this part of the personality, and the tantrum is over almost as quickly as it begins. More so, Taurus can sometimes be a skinflint, secretive and suspicious. And there's a self-indulgent quality about Tauruses, too. However, their sensual, loving and humorous nature often outshines the more difficult qualities of the sign.

The Taurus man or woman always keeps people guessing. Is this a cold-hearted stone of a person, or a fun-loving, sensual delight? Living, knowing, loving and/or working with a Taurus is always a surprise.

While traditional astrologers use books to calculate a personal birth chart based on the position of the Sun, Moon and planets at a distinct time, computer software has replaced most of this time-consuming work. The correct term for calculating a birth chart is to "cast" it. In order to fully comprehend the extent of traits, potential and attributes, the exact time and place of birth must be known and interpreted.

See also ASTROLOGICAL SYMBOLS; ASTROLOGY.

Further reading

Cosmic Connections. Mysteries of the Unknown. Alexandria, Va.: Time Life Books, 1990.

Goodman, Linda. *Linda Goodman's Sun Signs.* New York: Fawcett/Columbine, 1978.

Morgan, Chris. *Fortune Telling: How to Predict Your Own Future.* London: Quintet Publishing and Random House, 1992.

Omarr, Sydney. *My World of Astrology.* New York: Fleet, 1965.

———. *Taurus.* New York: New American Library, 1992.

Verlagsanstalt, Datura. *Taurus Astro Analysis.* New York: Grossett & Dunlap, 1976.

Woolfork, Joanna Martine. *The Only Astrology Book You'll Ever Need.* Landham, Mass.: Scarborough, 1992.

TEACUP READING
See TASSEOGRAPHY.

TELEPATHY *The direct experience of another person's mental condition or state of being; ability to perceive and receive information through a means other than the traditional senses.*

Some metaphysical writers refer to telepathy as "mind-to-mind" communication. Most people have, at one time or another, thought of a friend, only to have that friend suddenly call. Or you might have had the experience of knowing exactly what someone will say before he or she has spoken. These are examples of telepathy.

As with CLAIRVOYANCE and EXTRASENSORY PERCEPTION (ESP), telepathy is another term indicating awareness without the support of information or data. These are the thoughts or the knowingness of thought, emotions or visions from one mind to another mind, even at a distance. It is the divination of forthcoming events or circumstances without any outside assistance. Telepathy is often placed under the general category of ESP.

The word *telepathy* was coined in 1882 by Frederic W. H. Myers, a British psychical researcher and founder of the Society for Psychical Research. It originated from the Greek term *tele,* meaning distant, and *pathe,* meaning to feel from afar. According to Myers, this word best expressed the curious and unexplainable happening of thought transference.

Most civilizations have folklore and recorded incidents regarding telepathic communication, including Native American tribes. It is often pointed out by scientists that while telepathic occurrences are recorded, they have not been proved in labs and there is still no hard scientific evidence to prove their existence. Still, most people believe in some form of telepathy and may have had personal experience with it.

See also RHINE, JOSEPH BANKS, M.D.

Further reading

Cavendish, Richard, ed. *Man, Myth and Magic: An Illustrated Encyclopedia of the Supernatural.* Vol. 7. New York: Marshal Cavendish Corporation, 1970.

Feyer, Dr. Ernest C. *The Call of the Soul: A Scientific Explanation of Telepathy and Psychic Phenomena.* San Francisco: Auto-Science Institute, 1926.

Guiley, Rosemary Ellen. *Harper's Encyclopedia of Mystical and Paranormal Experience.* San Francisco: HarperSan Francisco, 1991.

Halbourne, Max. *Mental Telepathy and ESP Powers for the Millions.* Los Angeles: Sherbourne Press, 1967.

Hintze, Naomi A., and J. Gaither Pratt. *The Psychic Realm: What Can You Believe?* New York: Random House, 1975.

Thouless, R. H. *Experimental Psychical Research.* New York: Penguin, 1963.

Tyrrell, G. N. M. *Science and Psychical Phenomena.* London, 1938. Reprint. New York: University Books, 1961.

TEPHRAMANCY *Divination from the ashes of a combustible object.* ANTHROPOMANCY, *a variation, deals with the ashes of a human or animal sacrifice.*

Tephramancy is quite often grouped under the larger heading of PYROMANCY, divination by analyzing the flames of a combustible object. This ancient practice is also sometimes referred to as lapadomancy, lampandomancy and pyroscopy.

In tephramancy, after one meditates on the question at hand, he or she asks the universe for assistance, writes a question on a piece of paper and then sets it on fire. Divination comes through examining and analyzing the ashes or through "reading" the patterns and ash formations as one would read tea leaves.

Historically, the ashes of sacrificial victims and animals, as well as specific types of trees, have been used in this method. It is believed that the ancient Druids, who have been said to have burned enemies in order to practice a form of divination, may have also used tephramancy.

In some places in the rural United States and England today, ashes are consulted to predict the future. For example, an ash that resembles a bird might mean good news; an ash that looks like a heart might mean true love.

Other variations of fire, smoke and ash divination include divination by CAPNOMANCY (patterns of smoke made by burning various objects and/or sacrifices), CAUSIMONANCY (throwing flammable objects into a fire or onto hot coals), CRITOMANCY (burning of barleycorn), DAPHNOMANCY (divination by the crackle of burning laurel leaves), LIBANOMANCY (divination through incense smoke) and SIDEROMANCY (divination by interpreting the twisting and smoldering of pieces of straw when thrown on a red-hot grate).

See also MANTIC OBJECTS.

Further reading

Dey, Charmaine. *The Magic Candle*. Bronx, N.Y.: Original Publications, 1989.

Kittredge, George. *Witchcraft in Old and New England*. Cambridge: Harvard University Press, 1929. Reprint. New York: Atheneum, 1972.

Maven, Max. *Max Maven's Book of Fortunetelling*. New York: Prentice-Hall, 1992.

Nichols, Ross. *The Book of Druidry—History, Sites, Wisdom*. London: Aquarian Press, 1990.

Opie, Iona, and Moira Tatem. *A Dictionary of Superstitions*. Oxford: Oxford University Press, 1992.

Pajeon, Kala, and Ketz Pajeon. *The Candle Magic Workbook*. New York: Citadel Press, 1992.

THEOMANCY *Ancient Hebrew belief of divination by studying the mysteries of the universe.*

It was believed that by studying the mysteries of the universe, or divine majesty, and through seeking the sacred names in the universe, one could have power over angels and guides, demons and other deities. It was through this power that one could control nature and work miracles. Theomancy is no longer considered a viable prognostication method. The exact details of how it was performed, perhaps through ritualistic magic, have been lost in time.

See also KABBALAH; LEON, MOSES BEN SHEM TOV DE; LEVI, ELIPHAS.

Further reading

Fortune, Dion. *The Mystical Qabalah*. 1935. Reprint. York Beach, Maine: Samuel, Weiser, 1984.

Franck, Adolphe. *The Kabbalah*. New York: Bell, 1978.

Giles, Cynthia. *The Tarot: History, Mystery and Lore*. New York: Paragon House, 1992.

Ponce, Charles. *Kabbalah: An Introduction and Illumination for the World Today*. Wheaton, Ill.: Theosophical Publishing House, 1973.

Schmaker, Wayne. *The Occult Sciences in the Renaissance*. Berkeley and Los Angeles: University of California Press, 1972.

Scholem, Gershom. *Origins of the Kabbalah* (translation). Princeton, N.J.: Jewish Publication Society, 1987.

THEOSOPHICAL SOCIETY *Metaphysical organization founded by Madame Helena P. Blavatsky and Henry Steel Olcott in New York City.*

Founded in 1875, the society was based on a number of ancient teachings including those of Pythagoras, Plato, the Gnostics and the Neoplatonists. The society had three main goals: (1) to support the unity of humankind without distinction of race, color, religion or social position; (2) to study the ancient religions to compare and then select ethics for the universal understanding of religion; (3) to study and promote the study of psychic powers so that all people could develop their psychic abilities.

Madame Blavatsky was directed to form the organization in 1875 by a spiritual master known as Master Morya. Blavatsky left her home in England to travel to the United States to investigate psychic disturbances on a farm in Vermont, having been alerted about them through an article in the *New York Graphic* written by Henry Steel Olcott. Blavatsky and Olcott became colleagues and friends and continued to research the occult.

On March 9, 1875, Olcott had received a letter written in gold ink on green paper that was signed "Tuitit Bey, Grand Master of the mystical Brotherhood of Luxor." Olcott was instructed to study the occult with Blavatsky; over the following three or four months, he continued to receive letters directing his metaphysical education.

The group's name was suggested by Charles Sotheran, then an editor of the *American Bibliopolist*. It comes from the Greek *theos,* meaning "a god," and *sophos* for "wise," or divine wisdom. It has been used to describe various esoteric and mystical systems adopted by Blavatsky and Olcott to represent the goals of the society.

In September of that year, Olcott and Blavatsky formed the Theosophical Society. Blavatsky was a very popular psychic and a celebrity. During the first two years, the society drew in many people who were curious about the charismatic H.P.B. After only two years, public interest in the society waned. It wasn't until Blavatsky and Olcott went to India, where Blavatsky was psychically directed to contact spiritual guides, that the organization once more became popular. However, Blavatsky's credibility came under scrutiny, and she and others in the Theosophical Society were accused of defrauding the public; the claim was that their messages from the Indian master had been staged. Though fraud was never proved, the charges did undermine the plausibility of all involved.

Krishnamurti, a Indian whom those in the Theosophical Society believed to be the next messiah, was considered to be the incarnation of Lord Maitreya, the long awaited Buddha. He brought thousands into the society by convincing them that he was the next Buddha, and continued to be a leader in the organization after he established a U.S. headquarters in Ojai, California, near Los Angeles. However, Krishnamurti became disenchanted with the direction of the movement, since he believed that there wasn't just one way to spiritual knowledge but many. He left the organization in 1930.

Many notable people have studied with the Theosophical Society, including Thomas Alva Edison, William Butler Yeats, Rudolph Steiner and Mahatma Gandhi.

Today there are more than 40,000 members of the society worldwide, with approximately 6,000 in the United States. The Theosophical Society of America is headquartered in Wheaton, Illinois; the United Lodge of Theosophists is located in Los Angeles; the Theosophical Society is in Covina, California, and the International Group of Theosophists is also located in the Los Angeles area.

See also BLAVATSKY, HELENA P.; KRISHNAMURTI; OLCOTT, COLONEL HENRY STEEL; STEINER, RUDOLPH.

Further reading

Caldwell, Daniel H., ed. *The Occult World of Madame Blavatsky: Reminiscences and Impressions by Those Who Knew Her.* Tucson, Ariz.: Impossible Dream Publications, 1991.

Mather, George A., and Larry A. Nichols. *Dictionary of Cults, Sects, Religions and the Occult.* Grand Rapids, Mich.: Zondervan Publishing House, 1993.

Ryan, Charles J. *H. P. Blavatsky and the Theosophical Movement.* Pasadena, Calif.: Point Loma, 1975.

Woolfork, Joanna Martine. *The Only Astrology Book You'll Ever Need.* Landham, Mass.: Scarborough, 1992.

THERIOMANCY *Divination by studying the behavior of animals.*

Theriomancy is a less common name for alectryomancy (divination by observing animals in the wild as well as domesticated creatures) and apantomancy (divination by chance encounters with animals).

In various times and cultures every animal has probably been used in a prognostication method. More than 2,400 years ago, the Etruscans practiced theriomancy by utilizing a hen or rooster. Babylonians used beasts of burden. By splashing water three times on a sleeping ox's head, a psychic was said to be able to divine, through the animal's 17 possible reactions and types of responses, the answers to the question at hand. The Hittites of Asia Minor and Syria used alectryomancy in studying the movements of an eel within a tank of water.

Forms of observing animals in order to foretell the future are still used today. In the central African tribe of Zande, questions are answered through the movement of ants. In Polynesia crimes are traditionally solved when a beetle is allowed to crawl over the grave of the murder victim. Supposedly the beetles' tracks reveal the murderer's name and/or identity. One can have one's future told by a fortune merchant's trained bird in cities throughout the world. The querant asks a pertinent question and releases his or her thoughts to the universe, and the bird picks an answer from the papers hanging from a rack or branch. The paper is said to reveal what the universe wants the querant to know. Of course, there is a price tag attached to this practice; that's how the vendor makes money.

There are a number of other mantic arts that involve observing animals. It is interesting that even today, some people believe that by observing the behavior of dogs, for example, one can predict earthquakes. Some scientists think that when migratory birds leave their summer habitats early, this indicates a harsh winter ahead.

Theriomancy is still practiced in various parts of the world. From black cats and white horses to bats and doves, much superstition and "luck" is told from the behavior of animals. In the United States, whether or not a groundhog sees its shadow on February 2 indicates how many weeks of winter remain. The result of that famous four-footed prognosticator's vision is broadcast throughout the country. Other lucky omens concerning animal encounters include meeting a goat or a flock of sheep (and making a wish when seeing the black sheep in the flock) and seeing a white horse in a field. Unlucky animal omens range from hearing a bat squeal as it flies overhead to meeting a hare (but only if you are a sailor on your way to your ship).

See also ALECTRYOMANCY; APANTOMANCY; FELIDOMANCY; HIPPOMANCY; MYOMANCY; OPHIMANCY; ORNITHOMANCY; ZOOMANCY.

Further reading

Bardens, Dennis. *Psychic Pets.* Boca Raton, Fla.: Globe Communications, 1992.

Green, Marian. *The Elements of Natural Magic.* Dorset, England: Element Books, 1989.

Logan, Jo, and Lindsey Hodson. *The Prediction Book of Divination.* Dorset, England: Blandford Press, 1984.

Stewart, R. J. *The Elements of Prophecy.* Dorset, England: Element Books, 1990.

THIRD EYE   *The sixth of the seven chakras in Kundalini yoga.*

The *third eye* was a term coined by mystical author Lobsang Rampa (the pseudonym of writer Cyril Henry Hoskin) in a best-selling book called *The Third Eye.*

Lobsang Rampa states that the third eye is located slightly above the eyebrows and in the center of one's forehead. It is thought by many psychics and those who study paranormal phenomena to be the center of psychic powers.

Further reading

Cavendish, Richard, ed. *The Encyclopedia of the Unexplained.* New York: McGraw-Hill, 1974.

Drury, Nevill. *Dictionary of Mysticism and the Esoteric Traditions.* Dorset, England: Prism Press, 1992.

Jones, Lloyd K. *Development of Mediumship.* Chicago: Lormar, 1919.

Kardec, Allan. *The Book of Mediums.* York Beach, Maine: Samuel Weiser, 1970.

Magical Arts. Mysteries of the Unknown. Alexandria, Va.: Time Life Books, 1990.

TIROMANCY   *Divination by examining and interpreting the holes or mold on or in cheese.*

Also sometimes referred to as tyromancy, it is no longer practiced today though it was a popular mantic art throughout medieval times. Because there were no food preservatives, the cheese of the Middle Ages probably bore very little resemblance to that which we buy at the supermarket today. In addition to the usual spoilage, cheese was also blended specifically to accumulate mold spores, as with blue cheese; early cheese makers also processed the cheese less, and it naturally came with more holes.

The exact nature of the divination process has been lost in time, but most likely the mold or holes were "read" much like one reads tea leaves or coffee grounds. For example, if after posing a question to the universe, one saw a heart shape in the cheese, it might mean love. If one saw a letter, it might have indicated that news was on the way. The image of a baby often indicated an unexpected change or a series of interruptions. An egg, or perhaps a basket of eggs, might reveal prosperity beyond one's hopes and dreams.

See also GEOMANCY; TASSEOGRAPHY.

Further reading

Ancient Wisdom and Secrets Sects. Mysteries of the Unknown. Alexandria, Va.: Time Life Books, 1990.

Bletzer, June G. *The Donning International Encyclopedic Psychic Dictionary.* West Chester, Pa.: Whitford Press, 1986.

Morgan, Chris. *Fortune Telling: How to Predict Your Own Future.* London: Quintet Publishing and Random House, 1992.

Rossbach, Sarah. *Feng Shui: The Chinese Art of Placement.* New York: Arkana/Penguin, 1991.

Showers, Paul. *Fortune Telling for Fun and Popularity.* Philadelphia: New Home Library, 1942.

TRANCE   *Altered state of consciousness.*

In metaphysics, a psychic may go into a trance in order to channel information from a spirit who is a master. He or she may enter a trance to find and provide information said to be stored in the AKASHIC RECORDS.

It is believed that in a trance, one's powers of concentration are greatly increased and subconscious memories can come to the forefront. Sometimes during a trance another entity takes over the psychic's body and speaks through his or her voice. JZ Knight's Ramtha is an example of a spirit who has been channeled by a psychic during a trance. Psychics sometimes do not recall what has happened when they are in a trance; however, it is not necessary to be in a trance to use one's psychic powers. A psychic may or may not go into a trance during PSYCHIC READINGS.

The American psychic Edgar Cayce (1877–1945) is said to have had the power to examine the Akashic Records while in a trance.

See also CAYCE, EDGAR; CHANNEL; CLAIRVOYANCE; GARRETT, EILENE; KNIGHT, JZ.

Further reading

Angoff, Allan. *Eileen Garrett and the World beyond the Senses.* New York: Morrow, 1974.

Bailey, Alice. *A Treatise on White Magic.* New York: Lucis, 1951.

Bletzer, June G. *The Donning International Encyclopedic Psychic Dictionary.* West Chester, Pa.: Whitford Press, 1986.

Cavendish, Richard, ed. *The Encyclopedia of the Unexplained.* New York: McGraw-Hill, 1974.

Cayce, Hugh Lynn, ed. *The Edgar Cayce Collection.* New York: Bonanza Books, 1986.

Klimo, Jon. *Channeling: Investigations on Receiving Information from Paranormal Sources.* Los Angeles: Jeremy P. Tarcher, 1987.

Knight, JZ. *A State of Mind: My Story.* New York: Warner, 1984.

McDermott, Robert, ed. *The Essential Steiner.* San Francisco: Harper & Row, 1984.

TRANSATUAUMANCY   *Divination through chance remarks overhead in a crowd.*

In this method, which was practiced along with many other ancient prognostication methods during Egyptian and early Roman times, the remarks are interpreted to reveal something other than their original meaning or to give guidance concerning a question. For example, if one overheard a worker say, "The well is going dry," a psychic of the time might have interpreted it to mean the government's treasury was running low, a theft of the king's wealth had occurred or the queen could no longer bear children.

A variation of transatuaumancy is cledonomancy, the art of knowing what will be said in the first few minutes of a conversation and predicting the future by the context of the remarks. Both of these arts are considered to be part of CLAIRVOYANCE.

Further reading

Alleau, Rene. *History of Occult Sciences.* London: Leisure Arts, 1965.

Butler, W. E. *How to Develop Clairvoyance.* 2d ed. New York: Samuel Weiser, 1979.

Guiley, Rosemary Ellen. *Harper's Encyclopedia of Mystical and Paranormal Experience.* San Francisco: HarperSan Francisco, 1991.

LeShan, Lawrence. *The Medium, the Mystic, and the Physicist: Toward a General Theory of the Paranormal.* New York: Viking, 1974.

TWENTY-ONE TAROT CARD SPREAD   *In tarot, a card spread that receives its name through the use of 21 cards.*

The Twenty-One tarot card spread is said to be excellent for a thorough reading. According to tarot card readers, this spread is especially valuable in providing a long-term, in-depth view of an individual's life. It is used to answer questions and provide advice on present situations; domestic fronts; one's hopes, ambitions and anticipations; future and unexpected events, the immediate future as well as what will happen in the long-term. Other spreads, such as the Gypsy and the Seven-Point Star, provide a quick view of the querant's future or answer a few questions.

For this method, all tarot cards are utilized. They are shuffled by the querant while he or she considers the questions to be asked. Sometimes one card is picked by the querant before the reading. He or she will look closely at all the cards, and the one that "speaks" to the querant (i.e., seems especially intriguing or inviting) should be used as the significator. This is the card that is believed to represent the querant. It is placed faceup near where the cards are spread on the table, often to the right of the spread.

After the cards are shuffled and meditation has occurred, the querant (or the reader, depending on the preference or situation) begins to deal the cards. All cards are dealt facedown and are not turned over until the reading begins.

The first card is placed in the top right corner of the table, the second to the left of the first; this placement continues through the first seven cards. The eighth card is placed directly beneath the first card, closer to the querant, and another row is formed. The third row begins with the 15th card, which is placed in a vertical row with the first and eighth card.

Reading the cards from the right to the left:

The first vertical row of three (cards 1, 8, 15) are said to indicate one's present situation.

The second vertical row of three (cards 2, 9, 16) are said to indicate one's relationships.

The third vertical row of three (cards 3, 10, 17) are indications of what is happening regarding hopes and dreams.

The fourth vertical row of three (cards 4, 11, 18) are reflections on one's expectations and ambitions.

The fifth vertical row of three (cards 5, 12, 19) tells of unforeseen incidents, chance events, things that will affect the querant.

The sixth vertical row of three (cards 6, 13, 20) tells the querant what is currently taking place in his or her life. These occurrences may be things of which the querant is unaware or they may be happening to verify that he or she is on the right pathway.

The seventh vertical row of three (cards 7, 14, 21) reflects the future and what it may hold.

See also ARCANA; CARTOMANCY; LEVI, ELIPHAS; TAROT.

Further reading

Buckland, Raymond. *Secrets of Gypsy Fortune Telling.* St. Paul, Minn.: Llewellyn, 1988.

Giles, Cynthia. *The Tarot: History, Mystery and Lore.* New York: Paragon House, 1992.

Morgan, Chris. *Fortune Telling: How to Predict Your Own Future.* London: Quintet Publishing and Random House, 1992.

Secrets of the Alchemists. Mysteries of the Unknown. Alexandria, Va.: Time Life Books, 1990.

Visions and Prophecies. Mysteries of the Unknown. Alexandria, Va.: Time Life Books, 1990.

UNDERHILL, EVELYN *(1875–1941)*
English mystic, poet and novelist.

From an Anglican upbringing, Underhill is said to have had a profoundly religious transformation in her late 20s that led her into the teachings of the Catholic Church. She taught philosophy and religion at Manchester College and at Oxford, England, and held an honorary doctorate of divinity from Aberdeen University.

Underhill's total fascination with religion and the Laws of the Universe led her to join the Hermetic Order of the Golden Dawn. She is best remembered for her metaphysical work *Mysticism,* first published in 1911, which explained her views of the roles of religion, philosophy, and the occult, including ceremonial magic. The book was readily accepted by psychics and philosophers of the time.

See also HERMETIC ORDER OF THE GOLDEN DAWN; LAWS OF METAPHYSICS.

Further reading

Cavendish, Richard, ed. *The Encyclopedia of the Unexplained.* New York: McGraw-Hill, 1974.

Drury, Nevill. *Dictionary of Mysticism and the Esoteric Traditions.* Dorset, England: Prism Press, 1992.

MacKenzie, Norman. *Secret Societies.* New York: Holt, Rinehart & Winston, 1967.

Symonds, John, and Kenneth Grant, eds. *The Confessions of Aleister Crowley: An Autobiography.* London: Routledge & Kegan Paul, 1979.

Wilson, Colin. *The Occult.* New York: Vintage, 1973.

UNIVERSAL LAWS *The principles of psychic and mystical sciences that are known to occur time and again. Also known as spiritual laws.*

The laws, which are functional as well as philosophical, are the doctrines and canons of esotericism. They are the basis of New Age teaching and philosophies, occultism, alchemy, psychic gifts and mysticism. Although they are complex and thought provoking, at the same time, at least at first, the descriptions seem too elementary. For example, Abram's Law states that all forms of matter possess a quality that puts them in touch with each other's signal. The Law of Catastrophe states that a severe turning point, that takes place abruptly, happens to everything in its season. Psychics encourage understanding the laws through meditation, by reading and studying the laws and other principles of metaphysics, and by making the laws part of one's personal philosophy.

See also LAWS OF METAPHYSICS.

Further reading

Bailey, Alice. *A Treatise on White Magic.* New York: Lucis, 1951.

Bletzer, June G. *The Donning International Encyclopedic Psychic Dictionary.* West Chester, Pa.: Whitford Press, 1986.

Cavendish, Richard, ed. *The Encyclopedia of the Unexplained.* New York: McGraw-Hill, 1974.

Cayce, Hugh Lynn, ed. *The Edgar Cayce Collection.* New York: Bonanza, 1986.

URIMANCY *Divination of yes and no answers through the use of lots to be cast, which were kept in a priest's breastplate.*

A prognostication method often utilized in ancient Israel, urimancy was most likely practiced by prophets and priests. At that time, wise people of the ancient tribes wore breastplates with a pocket that contained a Urim and Thummim (sometimes called Thummin). The Urim and Thummim were sacred articles, possibly knucklebones, flat disks or early forms of dice. Some biblical historians explain that the dice were the oracular knucklebones said to have been invented by Hermes. They were known to have been used as a sortilege method. (Sortilege is the technical term for casting of lots.)

In 1 Samuel 28:6, the Kings of Israel are said to govern their acts by the prophecies of the Urim and Thummim. Under Levitical law, high priests carried the objects in their "breastplates of judgement," required apparel when entering the tabernacle. The spirits of the holy place could enter the Urim and Thummim to direct the priests in their prophecies (Exod. 28:30). Other biblical references include Numbers 27:21 and 1 Samuel 28:6.

In Mormonism, the Urim and Thummim are two disks that are said to have assisted Joseph Smith. He used them, according to church records, when decoding the language inscribed on the golden tablets that are the basis for teaching the dogma of the Latter-Day Saints. According to Smith's account, the disks were attached to something that appeared to be "silvery bows" slightly resembling a pair of eyeglasses. Looking through these articles, Smith was able to translate the strange lettering on the plates, which then became the Book of Mormon.

Additionally, urimancy was a way to divine the future or to decide the innocence or guilt of an accused.

See also BIBLICAL PROPHETS AND DIVINATION METHODS; CASTING OF LOTS; SORTILEGE SYSTEMS.

Further reading

Bouqet, A. C. *Everyday Life in New Testament Times.* New York: Scribner's, 1954.

Mather, George A., and Larry A. Nichols. *Dictionary of Cults, Sects, Religions and the Occult.* Grand Rapids, Mich.: Zondervan Publishing House, 1993.

Miller, Madeleine S., and J. Lane Miller, eds. *Harper's Encyclopedia of Bible Life.* San Francisco: Harper & Row, 1978.

Tinney, Merrill C., ed. *The Zodervan Pictorial Encyclopedia of the Bible.* Grand Rapids, Mich.: Zodervan Publishing House, 1977.

Walker, Barbara G. *The Woman's Encyclopedia of Myths and Secrets.* New York: Harper Collins, 1983.

UROMANCY *Divination using urine.*

Urine was used by the ancient Greeks and Romans in place of water in order to scry the future. Uromancy is no longer in practice today.

Additionally, Pliny the Elder (A.D. 23?–79), the Roman naturalist and author of *Historia naturalist*, wrote about the power of urine to reverse a bad omen. Within this 37-book collection, he reported, "Among the counter-charms are reckoned, the practice of spitting into the urine the moment it is voided." In *Discoverie of Witchcraft* (c. 1584), the Scottish were instructed that to "unbewitch the bewitched . . . you must spet into the pissepot where you have made water."

Copromancy (foretelling the future from feces) was also practiced by the ancient Greeks, although details of the process have been lost in time.

Further reading

Bletzer, June G. *The Donning International Encyclopedic Psychic Dictionary.* West Chester, Pa.: Whitford Press, 1986.

Cumont, Franz. *Oriental Religions in Roman Paganism.* New York: Dover, 1956.

Maven, Max. *Max Maven's Book of Fortunetelling.* New York: Prentice-Hall, 1992.

Opie, Iona, and Moira Tatem. *A Dictionary of Superstitions.* Oxford: Oxford University Press, 1992.

VERNE, JULES *(1828–1905) French author and mystic.*

Verne is considered to be the "Father of Science Fiction," and his works are classics. Psychics like to point out that he did as well in the role of diviner of the future as many others who have taken more credit. In his books, Verne wrote about manned space travel years before it became reality. It is said that the details of the Apollo moon exploration program could have been outlined from his books *From the Earth to the Moon* (1865) and *Round the Moon* (1870). Verne's spaceship, the *Columbiad,* takes off from Florida with a three-man crew and splashes down in the Pacific Ocean. Verne's "trip" took 97 hours; Apollo 11's flight time into space was 97 hours 39 minutes. Another "coincidence" is that both spacecrafts suffered life-threatening loss of oxygen in flight. Additionally, Verne's description of the submarine the *Nautilus* predates submarine technology by a quarter of a century. Even nonmetaphysical authorities remark that his novels were "remarkably prophetic."

Verne was not alone in prognosticating future scientific events. A number of other famous scientists recorded their predictions; included on this list are Leonardo da Vinci and Sir Francis Bacon. Both foretold space travel long before the National Aeronautics and Space Administration was created in 1958.

Verne studied law in Paris, yet writing and the theater had a greater attraction for him. He successfully produced his first play under the patronage of Alexandre Dumas in 1850. Many of his works achieved popular acclaim during his lifetime. This genius of science fiction and prognostication even authored a series of romance novels. During his prolific 40-plus-year career, Verne wrote an average of one or more books a year.

Further reading

Glass, Justine. *They Foresaw the Future.* New York: Putnam's, 1969.
Mysteries of Mind, Space and Time: The Unexplained. Vol. 6. Westport, Conn.: H. S. Stuttman and Orbis Publishing, 1992.
Visions and Prophecies. Mysteries of the Unknown. Alexandria, Va.: Time Life Books, 1990.

VIA LASCIVA *In* PALMISTRY, *one of the less influential lines of the hand.*

Not found on all hands, the via lasciva is located slightly above the wrist toward the fingers. If it is straight, it is believed to indicate a personality that tires of details and bores easily. A long, straight, deep via lasciva is believed to reflect a person who has strong powers of persuasion. A curved line may indicate someone who has little self-confidence; a line that curves, beginning at the mount of Venus, is believed to reveal self-indulgent qualities. Should the line branch, palmists explain that the individual has the ability to make (and perhaps spend) a great deal of money.

Further reading

Altman, Nathaniel. *Palmistry Workbook.* New York: Sterling, 1990.

Cheiro. *Cheiro's Book of Numbers.* New York: Prentice-Hall, 1988.

———. *The Language of the Hand.* New York: Prentice-Hall, 1987.

Robinson, Rita. *The Palm: A Guide to Your Hidden Potential.* North Hollywood, Calif.: Newcastle, 1988.

VIA MYSTICA   *Latin term for "mystical way" or "mystical path."*

The ancient Greek philosophy the via mystica is the pathway back to the gods, heaven, nirvana or the Universe if one follows the laws of metaphysics.

See also LAWS OF METAPHYSICS.

Further reading

Bevan, E. *Sibyls and Seers: A Survey of Some Ancient Theories of Revelation and Inspiration.* London: Allen & Unwin, 1982.

Epstein, Perle. *Kabbalah: The Way of the Jewish Mystic.* Boston: Shambhala, 1988.

VICTORIAN LADY'S ORACLES   *Divination system created and popularized during victorian times.*

The Victorian Lady's Oracle is a board designed with symbols. With eyes closed, the querant asks a question, touches the board and waits for the universe to reveal the answer. The same types of divination systems are used in dominoes, dice and cards. Sometimes this type of prognostication is referred to as "magic tables" or "tables of fate."

There are a number of other systems that use a similar technique in order to foretell the future, and some psychics even practice the I Ching in the same manner: concentrating on a question, closing the eyes and allowing the finger to fall onto the 64 three-line patterns. These magical tables or ways of speaking to the universe through "oracles" were considered parlor games, yet like the Ouija board, psychics warn that one should take the information seriously. Posing serious questions in a thoughtful manner may provide the information desired.

See also OUIJA BOARDS; SORTILEGE SYSTEMS; TABLES OF FATE.

Further reading

Agrippa, Cornelius. *The Ladies' Oracle.* London: Hugh Evelyn, 1962.

Buckland, Raymond. *Secrets of Gypsy Fortunetelling.* St. Paul, Minn.: Llewellyn, 1988.

Palmer, Martin; Joanne O'Brien; and Kwok Man Ho. *The Fortune Teller's I Ching.* London: Century, 1986.

Walker, Barbara G. *The Woman's Encyclopedia of Myths and Secrets.* New York: Harper Collins, 1983.

VIRGO   *One of the 12 astrological signs of the zodiac. The symbol is the virgin.*

Those who are born between August 23 and September 22 are natives of the sign of Virgo and have specific traits indicative of the time and date on which they were born. Divination of events can also be charted through this astrological sign.

Astrologers divine what is in store throughout life through the time, date and place in which the individual was born as they coordinate the influences against other signs, the planets, the Sun, the Moon and other powers.

In traditional Western astrology, Virgo is the sixth sign of the zodiac. Those born during the period typically exhibit qualities that exemplify

VIRGO

This ancient symbol represents the astrological sign of Virgo.

a somewhat reserved and discriminating nature.

The native of this sign is industrious, the hard worker of the zodiac, but he or she is also ever curious. The Virgo individual needs to know how and why something works and often makes an outstanding engineer. It is said that Virgo's most likable trait is that of conscientiousness. Virgo always wants everything in perfect order and seems to have the unfailing energy to achieve this goal. Unless there are other strong aspects in his or her chart, the Virgo simply does not know how to wait until tomorrow to finish a project. Do it now is the Virgo's motto. Finding a way to keep everything neat and orderly at the same time he or she is living in the real world has been the undoing of many Virgo partnerships and marriages.

Virgo tends to be highly health-conscious and very concerned about his or her body. However, this sometimes tends to mean worry instead of purposeful activity. Virgos tend to be the hypochondriacs of the universe. As with their health and other areas of life and love, nothing is ever simple. According to astrologers, Virgo has two questions for every answer and often worries over nothing.

The sign of the zodiac in which an individual is born is responsible for only one fragment of the qualities he or she receives. Psychics are quick to point out that a general forecast solely on the stellar position of the Sun on the day an individual was born is unlikely to provide an accurate glimpse of the future.

While traditional astrologers use books to calculate a personal birth chart based on the position of the Sun, Moon and planets at a distinct time, computer software has replaced most of this time-consuming work. The correct term for calculating a birth chart is to "cast" it. In order to fully comprehend the extent of traits, potential and attributes, the exact time and place of birth must be known and interpreted.

See also ASTROLOGICAL SYMBOLS; ASTROLOGY.

Further reading

Cosmic Connections. Mysteries of the Unknown. Alexandria, Va.: Time Life Books, 1990.

Goodman, Linda. *Linda Goodman's Sun Signs.* New York: Fawcett/Columbine, 1978.

Morgan, Chris. *Fortune Telling: How to Predict Your Own Future.* London: Quintet Publishing and Random House, 1992.

Omarr, Sydney. *My World of Astrology.* New York: Fleet, 1965.

———. *Virgo.* New York: New American Library, 1992.

Verlagsanstalt, Datura. *Virgo Astro Analysis.* New York: Grosset & Dunlap, 1976.

Woolfork, Joanna Martine. *The Only Astrology Book You'll Ever Need.* Landham, Mass.: Scarborough, 1992.

VISION *A state of consciousness in which one can see images and prognosticate future events or interpret omens.*

Most CLAIRVOYANCE, the psychic ability to become aware of something or someone without any outside influences and without the normal perception of the senses, uses visions to relay information and thought. A vision is like seeing a picture without the use of outside influences. It may be a person, place, scene, article or even a continuing series of events and may be seen with or without the eyes being closed. Sometimes past lives are viewed. Visions usually occur during a changed state of consciousness such as meditation or a dreamlike state.

Throughout history, prophets, soothsayers, fortune-tellers, clairvoyants, spiritualists and those who consider themselves to be sensitive to other depths of thinking and knowing have experienced visions in order to provide information to the masses as well as to querants. Clairvoyance is the umbrella term to cover all the ways in which a psychic knows of coming events or things that have happened in the past. The soothsayer who tried to warn Caesar of the Ides of March is said to have had a vision of the ruler's impending death. Those who use crystal balls, such as Jeane Dixon and Dr. John Dee, typically see visions. Nostradamus is said to have seen visions while scrying in a bowl of water coated with a film of oil.

The Bible contains a number of references to visions and their interpretation. In Numbers 12:5–6, it is said, "And the Lord came down in a pillar of cloud, and stood at the door of the Tent, and called both Aaron and Miriam and they both came forth." In this case the Lord was a vision.

See also BIBLICAL PROPHETS AND DIVINATION METHODS; CLAIRVOYANCE; DEE, DR. JOHN; DREAM INTEREPRETATIONS; NOSTRADAMUS; PAST LIVES.

Further reading

Bevan, E. *Sibyls and Seers: A Survey of Some Ancient Theories of Revelation and Inspiration.* London: Allen & Unwin, 1982.

Butler, W. E. *How to Develop Clairvoyance.* 2d ed. New York: Samuel Weiser, 1979.

[Cayce, Edgar.] *Edgar Cayce on Dreams.* Virginia Beach, Va.: ARE Press, 1968.

McKenzie, John L. *Dictionary of the Bible.* Milwaukee: Bruce, 1965.

Psychics. Mysteries of the Unknown. Alexandria, Va.: Time Life Books, 1990.

VOODOO *A cultlike religion that employs divination as part of its practices.*

Voodoo (also known as vaudoux, vodun and vodoun) is an ancient practice that is shrouded with mystery, some of it generated by Hollywood moviemakers. The majority of those who practice the religion are centered in Haiti, but there are more than 50 million followers worldwide. Voodoo was originally practiced in part of the ancient African nation of Dahomey, and variations of the voodoo services were brought to the New World and the United States by slaves. The belief merges the principles of Roman Catholicism, tribal principles and West African doctrine, combining a pantheon of deities and various other mystical beliefs.

According to historians, one of the most important concepts of voodoo is divination. During the voodoo ceremony the hungan (religious leader, sometimes called a houngan) conjures up good luck, interprets situations, talks and brings forth benevolent spirits to help the initiated. According to practices, the hungan uses wangas (magical charms), and to an outsider the ceremony may seem more like sorcery or a theatrical performance with singing, shouting and gestures than divination or healing.

The hungan can also bring on evil and produce bad luck through the use of paquet, which is said to be able to induce death in an unlucky individual or one who is considered evil. The paquet is an abstract article, made of rags; this is the origin of the voodoo doll. Voodoo priests continue to use many ancient prognostication methods, including ceromancy.

See also CEROMANCY; TASSEOGRAPHY.

Further reading

Denning, Melita, and Osborne Phillips. *Voudou Fire: The Living Reality of Mystical Religion.* St. Paul, Minn.: Llewellyn, 1979.

Guiley, Rosemary Ellen. *Harper's Encyclopedia of Mystical and Paranormal Experience.* San Francisco: HarperSan Francisco, 1991.

Mather, George A., and Larry A. Nichols. *Dictionary of Cults, Sects, Religions and the Occult.* Grand Rapids, Mich.: Zondervan Publishing House, 1993.

Rigaud, Milo. *Secrets of Voodoo.* San Francisco: City Lights Books, 1969.

WAITE, ARTHUR EDWARD

(1857–1942) American-British mystic, historian, author and tarot card reader.

Born in Brooklyn, New York, Waite moved to England with his mother at an early age. He began his lifelong study of metaphysics while still in school. It is said that he was greatly influenced by the teachings of Madame Helena P. Blavatsky and Eliphas Levi. In his 20s, Waite joined the Hermetic Order of the Golden Dawn. Although he came from a strict Roman Catholic family, Waite grew up asking questions. He came to believe that all religions were downplaying their traditional mystical qualities.

Waite studied all the metaphysical arts, including tarot, in a practical manner rather than in a theoretical way. (The practical method answers a querant's questions on everyday living rather than answering only questions of a universal nature). He espoused the theory that through the study of the tarot and the images found in the cards, one could walk the pathway of knowledge and transformation. He also worked toward having the general public as well as those who were involved in mysticism see the tarot as a symbolic tool, in all its beauty and power.

In 1910, along with American artist and occultist Pamela Coleman-Smith, Waite created the best-selling and best known of all tarot card decks, the Rider-Waite deck (also known as the Rider Pack, since it was purchased by the Rider Company). It is very much in use today, available at most metaphysical shops.

In addition to the tarot card deck, Waite is best remembered for several books on magic, mystical beliefs and the occult. They include *Devil Worship in France: The Book of Ceremonial Magic, The Brotherhood of the Rosy Cross: The Real History of the Rosicrucians, The Holy Kabbalah, The Holy Grail* and *The Secret Tradition of Freemasonry.* Many believe that his most important work is *Azoth*, a volume on mysticism. His still-popular *A Pictorial Key to the Tarot* continues to influence readers and the public today.

Further reading

Giles, Cynthia. *The Tarot: History, Mystery and Lore.* New York: Paragon House, 1992.

MacKenzie, Norman. *Secret Societies.* New York: Holt, Rinehart & Winston, 1967.

Waite, Authur Edward. *Brotherhood of the Rosy Cross.* New Hyde Park, N.Y.: University Books, 1961.

———. *The Holy Grail: The Galahad Quest in the Arthurian Literature.* New Hyde Park, N.Y.: University Books, 1961.

———. *The Holy Kabbalah: A Study of the Secret Tradition in Israel.* New York: Carol Publishing Group, 1969.

———. *The New Encyclopedia of Freemasonry.* Combined edition. New York: Weathervane, 1970.

———. *A Pictorial Key to the Tarot.* New York: Carol Publishing Group, 1979.

WESTCOTT, DR. WILLIAM WYNN

(1848–1925) English psychic, author and Freemason.

Westcott took a series of Masonic writings and, along with MacGregor Mathers, developed a group of magical rituals and rites. These were the basis of the ceremonies practiced by the Hermetic Order of the Golden Dawn. Westcott and Mathers became leaders of the highest grade in the secret society.

Westcott is also remembered for his metaphysical books on the Kabbalah, including *An Introduction to the Qabalah* (written in 1910) and his translation of *Sepher Yetzirah* (in 1911). He also translated the works of Eliphas Levi (such as *The Magical Rituals of the Sanctum Regnum,* a book of ceremonial magic). He was the editor for the occult monographs known as Collectanea Hermetica, published by the Theosophical Publishing House in London about 1890.

See also MATHERS, SAMUEL LIDDELL MACGREGOR.

Further reading

Ancient Wisdom and Sects. Mysteries of the Unknown. Alexandria, Va.: Time Life Books, 1990.

Cranston, Sylvia. *H.P.B.: The Extraordinary Life and Influence of Helena Blavatsky.* Los Angeles: Jeremy P. Tarcher, 1992.

MacKenzie, Norman. *Secret Societies.* New York: Holt, Rinehart & Winston, 1967.

Symonds, John, and Kenneth Grant, eds. *The Confessions of Aleister Crowley: An Autobiography.* London: Routledge & Kegan Paul, 1979.

WOODRUFF, MAURICE *(1916–)*

British psychic.

Woodruff is most famous for his prediction of the election of John F. Kennedy, even before Kennedy was considering entering the presidential campaign.

It is said that Woodruff's clairvoyance is so reliable that when visiting the United States for the first time, he was asked by the press to provide the name of the winning horse in the Kentucky Derby. Woodruff knew nothing of horse racing; however, he kept smelling a heavy scent, even though there were no flowers or floral arrangements in the vicinity or women wearing perfume. Yet the fragrance lingered. Woodruff is quoted as saying, "Rose Bowl will be the winner," and, in fact, Rose Bowl won.

Woodruff was an amusing and witty writer; his books are often available at used-books stores. *Maurice Woodruff Futurecaster: The Secrets of Foretelling Your Own Future* is entertaining and enlightening.

Further reading

Burns, Litany. *Develop Your Psychic Abilities.* 1985. Reprint. New York: Pocket Books, 1987.

Vaughn, Frances. *Awakening Intuition.* Garden City, N.Y.: Anchor/Doubleday, 1979.

Woodruff, Maurice. *Maurice Woodruff Futurecaster: The Secrets of Foretelling Your Own Future.* Cleveland, Ohio: World, 1969.

X

XYLOMANCY *Divination using the arrangement of dry sticks.*

It is believed that xylomancy was originally used more than 5,000 years ago by Hebrew psychics as a divination method to foretell the future and interpret omens.

Some ancient volumes say specific sticks or dried logs were used in xylomancy; a question was asked, and the twigs were tossed in the air. Psychics deciphered the placement of the twigs in response to the question at hand. Another

XYLOMANCY
Xylomancy may be an adaptation of the I Ching.

method apparently used flat sticks and required that the bark on one side of the stick be removed. From 3 to 10 sticks were tossed in the air. If the sticks with sides not having bark fell facing up, the answer was yes, or a sign that the querant should move forward. If the sticks fell the bark side up, reverse was indicated; the answer was no, or the querant should not proceed.

Xylomancy may very well be an adaptation of I Ching. Some I Ching practitioners use yarrow sticks, which are thrown to the floor in order to divine the future. I Ching began well before written time (most likely prior to 2498 B.C.).

Another variation of xylomancy requires that sticks or dried logs be placed in a fire. The way the fire burns the logs is what is interpreted by the psychic. Other mantic arts use fire to foretell the future including capnomancy (divination by the patterns of smoke made by burning various objects and/or sacrifices), critomancy (burning of barleycorn), daphnomancy (divination by the crackle of burning laurel leaves), libanomancy (divination through incense smoke), pyromancy (divination achieved by staring into a burning fire) and sideromancy (divination by interpreting the twisting and smoldering of pieces of straw when thrown on red-hot grate; crushed dried peas were also used in sideromancy).

See also I CHING; SORTILEGE SYSTEMS; and other related mantic arts mentioned above.

Further reading

Bletzer, June G. *The Donning International Encyclopedic Psychic Dictionary.* West Chester, Pa.: Whitford Press, 1986.

King, Francis, and Stephen Skinner. *Techniques of High Magic.* Rochester, Vt.: Destiny Books, 1991.

Loewe, Michael, and Carmen Blacker, eds. *Divination and Oracles.* London: Allen & Unwin, 1981.

Logan, Jo, and Lindsey Hodson. *The Prediction Book of Divination.* Dorset, England: Blandford Press, 1984.

Opie, Iona, and Moira Tatem. *A Dictionary of Superstitions.* Oxford: Oxford University Press, 1992.

Visions And Prophecies. Mysteries of the Unknown. Alexandria, Va.: Time Life Books, 1990.

ZENER CARDS
Cards developed to test the powers of ESP.

The cards were created by Dr. J. B. Rhine and psychologist Dr. Karl Zener, when they were beginning their scientific research in the paranormal or metaphysical fields. The cards, which are still in use today, include five shapes: a star, a circle, three wavy lines, a square and a cross. A pack of Zener cards has 25 cards, five of each shape.

To test for ESP, the cards are shuffled. Cards are then held up to the subject with the shape facing the test administrator. The percentage of right answers as to the shape on the card is compared with a chance score. A score of five or more correct answers in each run (a test of all 25 cards) is said to indicate that the subject has psychic or ESP skills.

See also EXTRASENSORY PERCEPTION (ESP); RHINE, JOSEPH BANKS, M.D.

Further reading

Halbourne, Max. *Mental Telepathy and ESP Powers for the Millions.* Los Angeles: Sherbourne Press, 1967.

Rhine, Louisa E. *ESP in Life and Lab.* New York: Collier-Macmillan, 1967.

Richet, Charles. *Thirty Years of Psychical Research.* London: William Collins, 1923.

Thouless, R. H. *Experimental Psychical Research.* New York: Penguin, 1963.

ZOANTHROPY
Divination by observing and interpreting the flames of three lighted candles placed in a triangular position.

ZENER CARDS
Still popular today, Zener cards, as these shapes are known, were developed when Rhine and Zener began scientific research in the metaphysical fields.

Sometimes referred to as candle prophecies, lampandomancy, and lampadomancy, zoanthropy is a form of fire divination or pyromancy, the analysis of the shape of flames to foretell the future. It is quite logical that the interpretation of flames from a candle or a touch would become a prognostication method, since fire has played such an integral part in human evolution.

The Egyptians are said to have used zoanthropy about 1,700 years ago with only one candle. The ancient Greeks took the ancient practice and devised a variation that required three (sometimes four) specially blessed candles. With three candles set in a triangle shape, all wicks were lighted. The shape, height, appearance and movement of the flames were interpreted to foretell the future.

Although this and other candle divination methods are ancient, many still use them today. To practice zoanthropy, a question must be seriously considered by the querant and then asked, either aloud or silently. It is best done in a quiet room, without any breeze that might change the message of the candle flames. Then all the candles are lighted. Interpretations are based on the candles' appearances and behavior.

See also CANDLE PROPHECY; CAPNOMANCY; LYNCHOMANCY; PYROMANCY.

Further reading

Dey, Charmaine. *The Magic Candle*. Bronx, N.Y.: Original Publications, 1989.

Morgan, Chris. *Fortune Telling: How to Predict Your Own Future*. London: Quintet Publishing and Random House, 1992.

Opie, Iona, and Moira Tatem. *A Dictionary of Superstitions*. Oxford: Oxford University Press, 1992.

Pajeon, Kala, and Ketz Pajeon. *The Candle Magic Workbook*. New York: Citadel Press, 1992.

ZODIAC   *In astrology, the division of the sky into 12 signs.*

The zodiac is a narrow band of the heavens that circles the Earth. It is divided into 12 signs: Aries, Taurus, Gemini, Cancer, Leo, Virgo, Libra, Scorpio, Sagittarius, Capricorn, Aquarius and Pisces.

The astrological signs relate to the 12 constellations, or groups of stars, of the same name that are within the narrow band of the zodiac. The constellations are of differing sizes; the zodiac divisions are of equal sizes of 30 degrees. They form a complete circle of 360 degrees. Since ancient astrologers saw these constellations in specific forms, the zodiac got its name from the Greek word *zodiakos*, which means the circle of animals.

The center of the zodiac's band is marked by the path of the Sun around the earth. The Sun, Moon, and all planets except Pluto are within the circle of the zodiac.

Astrologers point out that while the shapes seen in the heavens are imaginary, the actual constellations are very real. Each sign of the zodiac has a fable and legend mixed with a good deal of Greek mythology, since much of the early astrological discoveries were made by the Greeks.

The stars were grouped in patterns as early as 3000 B.C. by Mesopotamian observers. They believed that the constellations represented various objects or animals such as the raven, serpent and goat. They charted and observed the heavens and their influence, especially on crops and seasons. The actual history of the zodiacal symbols is unknown, although they first appeared in Greek manuscripts.

The philosophy of the zodiac and the symbolism of the signs reached Egypt during the Greek dominations (third century B.C.). About this same time, there was a rapid blending of astrological doctrines throughout Babylon, Greece and Egypt. The doctrines incorporated a system of theories about the powers of the celestial bodies and their association with people, places, events and omens. The concepts spread to Rome, then on to Byzantium and India, and returned adding new spiritual insight.

See also ASTROLOGICAL SYMBOLS; ASTROLOGY; HOROSCOPE.

Further reading

Forrest, Steven. *The Changing Sky: The Dynamic New Astrology for Everyone*. New York: Bantam, 1984.

ZOOMANCY
*Divination by studying the behavior of animals is
called zoomancy.*

Goodman, Linda. *Linda Goodman's Star Signs.* New
York: St. Martin's, 1987.
———. *Linda Goodman's Sun Signs.* New York:
Fawcett/Columbine, 1978.
Luce, Robert de. *The Complete Method of Prediction.*
New York: ASI, 1978.
Wilson, James. *The Dictionary of Astrology.* New
York: Samuel Weiser, 1974.
Woolfork, Joanna Martine. *The Only Astrology Book
You'll Ever Need.* Landham, Mass.: Scarborough,
1992.

ZOOMANCY *Divination by observing the
behavior of animals.*

Zoomancy is a less common name for alectryomancy, divination by observing animals in the
wild as well as domesticated creatures, and apantomancy, divination interpreted by chance encounters with animals.

See also ALECTRYOMANCY; APANTOMANCY;
FELIDOMANCY; HIPPOMANCY; MYOMANCY;
OPHIMANCY; ORNITHOMANCY; THERIOMANCY.

Further reading

Bardens, Dennis. *Psychic Pets.* Boca Raton, Fla.:
Globe Communications, 1992.
Green, Marian. *The Elements of Natural Magic.* Dor-
set, England: Element Books, 1989.
Logan, Jo, and Lindsey Hodson. *The Prediction Book
of Divination.* Dorset, England: Blandford Press,
1984.
Stewart, R. J. *The Elements of Prophecy.* Dorset,
England: Element Books, 1990.

INDEX

Boldface page numbers indicate main essays. *Italic* page numbers indicate illustrations.

Hippocrates
  anthroposomancy 8
  maculomancy 143
  metopomancy 166
hippomancy 101, *101*
hips
  astrology, medical 20
  maculomancy 145
Hitler, Adolf
  Krafft, Karl Ernest 122
Hittites
  alectryomancy 5
  hepatomancy 99
  theriomancy 263
Hodgson, Richard
  Piper, Leonore E. 203
Holland *see* Netherlands
holsters 256
Home, Daniel Dunglas *102*, 102–103
  levitation 135
  psychic 208
Homer (Greek poet)
  halomancy 95
Hong Kong
  cleromancy 50
  feng shui 77
hooks 256
horns 256
horoscope 103–104
horses *see also* hippomancy
  Chinese astrology 46
  haruspicy 96
  hieromancy 98
  omens 188
  tasseography 256
  theriomancy 264
horseshoes
  hippomancy 101
  omens 187
  tasseography 256
Horseshoe spread (tarot) 104–105
Hoskin, Cyril Henry *see* Rampa, Lobsang
Houdini, Harry
  Ford, Arthur 79
  Home, Daniel Dunglas 103
houses 256
houses (astrology)
  horoscope 104
Howard, Henry
  selenomancy 235
human sacrifices
  anthropomancy 7
  capnomancy 36
  Druids 67
  epatoscomancy 72
  hieromancy 98

Huna (religion) 117–118
hunch *see* intuition; precognition
hurdles 256
hydromancy 105
hylomancy *see* psychometry
hypnosis
  Mesmer, Friedrich Anton 164
  regression 217

I

iatromancy 106
Ibn Gabirol 115
icebergs 256
Iceland
  Odin 185
I Ching 106–108, *107, 108*
  Laws of Metaphysics 127
ichthyomancy *108*, 108–109
Igorot (Philippine tribal group)
  shaman 237
Incas
  anthropomancy 7
  astrology 18
  crystal predictions 55
  epatoscomancy 72
  felidomancy 76
incense
  libanomancy 136
inconjunct (astrology) 17
index finger 78
India
  botanomancy 31
  cartomancy 37
  dominoes 62
  felidomancy 76
  karma 118
  Krishnamurti, Jiddu *see* Krishnamurti, Jiddu
  levitation 135
  podomancy 204
  Rajneesh, Bhagwan Shree 215–216
  Ramakrishna, Paramahamsa 216
Indian medicine bundle 109
infants *see* babies
influence lines 109–110 *see also* fate line; head line; heart line; life line
Ing (rune) 226
initials 256
insects 256
intestines
  anthropomancy 7
  epatoscomancy 72
intuition 110–111
Ireland
  Cummings, Geraldine 56
  Dunne, John William 68–69
  Garrett, Eileen 83
  Greatrakes, Valentine 91–92
  ichthyomancy 109

margaritomancy 162
  onomancy 190
iridology 111
irises (flowers) 256
iron 257
Iroquois Indians
  dream interpretations 66
  prana 205
Is (rune) 225
Israel, ancient 27
Israel, modern
  Geller, Uri 84–85
Italy
  Anselm De Parma 7
  Cagliostro, Allesandro di 33–34
    Levater, Johann Kaspar 134
  catoptromancy 40
ivy 257

J

jackals 5
jade 87, 182
Japan
  anthropomancy 7
  anthroposomancy 9, 10
  channel 44
  epatoscomancy 72
  haruspicy 97
  levitation 135
  scapulomancy 230
Jaquin, Noel 112
jars 257
jasmine
  capnomancy 35
jasper
  crystal predictions 55, 56
jaws 257
Jefferson, Thomas 220
jesters 257
Jesus
  auras 22
  Biblical prophets and divination methods 26, 27
  hieromancy 98
  ichthyomancy 109
jewelry *see also* gems
  psychometry 211
Jews and Judaism *see also* Kabbalah; Old Testament
  hieromancy 98
  Leon, Moses Ben Shem Tov De 132–133, *133*
  sciomancy 231
Jo-Hau (Chinese philosopher)
  graphology 90
Johnson, Lyndon
  Dixon, Jeane 62
Jones, Charles Stansfeld 112–113
Joseph of Cupertino, Saint
  levitation 135

Judge, William Quan 113
Judgment (tarot card) 156, *157*
jugs 257
Julian of Norwich
  Hilton, Walter 101
Jung, Carl G. 113–114
  astral plane 15
  astrology 19
  collective unconscious 52
  dream interpretations 66
  gnosis 89
  I Ching 107
  intuition 110
  Laws of Metaphysics 127
  out-of-body experiences 194
  precognition 205
  soul 241
  synchronicity 247–248
Jupiter (planet)
  astrological symbols 15
  numerology 182
Jupiter, mount of *see* mount of Jupiter
Justice (tarot card) 151, *151*

K

Kabbalah 115–117, *116*
  Abulafia, Abraham Ben Samuel 1
  catoptromancy 40
  gematria 85
  gnosis 89
  Jones, Charles Stansfeld 112
  Leon, Moses Ben Shem Tov De 132–133
  Levi, Eliphas 135
  numerology 180, 181
kahunas 117–118
kangaroos 257
Kaplan, Stuart 251
Kardec, Allan 118
karma 118–119
Karma, Law of 127
kegs 257
kelidomancy 119
Kellner, Karl 119
Ken (rune) 224
Kennedy, John F.
  crystalomancy 55
  Dixon, Jeane 62
  Woodruff, Maurice 274
Kennedy, Robert
  Dixon, Jeane 62
kephalonomancy 119–120
kerchiefs 257
kettles 257
keys
  clidomancy 51
  tasseography 257
kidneys
  astrology, medical 20

medals 257
meditation **162–163**
medium **163–164** see also
Cagliostro, Allesandro di;
Cummings, Geraldine; direct-
voice medium
Melanesia 63–64
Mercury (planet)
astrological symbols 15, 16
numerology 182
Mercury, mount of see mount of
Mercury
mermaids 257
Mesmer, Friedrich Anton *164,*
164–165
Mesopotamians
astragyromancy 14
Biblical prophets and divination methods 26
zodiac 278
Messing, Wolf
psychic 207
metaphysics **165–166** see also
Laws of Metaphysics
metopomancy *166,* **166–167**
Mexico
belomancy 26
ceromancy 43
gyromancy 94
hieromancy 98
mice see also myomancy
apantomancy 10
tasseography 257
Middle Ages
anthropomancy 8
anthroposomancy 10
botanomancy 31
ceromancy 43
cleromancy 50
clidomancy 52
dowsing 64
felidomancy 76
gnosis 89
onimancy 189
palmistry 196
shaman 237
sortilege systems 240
stolisomancy 244
tarot 250
tiromancy 264
Milarepa, Jetsun **167**
levitation 135
mystic 174
mimosa 30
ming (or other "fortune") sticks
167–168
mirror prophecy **168** see also enoptromancy
mirrors
catoptromancy 40–41
enoptromancy 71, *71*
scrying 233
mistletoe
botanomancy 30

capnomancy 36
Druids 67
Mitchell, Edgar D.
Geller, Uri 84
Mohammed (prophet of Islam)
66
moleomancy **168**
moles (birthmark) see also
moleomancy
maculomancy 143–144
molybdomancy **168–169**
money 257
money dreams 67
monkeys
Chinese astrology 46
tasseography 257
Monroe, Robert
astral plane 15
out-of-body experiences 194
Montgomery, Ruth 23
Moon
astrological symbols 15, 16
Cancer 34
numerology 182
selenomancy 235
tasseography 256, 257
Moon (tarot card) *156*
major arcana 156
Moon, mount of the see mount
of the Moon
Moon Children 34
moonstones
crystal predictions 56
Moore, Francis 19
Mormons (Latter-Day Saints)
laying on of hands 128
urimancy 268
Moses, Stainton 23
moss (color) 183
Motoyama, Hiroshi
past life 198
mountains 257
mount of Apollo **169,** *196,* 197
mount of Jupiter **169–170,** *196,*
197
mount of lower Mars 170, *196,*
197
mount of Mercury 170–171, *196,*
197
mount of Saturn 171, *196,* 197
mount of the Moon 171–172,
196, 197
mount of upper Mars 172, *196,*
197
mount of Venus 172–173, *196,*
197
mouth
anthroposomancy 10
maculomancy 144
mucous membranes
astrology, medical 20

Mullins, John 64
Murphy, Bridey **173**
muscles
astrology, medical 20
mushrooms 257
musical instruments 257
musical notes 257
Myers, Frederic W. H.
telepathy 261
myomancy *173,* **173–174**
mystics **174**
Abulafia, Abraham Ben Sam-
uel 1
Agrippa, Von Nettesheim,
Heinrich Cornelius 2–3,
13, 181
Albertus Magnus 4
Blavatsky, Helena P. see
Blavatsky, Helena P.
Catherine of Siena, Saint 39–
40, 174
Eckhart Von Hochheim
(Meister Eckhart) 70
Hartmann, Franz 96
Hilton, Walter 101
Lee, Ann 130
Lully, Raymond 142
Machen, Arthur 143
Mathers, Samuel Liddel
Macgregor 100, 162, 274
Milarepa, Jetsun 135, 167,
174
Rajneesh, Bhagwan Shree
215–216
Ramakrishna, Paramahamsa
216
Underhill, Evelyn 267
Verne, Jules 269
Waite, Arthur Edward 100,
273–274
mythology **174–175**

N
nails 257
names, personal see onomancy
Napoleon Bonaparte
anthroposomancy 9, 10
Le Normand, Madame 131
Napoleon III (France)
Home, Daniel Dunglas 102
natal horoscope **176** see also
birth chart
Native Americans see also specific tribal groups (e.g., Comanche)
apantomancy 10
dowsing 65
dream interpretations 66
epatoscomancy 72
Goodman, Linda 90
guide 92
iatromancy 106
Indian medicine bundle 109

shaman 237
Nau, Erika S.
Kahunas 117
Navajo Indians
Indian medicine bundle 109
shaman 237
navels 145
Nazis
Krafft, Karl Ernest 122, 123
sortilege systems 240
near-death experiences 114
neck
astrology, medical 20
maculomancy 144
necklaces 257
necromancy **177**
needles 257
Nepal
haruspicy 97
nephelomancy **177** see also aeromancy
Neptune (planet)
astrological symbols 15, 17
numerology 183
nests 257
Netherlands
Croiset, Gerard 53–54
nets 257
Neuberg, Victor
Crowley, Aleister 54
New Age
Kabbalah 116
laying on of hands 128
metaphysics 166
occultism 184
Newbrough, John Ballou **177–
178**
New England
aeromancy 2
capnomancy 36
daphnomancy 59
omens 188
New Testament
ophimancy 192
Newton, Isaac 220
Nicholas II, Czar (Russia)
Cheiro 45
Nicholas III, Pope
Abulafia, Abraham Ben Samuel 1
nigromancy **178**
nimbus
auras 21
ninja
levitation 135
nipples 145
Nomi, Masahiko
anthropomancy 8
noses
anthroposomancy 9
maculomancy 144
omens 187
tasseography 257